Capitalism, Jacobinism and International Relations

This book offers a radical reinterpretation of the development of the modern world through the concept of Jacobinism. It argues that the French Revolution was not just another step in the construction of capitalist modernity, but produced an alternative (geo)political economy – that is, "Jacobinism." Furthermore, Jacobinism provided a blueprint for other modernization projects, thereby profoundly impacting the content and tempo of global modernity in and beyond Europe. The book traces the journey of Jacobinism in the Ottoman Empire and Turkey. It contends that until the 1950s, the Ottoman/Turkish experiment with modernity was not marked by a peripheral or statist capitalism, as conventionally presumed, but by a historically specific Jacobinism. Asserting this Jacobin legacy then leads to a novel interpretation of the subsequent transition to and authoritarian consolidation of capitalism in contemporary Turkey. As such, by tracing the world historical trajectory of Jacobinism, the book establishes a new way of understanding the origins and development of global modernity.

EREN DUZGUN is Assistant Professor at the University of Nottingham, China Campus. His research focuses on historical sociology, political economy and international relations. His work has appeared in the *European Journal of International Relations*, the *Review of International Studies*, the *Journal of International Relations and Development* and the *European Journal of Sociology*, among other scholarly outlets.

LSE INTERNATIONAL STUDIES

SERIES EDITORS
George Lawson (Lead Editor)
Department of International Relations, London School of Economics
Kirsten Ainley
Department of International Relations, London School of Economics
Ayça Çubukçu
Department of Sociology, London School of Economics
Stephen Humphreys
Department of Law, London School of Economics

This series, published in association with the Centre for International Studies at the London School of Economics, is centred on three main themes. First, the series is oriented around work that is transdisciplinary, which challenges disciplinary conventions and develops arguments that cannot be grasped within existing disciplines. It will include work combining a wide range of fields, including international relations, international law, political theory, history, sociology and ethics. Second, it comprises books that contain an overtly international or transnational dimension, but not necessarily focused simply within the discipline of International Relations. Finally, the series will publish books that use scholarly inquiry as a means of addressing pressing political concerns. Books in the series may be predominantly theoretical, or predominantly empirical, but all will say something of significance about political issues that exceed national boundaries.

Previous books in the series:
Before the West: The Rise and Fall of Eastern World Orders Ayşe Zarakol
How the East Was Won: Barbarian Conquerors, Universal Conquest and the Making of Modern Asia Andrew Phillips
The World Imagined: Collective Beliefs and Political Order in the Sinocentric, Islamic and Southeast Asian International Societies Hendrik Spruyt
Socioeconomic Justice: International Intervention and Transition in Post-war Bosnia and Herzegovina Daniela Lai
Culture and Order in World Politics Andrew Phillips and Christian Reus-Smit (eds.)
On Cultural Diversity: International Theory in a World of Difference Christian Reus-Smit

Capitalism, Jacobinism and International Relations

Revisiting Turkish Modernity

EREN DUZGUN
University of Nottingham

CAMBRIDGE
UNIVERSITY PRESS

CAMBRIDGE
UNIVERSITY PRESS

University Printing House, Cambridge CB2 8BS, United Kingdom

One Liberty Plaza, 20th Floor, New York, NY 10006, USA

477 Williamstown Road, Port Melbourne, VIC 3207, Australia

314–321, 3rd Floor, Plot 3, Splendor Forum, Jasola District Centre, New Delhi – 110025, India

103 Penang Road, #05–06/07, Visioncrest Commercial, Singapore 238467

Cambridge University Press is part of the University of Cambridge.

It furthers the University's mission by disseminating knowledge in the pursuit of education, learning, and research at the highest international levels of excellence.

www.cambridge.org
Information on this title: www.cambridge.org/9781009158343
DOI: 10.1017/9781009158367

© Eren Duzgun 2022

First published 2022

A catalogue record for this publication is available from the British Library.

Library of Congress Cataloging-in-Publication Data
Names: Duzgun, Eren, 1981– author.
Title: Capitalism, Jacobinism and international relations : revisiting Turkish modernity / Eren Duzgun, University of Nottingham.
Other titles: Property, state and geopolitics
Description: Cambridge, United Kingdom ; New York, NY : Cambridge University Press, 2021. | Series: LSE International Studies | Revised version of the author's thesis (doctoral)–York University, 2016, titled Property, state and geopolitics : re-interpreting the Turkish road to modernity. | Includes bibliographical references and index.
Identifiers: LCCN 2021051137 (print) | LCCN 2021051138 (ebook) | ISBN 9781009158343 (hardback) | ISBN 9781009158350 (paperback) | ISBN 9781009158367 (epub)
Subjects: LCSH: Capitalism–Turkey–History. | Kemalism. | Radicalism–Turkey–History. | Civilization, Modern–19th century. | Civilization, Modern–20th century. | Historical sociology. | Turkey–Politics and government–19th century. | Turkey–Politics and government–20th century. | Turkey–Foreign relations. | France–History–Revolution, 1789–1799–Influence. | BISAC: POLITICAL SCIENCE / International Relations / General
Classification: LCC DR475 .D89 2021 (print) | LCC DR475 (ebook) | DDC 327.561–dc23/eng/20220215
LC record available at https://lccn.loc.gov/2021051137
LC ebook record available at https://lccn.loc.gov/2021051138

ISBN 978-1-009-15834-3 Hardback

For Destine Celal, my mother.

Contents

Acknowledgments

This book is the revised version of a doctoral thesis I embarked on about ten years ago at York University, Toronto. The Political Science Department at York was an intellectual heaven driven by curiosity, skepticism and progressive politics, which I most gratefully acknowledge. In a cutthroat PhD market that prioritizes research with immediate "relevance" and "impact," York provided me with the financial and intellectual resources to ask "big" questions, explore "large processes" and make "huge comparisons" in a way perhaps only a few places would dare to encourage their students today.

At York, I am most indebted to my supervisor Hannes Lacher. Hannes was the sharpest critic as well as the most generous supporter of this project. Indeed, the very idea of this book crystallized in his graduate seminars, and I have tried to build on and reformulate some of the theoretical questions Hannes raised in his own doctoral project. Ellen Meiksins Wood, whom I was very lucky to have on my dissertation committee for a while, was a continuous source of inspiration until the final penning of this book. Ellen fell ill and passed away before the completion of my thesis, but anyone who reads this book will understand the extent of my debt to Ellen from the frequency of references to her work, and from my critical endorsement of her particular interpretation of historical materialism. Upon Ellen's illness, I was fortunate that George Comninel accepted her place. George offered numerous invaluable insights, while saving me from making a couple of embarrassing errors about early modern European history. Kamran Matin, my external examiner, provided extensive comments that not only forced me to formulate my arguments much more clearly, but also guided the future development of my work, especially in connection to the field of International Relations. During my viva, Feyzi Baban and Greg Albo also made several important suggestions for improvement, which I have integrated into the revising of the book. More recently, Benno Teschke, Stephen Miller, Ruben Gonzales-

Vicente, Alp Yücel Kaya, Spencer Dimmock and Görkem Akgöz were all very kind to agree to read various draft chapters of the book; I benefited immensely from their comments and critiques. I am also indebted to George Lawson, the lead editor of this book series, for encouraging and supporting this project, as well as the two anonymous reviewers who provided helpful advice on the content and presentation of the argument. Thanks also go to John Haslam, Hannah Weber, Toby Ginsburg, Jane Bowbrick and Abigail Neale at Cambridge University Press and Vinithan Sedumadhavan at Straive for skillfully guiding me through the publication process.

Over the *longue durée*, I have received help, feedback and encouragement from many people at different stages of my academic life. Adam David Morton, Alexander Anievas, Andreas Bieler, Baran Gürsel, Can Cemgil, Ceren Ergenç, Charles Post, Claire Vergeiro, Ece Kocabıçak, Faruk Yalvaç, Galip Yalman, Gjovalin Macaj, Jeroen Duindam, Joseph Bryant, Jonathan London, Meliha Altunışık, Mustafa Türkeş, Necati Polat, Pınar Bedirhanoğlu, Ray Bush, Sabine Dreher, Sam Knafo, Sam Putinja, Sümerjan Bozkurt, Şebnem Oğuz and Zülküf Aydın deserve much thanks. On a more personal level, I am very lucky to have met some wonderful friends along the way. Special thanks are due to Aziz Güzel, Barbara Calvo, Ezgi Doğru, Erdem Akbaş, Frantz Gheller, Jessica Evans, Julian Germann, Licianny Matos, Lilian Yap, Lucy Angus, Nicole Swerhun, Rengin Ataç, Serdar Sözübek, Thomas Chiasson-Lebel, Vedat Altun and Zeynep Kaşlı. Fulya, my partner, witnessed the final stages of the completion of this book; I thank her for the love and joy she has brought into my life. Finally, to my family: Destine, Baran, Elif, Deniz and Woolly. Thank you so much for years of support, generosity and constantly reminding me what matters most. I love you so much.

1 | Introduction

No object of inquiry has been arguably more central to the development of the social sciences as "modernity." Understandably so, for, the very birth of the social sciences was deeply implicated in and integral to the modes of life and convulsions brought into being by modernity. Modernity made thinkable the compartmentalization of social life into ontologically distinct spheres such as the "economic," the "political," the "social" and the "international," with each sphere examined by a separate academic discipline. The transition to modernity usually came with a sense of unprecedented novelty and temporal distinctiveness, founded on paradigmatic transformations in conceptions of time, space and knowledge. For all of this centrality, however, modernity has remained a notoriously ambiguous concept. Whatever is meant by "modernity" and whether one chooses to emphasize the "bright" or "dark" side of it, it is usually used as a blanket concept to refer to a mixed bundle of transformations emblematic of the transition to the "modern" world, such as state formation, exclusive territoriality, capitalism, colonialism, imperialism, secularism, individualism, citizenship, nationalism, genocide, private property and industrialization. Indeed, thanks to this conceptual ambiguity, theorists have used modernity to add a sense of complexity to their analyses without pledging themselves to any monocausal conception of this composite transition.

The debate on the actual content of modernity and the timing and manner of its unraveling continues. Nevertheless, two particular aspects of modernity (i.e. its historical specificity and diversity) have become staples for most social and International Relations (IR) theory (albeit more so for the former than the latter). The historical specificity of modernity as an epochal shift from "past" to "present" (e.g. from "*gemeinschaft*" to "*gesellschaft*," and "status" to "contract") was a fundamental building block for virtually all nineteenth- and early twentieth-century social theory; and categories and assumptions grounded in the historical distinctiveness of modernity continue to mark the contemporary social sciences. Likewise, it has become commonplace to understand modernity as a highly interconnected and variegated process. Different sociohistorical and geopolitical legacies gave rise to distinct forms of modernities and new conditions of being "modern." In this sense, modernity has been a historically specific, internationally interactive and sociologically multilinear process all at once.

Indeed, speaking of modernity in the plural, emphasizing diversity, specificity and interconnectivity among multiple modernization projects, appears to be a fundamental correction to homogeneous, unilinear and Eurocentric conceptions of world history. Nevertheless, "diversity," "specificity" and "interconnectedness," by themselves, are by no means substitutes for social theory. The debate about how to theorize the differentiated origins and outcomes of modernity is complex, and competing explanations abound. In this book, I seek to intervene in this debate. I do so primarily by developing a *transdisciplinary* approach to the study of modernity. The importance of transdisciplinarity is rooted in the awareness that the history of modernity cannot be examined through the disciplinary divisions and categories created by modernity itself. Using these categories and divisions in an uncritical way tends to project the structure of modern society back into the past, which renders "historicization" impossible from the very beginning. Instead, we need to defy the methodological compartmentalization of social life, and subject already constituted spheres and logics of modernity to critical scrutiny. Rather than reading back the multiple spheres of contemporary life and studying their interrelations through "interdisciplinary" methodologies, we need to problematize the genesis of their differentiation from each other through a transdisciplinary methodology. Only through transdisciplinarity (and a holistic ontology) can we free historical time and space from the presuppositions of contemporary life. Only through a transdisciplinary methodology can we properly recover the history of modernity, theorizing modern processes in their unity and diversity.

To be sure, talking about transdisciplinarity and modernity is hardly a novelty. After all, crossing and overcoming disciplinary boundaries has long been on the agenda across the social sciences. In particular, scholars of IR and historical sociology have made several attempts in the past decades to bridge the analytically compartmentalized world of the social sciences as they have sought new ways of historicizing and theorizing the origins and development of the modern world (e.g. Wallerstein 1974, 2001, 2003; Ashley 1984; Block and Somers 1984; Cox 1986; Mann 1986; Tilly 1990a; Ruggie 1993; Walker 1993; Rosenberg 1994, 2013; Wood 1995; Hobden and Hobson 2002; Calhoun 2003; Teschke 2003, 2015; Lacher 2006; Buzan and Lawson 2015; Go 2016). That said, my contention in this book is that most extant approaches to IR and historical sociology have not sufficiently dispensed with the categories and assumptions borrowed from the modern present. In other words, existing accounts of modernity have failed to sufficiently turn to "real historical time," continuing to read back the presuppositions of contemporary social life.

My argument in this respect is driven by a twofold methodological critique: the critique of "presentism" and the critique of "internalism." The former critique is closely related to one of the key components of modernity – that is, capitalism. Of course, there have been many explanations for the relationship between modernity and capitalism, and a plethora of interpretations has been advanced over the years for the question as to what extent a history of modernity can be grounded in a history of capitalism. Yet, the more I examined the relevant IR and historical sociology literature, the more I found myself in agreement with an argument repeatedly made by such scholars as Karl Polanyi, Ellen Meiksins Wood and Robert Brenner: Much that has been written about the origins of capitalism tends to presume the prior existence of capitalism to explain its rise. That is, most approaches to IR and historical sociology, despite several differences and disagreements, are united by a common tendency to extrapolate back in history the logic and dynamics of the present economic order –capitalism. The critique of presentism is, in turn, firmly connected to the critique of "methodological internalism." For, by assuming the existence of autonomously and endogenously developing societies in history, "internalist" models of historical change abstract the "social" from its wider international context, thereby transhistoricizing the spatial binaries and hierarchies specific to modernity. This, in turn, not only perpetuates the false image of bounded societies, but also fundamentally obscures the interactive constitution of the modern world. In particular, the assumption of endogenous development tends to force sociological imagination into a straitjacket in which historical particularities are not seen as organic components of an interactively and cumulatively unfolding world history but viewed as "exceptions" or "aberrations" from a purportedly universal and unilinear framework of analysis.

This two-tiered critique, once systematically operationalized, turned out to be an important key to recovering the historicity and diversity of modernity, both inside and outside Europe. A departure from the vocabulary of transhistoricized concepts and categories allowed me to interpret (early) modernity's diversity and interconnectivity in a new light. More specifically, once I adopted a non-presentist and non-internalist conception of history, the conventional notion of a "unitary" Western modernity collapsed, which, in turn, generated significant implications for a rereading of world historical development. I understood that the rise of a pan-European "market civilization" was by and large a "myth" up until the early nineteenth century. While capitalism was developing in Britain during the early modern period, continental European states were not following their British counterpart with a time lag as often presumed. Although the rise of capitalist agriculture and later industry in Britain generated unprecedented geopolitical and fiscal pressures on the continent for emulation, this did not lead to an immediate convergence of socioeconomic forms. Mainland Europe, and perhaps above all, France, up until the end of the Napoleonic Wars, was marked by fundamentally different forms of rule and appropriation, which were absent in capitalist Britain and can hardly be explained by the dictation of any internal capitalist dynamics. Therefore, it became increasingly clear to me that instead of a more or less singular transition to capitalism in Western Europe, geopolitical conflicts, international connections and socioeconomic specificities led to the development of radically different modernities. In particular, revolutionary and Napoleonic France seemed to pose a formidable challenge, as well as a distinctive alternative to capitalism, which, even if short-lived and ultimately defeated, could not be subsumed under an overarching conception of "capitalist modernity. "

Clearly, I cannot claim originality for most of these historical insights. The conventional narratives of Western European history have long been criticized for reproducing idealized conceptions of the "Western path to modernity." Similarly, generations of historical sociologists such as Theda Skocpol (1979), George Comninel (1987), Ellen Meiksins Wood (1991) and Xavier Lafrance (2019a) have long argued that French society barely involved any internal capitalist dynamics before the French Revolution and even the revolution itself hardly cracked this noncapitalist social fabric in any decisive way. The revolutionary and Napoleonic state expanded and consolidated subsistence-oriented peasant proprietorship on land and paved the way for new forms of customary regulation of manufacturing activity. Likewise, the commercial and industrial classes were by and large dependent on income, rents and careers provided by the state. In this sense, the revolution did not institutionalize a (seemingly) self-regulating market, nor did it embark on a systematic commodification of land and labor. Instead, by expanding state-based rents and income, it retained the state's direct role as the main source of social reproduction. Unless one takes a (very) long-termist view, therefore, the revolution provided a contradictory, if not totally infertile, ground for the development of capitalism in France (despite engendering unprecedented changes in the form of state and economy).

What I found missing in this literature, however, beyond the recognition that the French Revolution was not directly triggered by and did not immediately lead to capitalism, was a systematic inquiry into the question as to what the process of (post)revolutionary French "modernization" was actually about. In other words, if 1789 was not a mere continuation of the absolutist past, nor could it be easily understood as a form of protocapitalism, what was to be made of its socioeconomic character and (geo)political innovations? For example, if the political and ideological novelties conventionally associated with the French Revolution, such as universal citizenship, universal equality, universal conscription and nationalism, had no immediate connection with the development of capitalist social relations – how to make sense of them?

Indeed, these questions turned out to be far more important than I originally anticipated. For, on the one hand, revolutionary and Napoleonic France seemed to have generated forms of mobilization and appropriation alternative to capitalism – hence, pointing to the birth of a radically novel form of being "modern." And on the other hand, the social forms and institutions created by the revolution became a model for subsequent modernization projects in and beyond Western Europe. Read together, the revolution and the Napoleonic period seemed to have instituted a socioeconomically opposing, geopolitically contending and potentially internationalizing project more than a century before the rise of Bolshevism.

The potential implications of such an argument were massive. Given that the French Revolution has long served as a template by which other paths to modernity are compared, rethinking the "original" French "path" might have paradigmatic implications for the multilinearity of world historical development. The debate on the social nature of the French Revolution, therefore, was not merely a historiographical one but concerned social theory as a whole. Also, given that the revolution itself became an international vector, inquiring into the revolution could provide new insights into the historicization and theorization of the "international" – that is, it might shed new light on the social content and developmental tempo of the modern international order. A deeper understanding of the results and legacies of the French Revolution could thus generate a new perspective on the international relations of modernity within and beyond Europe.

The following research therefore required two major interventions. First, I needed to find out what kind of social and institutional mechanisms buttressed the (post)revolutionary political, economic and military apparatus in France. Second, I needed to demonstrate the spatial and temporal reach of this project – that is, the extent to which it evolved into a world-historical force impacting the constitution and development of other modernization projects. As for the former task, Robbie Shilliam's early work provided an invaluable starting point. Shilliam (2009) shows that Revolutionary and Napoleonic France set in train a new mode of modernization that did not invoke the systematic commodification of the means of life. More precisely, the French elite, organized in and as the state, introduced the modern rights of the (male) "individual" in Revolutionary France, but did not condition the enjoyment of these rights to a property-ownership criterion (as was the case in Britain until 1918). Instead, under severe social and geopolitical challenges, they extended modern economic and political rights down to the lowest stratum of society by linking these rights to individuals' compulsory service in the newly formed "citizen-army." By conditioning the right to property and equality on compulsory military service, they not only substituted the logic of British participation in the public sphere – the propertied citizenship – but also led to the universalization and institutionalization of a new extra-market mechanism for acquiring income and status. Participation in the army, instead of "productive" utilization of property, gave individuals access to land and equality. Therefore, universal equality, universal conscription and the citizen-army in France were not simply the political/military components of a nascent capitalism; nor were they merely the aspects of an emergent "political modernity," as often assumed. Rather, they constituted the socio-institutional foundations of a new regime of political economy and property relations radically different from capitalism. Following Shilliam, I call this new mode of modernization "Jacobinism."

The citizen-army mobilized social forces and resources in a way the ancien regimes of Europe could not even dare to imagine. In that sense, Shilliam is certainly right in noting universal conscription as the hallmark of Jacobin (geo)political economy. However, Shilliam overlooks that mass conscription was not the only factor that bolstered the revolutionary state. The mobilizing vision of the revolution, despite periodic retreats from and popular reactions to it, was also pursued in the field of "education." The revolutionary- and postrevolutionary elites, while seeking to boost political unity and geopolitical competitiveness through a citizen-army, also attempted to integrate the common people into the state through public education. The French elite, unable or unwilling to subject the peasants to capitalist market imperatives, attempted to centralize and universalize education as an alternative mechanism to tap peasant labor and energies. In addition to the invention of the citizen-army, "public schooling" was envisioned as another extra-market mechanism to discipline and appropriate peasant bodies. This was in stark contrast to capitalist Britain, where the political/cultural mobilization of the lower classes was neither necessary nor desirable for the reproduction of the ruling elite. In Britain, the "market" could well discipline the poor and deliver geopolitical objectives; therefore, there was no need to "educate" the lower classes beyond voluntary and localized forms of vocational/industrial training (at least until the latter nineteenth century). Yet, in a context that could not systematically subject land and labor to market imperatives, universal education was intended to be another method of mobilizing and appropriating peasant bodies based on a new (geo)political pedagogy.

As a further implication, the politico-cultural mobilization of the lower classes through public education and universal conscription led, in principle, to the generalization of access to the state in France, which was the main source of social reproduction, unlike in Britain. In this context, the French elite employed new discourses of "nation," "religion" and "science" to universalize and restrict the lower classes' access to the state and property. As a result, in the making of French citizens, "nationalism" and "secularism," in a way unheard of in Britain, acquired entirely new meanings, turning into "developmental" ideologies and practices. Also, given the centrality of secularism and nationalism for the reproduction of Jacobin political economy, it is no wonder that Jacobinism brought about a continuous onslaught against the potentially contending sources and interpretations of political community and religion. In this sense, Jacobinism was marked by an elite-led and top-down process of nation-building, war-making and subject formation. Yet, for social and geopolitical reasons that I will discuss in the following chapters, Jacobinism also provided a breeding ground for the radicalization of lower-class demands, hence, involving an emancipatory dynamic.

In short, Jacobinism, in the face of social and geopolitical crises, developed and sought to generalize two geo-institutional responses to and substitutes for the "market." By revolutionizing the social basis of the army and school (rather than production), the Jacobin project engineered new nonmarket means to the acquisition of equality and property. Revolutionary and Napoleonic France witnessed the systematic subjection of the peasantry to "universal conscription" and "public education," and the concomitant birth of the "citizen-soldier" and "citizen-officer," endowed with land and state-generated income. "Mass conscription" and "public schooling" conditioned the social mobility and social reproduction of the poor to their successful socialization and disciplining in a new military/educational complex. Service to the state, rather than successful market competition, gave direct access to the means of life and provided the ultimate form of civic participation. As such, Jacobinism did not lead to a concentric extension of a more or less similar market project in France, but set in motion a qualitatively different modernity.

The international reverberations of Jacobinism can hardly be overstated. For, Jacobinism not only instituted a set of new rules of social and geopolitical reproduction that did not invoke the commodification of land and labor but provided a blueprint for other modernization projects. The geopolitical success of the Jacobin project (unstoppable until Waterloo) inspired other ancien regimes within and beyond Europe to selectively adopt, alone or alongside the capitalist project, the socio-institutional legacy of Jacobinism. For example, the economic and geopolitical challenges generated by capitalism and Jacobinism compelled most Western European states to pursue a

combined "capitalist–Jacobin project." They took steps toward commodifying labor and land while invoking popular sovereignty by introducing the citizen-soldier and citizen-officer as the new engine of the
military/administrative machine. However, the long-term result of this
mutually conditioning and contradictory course of development in the
Western European context was the gradual subordination of the
Jacobin forms to the emerging capitalist market in the course of
the nineteenth century. Put differently, capitalism, Jacobinism and
local social forms were combined in historically specific ways in
Western Europe, yet the ultimate result of these processes of socio-
institutional cross-breeding in nineteenth-century Western Europe was
capitalism. Capitalism, by and large, universalized itself in Western
Europe during the nineteenth century, ultimately assimilating the historical legacy of Jacobinism into its systemic logic (despite the persistence of "national" differences linked to the spatial and temporal
conditions of the transition to capitalism).

At first sight, therefore, Jacobinism, given its short life span and early
"retirement" in Western Europe, seemed to be a phenomenon that
belonged merely to a distant past, producing only minor consequences
for the constitution of the modern world as a whole. Yet, what if
Jacobinism was not merely a passive bystander to capitalism? What
if Jacobinism, under certain social and international circumstances,
could serve as a substitute for capitalism much longer than it did in
Western Europe? Indeed, what if, as Shilliam (2009: 55–6) intuitively
suggests, it was not capitalism, but its substitute, Jacobinism, that
introduced the majority of the world to the relations and institutions
of modernity? What is implied here is that Jacobinism might be as
much central to the constitution of the modern world as capitalism,
hence it is an important link in recovering the "lost history" of modern
social and international relations (Rosenberg 1996).

With these questions in mind, I turned to the history of the late
Ottoman Empire and Turkey to evaluate the spatial and temporal
reach of Jacobinism. There were two reasons for my case selection.
First, it is well known that the late Ottoman and early Turkish reformers took France as a reference point for their own modernization
efforts. Second, as the late Fred Halliday argued, the Ottoman and
early Republican modernizations were "arguably the greatest turning
point in the modern history of the Middle East" – that is, the Young
Turk Revolution and its early Republican offshoot in Turkey launched

or inspired the development of modern institutions in the Middle East, decisively reshaping the international relations of modernity in a wider regional context (Halliday 2005: 7). Therefore, a systematic inquiry into the late Ottoman Empire and Turkey could point to the ways in which Jacobinism, combined with the social-intellectual resources of an Islamic-Ottoman milieu, turned into a transnational vector that shaped the international relations of modernity in the wider Middle Eastern context. In short, an inquiry into Ottoman/Turkish Jacobinism could provide a new starting point to explore the quality of international sociality in the making of the modern Middle East.

That said, my turn to Ottoman and Turkish history, exciting though it was, immediately encountered a number of problems. Most conspicuously, I was surprised to find out that most of the macrolevel historical sociological analyses of Ottoman and Turkish modernity, albeit empirically very rich, were informed by idealized conceptions of Western European history. They rested on standard narratives of Western capitalist development, according to which the "modernness" of the Ottoman and Turkish experience was judged. As a result, the alleged peculiarities of the Turkish "path" to modernity – that is, its transition to "capitalism from above," its "conservative" modernization, its "peripheral" capitalism and "incomplete" bourgeois revolution, alongside the "persistence" of bureaucratic interests, "weakness" of bourgeois classes and so on – were all derived from a counter reference point that hardly existed in history. After all, even the most "archetypal" cases of bourgeois revolution and capitalist development from "below," England and France, widely diverged from the premises of the conventional narratives of the "rise of the West." Therefore, the puzzle to be unravelled was this: if Turkey's transition to modernity could not be understood just as another *Sonderweg*, an aberration from an idealized and unitary "Western" model of modernization, how to make sense of it?

Indeed, once I departed from the pan-European conceptions of "market civilization" and introduced into my analysis the concept of Jacobinism as a historically specific path, Ottoman/Turkish modernization efforts appeared in a totally new light. I realized that Ottoman modernization did not follow a single project of "Westernization," but rather that Ottoman and Turkish elites selectively appropriated, oscillated between and recombined with local social resources two inherently contradictory "development" strategies: capitalism and

Jacobinism. Over time, however, the reactions from "below" and interventions from "outside" increasingly forced the Ottoman/ Turkish state to consolidate the Jacobin model at the expense of market society. Significant steps were taken to define human existence away from the market, with participation in a mass army and public schooling, rather than competition in the marketplace, was understood as the basis of the subsistence and equality of imperial/Republican subjects. The cumulative result of the Ottoman/Turkish experiment with modernity (1839–1950), therefore, was not a "backward," "peripheral" or "statist" capitalism as often presumed, but a historically specific Jacobinism that bypassed capitalism (and communism) based on an alternative form of property and sociality.

Jacobinism thus proved to be longer lasting in Turkey than its birthplace. In particular, the Young Turk (1908) and Kemalist (1923) revolutions consolidated Turkish modernity as a late Jacobin progeny. The Turkish Revolution generated a political economy and subjectivity that was consciously designed to achieve a noncapitalist (and nonsocialist) form of late development. Like other modernization projects, however, the persistence of Jacobin social relations and institutions hinged on domestic and international balances of power, which were rapidly changing after World War II. In many ways, the 1950s signified the end of Jacobinism and the rise of a capitalist project in Turkey. After more than a hundred years of modernization, the Turkish elite finally found the (geo)political breathing space in which capitalist property relations could be established without the imminent danger of domestic rebellion and foreign invasion. That said, one should not presume capitalism's coming into dominance as a relatively smooth process. Capitalism was born in a Jacobin womb: the property relations that characterized the original Kemalist project were often invoked by different classes to limit and contest, as well as to produce capitalism. The preexistent social relations, institutions and values rooted in the early Republican experience (combined with the lateness and international context of capitalist transition) greatly complicated the development of capitalist social relations in Turkey.

Asserting the historical distinctiveness of Jacobinism, therefore, led me to advance a new historical narrative of the initial development and ultimate consolidation of capitalism in Turkey. I argue that while capitalism in Turkey was born in a Jacobin womb, from the 1970s onward, the blueprint for a capitalism "proper" was being drawn up elsewhere in an entirely non-Kemalist – that is, non-Jacobin – socio-intellectual milieu. Completely detached from the social and intellectual resources of the original Republican project, it was an Islamic sociopolitical movement, *Milli Görüş Hareketi*, or the National View Movement (NVM), that provided the blueprint for a novel capitalist development strategy, heralding the end of capitalism's complicated coexistence with Jacobinism in Turkey. By deducing modernity from an imagined Ottoman-Islamic past rather than revolutionary France, the NVM sought to unburden capitalist development from the legacies of Jacobinism. As the classes associated with and mobilized by this Islamic movement mustered power throughout the 1980s and 1990s, "secularism" turned into the main Republican bulwark against this new form of capitalism. This secular bulwark was taken down in 2002 with the election of Erdoğan's Justice and Development Party (AKP), and since then different Islamic movements not only jointly eliminated the last remnants of Kemalist populism/radicalism, thereby consolidating capitalism to a degree never achieved before, but also initiated a competitive and contradictory restructuring of the post-Kemalist order, which led to the failed coup of July 2016.

Overall, then, the book attempts to trace the antagonistic coconstruction (not cogenesis) of Jacobinism and capitalism in world historical development. It utilizes Jacobinism as a corrective to one-dimensional narratives of the transition to modernity, and by doing so, it contributes to a deeper understanding of the multilinearity of world historical development. Furthermore, through a systematic examination of Ottoman and Turkish modernizations, it provides the preliminary outlines of an alternative narrative of the transition to modernity in the wider Middle Eastern region, as well as offering a new account of the development of capitalism in Turkey. As for its significance for historical sociology, the book emphasizes the historicity of capitalism, while positing that the "international" is far more foundational to the construction of property forms and social orders. Regarding its contribution to IR, the book critically reconsiders the theoretical significance of sociological processes for a deeper understanding of the "international." It does not take the "international" as an ontologically distinct realm operating according to its own transhistorical laws, but explores the international nature of sociological processes and their implication in changing patterns of intersocietal interaction. By elaborating the social and geopolitical dynamics set in train by Jacobinism, the book shows that the expansion of the liberal international order was not an unproblematic process even in the West, but led to the emergence of radically distinct (geo)political projects that impacted the development of capitalism in and beyond Europe. As such, the book offers new ways of recovering international interconnections and differences, assisting us in restoring the history of the modern international system as a more polycentric, interactive and processual terrain. All combined, the book, guided by a transdisciplinary methodology, makes arguments and conclusions transdisciplinary in scope. In particular, it seeks to contribute to the rethinking and reconstructing of some of the foundational concepts and assumptions of historical sociology, Political Economy, IR, Middle Eastern Studies and Turkish Studies.

The Plan of the Book

The book unfolds in seven chapters. Chapter 2 outlines the methodological foundations for a *transdisciplinary* approach to the history of modernity. The crux of my argument is that any inquiry into the history of modernity requires historicizing and going beyond the methodological divisions and categories created by modernity itself. Parsimonious as it may be, compartmentalization of social life into distinct realms, such as the "political," the "economic," the "domestic" or the "international," runs the risk of transhistoricizing modernity's consequences, therefore undermining the process of "historicization" in the first place. In this sense, "historicization" is not just a call for going back to history. After all, as C. Wright Mills pointed out, all social sciences, in essence, are "historical" ventures "unless one assumes some transhistorical theory of the nature of history, or that man in society is a non-historical entity" (Mills 1959: 146). Instead of a mere return to history, historicization thus involves a process of freeing "history" from "transhistoricism"; it is a call to turn to "real historical time," distancing ourselves from the presuppositions and methodological divisions created by the contemporary world itself. In short, historicization of modernity is firmly connected to the transdisciplinarity of methodology.

In developing such a transdisciplinary approach, I have been guided by two recurrent methodological strategies, the critique of "methodological presentism" and the critique of "methodological internalism."

Both critiques relate to the awareness that much social and international theory is pervaded by a mode of explanation that naturalizes
and reads back in time the social and spatial parameters of the present.
Therefore, they aim to problematize and overcome the transhistoricization of concepts, divisions and dichotomies abstracted from the
modern present, for example, "inside" versus "outside," "political"
versus "economic," and "social" versus "international." Based on a
critical overview of historical sociology and IR scholarships, I argue
that the persistence of "presentism" and "internalism" across social
sciences leads to "evolutionary" and "unilinear" conceptions of the
transition to modernity. A systematic departure from presentism and
internalism enables us to explore the radical heterogeneity of diverging
paths to modernity, as well as the spatially and temporally connected
nature of modern transitions.

The theoretical and methodological points raised in Chapter 2 are
used in Chapter 3 to disturb evolutionary and unilinear readings of
"Western European modernity," with a specific focus on early modern
Britain and France. The chapter first documents the historical and
international context in which British capitalism and French
absolutism arose as two geopolitically related yet qualitatively different
paths to modernity. Then, it shows that the revolutionary and
Napoleonic years in France did not generate merely another form of
capitalism as often presumed, but a project of "substitution," which
led to the birth of a noncapitalist (and nonsocialist) political economy –
that is, "Jacobinism." Furthermore, Jacobinism did not only "revolutionize" France, but it was emulated and selectively adapted by other
states too, including the Ottoman Empire.

Each chapter on the Ottoman Empire and Turkey (Chapters 4–6)
introduces a different historical period, while at the same time taking
issue with different manifestations of internalism and presentism in
relevant literature. In Chapter 4, I argue that the cumulative result of
the eighty–year-long Ottoman experience with modern social forms
and values (1838–1918) was not a form of "peripheral capitalism,"
but the emergence of a novel project of modernity: a modernity that
not only substituted the relations of market society with the Jacobin
model, but also repeatedly recombined the latter with the resources of
an Ottoman-Islamic context. Chapter 5 focuses on the early
Republican period (1923–45). It contends that the original Kemalist
experiment with modernity cannot be understood as an "incomplete or

failed bourgeois revolution" leading to a form of "state capitalism," as often argued. Instead, the original Kemalist experiment with modernity is best understood as a Jacobin revolution that invoked (and limited) Jacobin forms of mobilization, appropriation and subjectivity, while deliberately sidestepping the institutionalization of capitalist social relations.

Chapter 6 discusses the origin and protracted development of capitalism in Turkey in the post–World War II period. I show how capitalist social relations began to penetrate the social fabric, and how the initial Kemalist project has been reinvented by different actors to contest and produce capitalism. In addition, the period after the 1950s witnessed the rise of a new capitalist class in provincial Anatolian towns organized in and through the Islamic NVM. Arguing against the conventional interpretation of the NVM, the chapter shows that these commercial groups neither supported an "artisan" or "statist" capitalism, nor did they merely raise an Islamic critique of the developing market society. Instead, the movement envisioned a novel political space as the foundation of a new capitalist industrialization strategy unencumbered by the spirit of earlier Republican policies. Although the NVM was unable to take control of the state from the 1970s to the 1990s, its conservative capitalist heritage was appropriated by the AKP, which has led to an unprecedented consolidation and deepening of capitalist social relations in Turkey since the beginning of the new millennium. Chapter 7 summarizes the argument of the book and considers its implications for IR and historical sociology.

2 | Modernity, Historicity and Transdisciplinarity

In this chapter I attempt to build a transdisciplinary methodology to historicize modernity. The need for transdisciplinarity stems from the idea that disciplinary divisions and categories (such as the political, the economic, the social and the international) are the products of modernity. Therefore, they cannot be used to study modernity's history, which would otherwise impose the structure of modern (capitalist) society onto a differently constituted past. I use a twofold methodological critique to problematize these disciplinary divisions and the attendant tendency to transhistorize the sociospatial parameters of the modern present: the critique of "methodological presentism" and "methodological internalism."

In the first two sections of this chapter, I develop the critique of presentism. Surveying a number of contributions to historical sociology, I argue that extant approaches to the history of modernity suffer (explicitly or otherwise) from transhistorically understood notions of "economy" and "politics." To take economics and politics as separate spheres, each driven by a distinctive rationality, transhistoricizes the outcomes of capitalism, hence reading capitalism back in history as an ever-present developmental tendency. I suggest that defining capitalism as "market-dependence" enables a historically specific and historically dynamic conception of capitalism, which, in turn, provides an entry point for a nonpresentist historicization of global modernity. In the third and fourth sections, I turn to International Relations (IR) and historical sociology to develop a critique of methodological internalism. I show that the burgeoning field of international historical sociology (IHS), and in particular the theory of uneven and combined development (UCD) , offers unique resources to supplant internalism. By merging the "social" and the "international" at an ontological level, UCD dramatically increases our capacity to capture the interactive, temporal and cumulative constitution of the modern world. In the fifth section, I show how to combine a noninternalist and nonpresentist conception of history, which, as I will demonstrate in the rest of this book, is vital for capturing the radical multilinearity of modernity in and beyond Europe.

Historicizing Modernity: Beyond Fragmented Methodologies

The history of "modernity" as an aesthetic concept can be traced back to as far as the seventeenth century (Sayer 1990: 9). "Modernity" as a sociological concept, however, has a more recent genealogy. "Modern society" as an object of inquiry has been one of the main preoccupations of social theory since the nineteenth century (Prendergast 2003). Witnessing the sociohistorical rupture brought about by capitalism, modern state formation and industrialization, classical social theorists attempted to uncover the underlying causes of this unprecedented transformation, offering distinct, yet at times converging, sociologies of modern society (Sayer 1990). Yet, although already anticipated in nineteenth-century classical social theory, "modernity" as a sociological concept has been been popularized by "modernization theory" of the 1960s (Woodiwiss 1997).

Modernization theory saw modernity as a process of gradual rationalization and differentiation of distinct spheres of social life. In the modernization view, political, economic and cultural spheres, each driven by a distinct set of values, interacted in specific ways in history that ultimately produced the "modern" world of economically industrial, politically liberal and culturally secular entities of the West. Specifying the stages of and preconditions to modernity in the West was then used to identify why these were absent elsewhere in the world (e.g. Lerner 1958; Rostow 1960). It is no wonder that in the modernization lexicon, geospatial differences were understood in terms of such hierarchical binaries as "developed" versus "developing," which were, in turn, instrumental in fostering the image of modernization as a unilinear and evolutionary developmental path through which all societies must pass. Modernity, in other words, was understood as a more or less singular process for all societies, while its developmental sequence and pattern was abstracted from the presumed historical evolution of an ideal type of modernity, which the United States supposedly epitomize.

Obviously, it has been a long time since modernity departed from the crudest versions of modernization theory (Knöbl 2003). Hardly anyone today in academia subscribes to the overtly unilinear and evolutionary narratives of social change. Contemporary approaches to modernization no longer understand modernity as a coherent and unilinear path; instead, it is now seen to exist in a multiplicity of forms, moving in competing, inconsistent and often alternative directions complicated by the relations of international hierarchy. In other words, social and temporal diversities are no longer seen as aberrations from an ideal type, but as constitutive and interlinked instances in the movement of global modernity (e.g. Mann 1986; Ashley 1989; Gilroy 1993; Eisenstadt 2000; Gaonkar 2001; Goody 2004; Hobson 2004).

Indeed, there is much to commend in these relatively more recent renditions that attempt to capture the multiplicity and interconnectedness of the modern experience. Yet, despite the diversity of attempts to clarify the social and temporal content of modernity, it remains remarkable that most of the contemporary approaches to modernity (and postmodernity) have reproduced the *fragmented methodology* of modernization theory. Their mode of inquiry still revolves around the assumption that societies function on the basis of a complex interplay of distinct spheres, webs or networks, each operating according to their own logic or rationality (e.g. economic, political, cultural or military). This fragmentation is usually defended on the basis of explanatory parsimony and causal flexibility, which arguably make for an intelligible and nonreductionist history of modernity (e.g. Mann 1986; Giddens 1987; Runciman 1989; Tilly 1990a; Hobson 1997; cf. Lapointe and Dufour 2012). Precisely here, though, we face a fundamental contradiction. Understanding modernity based on the interaction of preconstituted spheres of social life ultimately undermines our understanding of an essential feature of modernity: modernity's historical specificity. Let me explain.

If multiplicity is considered central to modernity, so is its historicity. According to Anthony Giddens, for example, modernity stands for a "particular discontinuity" in human history, a break from our previously existing perceptions of time and space, marked by fundamental changes in the "pace," "scope" and the "nature" of socioeconomic development (Giddens 1990: 4–6). Karl Polanyi tends to concur with this view by emphasizing the radical modernness of "market society." He notes that the rise of market society corresponds more to "the metamorphosis of the caterpillar" than "any alteration that can be expressed in terms of continuous growth and development" (Polanyi 1957a: 44). Clearly, modern transformation has never been a "quantum jump"; that is, the transition to modernity occurred rapidly but processually, bearing the traces of the previous political, economic and cultural forms (Goody 2004: 11). Michael Mann writes that modernity brought about "structural" changes, "often occurring within single lifetimes," yet it rarely "swept all away but were molded into older forms" (Mann 1993: 14–17). Thus, the protractedness of modernity aside, the historical specificity of modernity as an epochal shift from past to present has been a persistent reference point for social theory.

What is being exposed here is a discrepancy between what social theory wants to achieve and how it wants to achieve it. For, despite all the historical specificity attributed to modernity and all the different causes said to have impacted its emergence, social theory's fragmented vision of history diminishes our understanding of modernity's specificity. Consider Michael Mann's four-footed methodology and his narrative of the "rise" of the modern state and modern capitalism (Mann 1986). According to Mann, throughout human history, societies have been organized based on four distinct logics of power (ideological, economic, military and political). Such a differentiation of power networks stem from the diversification of basic human needs: economic power networks have been formed to meet the needs for "material subsistence"; political power to "settle disputes without constant recourse to force"; ideological power to provide "meaning and legitimacy"; and military power "to defend whatever they have obtained and pillage others" (Mann 1986: 14). These distinct power networks operate across borders, hence are not internally bounded (Mann 1986: 15). Likewise, a clear-cut separation of power networks hardly exists in the empirical world: "the character of each (network) is likely to be influenced by the character of all" (Mann 1986: 14–15). Yet, given the diversity of human needs, "a broad division of function between ideological, economic, military, and political organizations is ubiquitous," hence a transhistorical norm (Mann 1986: 18). Networks of power are autonomous and none of them have causal primacy. Yet, they also interact and overlap in a diversity of ways depending on historical and contingent factors, which lends world historical development its nonevolutionary and multilinear character. As such, Mann's methodology rejects monocausal explanations and breaks with the false image of separate and internally driven societies in history. These, in turn, allow (at least in principle) a departure from the evolutionary unilineralism characteristic of modernization theory.

Yet, it is questionable the extent to which Mann's methodology based on transhistorically separate spheres of social action can really depart from evolutionary models of social change and capture the historical specificity of modernity. To presume a priori the existence and interaction of institutionally separate power networks risks reading back the consequences of modernity, undermining the process of historicization from the very beginning.

Nowhere is this clearer than in Mann's narrative of the transition to capitalism and the modern state (cf. Teschke 2003: 121). According to Mann, the rise of capitalism and the modern state was rooted in the centuries-long reconfiguration of the ideological, political, military and economic power networks in medieval and early modern Western Europe (Mann 1986: 373). To be more precise, the rise of capitalism was underlined by the absence of a "unitary state" and the distinctiveness of the Roman-Christian legacy in Western Europe. While the fall of the Roman Empire caused the weakening of centralized political power, hence, decreasing demands for taxation, Christianity provided common social norms and a common social identity, thereby unburdening bourgeois classes from the high costs of political regulation. The fragmentation of imperial sovereignty also produced unprecedented geopolitical pressures among competing political units. This forced the holders of political authority to give up most of their redistributive functions and to confirm property rights in exchange for the bourgeois classes' support for war efforts (Mann 1986: 377–8). Once endowed with property rights and absolved from medieval polities' redistributive pressures, people obtained "autonomy and privacy sufficient to keep to themselves the fruits of their own enterprise and thus to calculate likely costs and benefits to themselves of alternative strategies. Thus, with supply, demand, and incentives for innovation well established," the path to Europe's "embryonic transition to capitalism" was cleared (Mann 1986: 409). Henceforth, capitalism and the protomodern state continued to mutually reinforce one another, the former by providing funds for war-making and state-making, and the latter by fulfilling "new pacification requirements" of a rapidly commercializing economy under new geopolitical imperatives (Mann 1986: 500–17). In sum, "(a)s the original dynamism of feudal Europe became more extensive, capitalism and the national state formed a loose but coordinated and concentrated alliance, which was shortly to intensify and to conquer both heaven and earth" (Mann 1986: 446).

Three important and interrelated problems ensue from Mann's narrative. First, according to Mann, whenever the holders of political/ ideological power secure private property and maintain order without encumbering the economy, people, by definition, adopt a capitalist logic of action; that is, they systematically exploit market opportunities, and progressively increase the degree of product specialization, productivity, technical innovation, commodity production and the size of a dispossessed "free" labor force (Mann 1986: 37). The problem with this approach is that private property, in different yet comparable forms, existed almost throughout history: it can be dated back to ancient societies and was certainly not exclusive to Western Europe (e.g. Goody 2004). There were well-defined property rights in certain parts of the non-Western world such as China, and furthermore, "there are many examples in history where protecting existing property rights actually had negative effects for (capitalist) economic development" (Vries 2012: 83). For example, what caused the transition to capitalism in the English countryside was not the existence of strong property rights per se, but the generalized precariousness of property rights (encoded in custom) that reinforced the arbitrariness of lordly power over the peasantry (Bloch 1961: 277). In France, by contrast, the existing rights on land were relatively more secure during the early modern period, and their codification and further strengthening after the French Revolution kept peasantry in place and agrarian capitalism at bay well into the nineteenth century (Brenner 1985a). Thus, the security of property rights alone is hardly an indicator of the character of socioeconomic relations prevalent in a given context. In other words, property rights by themselves tell us nothing, if anything, about the relational content and societal context of productive activity.[1]

Relatedly, prior to the emergence of market societies, property was not a "thing" in itself subjected to the laws of supply and demand. Its sale, status and function were not determined by the market, but customary rules, which were, in turn, vital to the reproduction of the wider military, judicial, administrative and political system (Polanyi

---

[1] For contrasting views on property rights in history, cf. North 1981: 22–3, chapter 11; Brenner 2006; Acemoglu and Robinson 2012: 429–30; Milonakis and Meramveliotakis 2012.

1957a: 72–3). In this sense, the prior presence or absence of markets
and private property "need make no difference" in the transition to a
"market society"; that is, "their absence, while indicating a certain
isolation and tendency to seclusion, is not associated with any particular development any more than can be inferred from their presence"
(Polanyi 1957b: 60–1). Therefore, a mere emphasis on the
strengthening of property rights assumes away the wholesale transformation necessary for the emergence of capitalist societies. Viewed
together, private property per se is far too general to be interpreted as a
necessary precursor of capitalism in history.

Second, equating private property to capitalism on an a priori basis
ushers in the transhistoricization and naturalization of capitalism. That
is, by uncritically equating private property to capitalism in history,
Mann tends to assume an ever-present capitalist potential rooted in
private property ownership. Private property is seen as part of a
transhistorical economic logic, which, if afforded with the right incentives, unfetters itself from the impediments that stand in its way. As
such, the prior existence of capitalism in some embryonic form is
presumed in order to explain capitalism's origins (Wood 1999;
Brenner 2006). Therefore, Mann, despite his claim otherwise, delivers
an evolutionary narrative based on the gradual "liberation" of a
pregiven human proclivity toward capitalism. This signals that
Mann's narrative is susceptible to the charge of what may be called
methodological presentism. That is, Mann takes as given and extrapo-
lates back in time the present form and logic of the economy – that is,
capitalism. The overall consequence is that in Mann's narrative, the
composite transition to modernity is, at least partly, conceived as
buttressed and conditioned by a transhistorical process of capitalist
rationalization. Modernity becomes part of the teleology underlying
the rise of capitalism. Modernity's historicity ultimately gets lost in the
"non-history of capitalism" (Wood 1997a).

Third, Mann's relapse into presentism is a logical result of his
fragmented methodology. By presuming the existence of functionally
differentiated networks of power in history, Mann tends to impose the
institutional divisions of capitalist modernity onto the precapitalist
past. For example, the conception of economy as an autonomous
sphere interacting exogenously with other spheres of life is specifically
a modern invention (Godelier 1986: 28). In nonmarket societies,
"there existed, as a rule, no term to designate the concept of economic"

(Polanyi 1957c: 71); for, "(n)either under tribal, nor feudal, nor mercantile conditions was there ... a separate economic system in society" (Polanyi 1957a: 74). The economy either "remained nameless" or had "no obvious meaning," for the economic process and prices were instituted through nonmarket means, such as kinship, marriage, age groups, status, political patronage, and so on (Polanyi 1957c: 70–1; Godelier 1986: 29). The economy began to emerge as a functionally, institutionally, conceptually and motivationally distinct sphere of life only when institutionalized markets compelled and induced economic action driven by a distinctive market rationality. It is the social relations and institutional arrangements of market society that gives the economy a practical significance in social life, an autonomous sphere governed (presumably) by laws of its own (Polanyi 1957c: 68).

Mann's fragmented methodology, therefore, is susceptible to viewing the past in terms of the present. Mann's fragmented methodology, for all its parsimony and causal flexibility, ontologizes the consequences of capitalist modernity, hence falling back into evolutionary explanations of world historical development. What is implied here is that an interdisciplinary methodology would not do the job, for interdisciplinarity presupposes the existence of an already fragmented world (Abbott 2001: 135; Lacher 2006: 169). Our ability to register the historicity of modernity hinges on imagining a nonfragmented ontology that would systematically counter methodological presentism. Therefore, there is a strong connection between the historicity of modernity and the transdisciplinarity of our methodology. This is to say that rather than treating the political, the economic, the military and the ideological as self-evident, separate and a priori categories, we need to comprehend their historically changing content and ultimate differentiation from one another.[2] In this sense, historicization of modernity is not just about bringing history back in, but requires a constant conversation between history and theory, a dialogue that can free our disciplinary categories and assumptions from the presuppositions of contemporary life (cf. Lawson 2007).

Karl Polanyi's substantivist approach to economic history represents a big step taken in this direction. According to Polanyi, the economy in

---

[2] Similar arguments have been made from a variety of disciplinary and theoretical angles, see Nicolaus 1973: 30; Anderson 1974: 402–5; Kosik 1976: 64; McMichael 1990: 385; Abbott 1995: 856–7; Emirbayer 1997: 287.

history cannot be analyzed based on formalistic categories and assumptions derived from market society. Reading back into history, the dynamics and motives underlying market society naturalizes and universalizes self-regulating markets, turning them into self-referential and self-birthing phenomena. This, in turn, narrates a world history in which past economies appear to be mere "miniatures or early specimens of our own" and markets seem to have "come into being unless something was there to prevent it" (Polanyi 1957c: xviii, 1977: 14–15). Immediately lost in this narrative, Polanyi argues, is the insight that the advent of self-regulating markets represented a watershed in human history. "[N]ever before our time were markets more than mere accessories of economic life." For, social reproduction was never dependent on exchange and production per se, but immediately tied to people's capacity to mobilize political, juridical, custom-based and territorial privileges and sanctions. In other words, kinship, custom, political/jurisdictional and territorial arrangements constituted economic relations themselves (Polanyi 1957c: 70–1). Therefore, even "where markets were most highly developed, as under the mercantile system," the economic system, as a rule, "was absorbed in the social system" and showed "no tendency to expand at the expense of the rest." In this sense, the self-regulating and self-expanding markets "were unknown in history; indeed the emergence of the idea of self-regulation was a complete reversal" of previously existing patterns of social reproduction (Polanyi 1957a: 71).

What Polanyi implies is that the development of market societies was not a logical extension of preexistent social and economic patterns, but rather the consequence of a fundamental rupture in millennia-old patterns of social reproduction. In order for self-regulating markets to self-regulate, the age-old communal systems of social and moral regulation had to be eradicated, a process that systematically subordinated the "natural and human substance of society," that is, land and labor, to market relations for the first time in history (Polanyi 1957a: 42). In other words, the market economy arose only when "land and food were mobilized, and labor was turned into a commodity." Only with the rise of institutionalized markets that systematically commodified land and labor did the economy begin to constitute (however fictitiously) a separate economic sphere that functioned according to its own rules. Therefore, it is only these new social relations and institutional arrangements that make relevant the "view of the economy as the locus of allocating, saving up, marketing surpluses" and "compel (ling) economizing actions." Furthermore, Polanyi promptly adds, all this is "nowhere created by mere random acts of exchange" but is an "institutional setup" (Polanyi 1957c: 240, 250–1, 255).

Unlike Mann, therefore, Polanyi tends to explain the emergence of capitalism in a way that does not already contain capitalism's logic or dynamic as part of historical explanation. The transition to capitalism had nothing to do with the gradual unfettering of a dormant transhistorical economic logic in history. Instead, an entirely unprecedented institutional mechanism was imposed on human beings, which led to the rise of the market economy and concomitantly to the appearance of the economy as a separate sphere of human action. At stake in Polanyi's analysis, therefore, is a departure from a presentist interpretation to a nonpresentist one – that is, from a transhistorically cumulating capitalism toward a conception of capitalism as a qualitative break in human history. Relatedly, Polanyi's substantivist conception of the economy works as an effective antidote to transhistoricism, as well as showing us how to "unthink" the fragmentation of our methodologies. By emphasizing the inseparability of the economy from other spheres of life in history, Polanyi insists on the unity of life experience, helping us imagine a nonfragmented methodology on which a transdisciplinary social science can be built and operationalized. By countering the false identification of the economy with its market form, Polanyi opens up a theoretical space, in which we can move beyond methodological divisions and begin to envisage a nonpresentist historicization of modernity.

All that said, however, Polanyi's departure from presentism ultimately remains mired in his somewhat economically determinist narrative of the emergence of market society. He writes that "[t]he idea of a self-regulating market system was bound to take shape once elaborate machines and plants were used for production." For "they (machines) can be worked without a loss only if … all factors (of production) are on sale, that is, they must be available in the needed quantities to anybody who is prepared to pay for them" (Polanyi 1957a: 42–3). Eventually, then, Polanyi views the emergence of market society somewhat as a function of cost-calculation and technological changes associated with the Industrial Revolution. Indeed, this is rather an abrupt lapse into economic-technological functionalism. While Polanyi acknowledged that capitalism cannot be treated as an inherent potentiality in human history, he failed to properly historicize the making of market society. An implicitly presentist narrative of the transition to capitalism undermined his otherwise forceful critique of *Homo economicus*.

From Marx to Marxism: Unifying the "Political" and the "Economic"

The contradictions and ambiguities that mark Polanyi's oeuvre perhaps find their strongest echo in Karl Marx's critique and method of the historicization of capitalism. On the one hand, it seems incontestable that Marx is a presentist. Although he never embarked on a systematic historical inquiry into the origins of capitalism, Marx tends to make economistic arguments in several early texts. He emphasizes the primacy of economic factors and actors in history as if the economic was already a separate sphere, the prime example of which is the infamous "base/superstructure" metaphor derived from the 1859 "Preface."[3] Likewise, in the *German Ideology* and the *Communist Manifesto*, he explains the emergence of modern social forms through the "rationalization of division of labor," crisis of the "relations of production" or the rise of "bourgeois classes" (Marx 1975: 8–9, 1976: 19) Perhaps this economistic tendency is not too surprising a consequence considering especially that the early Marx seems to have extensively relied on and appropriated the taxonomies of nineteenth-century liberal historiography, including a "stagist" history driven by the unilinear and transhistorical conceptions of "progress" (Godelier 1986: 99; Comninel 1987: 86, 2019: chapter 5).

In this sense, it is little wonder that several scholars have taken Marx and Marxism to task for their "irremediable" evolutionism/determinism. According to Anthony Giddens, for example, there is a strong tendency in Marx's theory of history to give priority to "production over other elements of social life," which ultimately results in an "evolutionary scheme" of history marked by transhistorical patterns

---

[3] From the *Preface to A Contribution to the Critique of Political Economy*: "The relations of production constitute the economic structure of society – the real foundation, on which rise legal and political superstructures and to which correspond definite forms of social consciousness. The mode of production in material life determines the general character of the social, political and spiritual processes of life" (Marx 1996a: 159–60).

of conflict and development (Giddens 1985: 88). Likewise, E. H. Carr argues that Marx wrote "as if economics and politics were separate domains, one (the latter) subordinate to the other (former), therefore unable to capture that 'economic forces are in fact political forces' in history" (Carr 1981: 116–17). In a similar fashion, Charles Tilly (1984: 79) contends that it is uncertain in Marxist analyses if the state and the organization of coercion in general have a logic of their own, or if they ultimately reduce to the logic of production. The conventional verdict, then, is that Marxism in all of its guises falls into some form of economic reductionism, hence presentism: "a non-reductionist Marxism is a non-sequitur" (Hobson 1998: 358; 2011).

Whether or not one agrees with these critiques, however, in Marx's mature accounts, the influence of presentist categories and the resultant economic determinism is countered by a consistent emphasis on the historical specificity of class societies and of capitalist society in particular. In the *Grundrisse*, for example, he accuses liberal political economy of presenting the economy "as encased in eternal natural laws independent of history," which were "then quietly smuggled in as the inviolable laws on which society in the abstract is founded" (Marx 1993: 87). Likewise, in volume 1 of *Capital*, he writes that the categories of liberal economy are not eternal but "forms of thought expressing ... the conditions and relations of a definite, historically determined mode of production," whose validity "vanishes ... so soon as we come to other forms of production" in history (Marx 1996b: 65).

In a similar vein to Polanyi, then, the late Marx argues against the eternalization and naturalization of capitalist social relations and economic categories. By implication, he too holds a strongly discontinuist view of the transition to capitalism. He stresses the submergence of economic transactions in extraeconomic processes (and vice versa), hence the inseparability of the economic and the noneconomic in precapitalist history (Marx 1997: 776–7). Relatedly, he notes that "[t]he original formation of capital does not happen, as it is sometimes imagined, with capital heaping up necessaries of life and instruments of labour and raw materials" (Marx 1993: 507). Put another way, the existence of wealth in the form "merchant capital" and "usurer capital" is "insufficient to explain" and indeed in some circumstances "stands in inverse" relation to the transition to capitalism (Marx 1997: 730–2, 444–50). Commerce and money can have a "solvent effect on traditional economic structures" but, by themselves, do not guarantee and indeed may hinder the development of capitalist social relations. Therefore, the transition to capitalism was not facilitated by economic processes per se; it did not have anything to do with money or market exchange, but it required a radical political intervention and social transformation. What was central to the transition to capitalism was "the expropriation of the great mass of the people from the soil, from the means of subsistence, and from the means of labour; this fearful and painful expropriation of the mass of the people forms the prelude to the history of capital" (Marx 1996b: 749). Only after such a process of "primitive accumulation" began, could the basic categories and assumptions of liberal political economy hold – that is, land and labor could be considered commodities and the assumption of a cost-saving, productivity-maximizing and labor-saving individual can be introduced into historical explanation as a general typology.

In short, Marx, in his later works, attempts to unfreeze his historical categories. He no longer views capitalism as something natural, slowly germinating in the interstices of precapitalist societies, ready to burst forth as the division of labor or the forces of production advance, but as an unnatural discontinuity founded upon an unprecedented reorganization of humans' relation to land and to one another (Marx 1996b: part 8). And it is indeed this recognition of the epochal difference of capitalism that allowed him in the *Ethnographic Notebooks* to explicitly deny that he had created a unilinear trajectory of historical development and the stagist view that non-Western societies such as Russia or India had to first follow a natural and preordained path to capitalism before building a socialist society (Anderson 2010: 228).

The overall point is that the late Marx's concepts are as substantivist as those of Polanyi; their meanings are not fixed but change in history; hence, they have a built-in potential to preempt presentism. Despite his contradictory legacy, therefore, Marx's critique exposes the historicity of economic relations, and by doing so, it has the potential to lay the basis of a transdisciplinary approach to historicizing modernity. Yet, to realize this potential, historical materialism has to first find a way to fully recover from the complications caused by the economistic models of historical development, and then to translate Marx's nonpresentist insights into a systematic narrative of the origins and development of the modern world. According to Ellen Meiksins Wood, for example, historical materialism would be better off completely dispensing with the base-superstructure model (instead of trying to modify and repro-duce it in different guises).[4] For a more accurate historical materialist understanding of modernity,

our current conceptions of the "political" and the "economic" must be subjected to critical scrutiny in order not to take for granted the delineation and separation of these categories specific to capitalism. This conceptual separation, while it reflects a reality specific to capitalism, not only fails to comprehend the very different realities of pre- or non-capitalist societies but also disguises the new forms of power and domination created by capitalism. (Wood 1995: 11)

Wood's remarks echo E. P. Thompson's suggestion that the alleged "superstructural" relations in fact constitute the economic "base" itself (Thompson 1995: 130). Law, moral codes, political institutions and forms of subjectivity are not "reflections" of, but constitutive of and central to the social reproduction of life and its "material" conditions (Thompson 1991a: 2). In this sense, a "mode of production" is not an economic structure that "social and cultural phenomena ... trail after ... at some remote remove" (Thompson 1965: 84). Instead, as Derek Sayer puts it, it is a particular "mode of life" that encompasses "the totality of social relations, whatever these may be, which make particular forms of production, and thus of property, possible" (Sayer 1987: 77). Phrased differently, production or the "base" cannot be "just 'economic' but also entails, and is embodied in, juridical-political and ideological forms and relations that cannot be relegated to a spatially separate superstructure" (Wood 1995: 61). In short, histor-ical materialism, thus construed, provides a holistic ontology of the

---

[4] Many attempts have already been made to modify the base-superstructure model in order to save historical materialism from the charge of economic determinism. The widespread appeal of Althusserian Marxism, for example, rested precisely on its allowing of political and ideological superstructures to be "dominant" in a given "conjuncture," and the postponement of the "determination by the economic" to the "last instance." However, this shift from "crude" to "remote economism" is hardly a cure for the problem itself (Lacher 2006: 30). Furthermore, when this inexorable economistic straitjacket becomes too rigid and attempts are made to relax it by injecting a greater degree of "relative autonomy" to superstructures, this then risks the "randomization" of history and social agency (Wood 1986: 31–5): "the base becomes a mere thing which can be safely ignored, while the relatively autonomous superstructures become too complex to analyze systematically and determination becomes 'overdetermination' verging on indeterminacy" (Holstun 2000: 91).

economic and the political, which then can be used to learn how to
think in "real historical time," how to think in noncapitalist terms and
how to historicize the transition to modernity without presuming a
transhistorical economic rationality.

Yet, our ability to operationalize this theoretical potential rests on
formulating a nonpresentist definition and a narrative of the origins
and expansion of capitalism (which Polanyi failed to deliver). In this
respect, we may allow Robert Brenner and Ellen Meiksins Wood to
carry some water for us. Both Brenner and Wood, the founders of a
distinct brand of historical materialism known as Political Marxism
(PM), begin their analyses by emphasizing the unity of the political and
the economic in noncapitalist history. Just like Polanyi and the late
Marx, both Wood and Brenner argue that production, appropriation
and distribution of surplus product and surplus labor – the economic –
was immediately tied to the political in precapitalist history. The
producer was not separated from the means of production; thus, the
extraction of the surplus product had to be obtained by noneconomic
means. Having a share of, investing in and being recognized by political authority was the only way to secure access to land and peasant
surpluses. Subsistence, exchange and accumulation immediately and
necessarily took political and geopolitical forms (Brenner 1985a; also
see Teschke 2003). In other words, prior to capitalism, there was no
spatial and temporal differentiation between political and economic
powers, that is, the moment of appropriation and the moment of rule
were fused. Political authority and political privileges were the most
immediate source of surplus extraction, commercial power and
income. Given the necessary fusion of economic and political powers,
the political elite was not qualitatively different from the economic
elite. They were species of the same genus.

How does PM explain the differentiation of the political and the
economic under capitalism? Wood views the development of capitalism "as the outcome of a long process in which certain political powers
were gradually transformed into economic powers and transferred to a
separate sphere" (Wood 1995: 40). That is to say, capitalism has
created the fiction of self-regulating markets by systematically cutting
off "essentially political issues" (e.g. the control of labor, land, production and property) from the political arena and displaces them to a
separate economic sphere (Wood 1995: 20). At the heart of the economic, therefore, rested a political, legal and violent process that led to

the historically unprecedented characterization of land and labor as commodities. From this perspective, capitalism cannot be seen as an economic phenomenon at all, but is based on the reorganization of political relations and the nature of social power in hitherto unexperienced ways that the economic in the end becomes conceivable as a separate sphere; and the state abstracted from the immediate relations of economic appropriation acquires a political form.

Obviously, this separation is strictly formal; the underlying unity of the political and the economic holds in capitalist societies too. That is, it is true that under capitalism, the relations of exploitation do not *necessarily* rest on extraeconomic coercion. Given the commodified nature of land and labor, the mere threat of unemployment and dispossession may be sufficient to ensure the continuity of capitalist appropriation and accumulation. Yet, this by no means excludes the *possibility* of the use of noneconomic means of coercion. Legally coerced wage labor, extremely authoritarian forms of social control and imperialist interventions are very commonly used to ensure the (geo)political basis of capitalist dominance and discipline. Equally important, in a sense, economic and political powers are even more strongly integrated in capitalism than they ever were previously. For the decisions concerning the allocation of labor and resources have never been more thoroughly subjected to the dictates of profitability and the production process has never been more closely regulated and managed (Wood 1981: 92). Likewise, the state is sine qua non for all market economies given its market-correcting, market-enabling and market-saving "interventions" into the economic sphere. Yet, even the language of "intervention" is suggestive of capitalism's specificity: only in capitalism do these spheres gain a self-referential character and the analytical division between the political and the economic parallels their institutional differentiation.

Against this methodological background PM attempts to formulate a nonpresentist definition of capitalism. Political Marxism does not see the mere existence of profit-seeking, commercial classes, wage labor or private property as necessary precursors of capitalism in history. All these phenomena, in different yet comparable forms, can be dated back to ancient societies; therefore, their unqualified equation with capitalism risks capitalism's transhistoricization and naturalization. By uncritically associating commerce, private property and wage labor with the existence of capitalism in history, we end up seeing capitalism present at all times and at all places (in embryo form), hence treating capitalism as if it were something intrinsic to human nature. Undoubtedly, this is not to deny that capitalism increases the volume of production, commerce and the size of a commodifiable workforce; yet, taking these as "necessary" indicators of the existence of capitalism in history simply collapses capitalism's consequences into its causes (Brenner 1977: 52; Wood 1999: 176–7).

According to PM, therefore, the transition to capitalism cannot be understood as the quantitative extension of any economic phenomena. Capitalism is not just more of the same thing. It is not just more trade, more markets, more private property or more wage labor, but the transitions to capitalism required a qualitative shift in the way societal relations were organized, such that the customary conditions of social reproduction were systematically undercut, and the market was made the ultimate basis for holding and expanding the means of life. In other words, transitions to capitalism did not follow a universal pattern, yet all transitions, in principle, required a strategic political intervention and an institutional setup to systematically eliminate nonmarket survival strategies so that the market could turn into the main institution responsible for social reproduction. In a setting that is becoming capitalist, therefore, land and labor are mobilized as commodities, and the market is no longer a space of "opportunity," where goods and services are occasionally sold, but turns into an "imperative" for social reproduction.

As such, capitalism presupposes the development of market-dependent societies, in which laborers and propertied classes are systematically forced and enabled to transform the conditions of production and subsistence according to market imperatives (Wood 2002). Put another way, capitalism as market-dependence signals the rise of a sociolegal order that is subsumed to the operation of market imperatives or the "law of value," that is, a form of society that systematically enables and compels producers and employers to increase the "ratio of unpaid labor to paid" and reduce the "socially necessary labor time" involved in appropriating "surplus value" (Post 2013). Such a conceptualization diverts our attention from transhistorical phenomena usually considered as preconditions to capitalism toward the ruptural processes of building market-dependent societies.

How did such a rupture occur in history? A fuller narrative of the transitions (and nontransitions) in Europe will be provided in Chapter 3; here it suffices to say that capitalism's first appearance in world history was an unintended result of social and geopolitical struggles in early modern England. A combination of factors, such as historically distinct forms of lordly solidarity, traditions of peasant resistance and lack of geopolitical opportunities, set off a process of transition in postfeudal England, during which the immediate unity of political and economic powers began to dissolve. In particular, following the social and demographic convulsions brought about by the Black Death (1340s), lords began to lose their extraeconomic powers in the face of heightened peasant resistance/flight. As a result, they had to increasingly rely on the king's legal authority to maintain their incomes and rule over the peasantry. In this context, peasants were able to change their conditions of servitude, yet they were not able to gain property rights to the lands that they customarily occupied. Taken together, from the 1450s, a new sociolegal order began to emerge in England, in which lords owned the land, yet they were unable to tap peasant surpluses through extraeconomic measures. Combined with their geopolitical losses on the continent, lords had no option but to increasingly resort to market-based measures to appropriate peasant surpluses and maintain themselves as lords. As such, they initiated a process that was to transform the millennia-old rules of accessing land. Lords, sometimes in cooperation and sometimes in conflict with the monarchy, began to systematically change the manorial custom, subjecting peasant tenants to competition for market-determined leases (Brenner 1985a: 49). This signalled a departure from the subsistence logic of agriculture toward a system-wide political-economic transformation, during which both the direct producers and the appropriators of their surplus became market-dependent. They were progressively compelled and enabled to specialize, accumulate, invest, innovate and maximize productivity and output in order to survive the market imperatives and to pay rents at market rates. Capitalism was thus born.[5]

[5] Compare this narrative with Wallerstein's historical sociology of the emergence of the "capitalist world economy." According to Wallerstein, lords and merchants, driven by commercial opportunities and profits, transformed the "mode of labor control" into wage labor in the "core" of the capitalist world economy, whereas the relative lack of commercial opportunities compelled the ruling classes in the "periphery" to use more coercive forms of labor control; peasants became serfs and were coerced into cash crop production in the "periphery" (Wallerstein 1974: 87–116). The transformation of property relations is therefore perceived by Wallerstein as a function of different levels of

In England, therefore, social actors "acted to reproduce themselves *as they were,*" and while doing so, this led to a contingent or unintended process of creating a market-dependent society (Wood 2001a: 58).[6] Elsewhere in Western Europe, no similarly contingent development of capitalism occurred during the early modern era. In France, for example, lords did not lose their extraeconomic powers of surplus appropriation, nor did peasants lose hereditary possession of their lands. The struggles within and among contending classes and polities considerably transformed the logic of appropriation and rule in early modern France, yet did not result in a qualitative break. No market-dependent society emerged from the interstices of the old. In its stead, capitalism began to spread to France and the states of continental Europe only from the nineteenth century onward and as a protracted process compelled (directly or indirectly) by the geopolitical pressures engendered by the success of Britain's capitalist economy (Wood 1991: 159–60).

By emphasizing the specificity, contingent emergence and geopolitically driven expansion of capitalism in history, PM breaks with the tendency to transhistoricize and naturalize capitalism. As such, PM provides a powerful check against methodological presentism.[7] Relatedly, as I will show in the next chapters, by countering the transhistoricization of capitalism, PM opens up new avenues for

profitability and the commerce-based division of labor. What is overlooked by Wallerstein is that profit-seeking, markets and commercial classes are not synonymous with capitalism. Depending on the preexisting context of social and international relations, profits accrued from commercial activity may empower a variety of actors and initiate a multiplicity of processes, hence not necessarily leading to capitalism (Brenner 1977; also see Skocpol 1977).

[6] Here, "contingency" in no way means mere accident or luck of a purely external and nonsociological nature (for a critique of approaches that explain the rise of Europe through a series of fortunate accidents, see Bryant 2006). Rather, it is a social phenomenon that is related to the open-ended character of class and geopolitical struggles and can be explained by analyzing the variations in the degree of self-organization of the ruling and producing classes (Brenner 1985a: 36).

[7] Several scholars have argued that even if PM breaks with the tendency to transhistoricize and naturalize capitalism, its understanding of capitalism as market-dependence is too "narrow," derived only from the experience of northwestern Europe (inter alia Anievas and Nişancıoğlu 2015: 22–9). A thorough discussion on PM and its (alleged) Eurocentrism falls beyond the scope of the present book. For a defense of PM, see Duzgun (2018a, 2020).

reconsidering the radical multilinearity of the world historical development.[8] All that said, however, it is still not clear the extent to which Wood and Brenner, the first generation of PM, could provide a transdisciplinary methodology adequate for the historicization of modernity. The problem is that although the critique of presentism does a good job in taking us beyond the timeless notions of the economic and the political, it fails in one important aspect. The critique of presentism with an exclusive focus on politics and economics does not take us far in explaining the constitution of the spatial parameters of the modern world. For, the modern world is characterized by the spatial differentiation of an international sphere from the social realm, as well as by the separation of politics and economics. Therefore, the "international" and the "social," just as the "economic" and the "political," are not to be taken for granted, but historicized for a more complete understanding of the origins and development of global modernity. In short, if the historicization of modernity is connected to our ability to problematize the institutional and analytical divisions created by modernity itself, the second step in this direction involves overcoming the analytical bifurcation between the social and the international. The critique of methodological presentism needs to be combined with the critique of methodological internalism. This signals the need to further deepen our ontology in ways to capture the coconstitution of social and international processes in history. A discussion on IHS is in order.

International Historical Sociology: Unifying the "Social" and the "International"

"In a basic sense," writes Theda Skocpol, notwithstanding the structuralist-functionalist interregnum of the postwar period, "sociology has always been a historically grounded and oriented enterprise" (Skocpol 1984: 1). Necessarily so, for, as Charles Tilly remarks, "to the degree that social processes are path-dependent – to the extent that

---

[8] For more recent PM-influenced historical sociology scholarship (see Teschke 2003; Lacher 2006; Dufour 2007; Gerstenberger 2007; Patriquin 2007; Hoffmann 2008; Kennedy 2008; Post 2011; Knafo 2013; Dimmock 2014; Bauerly 2016; Evans 2016; Isett and Miller 2016; Zacares 2018; Lafrance 2019b; Post and Lafrance 2019; Pal 2020; Salgado 2020a).

prior sequence of events constraints what happens in time – historical knowledge of sequences becomes essential" (Tilly 1991: 86). Sociology, then, is an inevitably historical venture. And, as Philip Abrams notes, the opposite applies too. Sociology is bound to be "concerned with (historical) eventuation, because that is how (social) structuring happens ... , (just as) history must be theoretical, because that is how structuring is apprehended." In this sense, historical sociology is not to be understood as some "interdisciplinary flag-waving and territorial-wrangling between historians and sociologists," but it is the core of both disciplines. Therefore, instead of trying to "give historical work more 'social context' or ... sociological work more 'historical background,' 'there might be much more to be gained by reconstituting history and sociology as historical sociology,'" a transdisciplinary enterprise (Abrams 1982: xi, 2, ix; also see Bryant 2005: 71).

A transdisciplinary historical sociology seems essential to the comprehension of the social. Nevertheless, the social offered by social theory has long been criticized for lacking an international dimension (Rosenberg 2016a: 19–20). As far back as 1958, Ralf Dahrendorf contended that contemporary sociology remained wedded to a utopian image of society as a self-sufficient and internally consistent unit, hence analytically "suspended in time and space, shut off from the outside world" (Dahrendorf 1958: 117). In 1973, Antony Giddens noted that "[t]he primary unit of sociological analysis, the sociologist's 'society,' has never been the isolated, the 'internally developing' system which has normally been implied in social theory." In this sense, "[o]ne of the most important weaknesses of sociological conceptions of development since Marx has been the persistent tendency to think of development as the 'unfolding' of endogenous influences within a given society." This is a fundamentally misleading assumption, according to Giddens, for, external factors are not just "an 'environment' to which the society has to adapt," instead the outside is always combined with the internal, "determining the transformations to which a society is subject" from the very outset (Giddens 1973: 265). Two decades later, Friedrich Tenbruck echoed Giddens, expressing dissatisfaction with sociology's internalist bias. Tenbruck argued that despite several attempts to recognize the international dimension of social transformation, sociology has remained rooted in "internalist histories," which blur "the fact that all societies are, in their internal constitution, already externally conditioned and mostly tied in with other societies" (Tenbruck 1994: 91). Therefore, what is needed is a

revision of sociological concepts and theories which must no longer start with the concept of an independent "society" but from a *plurality of societies* with their intersocietal relations and conditioning and other boundary-transcending processes of societalization, so that the existing nature and degree of interdependencies enter the conceptual apparatus and problem definitions. (Tenbruck 1994: 81, my emphasis)

In short, for all its diversity, social theory, both classical and contemporary, seems to be marked by what may be called *methodological internalism*.[9] Internalism tends to take the assumption of self-contained societies as an ontological given, hence reading back in history the sociospatial consequences of modernity, that is, *relative territorial exclusivity and societal fixity.* Indeed, against this internalist bias, since the 1970s, several historical sociologists have offered intersocietal or international perspectives on world history (Anievas and Matin 2016: 2–3). The voluminous works of Perry Anderson (1974, 1978, 1992), Michael Mann (1986, 1993, 2012), Immanuel Wallerstein (1974, 1980, 1989, 2011), Theda Skocpol (1979, 1994) and Charles Tilly (1984, 1990a) have all had an explicitly internationalist orientation. For example, Perry Anderson, in his work on modern revolutions, notes that revolutions "were historically interrelated, and the sequence of their connexions enters into the definition of their differences. Their order was constitutive of their structure" (Anderson 1992: 116). Anderson, thus, emphasizes the cumulative impact of international relations in constituting sociological differences (and vice versa). By doing so, his analysis seeks to challenge what he calls "chronological monism," that is, a "uniform temporal medium" in which "events or institutions appear to bathe in a more or less continuous and homogeneous temporality" (Anderson 1974a: 9–10). Anderson's effort to theorize "real historical time" mirrors Tilly's warning that the treatment of countries as "distinct societies, each having its more or less autonomous culture, government, economy, and solidarity" is bound to create an image of development "in natural-history form: stages, sequences, transitions and growth"

---

[9] The problem of methodological internalism has taken different names across the social sciences, such as "methodological nationalism" in sociology (Smith 1979) and the "territorial trap" in geography (Agnew 1994).

(Tilly 1984: 11, 98). All in all, then, for the past four decades, historical sociology has taken an international turn, which enabled not only a departure from the fiction of separate societies in history, but also from the assumption of a more-or-less unilinear sequence of "progress" toward modernity.

That said, while recognizing the relevance of the international, historical sociology has yet to sufficiently incorporate the question of temporality and internationality to the study of the social.[10] For example, Skocpol's "intersocietal approach" and Wallerstein's "world-system" analysis have both probed the question of how to explain local/national particularities in a deeply interconnected international order. Yet, both frameworks have proved to be problematic. On the one hand, Skocpol strongly endorses the international dimension of social change, yet in her work the international still figures as an "extra-social" phenomenon (Matin 2013a: 7–8). In Skocpol's model, international relations impact revolutionary transformation within states, yet it is not clear if the opposite also applies. The social seems to carry no weight in defining international dynamics. As a result, nowhere in Skocpol's analysis does the cumulative impact of international relations enter her explanation of what societies are and how they transform (Teschke 2003: 123; Rosenberg 2006: 310; 2008: 85; Shilliam 2009: 31; Matin 2013a: 8; Go and Lawson 2017: 26). On the other hand, in Wallerstein's world-system theory, analytical units are not discrete; they are all interrelated (albeit unevenly) within a web of global division of labor, which dictates its own internal imperatives to its parts. Sociospatial differences (modes of labor control, type of state, etc.) across these units are understood in terms of the reproductive requirements of the world economy. A region's role in the international division of labor, which is determined by the timing of its incorporation into the world economy, defines its historical specificities (with little attention paid to how historical specificities

---

[10] Clearly, the concept of society or the social should not be taken for granted; for both concepts refer to a historically specific way of structuring of social relations (and in this sense, both concepts are sociologically and ideologically loaded; Owens 2015). Yet, society or the social can still be thought of in a way that overturns the methodologically internalist/nationalist connotations of these concepts. As will become clear in the next pages, UCD provides precisely that: it uses the concept of society (and development) only to undermine the singular ontologies of society and unilinear conceptions of development (Rosenberg 2016b).

themselves could impact a region's "mode of incorporation"). Wallerstein's "international," therefore, tends to operate in a way that reduces sociospatial specificities to the functional requirements of a presumed whole/totality (cf. McMichael 1990). Sociospatial specificities enter Wallerstein's historical narrative only as spatially differentiated versions of an all-encompassing conception of capitalism, such as "peripheral capitalism," "semi-peripheral capitalism" and so on. As such, Wallerstein tends to overlook the possibility of alternative developmental paths, obscuring the multilinearity of world historical development.

What transpires from this discussion is that neither an extrasocial nor an overarching conception of the international provides a viable alternative to the internalist and unilinear accounts of world historical development. Neither Skocpol nor Wallerstein takes us far in understanding the international as part of an evolving historical continuum. Thus, neither scholar can assist us in fully recovering the temporal, sequential and intersocietal dimensions of global modernity. This failure hints that the critique of internalism has to go beyond the empirical acknowledgment of the international. Making the international intelligible in historical and sociological terms requires a deeper ontology that involves the international not just as an ad hoc addition to, but as an organic and constitutive part of social reality from the very outset (Rosenberg 2006). In other words, providing an alternative to internalism (and unilinearism) rests on our ability to formulate a transdisciplinary methodology that simultaneously plumbs the social in the international, and the international in the social. In addition to battering the demarcations between the political and the economic, therefore, we need to find a way to conceptually interiorize the international into the social and vice versa.

As shown earlier, historical sociology by itself has proved unfit to sufficiently fulfill this theoretical requisite. How about IR? International Relations, given its disciplinary focus on the international, seems well-positioned to shed light on this methodological problem. Yet, even a perfunctory glance immediately reveals that for most IR scholarship, the international is an unproblematic category, an independent variable devoid of sociotemporal content, an unmalleable space governed by a timeless logic of geopolitical competition. Of course, this does not mean that mainstream IR does not do history. Yet, history plays into mainstream IR only in an instrumentalist way: "history is used not as a means to rethink the present, but as a quarry to be mined only to confirm the theories of the present" (Hobson 2002: 5). For example, Thucydides' discussion of the Peloponnesian War or the shape of medieval geopolitics are often invoked in order to exemplify and corroborate the alleged timelessness of such IR concepts like anarchy and balance of power (Waltz 1979: 118; Keohane 1986: 7–8). Rather ironically, then, history in IR is used in a way that undermines the historicity of IR's own subject matter – the international. International Relations uses history to support its transhistorical claims about the nature of intersocietal relations, and as such it turns history into a mere "background narrative to be coded within pre-existing theoretical categories" (Lawson 2012: 205).

Of course, several alternative accounts have been already offered to (re)claim the historicity of international or intersocietal relations. In particular, the last three decades have witnessed numerous attempts to advance historical sociology as a critical approach to IR (HSIR). Through a sustained engagement with historical sociology, HSIR scholars have not only developed a deeper understanding of the socio-temporally changing character of international processes, thereby going beyond the timeless and static logic of anarchy, but have also asserted the relevance of IR for processes conventionally explained through internal sociological factors such as nationalism, racism, industrialization, revolution, and democratization (inter alia Yalvaç 1991; Rosenberg 1994; Halliday 1999; Hobden and Hobson 2002; Teschke 2003; Lawson 2004; Lacher 2006; Dufour 2007; Morton 2007, 2011; Bhambra 2010; Zarakol 2011; Green 2012; Lacher and Germann 2012; Matin 2013a; Anievas and Nişancıoğlu 2015; Buzan and Lawson 2015; Evans 2016; Morton and Bieler 2018). As such, HSIR has provided new insights into the coconstitution of the social and the international, which other critical approaches to IR that are underpinned by a strongly subjectivist epistemology are not able to deliver (Walker 1993; Wendt 1999). In particular, the scholars informed by poststructuralist perspectives have powerfully revealed the role of power-knowledge connections in the making of IR as a modern discipline (Tickner and Waever 2009; Vitalis 2015), yet, they also shied away from a macrohistorical sociological understanding of the constitution of the modern social and international order, which is the gap HSIR seeks to fill (Matin 2013b).

That said, despite the long-standing rapprochement between historical sociology and IR, HSIR has turned into a truly "transdisciplinary" enterprise only in the last decade. The late Fred Halliday was the first IR scholar who openly asked how to theorize the mutually constitutive character of social and international relations. As early as 2002 he hinted at the need for a "unified" theory of "international sociology" to better explain the simultaneity of the social and the international (Halliday 2002). Until more recently, however, Halliday's call for an "international sociology" remained merely a fleeting reflection. Halliday himself planted the seed of a unified theory, yet never gave it a systematic treatment. Justin Rosenberg's reworking of the concept of uneven and combined development has precisely addressed this gap in HSIR. Over the past decade, Rosenberg's endeavors, alongside other valuable contributions, have led to the birth of International Historical Sociology as a new subfield (Rosenberg 2006; Hobson et al. 2010).

Uneven and Combined Development: Modernity, Temporality, Multilinearity

If the theoretical interiorization of the international to the social is central to the development of IHS, the theory of UCD provides the tools for such a conceptual digestion. This theoretical framework was originally formulated by Leon Trotsky to make sense of the "peculiarity" of the Russian path to modernity.[11] International Relations scholars have systematized and expanded on Trotsky's insights to overcome the ontological binary of the social versus the international. The point of departure for UCD is the assumption that the world always contained not one but a multiplicity of polities and societies endowed with different social, institutional and environmental charac-

---

[11] In formulating UCD, Trotsky's main concern was to find an answer to the question as to why the socialist revolution did not happen in the industrialized core of Western Europe, but Russia. Trotsky broke away from the evolutionary and "stagist" readings of Marxism (present in the early writings of Karl Marx and turned into "iron laws" by Stalin) by bringing in the catalytic and complexifying impact of international relations on the transformation of social relations. According to Trotsky, modern history cannot be understood as a linear and homogenizing process of bourgeois modernization, precisely because capitalist modernization takes place in the context of the competitive relations of an already existing and unevenly developed system of states.

teristics; therefore unevenness is an enduring feature of human history. Furthermore, unevenness, which is inherent in the condition of societal multiplicity, leads to a continuous process of combination. That is, pressures generated by intersocietal unevenness compel geopolitically "less developed" societies to learn from and selectively combine with local social resources the "best" aspects of geopolitically more "advanced" societies. If they survive this process, they can mobilize existing institutions to execute novel tasks, and through this process of "substitution," they can attempt to make up for the institutions and relations that, while available to the geopolitical enemy, are missing at home. Combined development (and substitution) thus points to a process in which a geopolitical enemy becomes a teacher, showing the kinds of transformations that would facilitate a geopolitical "catch-up" (e.g. Anievas and Nişancıoğlu 2015: 50; Matin 2013a: 19). These attempts at "learning," "substitution" and "catch-up" ultimately result in the emergence of various combinations of the domestic and the foreign, which, in turn, reacts back on the international, leading to the transformation of the initial conditions of unevenness.

At a conceptual level, then, UCD accomplishes three interrelated things. First, in this analytical framework, unevenness, hence inter-nationality, is not merely an afterthought, but an organic component of the social from the beginning. The international is not something that enters the analysis from without as a suprasociological category. Instead, UCD postulates a conception of the international that is diachronic and interior to sociological processes themselves. Second, UCD facilitates a historically dynamic conception of international relations, which, in turn, furnishes us with a conceptual key to moving beyond the world of historical exceptions, deviations and *Sonderwegs*. In other words, by capturing the cumulatively changing nature of international relations, UCD frees sociological imagination from a framework of analysis in which historical particularities are seen as exceptions or aberrations from a purportedly universal history, and by doing so, it turns the alleged exceptions into organic and constitutive parts of world history. Third, through a historically dynamic concep-tion of the international, UCD unlocks the historically changing rules of entering modernity, thereby countering one-dimensional and unilinear conceptions of the constitution and development of the modern world. Read together, through UCD, international interactivity, alterity and multilinearity necessarily enter the ontological constitution of what we call historical "development."[12]

In short, UCD departs from the internalist conceptions of social change and equips us with an important tool to build a historically dynamic and sociological IR theory. Through UCD, a cumulatively changing international system is advanced, which, in turn, logically and historically undermines unilinear conceptions of modernity (Anievas 2015: 845). Clearly, UCD is not alone in its attempt to supplant unilinear conceptions of modernity. Two approaches are especially noteworthy: multiple modernities and postcolonialism (cf. Matin 2013a: 2). According to the multiple modernities paradigm, modernization has been "shaped in each society by the combined impact of their respective historical traditions and the different ways in which they became incorporated into the new modern world system" (Eisenstadt 2000: 15). In other words, different historical and international legacies have engendered distinct forms of modernity, hence the inherent plurality of modernization experiences and the inapplicability of Western modernity as a world historical yardstick. In a similar vein, postcolonial theory (particularly its subaltern variants that take Marxism as one of their primary interlocutors) rejects "any universalist narratives of capital" by positing the contested, heterogeneous and hybrid character of colonial modernity. By registering the spatially differentiated nature of capitalist social relations, postcolonial theory invokes difference and interconnectedness as ontological conditions, thereby conceptualizing capitalist modernity away from cultural particularism and homogenizing universalism (Chakrabarty 2000: 9–21, 70, 85).

In approaching the question of historical difference, both the multiple modernities paradigm and postcolonial theory repudiate unilinearism, acknowledging the contested and spatially interactive experience of global modernity. In this respect, both approaches share many affinities with IHS. Yet two important differences remain. First,

---

[12] The concept of "development" is surely one of the "organizing myth(s) of our age" (McMichael 2000: 668). Yet, in a framework informed by UCD, development is not used to bolster a stagist understanding of history in which development has a unilinear direction. To the contrary, the uneven and combined character of development is a constant reminder of development's multilinearity and heterogeneity in world history (Rosenberg 2020; cf. Blaney and Tickner 2017).

although these approaches are underscored by an internationalist critique, their proponents (like the historical sociologists discussed earlier) leave the international "analytically unpenetrated," that is, the international itself remains "untheorized in sociological terms" (Rosenberg 2006: 310; 2008: 85). This, in turn, limits their ability to illuminate the cumulatively developing content and hence the multi-linearity of global modernity (Matin 2013a: 2; Anievas and Nişancıoğlu 2015: 39–42; Buzan and Lawson 2015: 59–60, 330). Second, while existing approaches tend to take "European modernity" at face value, IHS problematizes it. For example, Alexander Anievas and Kerem Nişancıoğlu argue that postcolonial theory suffers from "lack of any substantive engagement with the question of how capitalism emerged" in Europe "before being subsequently expanded globally." They insist that "in order to truly 'provincialize' Europe we must dissect European history itself, and there is no more central myth to be dissected than that of narrating European history around the history of capitalism" (Anievas and Nişancıoğlu, 2015: 40). This echoes Sandra Halperin's warning that without deconstructing "fictitious views of Europe's development and history" a mere emphasis on multiplicity and hybridity falls short in overcoming unilinear conceptions of historical development (Halperin 2006: 60). Likewise, Kamran Matin writes that postcolonial theory successfully reveals the differentiated, hybrid and ambivalent character of colonial modernity, yet it "does not account for, or even address, the initial crystallization of ... capital in Europe," thereby failing to explain the heterogeneous constitution of the origins of capitalism (Matin 2013a: 364).

In short, theorization of a truly multilinear account of global modernity is firmly connected to our ability to undermine "the myth of European modernity." No doubt, one of the most sophisticated attempts in IHS seeking to problematize "European" modernity is the work of Anievas and Nişancıoğlu (2015). According to Anievas and Nişancıoğlu, any explanation of the origin and consolidation of capitalist modernity in Western Europe has to move beyond the "internalist" conceptions of social change (2015: 55). Internalism "presupposes a discrete and hermetically sealed European history," hence perpetuating the image of the European transition to capitalism as an "exceptional, pristine and autonomous" process (2015: 40). In advancing their critique of internalism, Anievas and Nişancıoğlu use the critique of the concept of "bourgeois revolution" as one of their main entry points. The conventional narratives of the "rise of the west" have long considered bourgeois revolutions as one of the main drivers of modernities in the West. In this conception, it has been assumed that the "bourgeois" classes, increasing their weight in the economic and political life through the early modern period, gradually tipped the balance of power against *ancien regime* forces, leading to the establishment of liberal economic (and political) institutions characteristic of Western modernity. Anievas and Nişancıoğlu are well aware of the widely held empirical dissatisfactions with the conventional interpretation of this concept (2015: 177–8). Following the revisionist historiography of the last fifty years, they argue that neither in the West nor in the non-West were there strong bourgeois classes dedicated to carrying out their "historic mission" of transforming society along capitalist lines. Most bourgeois revolutions in the West, such as the French Revolution, "were not heralded by the ascendancy of a distinctly capitalist bourgeois class; during the revolutions, the bourgeoisie were not in the lead of the movements and were often found on the opposing sides; [and] after the revolutions, the bourgeoisie did not hold power and were often further removed from state control" (Anievas and Nişancıoğlu 2015: 177).

For Anievas and Nişancıoğlu, what rests behind the inflation of bourgeois agency in orthodox accounts of bourgeois revolution is that they subscribe to internalist interpretations of historical change, which occludes the uneven and combined character of revolutionary processes. Anievas and Nişancıoğlu seek to move beyond the problem of internalism and lack of capitalist agency that troubled the conventional conception of bourgeois revolution by: (1) bringing (geo)political relations into the making of bourgeois revolutions; and (2) focusing on the consequences of, rather than the intentions or composition of the agents involved in, revolutions. According to this "consequentialist" reading, it is, in fact, futile to look for the involvement of a capitalist bourgeoisie in order to identify bourgeois revolutions, for the bourgeoisie's rise to power, both inside and outside the West, was complicated by the UCD of capitalist social relations. That is, the spatially "uneven" development of capitalist social relations generated geopolitical pressures on "backward" ruling classes in Europe, forcing them to initiate or precipitate capitalist transformation in their own societies. Geopolitics, not the bourgeoisie, was thus the driving force behind bourgeois revolutions. Old social forms were combined with new ones under geopolitical duress, which marked the inherently contradictory and internationally driven character of capitalist development. From this perspective, then, the ideal-typical models of bourgeois revolution are, by definition, misleading (Anievas and Nişancıoğlu 2015: 199–205; also, see Davidson 2012: 508–9). The implication is that given their "uneven and combined" character, bourgeois revolutions, both inside and outside the West, should be disassociated from the image of a "revolutionary" bourgeoisie executing its historical "mission" and a clear-cut ascendant capitalism. Bourgeois revolutions should be conceptualized more flexibly, judged only according to their long-term developmental outcomes, that is, according to the degree to which they fostered "a distinctly capitalist form of state" and "an autonomous center of capitalist accumulation" (Anievas and Nişancıoğlu 2015: 177; for similar interpretations see Morton 2011: 46; Davidson 2012: chapter 19; Allinson and Anievas 2010).

Anievas and Nişancıoğlu thus advance UCD as a conceptual remedy for the problem of internalism and highlight the usefulness of UCD to dismantle stylized assumptions about Western European modernity. Yet, it is equally important to note that UCD underlined by consequentialism succumbs to a form of presentism, which in turn obscures the heterogeneity of social forms generated by bourgeois revolutions. According to the consequentialist interpretation, it is (long-term) outcomes, not agents or causes, that identify a revolution's socioeconomic character. From this angle, revolutions are "capitalist" as long as they launch a long-term process of removing "obstacles" to the development of capitalism. Therefore, bourgeois revolutions, however imperfectly and belatedly, from below and otherwise, are construed as leading to capitalism from the very outset. What bourgeois revolutions facilitated, then, was nothing but "capital insert[ing] itself into ... an uneven developmental process, gradually gaining mastery over it" (Allinson and Anievas 2010: 473), or "assimilations to modernity" through "processes of primitive accumulation" (Morton 2007: 607).

The implication is that the consequentialist readings of bourgeois revolutions tend to freeze the social content and meaning of revolutionary processes with an overdose of a priori logic of capitalist development. Uneven and combined development, propelled by a consequentialist mode of explanation, allows social agents to act only in the shadow of a (distant) capitalist future (Teschke 2005: 5–6;

Matin 2013a: 48–9; Duzgun 2018b). In this sense, consequentialism acts as a form of presentism: it reads capitalism backward by overburdening the agents of revolutionary change with a pregiven conception of capitalism. The implication is that the presentist or consequentialist readings of history tend to undermine the methodological premises and empirical promises of UCD. For example, contrary to their self-proclaimed antiunilinear conception of world history, Anievas and Nişancıoğlu's consequentialist reading of UCD is able to concede heterogeneity within Western Europe only within an all-absorbing conception of capitalism. They tend to overlook that bourgeois revolutionary processes even in the West might lead to an amalgamation of conflicting interests, intentions and principles, which, in turn, may generate contradictory results for the development of capitalism. In consequentialist accounts, as a result, social and geopolitical complexities, uncertainties and noncapitalist alternatives that might arise during revolutionary processes get lost in an all-absorbing and pregiven conception of capitalism. Anievas and Nişancıoğlu consequently build a historical narrative in which all modernization projects with a bourgeois component are reduced to different instances of a single transitional social type, all moving at different speeds and by different paths toward capitalist modernity. Taken as a whole, Anievas and Nişancıoğlu's interpretation of combined development rules out from the very beginning the possibility of alternative noncapitalist (and nonsocialist) modernities.

"Alterity" is thus subordinated to "posterity" in consequentialist accounts. The cost of this failure is high. For example, as I will elaborate in Chapter 3, such a tendency to project the logic of capitalism backward severely occludes the combined character of one of the most critical junctures in modern European history, the French Revolution. For, irrespective of the continuing historiographical debate as to whether the French Revolution facilitated the development of capitalism,[13] it is certain that the revolution also gave birth to novel social forms that had contradictory implications for the development of

---

[13] For views within IHS that emphasize (explicitly or otherwise) the noncapitalist nature of absolutist and revolutionary France, see Teschke (2003, 2005), Matin (2013a) and Shilliam (2009); for a contrasting view, see Anievas and Nişancıoğlu (2015). For an empirical and theoretical assessment of these two rival positions from non-IR perspectives, see Comninel (1987) and Miller (2012), cf. Davidson (2012).

capitalism, that is, forms that were absent in capitalist England and cannot be easily explained by the dictation of any capitalist rationality, such as the consolidation of small peasant ownership, universal conscription, universal citizenship and equality, universal education, and popular conceptions of the "nation" (e.g. Skocpol 1979: 175–9; Furet 1981: 119–20). Surely, to make such an argument, one does not have to go as far as some scholars who totally deny the relevance of the French Revolution for the development of capitalism (e.g. Comninel 1987). Yet, what needs to be acknowledged is that consequentialism or presentism tends to obscure the fact that even in Western Europe, different social forms were created under geopolitical duress, which attempted to "substitute" (at least for a while) capitalist modernity with noncapitalist (and nonsocialist) forms of rule and appropriation (Shilliam 2009: chapter 2; Matin 2013a, 2019; Duzgun 2018b, 2018c). Such an oversight causes even one of the most radical and innovative periods in French history, that is, "the Jacobin phase of the French Revolution," to be reduced to a form of "proto-capitalism" (Rosenberg 2007: 478).

In short, for a truly multilinear conception of modernity we need to avoid the methodological trap of presentism. The critique of internalism without a full-on critique of presentism fails to save us from the trap of unilinearism. The history of global modernity must be conceptualized without presuming the necessary arrival of capitalism in the West as well as in the non-West. We need to be able to historicize and internationalize "multiple modernities" without falling back into presentist conceptualizations of capitalism's rise and development. As I will show later, IHS, once freed from such retrospective readings of history, will be able to reveal with more precision the spatially and temporally interactive character of world historical development and the multiplicity of modernities generated therein.

Renewing International Historical Sociology

At this point what is becoming clear is that IHS and PM must join forces for a noninternalist and nonpresentist conception of global modernity. International Historical Sociology needs PM to avoid circular explanations of capitalism's rise and expansion, while PM needs IHS to systematically signpost the temporal, processual and sequential dimension of global modernity. International Historical Sociology and

PM provide two complementary entry points to the process of historicization of modernity. Political Marxism's conception of capitalism as market-dependence focuses on the political/legal/institutional moment of the origin of capitalism, thereby diverting our attention from transhistorical phenomena usually considered as preconditions to the birth of capitalism such as commerce, wealth or wage labor. It argues that only when people are enabled/compelled to depend on the market for their means of subsistence, does capital begin to invade the productive process and systematically alter the conditions of life.

In addition to capitalism's historicity, PM recognizes capitalism's international dimension too. That is, PM insists that there can be no "transhistorical laws" governing the path to capitalism, because of the changing intersocietal context of capitalist transformation as well as the variations in social reactions from "below." For "once breakthroughs to ongoing capitalist economic development took place in various regions these irrevocably transformed the conditions and the character of the analogous processes, which were to occur subsequently elsewhere" (Brenner 1985b: 322; see also Brenner 1986: 29). In other words,

once capitalism was established in one country ... its development in other places could never follow the same course it had in its place of origin. The existence of one capitalist society thereafter transformed all others, and the subsequent expansion of capitalist imperatives constantly changed the conditions of economic development. (Wood 1998: 30)

Thus, by recognizing the cumulatively changing character of international relations, PM defies transhistorical interpretations of market-dependence. This implies that while market-dependence signifies the minimum sociolegal prerequisites to the existence of capitalist social relations, its focus cannot be on any static phenomena/policy. For example, equating capitalism to wage labor per se tends to obscure that under certain sociolegal circumstances, nonwage forms (such as commodity production based on nonwaged family labor) can and have permitted "a more or less direct transition to capitalism" without widespread dispossession of the workforce (Brenner 1977: 52; Wood 2001b: 176–7). Therefore, depending on past socioinstitutional legacies and the timing and international context of capitalist transition, the mechanisms that ensure market-dependence take different forms. The socioinstitutional content of market-dependence is not fixed, but cumulatively changes. As a consequence, PM neither sets up pregiven norms for the transition to capitalism, nor does it treat subsequent transitions as counter models to privileged ideal types.

All this hints at PM's potential to incorporate the international into the explanation of the social. However, it is important to note that even if the international and temporal dimension of social transformation is somewhat present in Brenner and Wood's work, neither Wood nor Brenner were IR scholars, therefore they did not address the question of the international in a systematic way that would fulfill IR's own disciplinary considerations. In other words, they both remained "comparativists," for whom the question of difference was more important than the question of interconnection. Indeed, this has been the lacuna that Political Marxists who work in the field of IR have acknowledged and sought to fill (inter alia Teschke 2003; Lacher 2006). Political Marxism in IR has moved beyond Brenner and Wood's comparativist focus by highlighting the generative impact of the international on the processes of early modern state formation and vice versa. They have problematized the common conception of the simultaneous emergence of capitalism and the territorial state, and in doing so, they have revealed the role of temporally specific and interactively developing strategies of spatialization in the constitution of the modern international order (Teschke 2003: 265; Teschke and Lacher 2007: 569).

In fact, in emphasizing the temporal and interactive character of world historical development, PM in IR even invoked the concept of uneven and combined development in the early 2000s. For example, Benno Teschke wrote in 2005 that combining PM "with the theorem of socially uneven and geopolitically combined development" can facilitate a deeper understanding of "the nationally specific and diachronic, yet cumulatively connected and internationally mediated nature of capitalist transitions" (Teschke 2005: 13, 21). Of course, this disciplinary reorientation via uneven and combined development intended to further clarify PM's relevance for IR. Yet, the opposite is also true. Teschke's use of UCD was based on the precondition that UCD itself was sterilised from transhistorical assumptions about capitalist development (Teschke 2014: 34–6).

Unsurprisingly, the issue of "historicity" has since remained the main bone of contention between the theoreticians of PM and UCD. While some UCD theoreticians have begun to rebrand the concept since the mid-2000s as a general theory of international relations, PM and other critics have argued against the formalization of UCD as a transhistorical concept (Rioux 2009; Teschke 2014). In particular, the insistence to conceptualize UCD as a postpositivist substitute for "anarchy" has countered the concept's earlier claim to specify the role of social agency in the constitution of social and international orders. The underspecification of social agency, in turn, runs the risk of emptying the historical-sociological content of the international: the "how" and "why" of the international, that is, how and why social and international dynamics evolved across time and space, and the exact mechanisms of this transformation, tend to disappear in narratives informed by an agent-less framework of international historical change (Rioux 2015; Duzgun 2021). Uneven and combined development, albeit extremely innovative, eventually risks becoming just another word for "multiplicity," "interconnectedness" and "hybridity," losing its explanatory power and theoretical significance grounded in historical materialism (cf. Matin 2013a).

Yet, does it have to be like this? In my view, no. For, UCD, in principle, points to an agency-led transformation during which the geopolitically less-developed society learns from and selectively adopts the traits of a geopolitical foe. In other words, UCD is underlined by a process of intersocietal learning, emulation and substitution; therefore logically and historically presupposing "active social agency" as the driver of social and international transformation. Therefore, as long as UCD is operationalized in a way that highlights the agential struggles over the organization of space and the concomitant acts of intersocietal comparison, intersocietal learning and substitution, it has the potential to dodge the charge of asocial readings of international change (Duzgun 2021).

In short, UCD, if freed from transhistorical assumptions, can serve as a constant reminder of the interactive and cumulative character of international social change, hence facilitating with greater ease a history-in-motion. In this sense, I suggest, IHS and PM, combined together, can activate a nonpresentist and noninternalist methodology adequate for the historicization of global modernity. On the one hand, UCD allows PM to signpost more systematically the temporal, sequential and cumulatively developing content of global modernity. Political Marxism, underpinned by UCD, traces temporal processes diachronically, hence decisively departing from the logic of synchronic comparisons. On the other hand, UCD, underpinned by PM, focuses more systematically on the historically specific sociospatial struggles, hence enabling a deeper understanding of sociohistorical causality, which is a prerequisite for international historical sociological imagination to develop. Uneven and combined development, combined with PM, stops seeing capitalism as somehow always in the air, waiting to be unravelled once favorable commercial or demographic developments take place. As a consequence, it ceases viewing multiple modernities as differentiated moments of subterraneously developing capitalisms, but as the multiplicity of attempts at emulating, selectively adapting or completely substituting capitalism (Teschke 2003; Shilliam 2009; Matin 2013a, 2020).[14] In the rest of this book, I will flesh out a historical narrative informed by these theoretical insights.

Conclusion

The political, the economic, the social and the international are specifically modern categories, each considered to be the subject matter of a distinct academic discipline. The starting point of this chapter was the claim that historicization of modernity was not feasible without problematizing and moving beyond the disciplines and categories created by modernity itself. The process of "moving beyond" implies that the history of modernity cannot be studied through fragmented or interdisciplinary methodologies. For, fragmented methodologies, even when they emphasize the interaction between multiple social spheres and academic disciplines, remain committed to a problematic ontology that takes as given the structure of modern society, which ultimately impoverishes our understanding of the past, present and future. What is at stake, therefore, is not a mere modification or a quick fix, but a complete overhaul of the process of historicization based on transdisciplinary methodologies. Transdisciplinarity is the key to developing a holistic ontology that does not see the past as an homunculus of the present both in social and spatial sense.

In developing such a transdisciplinary approach, I have used two methodological critiques, the critique of methodological presentism

---

[14] Hannes Lacher, 2015. "Polanyian Perspectives on Global History," unpublished paper, presented at Max Planck Institute for Social Anthropology, Halle, Germany.

and the critique of methodological internalism. Of course, several scholars in historical sociology and IR have advanced similar methodological critiques, charging conventional approaches with a tendency to read back the analytical binaries that characterize the modern present (e.g. Rosenberg 1994, 2013; Hobson 2002; Buzan and Little 2010; Anievas and Nişancıoğlu 2015; Go and Lawson 2017). Yet, these two modes of critique have yet to be sufficiently combined into a single analytical framework that scrutinizes the specificity, temporality and multilinearity of world historical development. I have proposed that an IHS, underpinned by PM, can deliver the promise of a truly nonpresentist and noninternalist conception of world historical development.

3 | Capitalism, Absolutism, Jacobinism
The International Relations of Modernity

In this chapter I will challenge the evolutionary and unilinear conceptions of Western European modernity by exploring the historical specificity of and intersocietal connections that produced the French Revolution. I will begin by substantiating the argument that early modern Western Europe witnessed the development of two radically divergent trajectories of class- and state-formation: capitalism in Britain and absolutism in France. The geopolitical tensions between capitalism and absolutism escalated particularly during the eighteenth century, repeatedly exposing the vulnerabilities of French fiscal and military power vis-à-vis Britain. This geopolitical backwardness led the French ruling elite and intellectuals to continuously debate how an English-like polity could be created on absolutist soil. A process of uneven and combined development thus began, which prompted the French reformers and intellectuals to look for ways to selectively emulate or substitute British capitalism.

Emulation, even if selective, proved to be an impossible task, though. The fundamental problem that confronted French elites and reformers was the policy of enclosures that empowered Britain geopolitically. Enclosures had produced a market-dependent society in England by the eighteenth century, generating a novel system of rule, appropriation and a new political subjectivity, the "abstract individual." As the "self-regulating" markets became the primary institution responsible for social reproduction, economic exploitation was no longer *necessarily* secured by the relations of political coercion and political inequality. With direct producers losing their customary rights over land, the very political processes through which surplus was extracted could take an ostensibly nonpolitical and contractual – that is, economic – form. Consequently, the relationship between appropriators and producers could, in principle, be viewed as a relationship between equal and abstract individuals.

Indeed, abstract individuals, unburdened from political inequalities and communal obligations of the past, were conceived by French reformers as the sociological basis of British economic productivity and geopolitical competitiveness. However, neither enclosures nor political equality was easily transferable to absolutist France. There was no market-dependent society; issues concerning property and income were immediately and necessarily tied to one's position in the system of political hierarchy and privilege. The relations of political inequality constituted the very basis of the French economy. Therefore, creating a British-like society underlined by abstract individuals required a fundamental overhaul of the relations of authority and property constitutive of the absolutist regime.

Indeed, this proved to be impossible in the eighteenth century, jeopardizing the position of reformers themselves. Without enclosure, as Shilliam (2009) argues, the only way to theoretically justify and practically contain the abstract individual was to condition the individual's right to property and equality to their service to an "abstract collectivity." The impossibility of emulating English enclosures on the one hand and the increasing geopolitical pressures on the other made eighteenth-century France the breeding ground for imagining a variety of abstract collectivities, such as "general will," "nation" or "humanity." And if these abstract collectivities were formulated (at least partly) as a response to the international unevenness generated by British capitalism, the French Revolution, under immense social and geopolitical pressures, radicalized and materialized these abstractions by innovating new methods of empowering and containing the abstract individual, which led to one of the most radical projects of substitution in world history – Jacobinism.

In short, rather than a unilinear extension of the market project from England to France, the Anglo-French contestation, and the concomitant processes of uneven and combined development sharpened and restructured existing sociohistorical differences, ultimately leading to the formulation of a qualitatively different regime of property and modernization in France. Jacobinism was neither absolutism nor capitalism, but combined and bypassed both based on a new form of sociality and political economy. It produced novel social, economic and geopolitical dynamics that gave modernity a radically multilinear texture.

As such, the approach taken in this chapter will build on and, in some respects, depart from the existing revisionist literature on the

French Revolution. We have come a long way since revisionist historiography rendered indefensible the old interpretations of bourgeois
revolution (e.g. Cobban 1964). For a long time, Marxists and non-
Marxists alike tended to associate the revolutions of the West with the
rise of bourgeois classes. According to these narratives, the revolutionary modern transformations in the West were carried out under the
aegis of "strong" bourgeois classes whose leadership during the revolutionary processes facilitated the full development of capitalist social
relations as well as the liberal political-cultural transformation characteristic of "Western modernity." After the revisionist turn, however,
even the most paradigmatic cases of bourgeois revolution – France and
England – lost their paradigmatic status. That is, revisionist
historiography has shown that even in the "classical" cases of revolutionary transformation, the bourgeoisie was not as capitalist and
democratic as traditionally assumed and capitalist development massively deviated from what was previously held to be the norm (e.g.
Mayer 1981; Blackbourn and Eley 1984; Comninel 1987; Wood 1991;
Halperin 1997; Davidson 2012). Most notably, in the case of France,
the engine of revolutionary transformation was not an idealized bourgeoisie, that is, a revolutionary capitalist class overthrowing feudalism,
but landowners, state officials and lawyers. Failing to find a "proper"
bourgeoisie and bourgeois revolution, most revisionist scholars have
either turned to the cultural interpretations of the revolution, which
negate the material dimension of revolutionary quarrels all together in
favor of purely ideological or cultural explanations (e.g. Baker 1990),
or shifted their emphasis from the significance of bourgeoisie to geopolitics as the catalyst of the transition to capitalist modernity.

In the field of historical sociology, undoubtedly, one of the most
influential contributions to the geopolitical interpretation of the French
Revolution was made by Theda Skocpol's *States and Social
Revolutions* (1979). In her analysis of the French Revolution,
Skocpol considerably modified the idea of bourgeois revolution by
emphasizing the catalytic impact of (geo)political relations in bringing
about the revolution and complicating its capitalist character.
According to Skocpol, in prerevolutionary France, distributional tensions between the aristocracy and the monarchy, aggravated by geopolitical defeats and challenges, caused the diminishing of ruling-class
authority in the countryside, which, in turn, opened up room for
maneuver for peasant mobilization. Given the pivotal role played by

the peasantry, combined with the threat of counterrevolution from "inside" and "outside," the French Revolution ultimately took a *dual* character. On the one hand, the revolution can be considered capitalist in the broad sense that it consolidated private property rights and destroyed regional, corporate and guild barriers to the formation of a unified national market. On the other hand, however, the popular and military pressures generated even "more striking and far-reaching transformations in the French state and national polity," which cannot be explained straightforwardly by capitalist class interests (Skocpol 1979: 179). In other words, the French Revolution, "by virtue of both its outcomes and processes ... was as much or more a bureaucratic-military, mass-incorporating and state-strengthening revolution as it was (in any sense) a bourgeois revolution" (Skocpol 1979: 179).

The argument presented here agrees with but at the same time goes beyond Skocpol's (geo)political interpretation of the French Revolution in two ways. First, the book emphasizes more systematically the centrality of international relations in generating modernizing impulses. In particular, it draws attention to the role of the Anglo-French contestation and interaction in the production of novel social and institutional forms in France. Second, given its nonpresentist premises, my argument reads the dual or combined character of the French Revolution in a different light. It does not see private property or abolishment of guilds as necessary indicators of the emergence of capitalist social relations. The resistance to presentist readings of capitalism, in turn, helps us clarify the historical specificity and world historical significance of the "bureaucratic-military, mass-incorporating and state-strengthening," that is, Jacobin, aspects of the French revolution more systematically than done by Skocpol.

The "Great Divergence" in Post-Feudal Europe: England versus France

Toward the end of the fifteenth century, England emerged as a country where the traditional rules of accessing land and dominant conceptions of property began to undergo drastic changes. Before 1450, no conception of ownership existed; each parcel of land was hierarchically distributed among different individuals, that is, interlocking forms of "possession" were in place that allocated differential access to different actors in the feudal hierarchy, such as the king, overlords, lords and peasants (Berman 1983: 454–5). Since "land could sustain multiple overlapping claims by many individuals . . . [t]he primary relation of an individual to land . . . could be maintained without physically excluding others. Indeed, land had little value to the rightful holder if others were entirely excluded" (Seipp 1994: 86–7). Land was an organic extension of such a community, in which individuated, impersonalized and strictly demarcated forms of property had no place or meaning (McNally 2011: 42–3). Likewise, the land rent was fixed and the peasantry had usufruct rights over land; therefore, English lords could maintain their income and status only through nonmarket means – that is, they could not increase their revenues by raising rent or investing in land; instead, they had to increase their extraeconomic powers and extend their juridical/territorial privileges to extract peasant surpluses and maintain themselves as lords. Therefore, exploitation and accumulation necessarily and immediately took a political form.

From the mid–fifteenth century onward, however, things began to change in the English countryside. Due to increasing peasant resistance to lordly jurisdiction, combined with the increasing exhaustion of geopolitical opportunities on the continent, English lords began to lose their political appropriative powers. Lords were no longer able to use their own political, juridical or territorial privileges to extract peasant surpluses, nor could they challenge the monarchy to make up for their losses (as did lords in France). They had no option other than to turn to king's law (common law) to be able to exercise authority over peasants and maintain their sources of income. The common law officially extinguished most of the autonomous juridical/political powers exercised by lords over the peasantry; yet it also recognized and amplified the exclusiveness of lords' economic power over the land occupied by peasants (Duby 1968: 194–6; Comninel 2000: 29–30). What was at stake therefore was the development of a distinct division of labor between the monarchy and landlords. Lords accepted the monarchy's political/juridical powers, giving up their centrifugal ambitions (if they had any), while the common law reinforced lords' economic power to tap peasant surpluses.[1] In developing their appropriative powers

---

[1] This does not mean that there were no more disputes among lords and the monarchy (e.g. the Wars of the Roses). Yet the issues arose less among the alternative holders of political-military authority, and were more centered on the struggles over the control of a centralized political authority. For "what English lords lacked in the form of feudal jurisdiction, they possessed as participants in

through the common law, English lords, from the mid–fifteenth century onward were inclined to raise their revenues through their possession of and investment in land, rather than mere extension of their juridical/territorial privileges. This was also facilitated by the existence of a middle peasantry, some of whom were wealthy enough to lease, work and invest in the lords' land (Brenner 1985a: 49; 1985b: 300). In this context, landlords and wealthier peasants began to restructure agrarian production through the enactment of common law against the law of manor – that is, the custom (Comninel 2000: 46).

Underlying the reorganization of custom were enclosures. Enclosures were neither a mere quantitative engrossment, nor a technical process of fencing of land. In fact, early enclosures transformed neither the form of tenure nor led to concentration of land, that is, customary tenants remained in place for a long period of time, yet without the customary rights that used to bind them to land (Thompson 1991b: 238–9; Comninel 2000: 31–2). Enclosures enforced that only those who could pay increasing rents could retain the land, and those who could not were to leave it. Land tenure, thus, was no longer custom-determined but made conditional on the tenant's ability to compete in the market place, and transform and invest in production. Consequently, from the 1450s, lords began to enclose the land by subjecting peasant tenants to competition for leases (Brenner 1985a: 49). Tenants had to improve the productivity of their estates to be able pay market-determined rents and to outcompete other bidders in the marketplace (Brenner 1985b: 301). The market was no longer a space of opportunity where surplus product and surplus labor was occasionally sold, but became an imperative for peasants' access to land. In order to ensure their subsistence and generational security, peasants could no longer rely on the age-old custom, but had to continuously transform the space and scale of production. They had to respond to the pressures of the marketplace by specializing, innovating and improving productivity.

Expropriating customary rights and subjecting the peasantry to market imperatives was not a peaceful process, but achieved usually through violence, threat of eviction, intimidation and interference into

royal justice and in the legislative role of the parliament"(Wood 1991: 48; Brenner 2003: 658–9). For a more nuanced and recent discussion of the relationship between royal and lordly powers in early modern England, see Dimmock (2019).

the viability of peasant production (Dimmock 2014: 182–3). Several peasant rebellions broke out, but to no avail (Brenner 1985a: 48).

Large parts of the population eventually became market-dependent through the early modern period in England. As much as 70 percent of arable land was already enclosed by 1700. Competitive pressures unleashed by enclosures resulted in unprecedented increases in labor productivity and agricultural production. This was accompanied by a massive upsurge in total population and by an equally dramatic decline in the number of people living in the countryside.[2] A deep and integrated domestic market emerged beyond the consumption of luxury goods, so did a market-dependent population and a reserve of landless laborers discharged from the agrarian sector (Parker 1996: 223–31). Combined with the profits accrued from slave trade and colonial conquests, all of this generated the economic momentum that led up to the Industrial Revolution (Wood 2001b). In short, the initial emergence of capitalism in England was a matter of social and geopolitical actors "involuntarily setting in train a capitalist dynamic while acting, in class conflict with each other, to reproduce themselves *as they were*" (Wood 2001ba: 52). As land was systematically and often violently divorced from its former political-legal embellishments, a new society governed by a distinct mode of property and rule began to crystallize in early modern England, heralding the contingent arrival of capitalism.

In France, just as in medieval England, every piece of land had multiple and partial owners who were connected to one another in a system of feudal privilege, dependence and hierarchy. Land was usually split between tenants endowed with use-rights and lords who were simultaneously the superior of those tenants and the dependents of a multiple strata of overlords (Blaufarb 2016: 4). From the fifteenth

---

[2] The total population increased by 350 percent from 1500 to 1800, while the proportion of the agrarian population dropped from 76 to 36 percent. The population grew in continental Europe by 50–80 percent during the same period, while the proportion of agrarian populations remained more-or-less the same (around 80 percent) (Overton 1989: 9, 13f.). As a result, "(o)ver half the total urban growth in Europe (between 1670 and 1750) occurred in England, a country with less than 8 per cent of Europe's population" (Parker 1996: 211). As an indicator of the growth of labor productivity in England, 100 persons engaged in agriculture provided food for 132 persons living in urban sites in 1520, and the ratio increased to 100:248 in 1800. In France, the ratio was 100:138 in 1520, which increased only to 100:170 in 1800 (Wrigley 1985: 720–6). Unsurprisingly, seventeenth-century demographic and commercial crisis in Europe had a much milder impact on England than its continental counterparts.

century onward, French lords, like their English counterparts, faced a decline in their juridical/military powers, that is, they were unable to increase their incomes by increasing labor services from the defiant peasantry. Yet, French lords, unlike the English, remained divided on questions of property and rule; hence, they were not able to transform the customary conditions of land tenure (Wolf 1997: 121). In consequence, enclosure was not an option; lords were not able to change the conditions of access to land. Instead, lords, in competition and collaboration with monarchs, and under intense geopolitical pressures from "outside," were to reorganize ruling-class power based on a new mode of political appropriation. They were to turn to the monarchy to reinforce their hold on the peasantry. Lords and the monarchy were to strike a new balance in a relatively centralized regime of appropriation, that is, the tax/office structure of the absolutist state (Anderson 1974: 18–19; Brenner 1985b: 263).

What underpinned the absolutist economy was a massive network of patronage and privilege built upon a market for venal offices. As a way of integrating the aristocracy and the crown, administrative-judicial posts and fiscal rights on land were put on sale as hereditable and vendible possessions. Many official posts could be bought and sold in an "open market," that is, a market not exclusive to the nobility. Like nobles, therefore, large numbers of the bourgeoisie, heavily involved in commercial and financial activity, competed to purchase a share of state power (Beik 1985: 335–6). For, given the persistence of peasants' customary rights over land, only political leverage within the state, rather than production per se, could secure and advance commercial and financial interests (Parker 1996: 53; Beik 2009: 65). Likewise, since enclosure was not an option, engrossment of land became the main ruling-class strategy in the countryside. Landlords, both of commercial and aristocratic origin, pushed back the extent of peasant holdings, consolidating big commercial farms by "squeezing" the land directly held by peasants (Beik 2009: 41, 63).[3] However, this "urban

---

[3] According to one estimate, the peasantry in France in the early seventeenth century possessed about half the land and worked most of the rest; the nobility owned about 20 percent, the bourgeoisie 15 percent, the clergy 10 percent (Parker 1996: 52). And on the eve of the revolution, peasants still constituted 85 percent of the population. And the land, whether possessed by the peasantry or rented out by landlords, remained extremely fragmented and scattered in comparison to England (Skocpol 1979: 55; Mooers 1991: 53).

colonization of the countryside" did not initiate a capitalist growth dynamic (Parker 1996: 53; Beik 2009: 65).[4] For the expropriation of land did not translate into the systematic expropriation of customary rights (Gerstenberger 2007: 456). Agrarian production and prices continued to be bound by the subsistence requirements of peasant holdings (Skocpol 1979: 55; Brenner 1985b: 313; Comninel 1987: 189–90).[5] Impoverished by the rent and tax demands of the ruling classes, a massive class of land-hungry peasants emerged, which severely restricted the expansion of the home market beyond the consumption of luxury items.[6] Of course, not all peasantry was poor: just as in England, in France too there was "a middle peasantry on relatively quite large holdings" that could potentially respond to market imperatives by investing in and transforming the conditions of production (Brenner 1985b: 300). Yet, even in the most affluent parts of France, such as in the Paris Basin, where most of France's so-called capitalist farms with wage labor were concentrated, no change occurred in the rules of accessing land, which could have otherwise forced, enabled and permitted peasant family units and big landlords to produce competitively, reorganize production, release labor and systematically transform the conditions of production (Brenner 1985a: 62–3 footnote 111; 1985b: 300–2; Miller 2012: 153–4).[7]

---

[4] And precisely in this context of urban colonization of the countryside, the revival of the complex categories of Roman law gained momentum, as more definite answers were demanded by royal justice for questions rarely raised before: Who was the owner of a tenure, the noble, the peasant tenant or the bourgeois? And yet again, no matter who owned the land, by the eighteenth century, it had become commonplace among French lawyers that the peasants were the "true proprietors" (Bloch 1966: 128–9; Beik 2009: 26). Rent, therefore, could be extracted through various forms of private property arrangements ranging from money-lease to sharecropping and yet without transforming the customary possession of land (Comninel 1987: 194).

[5] As a result, despite the rise of larger units of production, agricultural productivity (not output) remained almost stagnant (De Vries 1976: 67). This echoes David Parker's argument that eighteenth-century expansion of French agriculture was caused by an increased output following a severe subsistence crisis, not by the emergence of a more productive agriculture (Parker 1996: 210).

[6] By contrast, in early modern England, the dissolution of hereditary peasant tenancy developed simultaneously with the rise of consumer demand for the myriad small goods. Thus, "(p)urchasing power and productive capacity were . . . mutually sustaining" (Thirsk 1978: 174–5).

[7] Even the more optimistic historians who argue for the capitalist character of the Paris Basin recognize that in terms of labor productivity, overall French growth

Consequently, the overall dynamic of agrarian relations further reinforced the politically constituted character of bourgeois and noble fortunes (Miller 2008), thereby perpetuating the widely recognized structural problems of the French economy, that is, its peasant-based character, agricultural underinvestment, relative lack of specialization, interregional transportation problems, institutional inefficiencies and so on (Skocpol 1979: 54–64).

In the absence of an organized and system-wide political intervention into the prevailing property relations, mercantilist policies, which involved protectionist, regulatory and colonial measures, did not generate the kind of investments that could have otherwise unified and deepened the internal market.[8] Monopoly trading and manufacturing companies boosted profits only by securing politically maintained price differentials, hence, systematically excluding economic competition both abroad and at home. Better put, commercial competition was much less a matter of transforming the conditions of production and underpricing rivals than of direct political/ military control of markets.[9] Tariffs and subsidies eventually degenerated into mere fiscal, provisionist and redistributive devices (De Vries 1976: 250–1; Parker 1996: 44–5). Private property and accumulation of wealth were certainly existed prior to the development of capitalism, but neither of them in prerevolutionary France presupposed capitalist property and capitalist accumulation within itself as a developmental tendency. Quite the contrary, for capitalist property to develop, the dominant forms of private property, either in the form of commercial/

was low, 27 percent during the period 1500–1800, while it doubled in England during the same period (Hoffman 1996: 135–6).

[8] Mercantilist policies and colonialism certainly contributed to the rise of capitalism in Britain. Yet, this was mainly because they coincided with, if not predated by, the development of capitalist property relations (Parker 1996: 32–4; Wood 2001b: 49). That said, unless these sociospatial differences are taken into account, mercantilism, as a category that embraces the economic thought and practices of several nations across Europe, loses most of its explanatory value (McNally 1988: 23).

[9] In England, likewise, big merchants, organized in chartered monopolies, were not the pioneers of, but actually opposed the capitalist reorganization of society. In a series of events leading to the English Revolution of 1688, big monopoly merchants consistently opposed the capitalist landed class and the competitive reorganization of trade. Parliament, after the revolution, immediately broke these monopolies, constituting a more competitive colonial trade that induced capital investment overseas (Brenner 2003: 648–86).

manufacturing monopolies or venal office, would have to cease to be the main source of private appropriation (Gerstenberger 2007: 27). Absolutism was thus not a continental variant of capitalism. It was a historically distinct path out of feudalism that neither involved nor necessarily led to the development of capitalist social relations.[10] That said, the main impetus toward capitalism in France was to come not from within, but from without: military pressures, generated by Britain's capitalist economy, would make necessary the transformation of and showed an alternative to extant property relations in France. This was an alternative that French *économistes* so meticulously theorized in the eighteenth century, but which could only be materialized in the following century, that is, only after the absolutist state was no more (more on this later).

The (Geo)politics of Capitalist Modernity: "The Improvement of Property"

In parallel to their differential developmental trajectories, conceptions of property, law and culture radically diverged in early modern England and France. As argued earlier, in England, politically constituted and collectively regulated leases began to fade away from 1450 onward, as lords began to lease their demesnes based on prices determined by market competition. At stake in the transformation of property relations, therefore, was the destruction of rights and obligations embedded in the customary possession of land. From the 1490s onward, consequently, English lawyers began to perceive land less in terms of feudal mutual obligations, and more in universal, abstract and individualist terms (Seipp 1994: 34). By 1640, "land ... was much

---

[10] The conventional view holds that absolutism represented an interregnum before the final collapse of feudalism and the full-fledged unfolding of capitalism, hence, combining elements of both types of society (Anderson 1974: 113; Giddens 1985: 100, also see, Keyder 1983: 31–47). In consequence, the approximately three centuries–long existence of absolutism is read as some sort of protocapitalism, that is, in terms of the arrested development of bourgeois society, the aristocratization of bourgeois classes and the inefficient institutions that created a "court capitalism," thereby failing to further advance a bourgeois economy and so on. Obviously, grafting capitalism on to absolutism does not explain but reposes the question of the social character of absolutism. And behind the teleology inherent in this mode of argumentation lies the unqualified equation of the bourgeoisie and private property to capitalism. For a critique, see Teschke (2003: 151–65).

more clearly becoming capital, a profit yielding investment, rather than primarily a source of service, or followers, or royalty" (Corrigan and Sayer 1985: 73). And finally by 1750, as Thompson notes, property was already taken for granted by law as a "thing" in itself, totally alienable and with no consideration for mutual obligation or general good (Thompson 1991a: 135).

Underlying the transformation of property relations was an institutional setup that generated dramatic changes in the organization of politics and custom. The monarchical state was heavily involved in and actively promoted the construction and consolidation of capitalist social relations. This became especially pronounced after the Civil War as parliament took a decisive pro-enclosure stance: "no government after 1640 seriously tried either to prevent enclosures, or even to make money by fining enclosers" (Hill 1992: 69–70). And perhaps the clearest example of political and violent enactment of capitalist property relations was the Black Act (1724) that "criminalized long standing habits of protest," while leading to an unprecedented expansion of capital offenses for "even the most trivial of infractions" such as "poaching," "stealing a deer" and "firing a weapon indoors" (Zmolek 2019: 78).

The Act registered the long decline in the effectiveness of old methods of class control and discipline and their replacement by one standard course to authority: the example of *terror*. In place of the ... manorial and corporate controls and the physical harrying of vagabonds, economists advocated the discipline of low wages and starvation, and lawyers the sanction of death. Both indicated an increasing impersonality in the mediation of class relations, and a change, not so much in the "facts" of crime as in the category – "crime" – itself ... What was now to be punished was not an offence between men ... but an offence against property. (Thompson 1990: 206–7, my emphasis)

No wonder that under the terror of enclosure (combined with the violent suppression of agrarian and artisan riots), village communities and town guilds that were organized around customary rights and religious confraternities began to dissolve through the sixteenth and eighteenth centuries. In this regard, post-Reformation England witnessed not only the formation of a state-controlled and unified Church, but also an assertive parliament "urged on by a religious movement that was determined to narrow religion to its essentials,"

a process at the end of which people like John Locke could assert that
"society was bound together by agreement on things like property,
rather than on god" (Sommerville 1992: 143). For this, the "god of
work" had to cease to be conceived as the "devil," and "work" had to
become an end itself (Hill 1961: 294). All customary entitlements, for
example, access to common lands and alms from neighbors, had to
become markers of laxity, corruption and immorality (McNally 2011:
47–8). Rights and obligations over social reproduction had to be
transformed and assimilated into the impersonal mechanism of the
supply and demand of "things."

One testimony to the gradual disappearance of common purpose
from economic processes was the increasing popularity of mechanical
analogies and abstract conceptions of individuality in discussions of
property, society and the state (Hill 1992: 207–8). English intellectuals
and scientists of the early modern era worked out an image of society
as a multitude of free individuals collected together by a sovereign
power and increasingly governed by an "invisible hand"; a machine-
like market that functions according to its own rules. This was a
radical departure from the personalized image of the body politic
based on the divine harmony of naturally unequal men united to each
other by mutual obligations. Entailed in this reimagination of social
reproductive relations was the bourgeoning "culture of improvement."
Improvement, already "an integral part of English culture" in 1700,
"privileged certain kinds of public and private behavior above others,
encouraging innovative, industrious, and in every sense profitable
activities, while discouraging their opposites" (Slack 2015: 7–8).
Represented most powerfully by Locke's political theory and the new
"science of political economy," the culture of improvement pervaded
the intellectual scene in early modern England, generating novel conceptions of property, right and equality (Wood 2012b: 306–7).
Property could now belong only to those who could use it "productively" and indeed one's "responsibility" to use property productively
could now overrule another's right to subsistence. Furthermore, the
improvers of property were considered "equals" and granted civic
status in the newly emerging public place, while the rest were not. In
the early modern England, therefore, "improvement" of property
became an ethical right and responsibility and continued to be a
constant reference point for political discussions on "national" interest
and democracy (Slack 2015: 7–8).

Relatedly, despite differences in their sources of income and wealth, the members of the English ruling elite during the early modern period were becoming "a single economic class" whose power increasingly stemmed from "the possession of capital they employed for the end of profit and further accumulation" (Stone 1965: 52; also see Moore 1966: 19; Hill 1992: 19).[11] In this context, it is hardly surprising that the state began to be defined in clear opposition to property, for lords had no immediate need to use the state and state-office for appropriation (Brenner 1985b: 298; 1989: 304; 2003: 652). Better put, although the use of state-office for private gain continued,[12] the state-office was no longer of itself the direct and major instrument of surplus appropriation, hence a distinctly political state could be imagined. Likewise, the capitalist transformation of English agriculture led to the generalization of the market as the main access to the means of life,[13] thereby "unburdening" landlords and peasants from the communal rights/obligations that used to bind them to land. As property was separated from the earlier networks of interpersonal dependence and turned into a value in itself, an abstractly understood individuality, empowered by the right to "improvement," began to inform new forms of subjectivity. Property ownership per se, rather than a politically given communal duty, could be the basis of social existence and was considered for a long time as the only criterion for citizenship,

[11] Indeed, their power and unity was further consolidated after the Glorious Revolution, when the independent politicojuridical power of the Crown was effectively subjected to parliamentary control, so much so that the king began to be perceived merely as another member of the propertied class and the parliament (Corrigan and Sayer 1985: 79–80).

[12] The historical specificity of "corruption" in early modern England is best understood when it is compared to the nature of public–private power in early modern France. As I shall discuss later, in France "[s]tate office was a form of private property . . . therefore, private appropriation was a 'primary' function of the state, not an alien growth, not merely a corruption, not just a parasitism, but the thing itself" (Wood 1991: 27).

[13] While the commodification of land and labor at home opened the possibility of extracting surpluses by economic means, the English ruling classes did not necessarily give up extraeconomic forms of surplus extraction all together. In particular, colonialism and the concomitant forms of labor control such as forced labor and slavery galvanized the bourgeoning internal market, facilitating the processes of industrialization in England/Britain. The English ruling class had no problem whatsoever with applying the worst forms of violence and subjugation, especially when the colonized peoples were incapable of resisting them (Wood 2005: chapter 4; Lacher 2006).

political equality and membership in the English "nation." As property owners were economically united and politically equal to one another, they were able to give a unified "national form to their social interests." In this sense, nation was nothing more than an expression of the unity and equality of the propertied classes. As I will show later, this was in stark contrast to continental European states where relatively fractured forms of intraruling class politics could potentially force ruling elites to imagine and try to materialize more inclusive and popular notions of sovereignty and nation (Dufour 2007: 594).

Relatedly, given their coordination and economic sources of income, the intraruling class struggles in early modern England for a long time did not generate a strong tendency to establish a large army and bureaucracy (Brewer 1989: 64–87). A permanent army or a large bureaucracy was neither indispensable to the internal reproduction of the lordly classes nor rendered necessary by external factors (given also its relative insulation from continental war-making, especially during the Tudor period). Tax levels ultimately remained quite low at almost a quarter of those in France in the early seventeenth century, hence England's relative "inability" to man a centralized administrative/fiscal system (Hill 1961: 51). Therefore, oft-cited "idiosyncrasy " of the early modern centralization of the English state, that is, its "small bureaucracy," "limited fiscality," with "no permanent army" (Anderson 1974: 127), was rooted precisely in the power of the private holders of property and their relatively united struggle to protect private rights of appropriation from royal interference (Teschke 2003).

Emerging thus was a capitalist economy with a distinctly political state and a new collective and individual subjectivity. It is true that some aspects of this picture began to change from the end of the seventeenth century onward (Teschke 2003: chapter 8). In particular, under the geopolitical pressures emanating from the rise of absolutist powers on the continent, England was compelled to develop a competitive military-fiscal apparatus, a new foreign policy and new forms of political unity and subjectivity akin to its continental rivals. Yet, the emulative restructuring of the state and society under geopolitical imperatives did not result in another form of absolutism, but took a peculiarly British form. For one thing, given its buoyant domestic market and high levels of productivity, the state in Britain potentially had a larger tax base and was able to attract larger loans from the economic elite with less resentment than anywhere on the continent, especially in France (Parker 1996: 218–20). The emerging capitalist market enabled a qualitatively different fiscal base, which would eventually allow Britain to supersede its continental rivals militarily. Furthermore, the fact that the propertied classes were much less dependent on (geo)political means of appropriation meant that they could increasingly spare themselves from costly and militarily risky ventures on the continent. Instead of getting bogged down in costly intra-European disputes, Britain could commit its military resources to controlling the seas and overseas colonies while acting as the "balancer" on the continent (Teschke 2005: 17–18; 2019; Lacher 2006: 92).

Similarly, unlike continental Europe, the Church and the monarchy in Britain were already subjected to parliamentary control and capitalist discipline. The monarchy and the Church posed no serious challenge to the propertied classes and their dominant modes of appropriation (especially after the Glorious Revolution), hence, under geopolitical dictates, they could be reendowed with ideological support and value (in ways unimaginable in continental Europe, and especially in stark contrast to France). For this reason, the English ruling elite, by and large, substituted monarchical tradition and the Anglican Church for continental notions of state and nation. The cohesion of the body politic, organized based on economic relations, was well assured by the reinvoking of the most readily available forms of unity and inequality inherited from monarchical rule. In this context, reproducing monarchical/clerical tradition did not mean a return to the *ancien regime*; instead, it was a way of securing the stability of capitalism at home and worked as a geopolitical substitute for more populist continental notions of nation and state (Wood 1991: 31–41; 2012b: 179; Gerstenberger 2007: 318–19).

Read in this light, if any transition to "modernity" took place in Britain during the early modern period, it was the transition toward "capitalist modernity." This involved the emergence of a state increasingly rooted in and differentiated from civil society, an ethic of productivity, an abstract individuality, and a public space reproduced as part and parcel of the image of capitalist aristocracy. The propertied classes had no immediate interest in invoking an antimonarchical public space, nor did they need to envision a broader political community to challenge an inexorable internal or external enemy. By contrast, as I shall discuss later, most of the ideas, collective identities and institutions conventionally associated with (early) "modernity" had their origins not in capitalist social relations, but in their complete absence (Wood 1991: 18; Parker 1996: 203).

The (Geo)politics of Absolutist Modernity: "The Improvement of the Public"

In France, there were two main and interrelated features of the absolutist class structure that come to the fore: the persistence of peasant possession of land and the centrality of the state in obtaining ruling class incomes. The nobility and bourgeoisie owned over 50 percent of the land prior to 1789. While landholding was the main source of upper-class wealth, what guaranteed the continuation of their economic and political status was the sale of state-offices and the granting of fiscal immunities. In this regard, construing absolutism merely as political centralization lending weight to the monarchy would be misleading. For, while the Crown to a certain extent undermined the political/juridical autonomy of the nobility in the course of absolutist state-building, this was made possible only by granting the nobility patrimonial rights over state-office (Parker 1983: 26–7; Briggs 1998: 199). State-office itself, therefore, became "at one and the same time both an instrument for the extension of royal authority and a superb mechanism for the preservation of noble interests" (Beik 1985: 30–1).[14]

Office was as much the key to the reproduction of the bourgeoisie as to that of the nobility. The bourgeoisie did not differentiate itself from the nobility by seeking to establish an autonomous space of accumulation governed by an "improvement" ethic. Instead, their differences stemmed mainly from their differential access to state-office. Competition for fiscal and commercial privilege and a share of royal taxes persisted as the main means to the reproduction of the bourgeoisie and nobility alike (Taylor 1967: 491; Skocpol 1979: 59).[15] Therefore, it would be no misuse of words to say that the bourgeoisie and nobility were not two fundamentally opposing classes that

[14] At the time of Louis XIV, who is said to have coined the infamous phrase "L'Etat c'est moi!," the state involved merely 300 full-time commissioners and nonvenal officials as opposed to 45,000 venal office holders (Collins 1995: 93).
[15] It is, therefore, not without reason that by 1790 France was to become a country with the largest number of taxpayers and "the largest number and highest proportion of fiscal exemptions" in Western Europe (Bonney 2012: 93).

represented two different modes of life, capitalism and absolutism, respectively. Instead, the bourgeoisie and nobility in early modern France made up the opposing factions of the same noncapitalist ruling class (Comninel 1987: 194–6).

Relatedly, the relation of propertied classes to the state was never unambiguous in France. In England where ruling-class incomes were no longer immediately dependent on the use of the state as a means of appropriation, propertied classes were almost exclusively concerned with limiting state power over property. Yet, in France, given that ruling-class incomes were derived in and through the state, propertied classes had to confront the state both as a "competitor for and as a means to" accessing sources of income (Wood 2012: 151). Therefore, the struggle was much less about limiting state power than acquiring a privileged position in it or preventing others from doing so (Wood 2012). The flipside of this is that the fragmentation of the state among the holders of political/jurisdictional privilege made necessary an image of royal authority as the carrier of a "general" interest, that is, the interest of a "broader" political community (Jones 1995: 108, 138). And not so paradoxically, in the absence of a capitalist space of accumulation, those in opposition resisted state demands only by reasserting their equality of access to it and by invoking a more general interest in the name of a "higher" political community such as the nation or the people. What was at stake in constitutionalist debates in France, therefore, was not so much the protection of the private sphere from the state's encroachment but "transforming the 'private' state into a truly public thing" (Wood 2012: 170–1). The spiral effects of intraruling class struggles included a recurrent tension in French political discourse between privilege and equality and a continuous tendency to redefine the "general will" and "political community" in progressively popular terms. This was a phenomenon that, combined with new geopolitical pressures in the eighteenth century, would lend the public in France its most radical texture.

During the eighteenth century, Russia, Prussia and Britain rose as formidable geopolitical enemies, forcing French ruling classes to seek ways in which to rationalize the administrative apparatus and reorganize the system of taxation. Of these enemies, however, it was only Britain to which France would turn as a model. The British state, with its fiscal base rooted in a dynamic capitalist economy and home market, continually outspent and outcompeted France during what

some historians call the "Second Hundred Years' War" (1689/
1714–1815). Britain, especially after its involvement in the War of
the Spanish Succession, almost completely disengaged from territorial
claims on the continent (apart from the acquisition of certain strategic
posts on trading routes such as Gibraltar and Minorca) (Teschke 2003,
2019). It concentrated its geopolitical focus on naval power in order to
ensure unimpeded access for British commercial interests overseas.
This was combined by selective involvement in continental affairs in
ways to ensure that continental powers continuously fought one
another, thereby diverting their resources away from colonial operations (Brewer 1989: 178). Given the narrowness of its tax base,
colonial markets were much more important to absolutist France than
they were to capitalist England. In the course of the eighteenth century,
therefore, France fiercely reacted against British mercantilism overseas
while at the same time finding it increasingly difficult to sustain its
military superiority on the continent. Of the seven Anglo-French wars,
France lost six. Its only victory in the War of the American Revolution
provided nothing, but further added to the problem of war financing.
Despite widespread recognition of the need for fiscal reform, the fear
that changes could threaten fiscal/mercantile exemptions and privileges
left the elite "in a state of paralysis" (Parker 1996: 219).

The French elite was becoming increasingly aware in the course of
the eighteenth century of the comparative backwardness of their state
vis-à-vis Britain (Shilliam 2009: 37–43). By persistently defeating a
wealthier and more populous state like France, the British state
exposed the presence of a qualitatively different society across the
Channel. Britain became a constant reference for comparison for the
French elite, representing an order that is geopolitically more efficient,
yet which proved almost impossible to emulate. In approaching the
issue of geopolitical rejuvenation, the major problem confronting the
French ruling elite was how to reform the economy and the system of
taxation. In this context, from the 1740s, the French view of English
economic success had begun to shift from trade-based explanations
toward the "real economy" of England (Crouzet 1990: 137). The
productivity increases achieved in English agriculture drew the attention of a group of French agronomes and economists (physiocrats),
leading them to study and theorize the ways in which conditions of
capitalist agriculture could be created in France (Bourde 2013).
Especially after the humiliating defeat of the Seven Years' War, the

government also became more responsive to proposals for agrarian and fiscal reform, ready to take bold steps toward materializing physiocratic promises (Jones 1995: 128). However, it took only a decade or so for the French reformers to fully realize that any prospect of economic revitalization was conditional on the transformation of the entire social edifice of absolutism. Neither the customary rights of peasant possessors could be extinguished, nor the fiscal exemptions of the ruling elite be abolished. And indeed every attempt to adopt the social reproductive relations underlying the fiscal power of the British state would tend to threaten the political position of the reformers themselves (Bloch 1966: 222–3; Jones 2012: 112).

Despite the failure to emulate British enclosures, the debate on how to create a British-like society continued in eighteenth-century France. French Enlightenment philosophers found much inspiration in the works of Bacon, Locke and Newton and indeed a constitution similar to that of the British was increasingly perceived by French reformers as the key to national regeneration (Comninel 1987: 107; Wood 2002: 188–9). Yet, the general impression was that the process of transplanting the English constitution to France had to be selective and adjusted to local circumstances. For example, the physiocrats argued that "in an ill-ordered society" like France, "self-interested economic activity could rupture the social fabric" (McNally 1988: 123–9). The state, therefore, should actively create the conditions under which civic equality served the general welfare of the nation. Guided by "reason," the state had to educate "the public generally and the court specifically as to the true principles of economic and political administration" (McNally 1988: 123–9).[16] Like the *économistes*, most philosophes of the French Enlightenment, despite their evident admiration for it, also found "something unnervingly extreme about the English political

---

[16] In fact, Adam Smith agreed with the physiocratic opposition to the intrusion of selfish interests into the political sphere. However, while Smith held that certain classes such as the landed gentry had interests consistent with the general interest, the physiocrats argued for the constitution of an autonomous state against and above particular interests. This is another telling example of the socioeconomic differences between England and France in the early modern period. Adam Smith is not concerned about the capitalist transition. He can take for granted that the market functions as an integrative force and attributes to the state only a "corrective" role. Physiocrats, by contrast, had to assign the state a "generative" role, for their main concern was not the disciplining of an already existing market but its very "creation" (McNally 1988: 263).

experience" (Baker 1990: 178). Even the most Anglophile philosophers of the Enlightenment, such as Montesquieu, referred to England
as "a nation that could mobilize against its enemies immense fictional
riches, which the confidence and the nature of its government would
render real." Yet this also was a nation in which liberty by itself became
the main object of political life; therefore. the nation was "more easily
led by its passions than its reason" (Baker 1990: 176). Similarly, for
French reformers like Turgot and Necker, the doctrine of the rights of
man was the only norm on which the nation could be reconstituted; yet
to the nation they attached an important qualification: the hallmark of
the nation could not be individual will, but "reason" (Baker 1990: 127;
Stone 2002: 36–7). In short, while the increasing recognition of socioeconomic unevenness further irritated existing tensions within the
French ruling strata, the "improvement of property" and the "ethic of
profit" did not take root in France, for there was no capitalist property.
Rather, the French Enlightenment sought to substitute the improvement
of property for the improvement of the "reason," "state," "humanity,"
the "people" or the "nation" (Wood 2002: 188–9). In other words,
Britain gave new momentum to debates in France on how to reconcile
public with private interest, thereby promoting new conceptions of the
state, reason and the nation (Acomb 1980: 121–3; Baker 1990: 21–2).
In this sense, the eighteenth–century constitutional conflicts in France
can be understood (at least partly) as a series of struggles rooted in the
internalization of ideas imported from capitalist Britain.

   Yet this process of internalization and combination also hinted at a
radical departure from the British conceptions of sociality. To elaborate,
in Britain, self-interested economic activity based on the improvement
ethic was seen just as another way of serving the public. Moreover,
social reproduction was taken care of by the market, therefore the
relations of appropriation did not *necessarily* involve political inequalities and privileges. Therefore, the abstract individual, unencumbered by
wider social duties and entrusted to improve property, could become the
expression of public power. Mere ownership of property could underlie
the logic of political equality and representation. Nation or public was
no more than an agglomeration of abstract individuals whose freedom,
equality and unity was a function of their property. By contrast, in
France, property relations were directly sustained by the relations of
political inequality. Invoking British rights and equality in the land of
absolutism would mean the collapse of the entire political-economic

structure. Therefore, in the minds of French reformers and intellectuals, the political freedom and equality of the individual were affirmed in principle, but those rights were defined in friction with a duty toward an abstract collectivity, a truly public entity such as the nation (or the state). In other words, the impossibility of basing public power on abstract individuals led the elites to imagine abstract communities and enlightened sovereigns, both serving and served by individuals equipped with "reason." "Reason" mediated the substitution of nation for the individualistic conception of the public influenced by the British constitution. It forced the reformers to imagine a nation and a state as a "truly public thing" that would reform the old regime of privilege and boost its geopolitical competitiveness without the English-like contestation of "egoistic" interests. In the hands of the reformers, therefore, "reason" transformed the sociological referent of the public from the individual to the nation and sought to prevent the redefinition of the nation along more popular and radical lines (e.g. the radicalism most prominently propounded by Jean-Jacques Rousseau, more on this shortly).[17] The logic of social representation propounded by reforming elites sought to monopolize popular sovereignty in an enlightened or improved public space. This presented both a geopolitical alternative to the British form of social relatedness and a political response to popular claims to represent the nation in opposition to the crown (Baker 1990: 240–1).

If eighteenth–century French constitutionalism was as an attempt to restrain and bolster the absolutist state by way of an enlightened "abstract collectivity," Rousseau occupies a special place in this tradition. This is not only because he was arguably the most important figure in radicalizing the constitutionalist debates in France, but also because his writings had a deep impact on (though not universally embraced by) the Jacobins, especially Robespierre. Rousseau represented both a continuity within and a rupture from the constitutionalist tradition. He shared the constitutionalist concern for transforming the state into a

[17] Without doubt, nation is an amorphous concept. In France, it initially emerged as the contraposition to privilege, but whose privilege depended on the context. It could be used in support of provincial sovereignty and corporate orders as easily as of France as a whole (Fitzsimmons 1993: 30). Nation would acquire its most abstract meaning when the revolutionary deputies, in the face of urban resistance and rural/colonial revolts, merged the nation with the Third Estate as a whole, thus giving the nation its most heterogeneous and hence most universal character (Hampson 1991: 13–15).

"truly public" thing. Yet, unlike the mainstream of French constitution-alism, he refused to locate the public will in intermediate institutions. He identified private property as the principal cause of inequality, adversarial relations and ultimately "unfreedom." Therefore, while he attacked the proprietary character of the absolutist state as other constitutionalists did, he departed from them by locating the "general will" not in the "public council" or "assemblies of estates," but in the "people" as a broadly conceived social category (Wood 2012: 200).

Clearly, there was little embrace of the "radical" Enlightenment before the revolution. Nevertheless, this early modern legacy, especially that of Rousseau, largely shaped the way in which the revolutionary actors would make sense of and try to solve the underlying problem of geopolitical backwardness. For, unwilling/unable to differentiate political and economic processes, the agents of the revolution would have to confront the same dilemma that haunted the reformers of absolutism: How could they rejuvenate France without expropriating the traditional rights of the peasantry? How could they match the British fiscal-military power without replicating the British route to modernity? This required the creation of a new public with a historically specific combination of rights and duties. They had to find new ways in which the individual could be linked to the reproduction of a new political community. The logic of British participation in the public sphere – propertied citizenship – would be ultimately substituted by conditioning property and representation to compulsory military service and public education. In other words, the condition of entrance to British civil society would be universalized and militarized: It would be extended to an army of peasant proprietors with the condition of protecting the *patrie*. The revolutionary and Napoleonic state would materialize the eighteenth-century substitution project by militarizing it.

The French Revolution and the Rise of the Jacobins

Geopolitically exacerbated fiscal and constitutional crises gradually caused the collapse of the absolutist regime.[18] In June 1789, the Third Estate unilaterally transformed the Estates General into a National Assembly, laying the institutional foundations of a new mode

---

[18] My arguments in this section have benefited significantly from Shilliam (2009: chapter 2).

of representation and collectivity. The conquest of national sovereignty, however, was initially carried out in a somewhat reformist
fashion. The Third Estate, whose members were drawn mainly from
bourgeois landowners and professional office holders, represented the
less advantageous segment of the ruling class (Lucas 1973: 118). That
is to say, their interests, as with the interests of the First and Second
Estates, lay in the continuity of political modes of surplus appropriation, though they were relatively disadvantaged in accessing the
sources of income. Therefore, the conflict in June 1789 erupted mainly
as an intraruling class issue (Comninel 1987: 200). A more equitable
distribution of the tax burden, a doubling of the Third Estate and
voting by head were demanded. The Third Estate wanted a more
significant role in regenerating the realm; yet it did not seek to challenge privilege as an institution (Fitzsimmons 1987: 294; Jones 1995:
178). What forced the revolution to shift from mere intraruling
class negotiations and to embrace a more universally understood
sovereignty was "the combination of the counter-offensive of the
Ancien Regime and anti-privilege pressure from below" (Lucas
1973: 125).

Over the summer of 1789 urban populations mobilized against
worsening socioeconomic conditions, which led to a decisive defeat
of royal attempts at reconstituting the absolutist order. Meanwhile, the
peasantry also began to attack everything that threatened their existence in the countryside. They burned chateaux and the archives containing seigniorial dues, occupied their lost commons and invaded
forests (Lefebvre 1961: 129–32). Faced with pressures from below,
the Third Estate had two options. It could either support the royal
repression of the common people, thereby potentially contributing to
the undermining of its own position vis-à-vis the monarchy, or alter-
natively it could lead the people to undermine the regime as a whole.
August 1789 witnessed the *reluctant* realization of the latter option.
Through the Declaration of the Rights of Man and Citizen, the
National Assembly affirmed individual liberties, representative government, elections and the separation of powers as the principles of the
new regime. Yet, while venality of office, fiscal and regional privileges
were all categorically dismissed as remnants of the old order, the
National Assembly could only *conditionally* proclaim the destruction
of "feudalism": noble/clerical dues and rights over land practically
remained in place, that is, peasants still had to make exorbitant

redemption payments to redeem the lands that they customarily occupied (Woloch 1994a: 24–5).

In principle, then, elimination of noble privilege made imaginable a united public space based on individual liberty and civic equality, hence constituting an important step toward a British-style constitution and national sovereignty. And yet, unlike Britain, the free and equal individual in France was created merely by "political decree," that is, in the absence of a capitalist transformation (Shilliam 2009: 43). Despite the formal denunciation of the feudal system, the new regime, in practice, could neither destroy peasant usufruct (*censives*), which was a form of property within the hierarchy of privilege, nor sought to suppress seigniorial dues without compensation. The interests of the bourgeois landowners, as well as the fear of external and internal reactions to the revolution, rendered impossible the unconditional elimination of seigniorial dues and forced the National Assembly to make concessions to peasant demands for subsistence (Jones 2012: 113–14, 135).

The Assembly thus embraced the constitutional rights and liberties of the abstract individual in a noncapitalist society. And in such a context, political and economic rights were fused, that is, one's right to political equality was in immediate contradiction to another's right to enjoy their property. Therefore, the free and equal individual could become the basis of a new public space in France only if their constitutional rights and liberties were balanced by constitutional duties. In the absence of a society wherein self-interested "abstract" individuals may produce beneficial social and geopolitical effects, the rights of the individual had to be reformulated in such ways as to involve obligations for the welfare of an abstract collectivity – that is, the nation (Shilliam 2009).

And it is scarcely surprising that every major legal/constitutional text written after 1789 reproduced the inherent tension between property and equality, constantly shifting the rights and duties of the individual. While unleashing the rights of citizens, the Declaration of 1789, for example, set forth obligations to contain them according to the requirements of the general will. Likewise, the constitution of 1791, in theory, "brought into being one of the most participatory and democratic national communities in the world" by basing the electorate on taxes rather than on property (Fitzsimmons 1993: 37). Keeping the liability to direct taxation at low levels, the National Assembly extended liberty and equality far down the social order, creating a reservoir of (male) citizens that included many on the "poverty line" (Fitzsimmons 1993). And yet the same constitution could not help but halt the empowerment of new citizenry by dividing them into two groups: a minority of "active" citizens who were qualified to exercise rights and liberties; and a majority of "passive" citizens "endowed" with duties only (Sewell 1988). At this early stage of revolution, then, liberal rights could prevail only when based on a seemingly contradictory, yet ultimately necessary, mode of subjecthood, that is, based on a hierarchical allocation of duties among "equal" citizens.

The initial fissure opened between rights and duties, however, began to deepen as the old socioeconomic problems resurfaced. For, contrary to the expectation that the "equal" citizens would be willing to tax themselves, the members of the National Assembly consistently "confused tax reform with tax cuts" (Daunton 2012: 128). To restore public finances, the National Assembly issued paper money (*assignats*) based on the expected revenues from the sale of confiscated ecclesiastical lands. With the fiscal power significantly constrained, however, *assignats* rapidly depreciated, falling to "less than 1 per cent of their face value by 1796" (Daunton 2012: 129). The resultant hyperinflation and food scarcities began to afflict rural and urban citizens from the start of 1792. Price-fixing riots erupted in cities in early 1792, while peasant insurrections posed a serious challenge to the regime in the countryside. "Differently from in 1789," the popular anger was "directed no longer against the 'aristocrats' but against all the rich" (Gerstenberger 2007: 548).

Deteriorating domestic conditions were also breeding the fear of colonial disintegration and counterrevolutionary strife backed by foreign powers. The assumed linkages between the revolution's internal and external "enemies" were increasingly confirmed by the Habsburg and Prussian hosting of French émigré nobles and their open declaration of support for the embattled royal family. Likewise, the slave revolt in Haiti further stirred geopolitical fears as soon as it was revealed that loyalists in Saint Domingue bargained with the British for protection (Go 2016: 124–5). The geopolitical fault lines finally cracked during early 1792 when Vienna, hard pressed by the Russians in the East, demanded the disbanding of the French army on the frontier of the Habsburg Empire and the almost complete restoration of the old order in France (Stone 2002: 164–6).

In these dire social and geopolitical circumstances, the leading faction in the National Assembly, the Jacobins, became more responsive to popular demands and began to play a greater role in steering revolutionary politics. The Jacobin Club (or the Jacobins) was initially established as a body for debating constitutional matters among deputies, professionals and the bourgeoise; in short, a club for the well-off. The Jacobins in the Assembly were a loosely formed heterogeneous group that included two parliamentary factions: the Montagnards and the Girondins. Considering their socioeconomic backgrounds, perhaps it is not surprising that both the Girondins and the Montagnards alike made indisputable claims for individual liberty and property. Given the threat of social unrest and foreign invasion, however, they also grew increasingly lenient over time to lower-class demands for equality and subsistence. For example, the Girondins, the leading Jacobin faction in the Assembly from 1791 to 1793, declared the unconditional abrogation of all rents or redemption fees in August 1792. Likewise, in the face of increasing "lawlessness" in the countryside (violent acts of land clearance, land occupation and price-fixing), they took measures to implement progressive taxation (Jones 1991: 105). These measures were designed to pacify and ease the burden on the poor while trying to mobilize them for the war endeavor. Despite this, the Girondins also remained determined that stability should not come at the expense of property rights. They continued to associate property with the right to profit (Gross 1997: 70–1, 148). They rejected proposals for systematic price controls and grain redistribution as "an intolerable infringement of individual liberty" and decreed the death penalty against whoever proposes "an agrarian law or any other law which subverts territorial, commercial or industrial property" (Gross 1997: 71, 122–36).

The Girondin rule, thus, began when property was still "triumphant." Yet, it would end with a radical redefinition of property. The year 1793 constituted a turning point in this regard. On the military front, the Republican armies were driven out of the Netherlands and were under increasing pressure on other fronts too as Britain and Spain entered the antirevolutionary coalition. Anti-Republican revolts broke out in several western and southern provinces, while inflation and food scarcities were undermining popular support for the government in Paris (Stone 2002: 161). In this context, what is particularly worth mentioning is the proliferation of "popular clubs" in the capital and the provinces. Unlike the restricted membership of Jacobin clubs, popular clubs reached far down the social scale, providing lower classes unprecedented opportunities for political engagement. Through the clubs, the common people familiarized themselves with new modes of socialization (involving debates, committees, voting and, above all, the rhetoric of equality and fraternity) and acquired an important opportunity for raising popular demands and local subsistence issues (Woloch 1994b: 314–15). The clubs gave everyone a chance "to act as citizens and patriots, be accepted as spokesmen for the national will, engage in controversy, make proposals, go to meetings, and make speeches" (Palmer 1985: 83). Likewise, as the popular clubs were pushing the Jacobins to radicalize their views on property and equality, the revolt in Haiti, combined with the British threat to French colonies, effectively pushed the question of slavery and "color" onto the revolutionary agenda. Slaves demanded freedom, equality and citizenship, thereby forcing and further contributing to the universalization of lower-class demands regardless of race and color (Bhambra 2016: 9; Go 2016: 125–8). All combined, from 1793 it was becoming increasingly evident to the Jacobin elite that no mere "combination of free markets and bayonets" was able to pacify the common people and stave off "foreign" invasion (Hirsch 1994: 214).

It is little wonder, then, when the Montagnards seized power from the Girondins in the summer of 1793 through a parliamentary coup, they could do so only by opening the Jacobin clubs to the lower segments of society (Feher 1987: 49). Urban poor, workers, artisans and farmers, radicalized in popular clubs, began to enter the Jacobin clubs in large numbers, functioning tacitly as the executive branch of the Montagnard government, responsible, above all, with provisioning the army and policing the markets (by force if need be). By implication, the sans-culotte demands for equality and subsistence entered the Jacobin conception of property and political economy (Palmer 2005: 34). Food shortages were no longer perceived to be the result of temporary market imperfections but as treason and counterrevolutionary plots (Sewell 1994: 266). As a result, the Montagnards carried out radical "market-correcting" measures – the "Terror" – which the Girondins had outright rejected, such as the imposition of the death penalty on hoarders, enactment of a general price ceiling (the *maximum*) and the compelled acceptance of the *assignats* at face value. In a similar fashion, the Terror's agrarian policy, although short of a comprehensive land reform, merged with some of the peasant demands. It permitted the partition of the lands of émigré nobles into smaller plots and the dismantling of the castles in order to provide land and shelter to the rural poor (Jones 1991: 130). Peasants were not the primary beneficiary of revolutionary land sales; yet definitely gained from the sale and partition of confiscated lands, which, according to one estimate, resulted in a 20 percent increase in the number of peasant holdings (McPhee 2006: 211). Likewise, the Jacobins enacted and reinforced partible inheritance laws. By prohibiting traditional primogeniture, that is, by dividing holdings equally among many heirs, they aimed not only to limit the power of large landowners, but also, to secure the minimum subsistence requirements of peasant holdings, hence contributing to the democratization of property that "equal citizenship required" (Higonnet 1998: 123).

Property and the Terror: Beyond Capitalism and Socialism

None of this led to a form of (proto)socialism, though. The leading members of the Jacobin movement (to the extent it can be seen as an integrated "movement") never considered abolishing private ownership of the means of production, nor were they willing to build a society based on "economic democracy." True, there were more radical Jacobins (including, most notably, Babeuf) who sought to radicalize Jacobin equality along socialist lines; yet, it is equally true that the leading cadres clearly rejected the idea of socialism (Palmer 2005: 284–6). Robespierre makes this point quite clear by repeating numerous times that "inequality of wealth is necessary and incurable evil" or "the equality of property is a chimera" (quoted in Gross 1997: 39). In like spirit, the Jacobin constitution of June 1793 declared private property "sacred," just as its revolutionary predecessor of 1791. Therefore, Jacobins, albeit "eager to please deserving artisans or peasants," were "fierce and self-assured when faced with opposition to the idea of private property" (Higonnet 1998: 86).

Not uncoincidentally, the aspirations of the Jacobin political economy are usually associated with what may be called an (authoritarian) welfare capitalism. For example, Higonnet argues that Jacobins "were determined to find their place between the rejected extremes of collectively held property and private greed." Although Jacobins understood that capitalism "could aggravate or generate social inequalities," so runs the argument, they believed that it could be accommodated to the needs of the individual and the nation (Higonnet 1998: 82–5). Their expectation therefore was that "civil society, with some small nudge, would reform itself," raising the poor to the level of the rich, rather than "lowering the rich to some draconian average" (Higonnet 1998: 123). Indeed, a glance at the 1793 constitution seems to lend credibility to this interpretation. The Declaration of the Rights of Man and Citizen of June 1793, while reacknowledging the "sacred" right to property, introduced a number of addendums: it stated that "no one can be deprived of *the least portion* of his property without his consent" (art. 19) and introduced "poor relief" and "public assist-ance" as a "sacred debt." As such, while dispensing with all property qualifications on equality (hence eliminating the active versus passive citizen distinction of the 1791 constitution), the constitution tacitly invented new rights, such as the "right to subsistence," the "right to minimum property" and the "right to work," all of which were con-sidered vital for the advancement of "social harmony," "public reason" and "common welfare."[19] From this angle, as Gross argues, Jacobin egalitarianism might be seen as an early case for welfare capitalism and even a precursor of "universal citizenship income" (Gross 1997: 12, 44, 164).

On closer inspection, however, claiming Jacobinism for welfare capitalism loses most of its persuasiveness. For capitalist market dynamics to unfold, there needs to be a clear hierarchy between prop-erty and subsistence. In other words, a market-dependent society can be created only when demands for subsistence and equality are clearly subordinated to the requirements of capitalist competition and accu-mulation – that is, capitalist markets can be established only when the customary conditions of social reproduction are systematically

---

[19] The Declaration of 1793 reads: Article 1: The aim of society is the common welfare. Article 2: These rights are equality, liberty, security and property. Article 19: No one can be deprived of the least portion of his property without his consent, unless a legally established public necessity requires it, and upon condition of a just and prior compensation. Article 21: Poor relief/public assistance is a sacred debt. Society owes subsistence to unfortunate citizens in adversity, either by procuring them work or by ensuring the means of existence to those who are unable to work. Article 22: Education is needed by all. Society ought to favor with all its power the advancement of the public reason and to put education at the door of every citizen. Article 23: The social guarantee consists in the action of all to secure to each the enjoyment and the maintenance of his rights: This guarantee rests upon the national sovereignty.

undercut, and the market is made the ultimate basis for holding and expanding the means of subsistence. Obviously, this is not to say that capitalism cannot help the poor, deliver welfare provisions and so on, but no market correcting measures can afford (at least not in the long run) to put the means of production and subsistence out of the market-place. Even the most generous welfare systems that provide extensive market-correcting policies are unable to offer recipients with a genuine "alternative to market dependence" (Esping-Andersen 1990: 22–3). Turning labor and land into commodities on a systematic basis is a prerequisite to providing (limited and temporary) protection to the least fortunate members of society. That said, Jacobin egalitarianism does not easily lend itself to such an interpretation. In Jacobin eyes, the right to existence had a clear primacy over the right to property:

What is the first object of society? It is to maintain the indefensible rights of Man. What is the first of these rights? That of existence. The first social law, then, is that which guarantees all members of society the means of existence; all others are subordinate to this; property has been established or guaranteed only to consolidate it; it is in order to live, in the first place, that one has property. It is not true that property can ever be in opposition to the subsistence of men. (Robespierre, paraphrased by and quoted in Feher 1987: 141)

This signals that while Jacobins' defense of the right to subsistence did not seek to annihilate property per se, it instated the primacy of the "right to subsistence" over the "right to property." The Jacobin egalitarianism was not a mere adjunct of an already existing market; it was not a simple conciliation of property rights with citizen welfare; it was not designed to tame the worst excesses of a market-dependent society. In other words, while Jacobinism declared subsistence as a constitutional right, it "did not act merely as an appendix to the rights of property," as did the English Poor Law (Shilliam 2009: 46). Indeed, the poor law was essential to the completion of the transition to capitalism in England without any major agrarian revolts after 1600. Yet the poor law did not seek to resurrect old common rights and direct access to land. It partially recompensed for the disappearance of customary rights yet was not a substitute for capitalist property rights (Patriquin 2007: 115). Jacobinism, however, reversed the capitalist hierarchy between subsistence and property in a revolutionary non-capitalist context: one's right to subsistence could now rule over another's right to "improve" property.

The first "social law" which overrides all others [is] "that which guarantees the means of existence to all members of society"... [O]wnership [is] but a means to achieving this end, to ensuring life, and thus ownership [can] never be in opposition to man's subsistence ... that everything which [is] essential to preserve life [is] "a property common to society as a whole," and "only the surplus" [can] be considered "an individual property." (Robespierre, paraphrased by and quoted in Gross 1997: 69–70)

What is implied here is that in the course of combining British and local social forms, the Jacobins, wittingly or otherwise, dropped the seeds of an entirely new (geo)political economy. Since they deemed "subsistence" "ontologically prior" to the "improvement of property," they "generated an anti-capitalist dynamic and a network of social regulation which, so long as it lasted, brought ... capitalist accumulation to a forcible halt" (Feher 1987: 141, 147). Therefore, the introduction of subsistence as a constitutional right marked not a continuation of, but a departure from, the "liberal" logic of the earlier phases of the revolution, "a departure as radical as socio-economically as politically" (Feher 1987: 146). In choosing between capitalism and socialism, Jacobins did not create a capitalism with human face, but made an original attempt at sidestepping the creation of a market-dependent society.[20]

More specifically, the chaotic state of affairs, created by domestic and international circumstances, forced Jacobins to imagine a new state, a new nation and a new political economy, all born out of an attempt to find a substitute social base to reproduce a noncapitalist body politic. Central to the development of this new political economy was a historically specific conception of property, through which the Jacobins sought to overcome the recurrent tension between economic liberty and political equality. They attempted to ensure the security of property by making it directly pertinent to one's subsistence. That is, property was no longer for the wealthy only, but turned into a

[20] Tellingly, the Jacobin conception of property was a sham in the eyes of liberal-conservative British philosophers of the time. Edmund Burke writes: "the characteristic essence of property ... is to be unequal. The great masses therefore which excite envy and tempt rapacity, must be put out of the possibility of danger ... [In France] of course, property is destroyed, and rational liberty has no existence." Likewise, Jeremy Bentham claims that "unfortunately, in most matters of property, the outcome of the French declaration of rights would be not to establish property, but to extinguish it – to render it impossible ever to be revived" (quoted in Feher 1987: 139–40).

precondition to one's "right to existence." No wonder, the easiest and fastest way of ensuring subsistence was to facilitate and strengthen the peasantry's customary rights on land (which no successor regime following the Jacobins would dare to change for a very long time). The Jacobin agrarian policies "hugely reinforced the small-scale character of landholding in France" with the expectation that "[s]mall scale landholding, despite its economically adversary consequences, would facilitate the creation of a rampart of peasant and artisan mini-proprietors who would hold counterrevolution at bay" (Jones 1991: 130, 110). Likewise, in urban centers, artisans and workers, despite the formal abolition of guilds in 1791, persistently "interpreted the revolution as a complete overthrow of the old labor regime," as an assurance of their customary rights and autonomy at the workplace (Lafrance 2019a: 117–18). While freed from the corporate hierarchical structures and master-artisans of the past, therefore, workers did not accept (for a long time) the logic and techniques of, hence their subsumption to, capitalist discipline at workplace. There was no growing "artisan capitalism" as conventionally assumed, for the legal abolishment of guilds did not lead to the actual disappearance of customary rights (Lafrance 2019a: 98–100, cf. Sewell 1980). Although poverty and threat of unemployment continued, "most workers could now freely and legitimately discuss the organization and execution of work with an employer to which they were not subordinated" (Lafrance 2019b: 114). They could organize the labor process by themselves or jointly with their employer as "equals," a principle validated by tribunals and that would have strong implications for the content of property rights encoded in the Code Civil of 1804 (more on the Code later).

Equally important, the question of "whose right to existence" was further clarified, even if briefly, during early 1794 after the failure of price controls. Through the Ventôse decrees, the Jacobins promised the property of "enemies" of the revolution to be distributed to needy "patriots." Property did not necessarily belong to those who "improve" or get a profit from it, but was universalized as a political right for all men who were "patriots." Therefore, the year 1794 gave "property a new foundation in law. It [created] a title to property which all citizens could attain by rigorous political action on a national scale" (Jaures, quoted in Feher 1987: 144). Indeed, property was now all the more "sacred" because it was both the safeguard of individual existence and a means to securing political unity and defending the nation (Hirsch 1994: 220).

Therefore, by attempting to link social reproduction to patriotism, the Montagnard rule signaled the institutionalization of a new form of property with totally new sociopolitical embellishments. Property was no longer understood as an economic right exercised by productive individuals only. But it was freed from those who "abuse" it and turned into a political entitlement for those who are socially and geopolitically useful to the nation. What was emerging in this liminal space was not a market economy, but a new moral economy under-lined by a new sense of social reciprocity and unity: an economy in which service to a universally understood nation (rather than market competition) gave access to the means of social reproduction and provided the "ultimate form of civic participation" (Woloch 1994b: 317). The nation was not a derivation of property as was the case in Britain, but vice versa.

At the center of this new system of production and redistribution was a conception of the state as "general fictitious proprietor." The state had no legal ownership of the means of production or land – in this sense it was a *fictitious* proprietor; yet by upholding the right to subsistence, it was tasked with supervizing and managing "matters (tendentially, all matters) involving property: in this sense, it was a *general* proprietor." In other words, the state "declared property as a social institution and was prepared to manage it on behalf of the Republican [i.e. patriotic] poor, without even making attempts at realizing that chimera, absolute or factual equality, let alone agrarian communism" (Feher 1987: 144–5, original emphasis). By implication, the state's role as the general fictitious proprietor was not limited to intervening in the economy from "outside," but it had to reconstitute private property based on new social and moral foundations. The state, not the marketplace, had to allocate property and at the same time to check and limit it for (geo)political purposes, which pointed to the unambiguously noncapitalist character of the Jacobin conception of economy (Feher 1987: 142–3).

All that said, for all its epochal character, the Montagnard rule lasted only thirteen months, and their successors would do everything they could to reverse the radicalism of the earlier period. Yet, the institutional innovations of this period, which I will probe in the next section, would well outlast the period of Terror. For, the socioeco-nomic system implemented during this short period, although designed to be temporary, would face social and geopolitical circumstances "which afforded either the continuation of the same or a violent collapse" (Feher 1987: 146). The "battle-tested" innovations of this period, despite emerging "from desperate improvisations in response to threats of rebellion and bankruptcy," would "endure beyond the Revolution and Empire" (Tilly 1990b: 52).

Substituting Capitalism: The "Citizen-Soldier" and "Public School" as Keys to Understanding Alternate Routes to Modernity

The Jacobin Terror neither expropriated nor slavishly accepted the rights of the propertied individual, but redefined them in ways conducive to French political unity and geopolitical competitiveness. The most immediate result of conditioning welfare to patriotism was levée en masse – that is, mass conscription. As mentioned earlier, the 1793 Jacobin constitution implicitly linked the enjoyment of citizens' right to property and equality to their service in the newly formed citizen-army. The creation of citizen-soldier thus signaled the introduction of new nonmarket means to acquiring land and political status. Undoubtedly, in practice, even the Montagnards were quite reluctant to interpret military service as a means of economic redistribution. They were afraid that establishing a direct connection between military service and land ownership could provoke property violations. Yet, they were also aware that "[m]en who possessed nothing" would refuse to go to war, for "that they had no property and no interest in defending the property of others." There was substantial sans-culotte agitation within the army, and soldiers would fight for the new patrie only if they received assurances for access to income and property (Bertaud 1988: 114). Therefore, the division of common lands into small parcels, the abolition of dues and rents, and the political attempts at ensuring the customary rights of the poor both in urban and rural areas must be seen as part and parcel of the logical connection established between military service and peasant reproduction.

A citizen-army was quite an unprecedented phenomenon in world history. "It was an idea exemplified in the ancient classical republics, and favored by Jean-Jacques Rousseau and other eighteenth-century thinkers, but until then never realized so fully on so large and portentous a scale as in France in the 1790s" (Palmer 1988: xii). Prior to the revolution, "wars (in Europe) had been the result of dynastic struggles for power, a kind of family quarrel within a ruling aristocracy ... They brought about no alteration in social structures and thus had minimal impact on society" (Halperin 2004: 73). Likewise, in the *ancien regime* of France, one's participation in the army was necessarily mediated by his membership in monarchical institutions, corporate bodies and investment in political privileges. Mobilization of the commoners for war was too risky for the ruling elite even to contemplate (Kestnbaum 2002: 122). The Montagnards' elimination of privileges and the universalization of military service thus combined military and political practice in a hitherto unprecedented way: "for the first time in French history men of rural origin predominated in the army in the same proportions as they did in civil society" (Woloch 1994a: 387). "Even the lowliest of those previously excluded from politics now had an unimpeachable claim to be included as an equal citizen solely by virtue of the military service he performed" (Kestnbaum 2002: 131). The army became the most unmediated point of access to the nation. Citizens became soldiers and soldiers citizens. The citizen-soldier was thus born.

The fall of the Jacobins in July 1794 heralded a sea change in many respects, but the citizen-soldier remained firmly in place. For, while the Thermidorian reaction (1794–5) quickly reversed many of the Jacobin "excesses" by, above all, bringing back the propertied franchise (Woloch 1994a: 98–9), it even more strongly reaffirmed the place of military service at the heart of the new body politic. Under the Directory (1795–9), participation in the armed forces turned into a precondition for being a part of the nation, regardless of property qualifications. That is to say, military service became the precondition to gaining citizenship for the propertied and the propertyless alike, the former as the elected and the latter as the elector (Woloch 1994a: 390).

Two broader and interrelated implications ensued with the consolidation of the citizen-soldier as the new subject. First, given the peasant origin of the new armed forces, military mobilization rendered almost impossible the expropriation of the peasantry, hence it could not be used to facilitate the opening of an intensive path of economic growth. As a result, while the state-appropriation and redistribution of peasant surpluses continued to be the main locus of ruling-class reproduction,[21] the Directory and then Napoleon had to channel popular energies outward,

---

[21] With the dissolution of office venality and fiscal privilege and the opening of the state to "talent," the bureaucracy expanded five times from 1792 to 1795 and doubled from 1795 to 1799 (Mooers 1991: 73)

that is, they systematically linked the reproduction of the new body politic to an increasingly aggressive regime of (geo)political accumulation.[22]

Second, if the citizen-soldier marked a fundamental transformation in the contours of political life, its collective expression, the citizen-army, heralded a revolution in war-making and state-building (Mjøset and van Holde 2002: 33). Despite widespread draft evasion, after the first levy in 1793, the French army reached 750,000 men, a number the combined coalition armies could hardly match. Born as a one-time emergency measure in 1793, the levée turned into a systematic annual exercise in 1798, incorporating around 3–3.5 million men in the armed forces until 1813. Of the young men born between 1790 and 1795, almost half of them served in the armies of Napoleon (Forrest 1989: 20). This means that peasant resistance to conscription was by and large broken by 1810 and Napoleon fully routinized the recruitment process, finally ingraining "the habit of conscription ... in the psychology of the young and the communities to which they belong" (Woloch 1994a: 432–3; Forrest 2002: 104–5). Perhaps more important than its quantitative enormity, however, the creation of a national army mobilized social forces that the *ancien regimes* of Europe could not dare to unleash. For conscription offered the popular classes "a newly authorized place in the regime as citizens: political recognition if not democracy, a way to participate in at least one of the state's chief endeavors, and a way ... to (however limitedly) appropriate the state as their own" (Kestnbaum 2002: 133). Likewise, "Napoleon fully exploited the meritocratic and democratic possibilities of the revolution" by retaining the principle of careers opened to talent both in military schools and on the battlefields, where daring soldiers and junior officers were rewarded "on-the-spot advancement" (Skocpol and Kestnbaum 1990: 23).

The novelty of this shift in state–society relations can hardly be overstated. Indeed, it was precisely this qualitative transformation that

---

[22] The Directory and then Napoleon found themselves in a situation of permenant war. They could not feed their soldiers, nor could they disband them unless alternative sources of employment were created. "The only solution was to continue the war, and order the troops to 'live off' the invaded lands" (Biro, quited in Stone 2002: 219). In this sense, the strategy of Permanent war can be considered "the French substitute for the industrial revolution" (Feher 1987: 46).

not only made possible the triumph of French armies (virtually unstoppable until 1814) but also rendered their success, at least for a while, irreproducible by others. British elites, for example, already traumatized by the "lawlessness" and "tyranny" of Cromwell's New Model Army in the seventeenth century, found inconceivable the idea of a French-like citizen-army on British soil (Martin and Lender 2015: 6–7). Also, Britain, with its capitalist economy and dispossessed "surplus" population, could match the threat of French invasion by simply hiring more foreign mercenaries, recruiting volunteers and reinforcing its naval power. "More fundamental reforms were neither necessary nor desirable" (Mjøset and van Holde 2002: 34). Therefore, Britain could "rely on the incentives of the marketplace to meet its manpower needs" (Mjøset and van Holde 2002: 36), that is, it could afford to buy soldiers without creating equal citizens, at least until the World War I. Prussia, on the other hand, traumatized by its defeat by the Napoleonic armies at Jena (1806), had no option, but was forced to (selectively) imitate Napoleonic conscription, which would cost her nothing less than a "revolution from above" (Mjøset and van Holde 2002: 35).

Therefore, through mass conscription, the French revolutionaries universalized the conditions of acquiring property and equality. Instead of property ownership, participation in the citizen-army became the main criterion for accessing the sources of subsistence and civility. No doubt, the levée was the most successful expression of Jacobin state-building and an important hallmark of the new civic order in France. Yet it was not the only one. The revolution extended its mobilizing logic into the field of education too. Public schooling was considered central to inculcating the civic values conducive to the Republican cause. The Convention, and then the Directorate, regarded public schooling as a means to creating the new citizen and regenerating the nation. True, they were never able to adequately fund universal public education since the requirements of war-financing quickly depleted the financial and human resources of the French peasant-based economy, leaving no sustainable financial basis for establishing a national system of education. Napoleon, likewise, focusing all his energy on conscription, could show only little interest in keeping up with the Republican insistence on public schools. The Bourbon Restoration could only modestly revive the Republican belief in universal primary education while dropping altogether its Republican content (Woloch 1994a: 232–6). All that said, what is perhaps more important than the limited and protracted development of public schooling was the specific vision underlying the educational reform attempts: a (geo)political pedagogy that links the education of all citizens to the reproduction of the state. In this sense, "the Revolution produced a permanent change of perspective among the governing elites of most political persuasions. Officials in every successive regime denounced the deficiencies of community driven, tuition-supported traditional popular education ... and clung to some notion of *instruction publique* as a potential antidote" (Woloch 1993: 148–9).

The point is that public education, just as universal conscription, came out as a substitute mechanism of disciplining and appropriating peasant bodies. Furthermore, it was a way of linking the right to subsistence and the right to equality to the service of the nation. For, when education became accessible to all subjects, it, at least in principle, brought to an end the systematic exclusion of the lower classes from the state and state-generated income (which was the main source of social reproduction in France, unlike in Britain). The need to mobilize and contain popular classes for the state, in other words, brought in its train the generalization of access to it, which, over time, led to the emergence of a large "citizen-bureaucracy." Education was thus a right and a duty at the same time. Education was both a substitute for and a part of the revolutionary process (Palmer 1985: 81). The school as a result gained an unprecedented importance in the formation of the successive regimes in France.

The novelty of *instruction publique* should not be overlooked. In Britain, for example, educational attainment remained entirely voluntary, locally based and privately funded well into the second half of the nineteenth century. The political/cultural mobilization of the lower classes was not necessary for the reproduction of the ruling class. The market could well discipline the poor and deliver geopolitical objectives; therefore, there was no need to educate the lower classes beyond voluntary and localized forms of vocational/industrial training (Vaughan and Archer 1971: 202–30). That said, this does not mean that the education system in France performed more effectively than that of its neighbors. For example, Prussia of the mid–nineteenth century, empowered by a rapidly capitalizing economy, excelled at public education (and universal conscription) much more effectively than the French (Mann 1993: 304). However, what is more important than the relatively protracted development of public schooling in France is the conditions and terms of its emergence. "Public school" emerged as an alternative Republican space to the old regime and the market, fostering forms of association in substitution of absolutism and capitalism. The revolution introduced universal education not only to bolster a geopolitical pedagogy, but as a geoinstitutional response to and ideological substitute for the market. In other words, what lent instruction publique its historical specificity was that, unlike other Western European countries, it was born of an attempt to engineer a noncapitalist form of sociality, which would continue to complicate the development of capitalist social relations well into the nineteenth century.

It was precisely from this market–school dichotomy that another important implication ensued. Underlying the critique of traditional schooling in France was an attempt at shaping the existing religious establishment and values according to new political and strategic objectives. The Church's role, in this regard, as the main provider of education, had to be repeatedly restructured to meet the state's changing strategic goals, which inevitably generated a constant tension between and within the clergy and the political elite. This by no means implies that the state necessarily pursued an anticlerical or antireligious policy; after all, Napoleon was quick enough to liquidate Republican anticlericalism by "cementing anew Church-state relations, in the process trying to enlist the parish clergy as his moral prefects" (Woloch 1994a: 431). Yet the point is simply that in France religion and politics had to be merged in novel ways to ensure social reproduction and to defend the nation. And whenever the existing cadres failed to deliver these objectives, as they would at Sedan (1870–1), anticlerical and antireligious tendencies could resurface. Thus, the modernizing vision could potentially turn into a secular one. In England, by contrast, a new mode of political/cultural mobilization was not necessary. Demands for secular schooling therefore could be formulated not against, but in addition to the Church. The state could accommodate demands for secular schooling without turning secularism into a developmental ideology (Vaughan and Archer 1971: 202–30).

To recap, army and school were not merely the components of an emerging "political modernity" driven by a "totalitarian utopianism" in France (Eisenstadt 1999: 50). Instead, they constituted the very foundations of a new geo(political) economy. By conditioning representation and social reproduction to compulsory military service and education, Jacobinism not only substituted the logic of British participation in the public sphere – the propertied citizenship – but also led to the universalization and institutionalization of a set of new extramarket mechanisms of acquiring income and status. Service to the nation, rather than successful commodity production, gave access to land and state-based income and provided the ultimate form of civic participation. In short, the condition of entrance to civil society and modern economy was universalized and militarized in a way that reinforced the decommodified character of land and labor. Property and representation were extended to an army of peasant proprietors, that is, citizen-soldiers and citizen-officers, with the condition of protecting the nation. As such, "the Jacobins set in motion a completely new *imaginaire*," that is, "an utterly novel and untried ... economic, political and cultural regime which set an enduring precedent, almost a blueprint, for revolutions to come" (Feher 1987: 132, 14).

Conclusions: Rethinking the Jacobin Model and the "International"

Enclosures had created a historically specific society and a novel mode of existence in England. Property was separated from the wider networks of sociopolitical relations on which human existence came to depend. One's enjoyment of property could now, in principal, be perceived as an accident, hence not a mere result of one's genetically located status in society. As a result, social space could be built in the image of the abstract individual; an abstractly defined individuality, equipped with natural and unimpeded rights to property, could become the expression of both the private and public powers. Property per se, rather than a politically given communal duty, could become the basis of social existence and political equality.

Geopolitical pressures generated by capitalist England had already made the abstract individual the reference point for attempts at reform in prerevolutionary France. However, it was not enclosure but the revolution through which France could institutionalize the rights of the abstract individual. This, in turn, led to the contradictory assertion of capitalist forms of sociality and property rights in a society where capitalist social relations were absent. The Jacobin Terror, not less radical than the English enclosures, provided a historically specific solution to this uneasy modus vivendi. It recognized the abstract individual by conditioning his rights to his duties toward an idealized abstract collectivity – that is, the nation. The nation, freed from the particularisms of the prerevolutionary period, thus turned into a substitute for the British mode of social relatedness. In this respect, the French invention of the citizen-army and public school developed as geoinstitutional responses to and ideological/political substitutes for the market in Britain. They were born of an attempt to engineer an alternative form of sociality in the course of substituting the nation for British civil society.

France developed a specifically modern conception of community, rule and economy as it sought to overcome its conditions of geopolitical backwardness. Jacobinism was not a mere derivation of capitalism or a continuation of absolutism. Instead, it was a historically novel combination of the two: the geopolitical coexistence and contestation between British capitalism and French absolutism produced Jacobinism as a historically specific (geo)political economy. Jacobinism was the cumulative result of the adaptation of the British abstract individual into France, which brought about the end of absolutism without leading to capitalism. Indeed, the constitutions of the revolutionary period and then the Napoleonic Code continued to reflect this uncomfortable balance caused by the existence of an essentially capitalist subject in a noncapitalist society. For example, in the British common law world, private law always had a clear primacy over public law: laws governing "justice" were subordinated to the laws governing land and property (Schwartz 1956: 252–3). By contrast, in revolutionary France, while legal texts repeatedly endorsed the inalienable character of *propriété*, such assurances never amounted to the subordination of public law to private law (Lafrance 2019a: 118–19). Even the Napoleonic Code continued to retain the hierarchy between private and public laws so much so that considering various limitations placed by the Code on private law, some legal scholars go as far as to argue that the French *propriété* was "perhaps no ownership at all" (Lewy 1956: 165).

With that in mind, it is perhaps scarcely surprising that the legal system in France "for much of the nineteenth century served actually to discourage remedial adjustments to property structures" (Jones 2012: 133; also see Miller 2019). In 1820, for example, of the nearly 80 percent of the population that lived in the countryside, almost 90 percent subsisted on five acres of land or less. Between 1826 and 1858, the number of smallholders increased by 27 percent, and the level of subsistence farming increased by 50 percent during the century as a whole (Mooers 1991: 72). A subsistence-oriented peasantry, coupled by a "rentier" landlord class, put definitive limits on labor productivity and the expansion and deepening of internal markets (Brenner 1985b: 312; Jones 1988: 254). Besides the lingering legacy of the revolution in rural France, the revolution also had a huge impact on the future trajectory of industrial relations. Thanks to the sociolegal rights that they gained during the revolution, factory workers, at least until the mid–nineteenth century, worked based on a contractual system that allowed them substantial autonomy at the workplace. They were "not paid ... according to their productivity. Their income derived from the sale of goods that they produced autonomously, using tools and spaces that they rented, under their own individual or collective supervision" (LaFrance 2013: 165). The industrial bourgeoisie did make some investment in industrial technology, yet without exercising control over the labor and only behind a blanket economic protectionism. French merchants and industrialists did not have a "productivity policy," nor did they have a plan to organize the labor process according to the dictates of market imperatives (Lafrance 2019a: 120). In this sense, despite the rise of an "industrialized" order, it is hard to talk about the rise of a market-dependent – that is, capitalist – society in France until the critical tariff reform of 1860. Through the tariff reform, the French state elite, desperate for scarce foreign currencies in order to build up railways and military power, selectively and decisively exposed French industry to international competition, thereby imposing a capitalist industrialization project from above (Lacher and Germann 2012: 116–17; Lafrance 2019b: chapters 2–4).[23]

In short, the transformation of French economy along capitalist lines would proceed as a very protracted affair, just as the "political modernization" of France would take several twists and turns throughout the nineteenth century (e.g. Weber 1976). Yet, the international envy and horror Jacobinism created until Waterloo would have a significant impact on the formation of modern states in and beyond Europe. The

---

[23] For an overview of the historiography concerning the nineteenth–century French economy, see Crouzet (2003), see also Lafrance (2019b: chapter 2).

results of the French adaptation of British civil society – citizen-army and public school – provided a blueprint for other modernization projects. They demonstrated to the *ancien regimes* in Europe and beyond the geopolitical viability of an alternative model of rationalization that "did not invoke the idiosyncrasies of British history as a prerequisite" (Shilliam 2009: 54). By bypassing Britain's capitalist transformation, France, however contradictorily, proved that dissolving particularistic interests into a radicalized abstract collectivity could improve political unity and geopolitical competitiveness. As such, by revolutionizing the social basis of the army and school (rather than production), the French model of modernization "informed a new comparative standard against which other political authorities would be judged, and judge themselves, as 'backward'" (Shilliam 2009: 55).

The demonstration effect of the competition between, and the direct geopolitical threat generated by, Britain and France compelled most Western European states to carry out a combined "capitalist-Jacobin project." For example, as Shilliam (2009) has shown, Prussian elites set in train both projects concurrently. On the one hand, they commodified labor and land, and on the other, they invoked universal equality by abolishing serfdom and introducing the citizen-soldier as the new backbone of their military power. Both moves were very risky for the ruling elites, for they not only required the destruction of customary rights and obligations, they also created two potentially contradictory agents of change endowed with different rights and duties: the propertied-individual and the citizen-soldier. Upholding the rights of the propertied individual, especially his right to use his property "productively," was central to the constitution of a new fiscal base marked by a market-dependent society. Yet, invoking popular sovereignty and equality through the citizen-soldier (and citizen-officer), if unchecked, might end up radicalizing demands for equality, thereby generating a reverse impact on the rights of the propertied individual and the "productive" use of property. Indeed, that is precisely what seems to have happened across continental Europe during the first half of the nineteenth century.

In France, the thousands of men released from army service into civilian life contributed to the renewal of sans-culotte as well as trade union activity. There, and also in Germany, Russia, and Spain, new, non-aristocratic republican, liberal, or reformist army officers sought to intervene in politics and, when they found their way blocked, joined the ranks of secret societies and radical movements (e.g. the Italian Carbonieri, German Conditionals, and Russian Decembrist conspiracy). Foot soldiers and officers alike figured prominently in revolts and putsches in 1819, 1822, 1825, 1834, 1839, and 1844, and in the Europewide revolutions in 1820, 1830, and 1848. The army itself was seen as a tool of the left after the (Napoleonic) wars: the sans-culotte and other foot soldiers saw it as the vanguard of democracy. The new military officers who owed their ascent to professional ability rather than wealth saw in its new forms of organization and knowledge the basis of a new social order. (Halperin 2004: 73)

That said, the ultimate outcome of these contradictory dynamics in Western Europe was the gradual subordination of the Jacobin forms to the emerging capitalist market. In the Prussian context, for example, radical manifestations of popular rule, in the course of the nineteenth century, were by and large repressed and gradually incorporated into a constitutional framework of mass politics. By confining popular conceptions of nationhood and citizenship to a distinct "political" sphere abstracted from the economic relations of appropriation, Prussian/ German capitalism not only significantly watered down the Jacobin appeal of these concepts, but also profoundly transformed them into antidotes for working-class radicalism and internationalism (Eley 2002).

The bottom line of this discussion is that Jacobinism, sometimes in competition and sometimes in collaboration with capitalism, set in train new social and geopolitical dynamics that affected the constitution and development of the modern social and international order. As such, Jacobinism radically heterogenizes the more-or-less singular conceptions of "Western European modernity." Yet, given that Jacobinism was rapidly defeated in Western Europe, its world historical significance seems still debatable. Jacobinism as a concept may be useful to make sense of a rather short episode in European history, but does it have any relevance beyond that, both geographically and temporally? What if Jacobinism indeed made its way into the non-European world and even outlasted its European predecessors? What if it was Jacobinism, instead of capitalism, that provided non-European societies with the organizing principles of modernity for most of modern history? The remainder of this book attempts to answer these questions through the case study of the Ottoman Empire and Turkey.

4 | *Disputing Ottoman Modernity (1839–1918)*

Having documented the uneven and combined developmental trajectories of Britain and France, in this chapter I will begin to explore the significance of Jacobinism for our understanding of the rise of multiple modernities outside Western Europe. To this end, I seek to identify the precise nature and concrete outcome of the "combined" character of Ottoman modernization. I will question whether or not the combined Ottoman project, just as its Western counterparts, eventually neutralized its own Jacobin aspect, boiling down to merely another form of capitalism. The chapter begins by analyzing the reasons for the Ottomans' geopolitical decline and their reform attempts in the face of rival projects of modernization. In the remainder of the chapter, I turn to discuss the Ottoman path to modernity, a brief summary of which is as follows.

Compelled by a series of geopolitical failures outside and faced by the threat of partition inside, the Ottoman ruling elites, from the 1840s onward, began to selectively import social and institutional forms connected to capitalism and Jacobinism. Both projects presupposed the dissolution of politicocultural privileges and obligations that came to constitute the Ottoman moral economy. By implication, capitalism and Jacobinism equally inflicted on the Ottoman ruling classes the fear of violent reaction and foreign intervention. Both projects also strongly conditioned one another, repeatedly producing sociopolitical tensions in the first phase of the reform period known as the Tanzimat (1839–76). The ruling elites, organized in and as the state, had to continuously negotiate the rights of the propertied individual and the rights of the citizen-soldier. Reconciling the inherent tensions between property and subsistence emerged as a task of pivotal importance and constituted the underlying logic of the first period of Ottoman reforms.

The project of reinforcing Ottoman political unity and strengthening its fiscal base by way of introducing capitalist social relations reached a deadlock toward the 1870s. Propertied classes' "inviolable" right to property became socially and geopolitically too risky for the state elite to press any further. As the first period of Ottoman experimentation with the relations of market society came to an end, the Ottoman central elite increasingly turned to the Jacobin project to foster political unity and geopolitical mobilization. Military service and public education, not the market, were instituted as the ultimate means to acquire political and economic rights. Social reproduction, in other words, was increasingly detached from the market and linked to individuals' contribution to the welfare and survival of the nation. As such, the nation emerged as a substitute frame of reference according to which economic relations and power was organized. The Young Turk Revolution of 1908, and the concomitant revolutionary Terror, consolidated this trend, leading to the progressive militarization of the rules of reproduction and the institutionalization of a form of private property with new communitarian embellishments. Therefore, my overall argument is that the cumulative result of the eighty-year-long Ottoman experience with modernity (1839–1918) resulted in the emergence of a novel project of modernity: A modernity that not only substituted the relations of market society with the Jacobin model, but also repeatedly recombined the latter with the resources of an Ottoman-Islamic milieu.

Before the chapter proceeds along these lines, however, a short clarification is in order concerning the historical sociology of the Ottoman Empire and Turkey. In this chapter, I rely on many inspirational historical-sociological accounts of the Turkish "road" to modernity. While immensely benefiting from their empirical findings, however, the interpretation offered here also counters some of the most commonly held theoretical assumptions about Turkish modernization. For example, in Marxian accounts of Turkish modernity, capitalism is almost unanimously presumed to be there starting from the nineteenth century, based on the intensification of commercial relations with Western Europe. Capitalism, albeit in a "peripheral" form, is assumed to have developed by virtue of the commercial ties linking the empire to the capitalist "world system" (e.g. İslamoğlu and Keyder 1977; Berberoğlu 1982; Keyder 1987; Pamuk 1987a; Kasaba 1988). As I will discuss later, what is overlooked by these world system interpretations is that integration into and production for the world market does not of itself necessarily lead to the development of capitalism. Based on the relative strength of contending classes and broader geoterritorial configuration of power relations, commercial expansion may engender outcomes other than capitalism. By uncritically equating bourgeoisie and trade to capitalism, Wallersteinian accounts tend to see capitalism as always present in history as a developmental tendency. As such, they adopt a presentist understanding of the rise of capitalism in the Ottoman Empire, which in turn renders empirically invisible the emergence of noncapitalist alternatives in the course of modern transformation.

In Weberian accounts, the emphasis shifts from the Ottoman Empire's peripheral capitalism to its patrimonialism. Patrimonialism is usually associated with the overdeveloped nature of the Ottoman state, its "strong state tradition" or Islamic understanding of justice and legal infrastructure inhibiting the rise of "strong" bourgeois classes. Unlike Western Europe, so runs the argument, in the Ottoman Empire, bourgeois classes remained "weak," which is then used to explain the underdeveloped state of civil society, the illiberal character of economic and political institutions, and the leading role carried out by the bureaucratic cadres during the processes of modernization (e.g. Heper 1985; Kaya 2004; Kuran 2004; Mardin 2006). The most conspicuous problem with the Weberian interpretation is that it is underlined by an idealized conception of "bourgeois agency" derived from a highly contested narrative of the rise of "Western European modernity." The bourgeoisie is considered to be the paradigmatic agent of capitalist modernity in Western Europe (modernity "proper"), which then serves as a yardstick to classify modernization projects elsewhere. Revisionist historiography of the last fifty years has decisively refuted the image of Western European modernity rising on the shoulders of bourgeois classes. Neither in England nor in France, the alleged archetypal examples of Western modernity, did the bourgeoisie have an unambiguous relation to capitalism and democracy. As shown in Chapter 3, in France, there was a rising bourgeois class, but this was neither led by nor resulted in an emergent capitalism for a long time. By contrast, in England, capitalism developed by and large in an aristocratic shell. A more-or-less unified class of capitalist aristocracy owning large swaths of land, not the big bourgeoisie or monopoly merchants, became the pioneer of the capitalist reorganization of society. Similarly, the weight of bourgeois classes did not automatically translate into support for the development of democratic institutions. The bourgeoisie sometimes pushed to reform the state,

and sometimes took a totally opposite stance, turning the liberal institutions of this era into the defenders of feudal privilege and conserva-
tism (Mayer 1981; Blackbourn and Eley 1984; Comninel 1987; Wood
1991; Halperin 1997; Brenner 2003). Equally important, methodologically speaking, the image of capitalist modernity driven by bourgeois classes perpetuates an internalist logic of explanation. Weberian
accounts see the bourgeoisie as the transhistorical carrier of capitalist
social relations, and consequently, the entire discussion on modernity
boils down to finding reasons for the absence or "weakness" of an
"internal" class agency. Class roles are theorized not through social
agents' relations to one another in historically specific contexts of
social and geopolitical reproduction, but primarily deduced from the
presumed "peculiarities" of Western and Ottoman value systems and
political cultures. Ultimately, the Weberian interpretations based on
(fictional) ideal types tends to lock off and store away a static, causally
unrelated and internationally insulated image of the Ottoman state and
society (for critiques, see Dinler 2003; Duzgun 2012, 2013, 2021).

In short, existing approaches to the historical sociology of the
Ottoman Empire suffer, to varying degrees, from presentism and
internalism. Departing from these methodological issues, this chapter
seeks to provide an alternative reading of "modernity" in the late
Ottoman Empire. It shows that the late Ottoman Empire can neither
be understood as a patrimonial state nor can it be conceptualized as
peripheral capitalism. Instead, the end result of the Ottoman experiment with modernity was a historically specific Jacobinism that combined and bypassed capitalism (and socialism) based on an alternative
form of property and sociality.

The (Geo)politics of Ottoman Centralization Attempts

In many respects, the Ottoman expansion into Anatolia and the
Balkans from the fourteenth to the sixteenth century took place as a
conservative process (İnalcık 1954: 103). That is, the Ottomans' rapid
Ottoman geopolitical advance became possible not only thanks to their
superiority in military affairs vis-à-vis other lordly classes, but also by
their inability to change local customs that organized agrarian relations in the newly conquered lands. For one thing, the Ottomans were
compelled to resort to "competitive fiscal moderation" to secure the
loyalty of the peasantry against other lordly classes in the Balkans as

well as in Anatolia, which made them more lenient toward the preservation of local customs that supported the existence of an independent peasantry (Sugar 1977: 96; Kafadar 1995: 131–2; Adanır 1998: 276). Furthermore, peasant populations were historically marked by age-old customs of village solidarity, self-rule and seminomadism; therefore in such a context where resistance, land clearance and peasant flight were viable options, resettling the peasant population was an impossible task without granting them hereditary usufruct rights and fixed rents (Adanır 1998: 290). In short, in the course of its geopolitical expansion, "[T]he weight of custom (and) tradition proved difficult for the Ottoman state even to modify, let alone discourage or dislodge, despite the best efforts ... in seeking to alter peasant behavior to conform with state expectations and administrative orders" (Murphey 2012: 28).

Despite their inability to restructure the status of the peasantry, however, the Ottomans were strong enough to incorporate the old ruling classes into the *dirlik* (or *tımar*) system, a system of nonhereditary fiscal units granted in exchange for administrative/military service. The state employed various strategies to assimilate dirlik holders into the Ottoman structure of rule and property (İnalcık 1978: 119). Through constant deportation and rotation, it prevented cavalry soldiers, provincial notables, turbulent nomads and judges from setting roots in their own social environment, thereby barring "the solidification of claims of land, resources and positions within family lines" (Kafadar 1997: 37–8). A vast army of the socially uprooted ruling class (*askeri*) was thus in the making from the late fourteenth century, which was in the long run to preclude the development of lineage-based solidarities, thereby ensuring the continuity of state control of land (Adanır 1998: 280).

Nevertheless, the dirlik system that marked the "classical" period of the empire began to erode during the early modern period under the pressure of centralizing absolutist powers. The wars with Austria and Russia especially revealed the growing military ineffectiveness of the tımar-holding cavalry force, confronting the government with the problem of financing a centralized army of salaried soldiers. Faced by territorial losses and chronic monetary shortages, the Ottoman state, from the eighteenth century onward, began to farm out the lands and fiscal resources formerly absorbed by dirlik holders. A variety of tax-farming contracts (e.g. *çiftlik* and *malikane*) were eventually introduced to restructure the state finances and army, which, in turn, transformed the balance of power between the Ottoman center and provinces. Tax-farmers, most of whom were high-ranking military/ religious bureaucrats and business elites based in İstanbul, had to systematically empower and rely on provincial notables (*ayans*) for the collection of tax revenues (Salzmann 2004). The ayans not only assumed important administrative/military functions in their own localities, but also exercised substantial autonomy, raised military troops and were involved in commercial agriculture, all of which point to a strong tendency throughout the empire toward the reinforcement of centrifugal forces and quasiprivatization of land (though nominally all ownership of land still lay with the sultan).

The growing interelite cooperation between the Ottoman center and peripheries, however, fell short in providing a fertile ground for the formation of stable ruling-class alliances that could have more success-fully squeezed and more strategically utilized peasant surpluses. In other words, in spite of the introduction of new sociofiscal practices that indeed lent some degree of unity to the surplus-receiving groups, no enduring compromise could be reached between the central elite and provincial notables, which could have united them against the peasantry. The centrality of the state in surplus appropriation and redistribution was retained, yet without major improvements in the self-organization of the surplus-receiving groups. Therefore, in the seventeenth and eighteenth centuries, the Ottomans neither fragmented into a "nobiliary anarchy" (like Poland) nor could turn into a "cen-tralized" absolutism: they could not form a relatively stable ruling-class pact that could have massively boost the appropriation of peasant surpluses (either by supersqueezing the peasantry as in France or by enserfing them as in Russia and Austria). Consequently, the central elite could hardly augment their extractive powers and reintegrate notables into a single regulative framework of appropriation. According to one estimate, for example, central elites and provincial notables engaged in tax-farming diverted from the state more than two-thirds of net tax revenue (Darling 2006: 129). Furthermore, they sheltered private wealth from taxation and confiscation by establishing family endowments (*vakıfs*). Originally pious foundations customarily spared from confiscation and exempted from certain state taxes in exchange for the provision of educational and social services, vakıfs turned into the main avenue for privatizing tax revenues (Findley 2006: 75). At the end of the eighteenth century, vakıfs, controlled by military officers, religious office holders and dervish brotherhoods, amounted to a third of the Ottoman state's total revenue and took up between two-thirds and three-quarters of state land (Barnes 1986: 83; Kuran 2001: 849). As a result, Ottoman geopolitical competitiveness gradually declined during the early modern period, which rendered progressively more difficult and necessary the "reform" of existing forms of rule and property.

In short, from the seventeenth to the early nineteenth century, Ottoman fiscal power was considerably limited by the rise of elite households (Karaman and Pamuk 2010). Given the lack of ruling-class coherence, various ayan rebellions broke out from the latter half of the eighteenth century. Furthermore, the attempts to reform the military and fiscal organization under geopolitical imperatives bore little fruit until the 1820s; the elite households and old military personnel, most notably the *janissaries*,[1] successfully frustrated these efforts and often removed sultans that were "too reformist" and their allies from power.[2] As a result, having missed out on the first round of fiscal and military reform, the Ottoman attempts at centralization from the 1760s would be not only compelled, but also strongly conditioned by the prior development of absolutism in Europe.

Clearly, besides the ayans and janissaries, the most immediate factor conditioning imperial centralization attempts was war. The southward contraction of Ottoman territories in the last quarter of the eighteenth century substantially reduced sources of revenue otherwise available for reform (Hanioğlu 2010: 22). More importantly, the military

---

[1] Given the fiscal strains of the late sixteenth century, janissaries, originally servile soldiers, had acquired the right to enroll their sons in the corps and engage in extramilitary occupations such as crafts and trades. Meanwhile, in search of a steady government income, petty artisans (*esnaf*) also entered the janissary regiments in large numbers, opening wide the doors of the ruling-class establishment to "commoners" (Mardin 1962: 139; Kafadar 1981: 91; Göçek 1996: 90–1; Tezcan 2010: 10). The *esnafization* of janissaries and the *janissarization* of artisans, yoked together, created a large group of artisan-soldiers, who not only played a key role in the struggle among elite factions and in voicing discontent against the sultan, but also inflated the number of people on the state's payroll, further straining imperial finances (Berkes 1964: 60–1; Mardin 2006: 33). According to one estimate, by the end of the eighteenth century, there were 400,000 janissary pay certificates in circulation, of which no more than 10 percent belonged to the janissaries who were campaign-ready (Aksan 2013: 341).

[2] Between 1600 and 1800, seven out of fourteen sultans were deposed as a consequence of ruling-class factionalism.

defeats and diplomatic negotiations resulted in the yielding of extraterritorial privileges to major European states. European powers, in competition with one another, not only gained commercial privileges that would considerably limit the Ottomans' ability to pursue an autonomous tariff policy, but also obtained protectorate rights over non-Muslim Ottoman subjects, which would lead to the "internationalization of the empire's inner tensions and confessional lines" (Kafadar 1997: 46). In short, in addition to loss of economic autonomy and tax revenues, the Ottoman reform attempts became further complicated by the fact that the interests of non-Muslim Ottoman minorities became increasingly tied to the ability of foreign powers to claim representation and jurisdiction within the Ottoman state (Göçek 1996: 93–7).

The unsustainability of the existing order and the destructiveness of intraelite competition were becoming increasingly clear to the Ottoman ruling elite from the 1770s onward. In particular, the two disastrous wars against Russia (1768–74, 1788–92) had revealed that geopolitical challenges could no longer be contained by traditional patterns of intraelite negotiation and bargaining. Russians had deeply penetrated into Ottoman territories south of the Danube, gained control over Crimea and Russian naval guns could now be heard from İstanbul. Defeat could no longer be confined to a distant battlefield, but began to threaten the whole body politic. As centralization became progressively harder to attain, the Ottomans would be compelled to resort to untraditional ways of rejuvenating the empire. It was at this juncture that the French Revolution erupted, the consequences of which were to frighten and inspire the generations of Ottoman reformers on how to transform the empire.

French Revolution and the Ottoman Empire: Between the Ayans and the Peasantry

My God! What kind of situation is this? Two of the barbers who shave me say that they are members of the artillery corps! If we call for soldiers, we are told "What can we do? There are no salaried soldiers to go on campaign." Let others be enrolled, we say, and we are told "There is no money in the treasury." If we say, there must be a remedy, we are told "Now is not the time to interfere with the regiments."

Thus expressed Selim III (1789–1807) of the need for and the difficulty of Ottoman military reform the year he was enthroned (quoted in

Aksan 2007: 184). This frustration with the sorry state of the Ottoman military was often characterized by a sense of backwardness felt in the sultan's reformist circle in relation to their most formidable enemy: By "borrowing Frankish devices," the reformers noted, "the Muscovite nation of inconsiderable animals has in thirty years reached the point of posing a danger to states five hundred or a thousand years old" (quoted in Hanioğlu 2010: 42). And yet, despite their admiration for the Russian army, the sultan and his entourage were equally aware that the same Frankish ways led to unbearable sociofiscal burdens in France, ultimately causing what they called the "rising of the rabble" – the revolution. After the revolution, France, according to proreform imperial bureaucrats, was "like the rumblings and crepitations of a queasy stomach," poisoned by principles consisting of "the abandonment of religion and the equality of rich and poor." "In a manner without precedent," Jacobins "have removed ... the regard for retribution from the common people, made lawful all kinds of abominable deeds ... and thus prepared the way for the reduction of the people of France to the state of cattle" (Lewis 1975: 66–71; Yeşil 2007: 290). The fear and admiration felt toward Frankish methods was further aggravated in 1798 when a Napoleonic army of less than 30,000 soldiers swiftly invaded and ruled the Ottoman territories of Egypt and the Ionian Islands for three years. And indeed, after this brief period of direct geopolitical confrontation and hostility, "the voice of France, no longer shouting in Greek or Arabic, became more audible in İstanbul" (Lewis 1975: 68–9).

The line between reform and revolution was thus frighteningly thin. Little wonder, for forty years or so following the revolution, the Ottoman sultans continued to keep their reforms attempts as "traditional" as possible. They imported new weaponry, hired new foreign (mostly French) military advisors and tried to vertically reorganize intraelite politics, while carefully avoiding any appeal to the "poisonous principles" that could have led to the "rise of the rabble." Yet, even these strictly "elite" and "military" experiments with reform proved to be very dangerous. The first sultan who made definitive inroads into political centralization and military reform was Mahmud II (1808–39). The sultan managed to integrate many lesser notables in Anatolia and the Lower Balkans into a relatively centralized structure of rule and appropriation. And indeed, it was this remaking of state power in the provinces that enabled Mahmud to muster resources to finally abolish the janissary corps in 1826. Despite these "successes," however, suppression of notables in other parts of the empire, especially in Serbia, Greece and Egypt, proved impossible. In both Serbia and Greece, the struggle between the centralizing state and provincial notables turned into a mutually destructive process that caused massive peasant flight, brigandage and rebellion (Aksan 2007: 282–94; Hoffmann 2008: 386). The result was the wide opening of both regions to the exercise of Russian protectorate rights over non-Muslim Ottoman subjects, which not only led to the (formal or informal) secession of Serbia and Greece from the empire, but also brought the Ottomans to the verge of virtual collapse. By 1829, Russian troops advanced into northern Anatolia and the southern Balkans, ultimately reaching the outskirts of İstanbul. The sultan was to save İstanbul from invasion only when Britain forced the Russians to sign a peace treaty and retreat to the Danube.

The lesson to be drawn from this experiment with centralization in the Balkans was clear: the threat of internal disorder strongly correlated with the threat of partition from outside (Hanioğlu 2010: 69). The process of centralization was strongly mediated by geopolitical struggles and could be achieved only by maintaining a delicate balance of class forces inside. Under geopolitical pressures, the sultan had no option but to set in motion a pattern of vertical reorganization that regularized and backed the appropriative privileges of the ayans, yet at the same time prevented their exploitation of the peasantry from destabilizing imperial rule. In other words, the success of Ottoman centralization was strongly dependent on stepping up and stabilizing the conditions of peasant exploitation, while simultaneously checking the geopolitically risky consequences of this new framework of ruling-class cooperation. Peasant surpluses had to be extracted without leading to peasant revolts that could undermine the empire's geopolitical position.

These considerations would be further compounded in the face of Egypt's rebellious governor, Muhammed Ali. For, if the Ottoman centralization efforts in the Balkans showed that the state's external reproduction was dependent on its ability to mediate the relation between the peasantry and landholding classes, this became even more crucial in the face of Egypt's new conscript army. That is, during her brief invasion, France had considerably weakened Egypt's ruling and military elite. Thanks to this legacy, Muhammed Ali, the new Ottoman governor of post-French Egypt, was able to completely eliminate traditional notables and tax-farmers. This, in turn, opened the way for a series of radical reforms, "many of which built on the Napoleonic precedent, while others were aided directly by France, the governor's only European ally" (Keddie 1994: 142–3). Freed from traditional notables, Muhammed Ali launched an ambitious project of military and fiscal centralization almost twenty years before Mahmud II dared to destroy the janissaries. Besides programs of education, commercial agriculture and industrialization, among Muhammed Ali's French-inspired reforms, the most ambitious one, which would generate grave consequences for his overlord in İstanbul, was mass conscription. Based on brutal measures aimed at breaking peasant resistance and preventing peasant flight, mass conscription in Egypt produced an army of well over 100,000 men during much of the 1820s–30s (Fahmy 1998: 163; Dunn 2009: 183). Emboldened by the successes of the new army in the Sudan, Hijaz and Greece in the 1820s, Muhammed Ali was confident enough in the 1830s to chase the sultanic armies to within a few days march of İstanbul; such that only diplomatic struggles among the major European powers over the future of the Middle East was to stop Egyptian armies from invading the Ottoman capital.

Cairo thus set a new standard of geopolitical competition for the Ottomans (almost three decades before the Russians began to "free" and "modernize" their serf-based army). Muhammed Ali's peasant soldiers became a source of inspiration and envy for the Ottoman elite, which hinted at the further complication of agrarian relations in the Ottoman Empire (Zurcher 1999: 80–1). The state's external reproduction was already highly dependent on its ability to mediate the relation between the peasantry and landholding classes, which, in the face of Egypt's universal conscription, became even more crucial. The question of how to "save" the empire was becoming increasingly complicated by the fact that the state had to empower tax-farmers to reinforce its fiscal base, but given peasants' new geopolitical role as soldiers, the state had to further mediate their economic and fiscal exploitation. The state's acute lack of manpower for a mass army was thus to entangle its reliance on and check of landholding class power over the peasantry. In short, the geopolitical reproduction of the Ottoman state was becoming increasingly dependent on the constitution of historically specific agrarian property relations. It was precisely in this geo (political) context that the sultan was to resort to "untraditional" ways of rejuvenating the empire and establish "modern" conceptions of property and subjecthood.

The Tanzimat as a Combined Project: Between Jacobinism and Capitalism (1838–1876)

The social and geopolitical considerations here documented were central to the introduction of two potentially contradictory projects of appropriation and rule – capitalism and Jacobinism – into the empire. During the first phase of Ottoman modernization (Tanzimat), the Ottomans made several attempts to strengthen their fiscal base by establishing the political-legal foundations of capitalism. To start with, they signed a series of free trade agreements with Britain (1838–41), which led to an exponential growth of commercial agriculture. By lifting state monopolies in foreign trade and reducing custom duties on exports, they gained British support against Muhammed Ali, increased their control over contraband trade and induced production in the countryside (Pamuk 1987a: 20; Ortaylı 1998: 99, 106–8). Likewise, the Imperial Edict of 1839, which officially launched the Tanzimat project, promised to introduce laws guaranteeing life, equality and property of all subjects (including non-Muslims), and by doing so, it sought to both preempt European claims over Ottoman minorities and to institutionalize the "free" and "productive" individuals of a capitalist order. In a similar vein, the Land Code of 1858 and 1867, as will be discussed later, ruled out traditional revenue claims on and collective/village rights to land, thereby taking an important step toward the legal privatization and individualization of landed property (İslamoğlu 2000: 29).

Thus, in the words of Sadık Rıfat Pasha, who was one of the key figures of the Tanzimat period, the early Ottoman reforms were rooted (at least partly) in the liberal belief that "civilization depends on the attainment of complete security for the life, property and honor ... of each nation and people, that is to say, on the proper application of the necessary rights of liberty" (Mardin 1962: 186–7; 2006: 160; Berkes 1964: 130–1; Lewis 1975: 132). Civilization, asserts Sadık Rıfat, is a "system" in which the states maintain peaceful relations and respect equality between each other, and at the same time they provide their subjects "with the opportunity to reap to the fullest extent the fruit of

their daily labor' and 'freely engage in the productive activities"
(quoted in Mardin 1962: 180–1). Tanzimat "civilization" was, then,
predicated on the fairly liberal assumption that all people, if freed from
political and geopolitical constraints, would lead to the flourishing of
the state and society as they pursue their selfish interests. However,
behind this liberal façade also stands a vague conception of "justice."
According to Sadık Rıfat, it is of utmost importance to contain the
"uncontrolled inequalities" entailed by "freedom." For "excessive
freedoms" as well as "tyranny" cause revolutions and turmoil, hence
undermining "justice," which is the source of "the power and life" of
all states (Mardin 1962: 179, 188). Therefore, Sadık Rıfat concludes
that "[i]t is impossible for a country ... (acting) contrary to law and
reason and equity and justice to be settled and enduring" (quoted in
Darling 2013: 161).

Ambiguous as it may be, "justice" was a necessary add-on to the
introduction of capitalist property rights in a noncapitalist setting.
"Justice" marked the anticipation that in the course of transition to
capitalism, class and geopolitical balances would require the Ottoman
political elite to pursue a highly "mediated" route to capitalist
modernity. In particular, the rights of the tax-farmer, who would
constitute the provincial backbone of the future propertied classes,
had to be defined in ways that were purified from "egoistic" tendencies. A substitute route to modernity had to be invented, in which
property would be "freely" enjoyed without causing "oppression."
As encoded in the Imperial Edict of 1839:

Every one shall possess his property of every kind and may dispose of it
freely, without let or hindrance from any person whatsoever ... [This should
not however] amount to handing over the financial and political affairs of a
country to the whim of an ordinary man and perhaps to the grasp of force
and oppression, for if the tax-farmer is not of good character he will be
interested only in his profit and will behave oppressively.

Given that, it is perhaps not surprising that the sultan had no
problem with seeing the Tanzimat as "guaranteeing ... the good order
of the land' and at the same time bringing 'equal justice for all' and
'protecting the weak" (Darling 2013: 162). Yet, it is important to note
that the ambiguity of the Tanzimat was not based on a mere reformu-
lation of the traditional Ottoman conceptions of justice that presupposed and dictated a passive reciprocity between the ruler and the

ruled (cf. İrem 2008). Instead, the ambiguity of Tanzimat justice stemmed from the simultaneous introduction of two historically distinct modernization projects empowering two contradictory political subjects. A closer look at the reform period reveals that the Ottomans not only took measures to institute the rights of the propertied individual, but also took the critical Jacobin step toward creating the citizen-soldier. From the Imperial Edict of 1839 until the end of World War I, every major legal text asserted the equality of *all* subjects, while attempting to introduce military service as a "universal" and "individual" duty. True, mass conscription grew as a protracted process; draft evasion was common and there were many exemptions from the "universal" levy, including non-Muslims and the members of the central elite.[3] Yet, what is remarkable is that with the Tanzimat, peasants, for the first time in Ottoman history, began to enter the Ottoman body politic in an unmediated fashion, that is, without the mediating role of semicorporate bodies such as the tımar holders or the ayans (Heinzelmann 2009: 108, 263–4; Yıldız 2009: 150). The mobilization of the lowest stratum was no longer based on the relations of a localized and personalized political community, but began to be understood within the framework of the universal rights and duties of a new political subject – the citizen-soldier. The *reaya* (the common people, or more literally the "herd"), had been systematically excluded from the military class and prohibited even from riding horses and carrying swords for centuries (Itzkowitz 1980: 40). Yet, under the (geo)political challenges discussed earlier, the common people were now to be armed and declared equal. Geopolitical reproduction of the ruling elite was therefore becoming dependent on the creation of a new political subject from the ranks of the rural poor, which would, in turn, qualitatively redefine the space of bargaining between the ruler and the ruled.

What is implied here is that the unqualified equation of Tanzimat reforms to capitalism tends to obscure the "combined" character of the Ottoman modernization attempts. The geopolitical unevenness forced the Ottoman reformers to inject into the domestic social fabric the logic of capitalism and Jacobinism concurrently. Both projects aimed to

---

[3] After four decades of enforcing conscription, the number of military troops increased from 24,000 regular soldiers in 1837 to 120,000 in 1849 and up to 206,000 in 1877, with a reserve army of 500,000 soldiers (Karpat 1972a: 278; Quataert 1992: 218).

create a universal political subject with equal rights and obligations, that is, they attempted to make property owners and peasants active participants of and directly responsible for the reproduction of the body politic as a whole. Yet, capitalism and Jacobinism were also contradictory: they sought to empower two conflicting subjects, the propertied individual and the citizen-soldier, whose "equality" and contradictory interests on land would complicate the unfolding of modernity. The Ottoman ruling classes had to continuously negotiate the rights of the propertied individual and the rights of the citizen-soldier. Reconciling the inherent tensions between property and subsistence emerged as a task of pivotal importance and constituted the underlying logic of the first period of Ottoman reforms.

Therefore, the Tanzimat did not seek to resurrect old patterns of reciprocity and justice in the Ottoman political economy, but justified and reacted to, and ultimately tried to reconcile capitalist and Jacobin social forms within the context of preexistent social relations. Indeed, from the very beginning, this internally contradictory and internationally conditioned character of Ottoman modernization was reflected in the manner in which the Tanzimat principles were implemented. To begin with, the universalization of the right to property and equality ushered in competing claims on land. On the one hand, many provincial notables claimed to own the villages that fell under the areas in which they had been authorized to collect taxes. In other words, tax-farmers attempted to subsume peasant lands into their private estates by using the Tanzimat principles that secured private ownership. Likewise, the tax-farmers' utilization of the Tanzimat for their own benefit was countered by peasants, who rebelled in many parts of the empire by radicalizing the Tanzimat principles concerning equality (Aytekin 2012: 191–228; 2013: 315–18). Peasants construed the Tanzimat as giving them land, relaxing tax demands, saving them from tax-farmers' oppression and so on (Ortaylı 1998: 120).

Eventually, the competing claims to land ownership, combined with the conscription demands of the state (enacted through the conscription law of 1846), caused large-scale and long-lasting peasant unrest in many parts of the empire, most notably in Bulgaria (1841–50, 1875–6), northern Anatolia (1840s–60s), Lebanon (1858–61), Palestine and Syria (1852–64), and Bosnia (1850, 1874–5) (Quataert 1994: 877; Aksan 2007: 416–31; Aytekin 2013). Moreover, without the support and assistance of the provincial notables, tax collection utterly collapsed in the countryside (Shaw and Shaw 1977: 96). The core danger anticipated by the Ottoman reformers, then, proved to be very real. Attempts at simultaneously creating the propertied individual and the citizen-soldier ended up corrupting the developmental and geopolitical promises of modern subjecthood. The process of formulating the Ottoman equivalent of the citizen-soldier and the propertied individual, in other words, caused further popular disengagement from the reform project. The state could neither afford to alienate tax-farmers' right to property, nor could it give them full support against the peasants' demands for equality.

The Tanzimat tried to stabilize this uneasy *modus vivendi* in a number of ways. Reformers were usually unwilling to restrain tax-farmers' demand for land. For they were well aware that agricultural productivity, investment and increases in imperial revenues depended on individualizing property and lifting restraints on the inheritability, size, sale and the use of private landholdings. Yet, in the meantime they were also "engaged in a continuous balancing act between the exigencies of a rule of justice (read absence of social strife) and a rule of property" (İslamoğlu 2000: 33–4). During the first half of the nineteenth century, such a balancing act included a number of protective measures, and above all, the importation of Napoleonic inheritance law, which institutionalized the "partage" on Ottoman soil, that is, it ensured the customary rights on land by prescribing partible inheritance regardless of the gender of heirs (Shaw and Shaw 1977: 96; Ortaylı 1998: 216; cf. Kocabicak 2022). Besides stipulating individual title to land in order to increase agricultural productivity, the Tanzimat thus simultaneously moved in the opposite direction by trying to secure the minimal subsistence for cultivators. This was definitely not an act of benevolence; yet the requirements of geopolitical reproduction forced the state to take measures to maintain the generational security of the peasant holding as a unit of conscription. Furthermore, given European powers' protectorate rights on Ottoman minorities, especially in regions where the struggle over land occurred between Christian cultivators and Muslim tax-farmers, any disruption of internal order could make the empire vulnerable to European intervention, which aggravated the reformers' rather "dispassionate view of individual property rights." In sum, during the first half of the nineteenth century, the Ottoman reformers' utmost concern was to introduce private property without "allow(ing) disputes over property to be translated into political conflicts" (İslamoğlu 2000: 33–4).

Keeping property politically sterile did not necessarily deliver a balanced fiscal sheet, however. Imperial revenues, albeit improved, were far from meeting the costs of military and administrative centralization. This situation further worsened in the face of the Crimean War (1853–6), at the end of which the Ottomans faced a tremendous fiscal burden: Whereas the cost of Ottoman participation far exceeded Ottoman revenues, the allied victory against Russia brought no substantial benefits in return (Shaw and Shaw 1977: 97). In response to these fiscal and geopolitical challenges, and to pacify its wartime allies, the Ottomans initiated another bold reform attempt with the declaration of a renewed Imperial Reform Edict in 1856. The Edict of 1856 expressed commitment to the realization and expanded the scope of the Ottoman combined project, that is, it pledged to carry out reforms that aimed to realize both the fiscal and military potentials, which British enclosure and French Jacobinism had unleashed, respectively.

The guarantees promised [by the Edict of 1839] to all the subjects of my Empire ... for the security of their persons and property ... are today confirmed and consolidated, and efficacious measures shall be taken in order that they may have their full and entire effect ... Everything that can impede commerce or agriculture shall be abolished ... Non-Muslim subjects shall, as well as Muslims, be subject to the obligations of the Law of Recruitment ... it shall be lawful for foreigners to possess landed property in my dominions, conforming themselves to the laws as the native inhabitants.

The clearest manifestation of this promise of property came with the Land Code of 1858. The Code, first and foremost, ruled out traditional revenue claims on and collective/village rights to land, thereby taking an important step toward privatizing and individualizing property (Mundy and Smith 2007: 46). Put another way, it "signified the separation of the ownership claims from the former revenue and use claims, thus establishing (individual ownership) as the singular and absolute claim over land, only to be restrained by the taxation claims of the state" (İslamoğlu 2000: 29). This determination to institute property rights went one step further than the laws issued in the 1840s, for the Code and two subsequent decrees issued in 1860 and 1869 not only permitted foreigners to own land, but also allowed mortgage of land for payment of taxes and payment of debt to individuals. The Code, therefore, officially lifted restraints on dispossession of

the peasantry by permitting the alienation of land in case of indebtedness (Güran 1998: 141–2). In addition, concomitantly with the Land
Code, the Provincial Law of 1864 introduced the principle of representation for the propertied classes: Wealthy provincial notables
gained some degree of legitimate voice in local affairs as the central
state allowed them to send their representatives to newly established
provincial administrative councils. While the provincial law thus
sought to reintegrate propertied classes into a legal framework of
appropriation and taxation, it also provided them with some political
leverage over their peasant tenants (Shaw and Shaw 1977: 90–1;
Kayalı 1995: 266).

Meanwhile, the Jacobin project was unfolding too under new geopolitical imperatives. Russia, traumatized by its failure in Crimea, had
embarked on a complete overhaul of its military-agrarian system based
on the elimination of serfdom and the introduction of universal
conscription (Aksan 2007: 437). The success of Prussia's popular
conscription against Austrian armies in 1866 also impacted the
Ottoman perception of military reform (Aksan 2007: 478; Çadırcı
2008: 52). Taken together, these forced the Ottomans to reconsider
the social basis of their geopolitical reproduction, which ultimately led
to two new initiatives: the Conscription Law and the Nationality Law,
both promulgated in 1869. The Nationality Law aimed to connect all
Ottoman subjects in a way unmediated by special community privileges, and to avoid interference from European states on the pretext of
protecting Ottoman non-Muslim subjects (Üstel 2004: 26–7). And
while the Nationality Law was a milestone in decorporating
Ottoman political life based on a common and equal Ottoman
citizenship, the military reform reaffirmed the duty of all equal citizens
to serve in the army. Although the conscription law continued to allow
the obligation to be transmuted into cash, and the non-Muslim reaction to it eventually remained insuperable due to the threat of foreign
intervention, the military reform of 1869 marked a decisive expansion
of popular conscription, especially among Anatolian Muslim peasants
(Moreau 2010: 17).

Given the simultaneous deepening of Jacobin and capitalist projects,
little wonder the seemingly contradictory character of agrarian relations also persisted after 1858. For one thing, despite its promise for
the productive utilization of property, the Ottoman Land Code hardly
amounted to "enclosure," that is, it did not expropriate peasant's

customary rights on land. While taking steps toward establishing private property in land, it also involved several affirmative references to the age-old custom that legalized peasantry's right to use the land (Çakır-Kantarcıoğlu 2018: 134). Also, ongoing peasant unrest in the provinces and the threat of European intervention rendered impossible the full implementation of the Code (Quataert 1992: 214–15). Indeed, toward the end of the 1860s, the Ottoman ruling classes seemed to have tacitly agreed that they would not be able to implement the Land Code without protecting from forced sale "the roof over the cultivator's head and a basic amount of land required for survival." They eventually sought to institute private property in many parts of the empire without overriding peasants' access to land. Despite widespread peasant indebtedness, the alienability and disposability of land was codified without allowing the seizure of the house and land of the cultivator against debt (İslamoğlu 2000: 33–9; Mundy and Smith 2007: 47). Likewise, laws and decrees concerning conscription consistently specified that those who chose to buy their way out of military service had to pay the exemption tax without selling their plots of land (Shaw and Shaw 1977: 100; Zurcher 1999: 87; Heinzelmann 2009: 156). By preventing conscription from causing dispossession, the state therefore linked its external reproduction to the maintenance of peasant subsistence. Moreover, from 1869, all of these sociolegal tendencies began to echo in the first Ottoman civil code, *Mecelle*. After having seriously considered the option of translating and directly adopting the Napoleonic Code, the Ottomans eventually decided not to. Instead, they selectively borrowed French civil code and selectively codified Islamic law (Rubin 2011: 30–1, 154–5). With regards to property rights, the result of this "combined" civil code, just as the Napoleonic Code, was the encoding of property law and the law of contracts within the terrain of and as only complementary to administrative law (İslamoğlu 2000: 10).

Therefore, two contradictory tendencies were at play during the Tanzimat, one was pushing for the realization of the capitalist project, and the other attempting to secure the sociolegal basis of the citizen-soldier. But, what was the overall outcome of these seemingly contradictory sociolegal developments during the Tanzimat period? Despite the persistence of customary rights on land, did capitalism indeed take off on the shoulders of "petty commodity producers" and sharecroppers, as conventionally presumed? How successful or willing was the Ottoman state in initiating and sustaining a capitalist restructuring of social relations and institutions? This is what I will question in the following section.

Sharecroppers, Peasants and Landlords: Toward a Market-Dependent Society?

The period from the encoding of the Ottoman Land Code of 1858 to the promulgation of the first Ottoman constitution (1876) is particularly decisive in tracing the trajectory and determining the outcome of the Ottoman combined project. For, this period, as mentioned earlier, not only witnessed a two decades-long agricultural boom, but also the Land Code and two subsequent decrees issued in 1860 and 1869 reaffirmed the security of property. The conventional argument about the Tanzimat's socioeconomic outcome is that the Tanzimat initiated a process of transition to (peripheral) capitalism based on "merchant capital" and "petty commodity production." The criterion used to identify (peripheral) capitalism, in many ways, boils down to "production for the market." For example, Şevket Pamuk, a prominent economic historian of the Ottoman Empire, writes that the unequal relations between peasant and merchant that involve market processes are capitalist by definition (Pamuk 1987a: 86). Based on this assumption, Pamuk argues that the intensive commercialization of Ottoman agriculture on the one hand and the central state's endeavor to preserve peasant holdings on the other led to the expansion of smallholding peasants as "petty" commodity producers (Pamuk 1987b: 185). Similarly, for another leading scholar of Turkish studies, Çağlar Keyder, what facilitated "the long duration of peripheral transition to capitalism" in the Ottoman Empire (and then Turkey of the 1920s) was the character of "merchant capital" as well as the specificity of the Ottoman political institutions. While merchant capital "expand[ed] its area of operation within existing social relations," the Porte tried to uphold its "redistributive precapitalist concerns," which together "conditioned and influenced the pattern of installation of commodity production"' in the form of petty commodity producers (Keyder 1981: 127, 1–3; 1987: 30–1). In short, the majority of the rural population did not lose their land but instead became market-dependent small producers. Surely, in addition to the petty commodity producers, there were large commercial estates (çiftlik) cultivated by sharecroppers.

Located, in particular, in the most commercialized parts of the empire such as the Balkans and Western Anatolia, çiftliks provided a strong stimulus for the expansion of production for the world market. Yet, çiftliks for the most part were not the norm; "small landholdings predominated almost in all areas" (Quataert 1994: 863). Therefore, according to the conventional interpretation, peasants engaged in commodity production on their own land became the main agents of "peripheral" capitalist transformation in the countryside.

Clearly, the existence of small producers and sharecroppers may not necessarily inhibit the development of a capitalist society. Peasants and sharecroppers, depending on the larger social and institutional context, may become market-dependent without losing their land (e.g. Friedmann 1980; Post 2011). For this, however, two conditions must be present. First, we need to be able to show that certain sociolegal measures ensured that peasants and sharecroppers as well as surplus-receiving groups were losing the ability to reproduce themselves outside commodity production and becoming dependent on the market. In other words, peasant and sharecropping households must show a tendency to becoming an enterprise whose existence and expansion progressively depends on competitive reproduction in the marketplace and on their ability to invest in labor-saving tools and techniques so that we see a secular trend toward the capitalist reorganization of production according to the requirements of competition, profitability and productivity. This requires the increasing elimination of nonmarket access to land, provision of credit, stabilization of food and labor supply, building of irrigation networks, transport facilities and so on, so that productive units, no matter how small they are, would be compelled and enabled to systematically produce for the market, specialize output, invest in productivity-increasing tools and accumulate savings in order to acquire, maintain or expand their means of subsistence and production. Unless these conditions are met, and especially if land clearance is a viable option, small peasant households would systematically prioritize production for subsistence in order to insure themselves against draught, disease, bad harvest and so on. In other words, in the absence of alternative sources of food supply and credit, peasants may continue to occasionally sell their surplus product and surplus labor, but ultimately they would neither be able to make a systematic shift from the logic of "safety-first" agriculture, nor would they be able to invest in and progressively transform the means of production.

Second, in a context of labor scarcity or immobility, peasant production in sharecropping arrangements provide landowners with a low-cost option for securing harvest labor. And indeed, when the sharecropping unit is relatively big and the land/labor ratio is relatively high, one can expect fairly continuous involvement in commodity production. Despite extensive participation in the market, however, for sharecropping to be considered conducive to capitalism, the landlord and sharecropper, in principle, must be able and willing to organize the logic and space of production according to the dictates of market competition. In the absence of alternative sources of labor supply and, again, especially if land clearance is a viable option for the sharecropper, large estate owners would not be able or willing to change the conditions of production according to the market imperatives. For, the introduction of productivity-increasing measures would not only benefit the sharecropping landlord, but would also help sharecroppers pay off their debts and become "independent" peasants again. With no monopoly over land and no access to an alternative labor market, the sharecropping landlord would be more likely to choose not to invest in the means of production that could otherwise cause him to lose his only source of labor (Bhaduri 1973). Furthermore, under conditions of extreme indebtedness, it is true that sharecropping peasants may get "locked in" production for the market, yet given that almost the entire surplus product would accrue to the landlord/creditor, sharecropping peasants would be structurally incapable to accumulate funds and invest in labor-saving and productivity-increasing tools (Friedmann 1980: 177–8). Therefore, in the absence of a socioinstitutional transformation that would set free alternate sources of credit, sharecropping peasants, despite producing extensively for markets, would be inherently unwilling or unable to respond to fluctuating market conditions and incapable of reinvesting in land. Sharecropping, as such, put definite limits on the transformation of the labor process, deterring the introduction of labor-saving techniques and the capitalist reorganization of production.

The problem to be solved is then twofold: How successful was the Ottoman state at reorienting the peasant strategy of production for subsistence toward that of production of commodities? How able or willing were the Ottoman merchants, usurers and landlords at initiating a capitalist growth dynamic in çiftliks? Obviously, on big commercial estates, the character of sharecropping arrangements varied highly

according to the sharecroppers' relative position vis-à-vis the landowner and the state (Issawi 1980: 207–8). But from the 1850s onward,
it was becoming increasingly clear to the Ottoman central elite that
sharecropping provoked revolt, which, in fact, provided the social
basis for the nationalist movements that ended Ottoman control over
many Balkan provinces (where çiftliks, hence sharecropping, were the
most common) (Quataert 1994: 874, 878–9). Combined with the
increasing importance of the peasantry as soldiers, it does not require
great foresight to predict that the Ottoman elites perceived their geopolitical reproduction as closely tied to the prevention of sharecropping's destabilizing impact and to the stability and "freedom" of
smallholdings. Undoubtedly, the freedom of the sharecropper should
be approached with caution. While sharecropping "most often was
based on a 50-50 division, with the sharecroppers usually paying the
taxes before dividing the produce" (Pamuk 1987a: 93; Quataert 1994:
863), the sharecroppers' position depended highly on the sociolegal
patterns of appropriation historically prevalent in a given region as
well as the state's willingness and ability to extend protection to the
producer. For instance, in some parts of Kurdistan and the Balkans and
in some Arab provinces, where the Ottomans had never exercised
effective rule, sharecropping often led to forms of social labor verging
on serfdom (Quataert 1994: 866, 871; Kaya 2015). In either case,
however, the productive role of the sharecropping landlord was usually limited to the provision of land, credit and agricultural supplies
and the dictation of crop-mix. Although overburdened by taxes, rents,
debt and even labor services, the sharecropper began and completed
the production cycle themselves. Regardless of the size of the landholding, "free cultivators accounted for most agricultural production and
exports, even on the largest estates" (Quataert 1994: 864; also see
Keyder 1991: 12; Pamuk 2008: 389).

More importantly, "sharecropping result[ed] from a difficulty in
continuing with independent farming, rather than from land unavailability" (Keyder 1983: 132). That is to say, sharecropping was the
result of a bad harvest, a drought, a disease, a wedding, the death of an
oxen or a decrease in market prices, rather than the absence of available land (Keyder 1983). Eviction in a case of default was rare, but
even when a landlord evicted a sharecropper (which would definitely
be a prize for some sharecroppers), the latter always had the option of
accessing marginal lands owned by the state in exchange for taxes

(Keyder 1983). No landlord/merchant monopoly on land therefore developed, which otherwise might have facilitated the subsumption of sharecropping peasants to the market imperatives. Of course, we can safely assume that due to their rent and tax obligations, sharecroppers who suffered from extreme indebtedness were hugely vulnerable to the uncertainties of the marketplace (e.g. Aytekin 2008: 295). Yet, it is also reasonable to assume that under conditions of extreme indebtedness, most of their product was transferred to the sharecropping landlord, which depleted the funds otherwise available for the "improvement" of the land. Furthermore, given that for the most part the land was expandable and divisible by the peasantry, and indebtedness was usually the only source of labor supply, sharecropping landlords would have little incentive to improve the means of production. That is, for landlords, permanent indebtedness and usury provided an opportunity both to appropriate a larger share of peasant surpluses and to secure tenants for their land (Pamuk 1987b: 186). Investing in the means of production and improving the land could have increased peasants' ability to pay their debts and become independent peasants again, hence causing the disappearance of the only pool of labor power exploited by the sharecropping landlord. Read together, neither the sharecropping peasant nor the sharecropping landlord, despite their extensive involvement in the marketplace, had the ability to initiate a capitalist growth dynamic in the Ottoman countryside. As a result, the engrossment of commercial landholdings, which occurred partly as a response to rising world market prices (especially of cotton), and often to the detriment of small peasant holdings, did not lead to a qualitative transformation from subsistence to market-dependent agriculture. Landlords responded to market competition by increasing exploitation on the old basis; consequently, productive forces remained primitive, domestic investment scarce and productivity rates unchanged (Quataert 1994: 853). In short, sharecropping in the late Ottoman Empire remained inherently inimical to the development of capitalist social relations, representing a noncapitalist form of social labor.[4]

---

[4] The only exception to the persistence of noncapitalist property relations on large estates seems to be the region of Çukurova. As elsewhere, in Çukurova, commercialization and the formation of large landholdings did not result from or result in dispossession of peasant producers and was largely based on sharecropping arrangements. Unlike other commercial regions, however, sharecropping seems to be accompanied by successful mobilization of labor

All that said, however, it was not large estates, but small peasant production that prevailed in most areas as the basic unit of taxation and seem to have remained remarkably stable during the commercial boom and bust of the latter nineteenth century. In 1859, of all of the cultivable land in the Ottoman Empire, 82 percent entailed smallhold-ings, with the average farm size somewhere between 6 and 8 hectares, and roughly the same proportions applied in 1900 (Pamuk 1987a: 91). In Anatolia the "majority of private plots were less than 5 hectares" and "even such small plots were likely to be fragmented into tiny parcels of land in a number of different places around the village" (Owen 1981: 208). In Western Anatolia, which was one of the most commercially oriented areas of the empire, the average size of a peasant landholding varied from 1.2 to 8 hectares (Issawi 1980: 203; Pamuk 1987a: 100). Given the size of their land and the low levels of productivity, most peasants were extremely vulnerable to unfavorable weather conditions and taxation, which also rendered usury and peas-ant indebtedness a widespread and chronic phenomenon. Whatever was left after the tax collector and the usurer had taken their shares was hardly enough for subsistence. "The small producers frequently had to struggle to survive from one year to the next', with no prospect of 'capital improvements in land and implements" (Pamuk 1987a: 89).

If access to land had been mediated through the market and had cheap credit been sufficiently provided, the combined pressure of taxes and debt might have generated a capitalist growth dynamic in the Ottoman countryside by compelling and enabling a richer stratum of the peasantry to break the cycle of indebtedness, improve productivity,

power. From the 1890s, the Ottoman government accomplished a relative constancy and regularity in seasonal labor supply in Çukurova thanks to the forced settlement of nomadic tribes with no agricultural skills. This, in turn, must have encouraged sharecropping landlords (who were mainly non-Muslims with limited eligibility to acquire state office) to introduce labor-saving techniques and machinery into the labor process (Toksöz 2010: 144, 173), thereby enabling them to break away from the productivity-hindering nature of sharecropping arrangements. Given the increasing mobility of labor power and if everything had remained the same, sharecropping in the Çukurova region, therefore, could have been seen as a "transitional" form – that is, a form that permitted "a more or less direct transition to formally capitalist class relations ... under the pressures of competition on the market" (Brenner 1977: 52ff.). All that said, however, the trajectory of class and geopolitical struggles, and the consequent expulsion of the non-Muslim landlord class after 1909, would enable sharecropping relations to prevail once again in the region until the 1950s (Keyder 1987: 138).

market ever larger portions of their subsistence and to eventually oust the less competitive producers from the land. And in fact, especially during 1850–73 (and then 1896–1908), a high world market demand for agricultural goods, together with the relative improvement of rural security and the establishment of modern means of transport, encouraged peasants to extend production and participate in the market. Population growth, the sedentarization of tribes, the settlement of immigrants and the availability of cultivable land also contributed to the expansion of agricultural output, especially for grains, tobacco, raisins and cotton (Issawi 1980: 6; Quataert 1994: 844, 847). However, grains, primarily wheat and barley, far outstripped the production of other cash crops. Even in regions where nonfood crop agriculture was relatively developed, grains accounted for roughly 75–80 percent of cultivated lands (Quataert 1994: 844–6). In Western Anatolia, for example, the share of nongrain crops did not exceed 12 percent of total cultivated land at the beginning of the twentieth century (Pamuk 1987a: 96). How much of these grains were marketed? Despite the relative absence of reliable data, especially for the period before 1900, Issawi estimates that in the Ottoman Empire "even during the 1863 cotton boom, by far the greater part of the land was planted to wheat, barley and other grains, which were mostly consumed on the farm" (Issawi 1980: 200). Quataert similarly notes that although "enormous changes over time occurred in the agrarian sector," in 1900, most cultivators still "possessed small landholdings, engaging in a host of tasks, with their crops and animal products mainly dedicated to self-consumption" (Quataert 2005: 130–1).

Implied here is the persistence of the peasants' "subsistence logic." More important than the quantitative underdevelopment of market production, however, is to remember that there were no qualitative changes in the rules of accessing land, labor and credit that could have forced, enabled and permitted peasant family units to become dependent on the market, produce competitively, reorganize production and accumulate land in the face of their less competitive neighbors. For one thing, as in the case of sharecroppers, even in the most market-oriented areas, such as Western Anatolia, "uncultivated marginal lands were always available for purchase from the state at nominal prices or in return for regular payments of tithe for ten years" (Pamuk 1987a: 88). Furthermore, although some significant attempts were made by the state to extend low-interest credit to induce market production, these were far from satisfactory, as most of the agricultural support targeting the land-hungry and technologically backward peasantry was siphoned off by bureaucrats, local notables and big landlords (Owen 1981: 202; Quataert 1994: 871–2). Considering their relatively uninhibited access to marginal lands and lack of credit, peasants were neither under compulsion nor willing to devote the majority of their labor time to commodity production and reorganize their labor process according to the dictates of market competition. Despite their participation in the market, "basic subsistence considerations (remained) paramount and accordingly most decisions betray[ed] risk-avoiding behaviour" (Keyder 1983: 136). In other words, small family farmers, already distressed by their subsistence, chose not to subject their generational security to the uncertainties of the market. Instead they were "ready to exert and be content with very low levels of consumption which made it easier for them to retain their holdings" in the face of the tax collector and the usurer (Pamuk 1987a: 101; also see Ortaylı 1998: 226–7). Even when peasants were encouraged by high cash crop prices, their involvement in the market was sporadic. Tobacco production, for example, which became especially popular among small producers during the last quarter of the nineteenth century, was carried out by peasants who were "only marginally" involved in and "were able to withdraw from the market" (Koç 1988: 65–71).

In short, in the Ottoman countryside, no market-dependent society was developing conducive to the increasing commodification of the means of life. Agricultural households using family labor were consolidated, but without households becoming "petty commodity producers." Peasants were not becoming market-dependent, that is, their whose incomes not were dependent on their ability to "improve" production according to the market imperatives and to maintain and expand their lands at the expense of less competitive households. Of course, a richer stratum of peasants or sharecropping landlords might still get rich in this context (e.g. Kaya 2021), but they would not be able to initiate a process of capitalist accumulation given their inability to change the sociolegal basis of the "safety-first" agriculture, and their inability to systematically mobilize land, labor and credit. A systematic political intervention was necessary to the conditions of social reproduction, which the Ottoman state was reluctant to initiate. In this regard, Çağlar Keyder's argument that in the Ottoman Empire "[a]n autonomously functioning economy where the law of value reigned had begun to grow in importance ever since external trade [and merchant capital] became significant" seems mistaken (Keyder

1981: 128). Instead, it would be better to conclude that no "petty commodity production" developed, and in fact, as Charles Post (2013: 88) hints at in a different context, the so-called merchant capital was not capital at all.

The route to improved agricultural productivity via systemwide trans-formation of peasants' customary rights therefore remained closed. The persistence of customary rights resulted in chronic labor shortages, undermining the investment climate from the very beginning. For example, there were massive inflows of foreign direct investment into land in Western Anatolia following the Land Code of 1867 – according to one estimate, a third of cultivable land belonged to the British in 1868 – and yet foreign investment totally retreated in the subsequent decades because of labor-power shortages, low effective demand, high wages and, above all, the reluctance of the Ottoman state to transform agrarian relations (Pamuk 1987a: 39, 68). Almost all foreign investment funds went into infrastructure projects, which gave "quick, high or at least secure returns," rather than flowing to production (Hershlag 1968: 33). As a result, an "extensive" economic development based on peasant squeezing, land clearance and settlement of seminomadic groups set in during the Tanzimat period with no prospects for "intensive" develop-ment based on (re)investment and productivity increases in land (Güran 1992: 233; Quataert 1994: 843).

Overall, during the Tanzimat, two contradictory projects with differ-ent stakes for peasant bodies were continuously played out; yet neither did capitalism undermine Jacobinism, nor did Jacobinism prevail over capitalism. Private property began to be instituted in many parts of the Ottoman Empire without overriding peasants' customary right to sub-sistence. The state's experimentation with capitalism and Jacobinism was to take a more decisive turn only in the following period.

From the Constitution to the Revolution: The Rise of Jacobinism (1876–1908)

Possession of lawful title is guaranteed. There can be no dispossession.

Article 21, The Ottoman constitution of 1876

Three decade-long attempts at reconciling the rights of the propertied individual and the rights of the citizen-soldier ended by producing a form of property that allowed neither a rate of productivity

characteristic of market society nor a system of geopolitical mobilization characteristic of Jacobinism. Approaching the 1880s, the Ottoman
state was thus at the brink of financial collapse. In order to finance its
skyrocketing military expenses, the Ottoman state increasingly turned
to foreign borrowing in the aftermath of the Crimean War, ultimately
defaulting on international debt in 1875 (Shaw and Shaw 1977:
155–6). In this context, the project of strengthening the Ottoman
fiscal/geopolitical base by way of an Ottoman form of capitalism
reached a deadlock and the Ottoman combined project took a more
decisive turn toward Jacobinism, the first step of which was the
Ottoman constitution of 1876.

At first sight, the constitution seems to be a "combined" text,
consisting of elements of capitalism and Jacobinism as the legal texts
of the Tanzimat period. For example, it built and expanded on the
earlier experience of provincial councils, which, during the 1860s, had
provided an advisory role and political representation to wealthy
provincial notables. While the provincial committees set up during
the constitutional period continued to consist of propertied groups of
diverse occupational, religious and ethnic backgrounds, they also
gained electoral capacity by sending their representatives to the newly
established House of Deputies. And the power of the House of
Deputies, despite being circumscribed in many ways by the sultanate
and the Executive (the Porte), was significant in one important respect:
The constitution granted the House of Deputies the right to supervize,
audit and, if necessary, dismiss government decisions on fiscal matters
(Shaw and Shaw 1977: 176–7). The constitution thus provided provincial elites with room for participation in central politics and gave
them considerable leverage concerning matters on property
and taxation.

That said, the constitution also had four critical Jacobin steps. First,
it equalized all subjects before the law, while reasserting the indivisibility of the empire (Article 1). The constitution called all citizens
"Ottomans" who have the same rights and owe the same duties
toward their country without prejudice to religion (Articles 8 and
17), therefore it foresaw the universalization of conscription regardless
of ethnoreligious and income differences. Second, the constitution
introduced popular elections; yet it did not confine political representation to the propertied classes. Based on the French election law of
1789, it expanded the scope of popular representation to "primary"

voters, that is, all men above the age of twenty-five who fulfilled a "vague" taxation requirement were allowed to vote for electors who then chose the actual deputies. Therefore, notwithstanding several problems involved in the actual elections, the constitution, *in principle*, created a system of "popular elections with relatively few suffrage restrictions," which compared favorably even with contemporary Western European countries (Kayalı 1995: 268–70). Third, the constitution (Article 21) "ensured the security of possessors [*mutasarrıf*] and not owners [*malik*] ... it stated that neither movable nor immovable property that was possessed [*tasarruf*] could be taken away from its possessors except in return for payment or in the event of its being required for public interest" (İslamoğlu 2000: 40).[5] In other words, while the previous Tanzimat documents sought to guarantee the right to property, the constitution ensured the security of possessors by prohibiting dispossession, thereby turning (minimum) subsistence into a constitutional right. Fourth, it introduced free education as a constitutional right and obligation (Articles 15 and 114).

The implication is that the constitution sought not only to universalize the political space beyond the representation of the propertied elite, but also to condition the freedom of the propertied individual to the maintenance of citizen subsistence. While prioritizing subsistence as a constitutional right, it introduced two extramarket institutions through which to obtain the means of subsistence – that is, conscription and education. As such, the constitution reset the conditions for Ottoman entry into modernity by officially introducing of the logic of Jacobin representation and property into the Ottoman body politic. Thereafter, equality and property would cease to be understood as the basis for universalizing the relations of the capitalist contract, but increasingly construed as the means to implementing Jacobin methods of appropriation and mobilization. In particular, reforming education and conscription would not only generate new spaces for political integration and mobilization, but would also signal the formulation of new rules of access to property. For the individual's participation in this new moral economy; that is, their right to land and subsistence was conditioned not on their ability to survive in the marketplace, but their

---

[5] Article 21 reads in Turkish as the following: "Herkes usulen mutasarrıf olduğu mal ve mülkten emindir. Menafii umumiye için lüzumu sabit olmadıkça ve kanunu mucibince değer bahası peşin verilmedikçe kimsenin tasarrufunda olan mülk alınamaz" (quoted in Gözler 1999: 30).

contribution to the geopolitical survival and their sharing of the geopolitical pedagogy of the state. By establishing a link between patriotism and material survival, the constitution provided the blueprint for a substitute route to modernity while suspending the option of market society.

All that said, however, the constitution remained a stillborn text. When the Russian armies appeared once again at the gates of İstanbul, Sultan Abdülhamid II (1876–1908) dissolved the parliament and shelved the constitution in 1878. The result of war was utterly disastrous for the empire. In spite of the ultimate Western diplomatic intervention in favor of the Ottomans at the Congress of Berlin, the empire was forced to pay a huge war indemnity and to surrender two-fifths of its entire territory and a fifth of its population. In addition to the loss of vital sources of taxation and manpower, the war accelerated the influx of Muslim refugees into the remaining Ottoman territories, which caused a massive strain on Ottoman finances (Shaw and Shaw 1977: 191–5). To add insult to injury, after the war the Balkans turned into a geopolitical "tinderbox." The newly emergent Balkan states, whose geopolitical aspirations far exceeded the petty territories that they gained at Berlin, would put constant pressure on the remaining Ottoman lands in Europe (Macedonia, Thrace, Thessaly and Albania); further complicating the difficult balance of power that the Ottomans were trying to maintain both within and without (Shaw and Shaw 1977: 191–5). Furthermore, the opening of the Suez Canal in 1869 had reduced the significance of the Ottoman Straits for British foreign policy, thereby mitigating the British fear of Russian control over the Ottoman Empire. Indeed, it was this growing British reluctance to preserve the status quo that first left the Ottomans wide open to Russian aggression during 1877–1878 and then would lead to the British occupation of Egypt in 1882 (Hanioğlu 2008: 131–2). While the Congress of Berlin, therefore, was part of this sea change in the British perception of the Eastern Question, it also marked the deprivation for the Ottoman state of a relatively reliable supporter in the international arena and the beginning of its rapprochement with a late capitalist–Jacobin progeny – Germany.

The irony is that under these dire fiscal and geopolitical challenges, Abdülhamid II, having killed the constitution, also had to revive the constitution's spirit of reform, especially in terms of its two main objectives: education and conscription. With regard to the latter,

Germany showed the Ottomans the future. Through their overwhelming victory against France in 1870, Prussia's conscript armies had not only sent grave geopolitical reverberations racing across Europe, but also forcefully reminded the European ruling classes of the virtues of universal conscription (Mjøset and van Holde 2002: 46–7). With the ghost of the citizen-soldier resuscitated once again in post-Napoleonic Europe, resulting in the competitive formation of conscript armies of unprecedented sizes, the Ottomans turned to Germany in the postconstitutional period for military expertise and help. The result was the new conscription law of 1886. In many ways, the new law still fell well short of universal conscription. The fear of revolt and foreign intervention, as well as fiscal concerns, prevented the suspension of military exemption fees, from which mainly non-Muslims and propertied Muslim subjects were eligible to benefit (Moreau 2010: 26–7). Despite the persistence of immunities, however, the law took an important step toward generalizing conscription among the Anatolian Muslim population: it conditioned the payment of exemption tax to the prior execution of three months of military service (Shaw and Shaw 1977: 100, 245–6). The significance of this legal detail lies in the fact that the law of 1886 put in practice, for the first time, the principle of equality between the propertied and the propertyless. The rich and the poor were equalized not through the relations of the capitalist contract, but in terms of their responsibility for the geopolitical reproduction of the Ottoman polity. Regardless of income differentials, therefore, military duty tended to become the indirect precondition for accessing property and to acquiring the status of modern subjecthood among the Anatolian Muslim populations (except in Kurdistan).

The intertwining of equality and property with conscription became even more pronounced among the lower classes, especially the refugees. The immigration of Muslim refugees from the lost Ottoman provinces, while initially disruptive, offered some relief to the problem of the scarcity of military manpower. In the wake of the Crimean War, the Ottomans had already issued relatively favorable refugee laws that gave plots of state land to immigrant families "with only a minimum amount of capital" (Shaw and Shaw 1977: 115; Pamuk 1987a: 105). Yet, under Abdülhamid II, an additional condition was set that newly arrived populations had to "fulfill the requirements of the Ottoman conscription system to acquire full Ottoman citizenship status." Thus at a time when the state encountered several difficulties in tapping manpower from native populations, a growing pool of a derooted and revanchist reserve army emerged, whose right to new lands was conditioned to fighting those who caused their displacement. Muslim immigrants thus began to substantially contribute to the Ottoman military power as "volunteers," as "volunteerism would confirm their rights to be granted land and status ... and further establish their legitimate residency in the Ottoman Empire" (Shaw and Shaw 1977: 246; Beşikçi 2012: 172–5).[6]

Linking geopolitical survival to peasant subsistence forced the Hamidian state to continue to be attentive to the precarious structures of social reproduction in the Ottoman countryside. On the one hand, taxation and usury, combined with the low productivity of peasant-based agriculture, left many cultivators in a state of permanent struggle for subsistence. On the other, the crisis of subsistence did not lead to a systematic process of dispossession either. It is remarkable that when the very subsistence of the peasantry was in jeopardy, the state was not willing to initiate a transformation of the conditions of access to land. Evictions were rare (Pamuk 1987a: 90). "Complaints that the default-ing peasants were not being arrested', though 'not unheard of," were infrequent (Pamuk 1987a: 90).The social conditions of geopolitical reproduction and heightening international economic competition, as well as the fear of revolt and the possibility of peasant flight, forced them to keep the peasantry in place (Ahmad 2009: 69–70). Considering their relatively uninhibited access to marginal lands and lack of credit, peasants were neither under compulsion nor able to devote the majority of their labor time to commodity production (despite their participation in the market).

Moreover, in urban centers, the state "compromised endlessly on the issue of guilds' position in the Ottoman economy" (Quataert 1992: 215–16). Although general price ceilings were lifted (except on

---

[6] The non-Muslim population and at least a quarter of the Muslim population remained exempt in the second half of the nineteenth century, leaving some estimated 12 million Muslims available for conscription. And while in Bosnia, Albania, Syria and Iraq conscription attempts foundered due to rebellious populations, the heaviest burden of conscription fell on the population of Turkic Anatolia, which grew by more than 2 million refugees from 1850 to 1900 (Aksan 2007: 479). "At the end of the nineteenth century, the wartime strength of the army was around 750,000 [soldiers] and by 1908, this had increased to 1,160,000" (Tokay 2019: 69).

important subsistence goods such as bread and meat), which was an important step toward undermining artisan solidarity, the state, afraid of social unrest, continued to recognize the monopolistic privileges of many artisan guilds throughout the nineteenth century (Ortaylı 1978: 125; 1998: 208–9). Given the persistence of peasants' and artisans' customary rights, it is scarcely surprising that Ottoman factories, few in number and despite considerable efforts to fund and sustain them, faced chronic labor shortages and extremely high turnover rates, which eventually frustrated the appetite for public and private investment in manufacturing (Clark 2012: 769).

In sum, conscription was still not comprehensive, nor was agriculture productive enough to create the human and fiscal resources needed for geopolitical regeneration. State revenues, already exacerbated by the worldwide depression of agricultural prices, consistently lagged behind military expenditures in the last quarter of the nineteenth century. Also, despite significant improvements in infrastructure and tax-collection, efforts to apply an income tax to the earnings of foreign and non-Muslim Ottoman merchants largely failed due to the opposition of the European ambassadors (Shaw and Shaw 1977: 225). In this context, Abdülhamid II turned to strengthen the second pillar of the Jacobin project charted by the constitution: he substituted public education for the capitalist market.

In the pre-Tanzimat Ottoman Empire, education for common people was voluntary and came to be provided by semiindependent religious orders and funded by pious foundations. Quran schools and medreses established in provincial centers educated provincial youth to be employed as the lower *ulema*, that is, cadres trained to provide basic services in law, education and mosques. By contrast, the higher ulema, especially from the eighteenth century on, originated exclusively from powerful religious households, and "were directly involved in political decisions." Education therefore was neither centralized nor had any significant impact on the circulation of authority and wealth from below to above (Mardin 2006: 87–8). With the Tanzimat's injection of equality into the Ottoman body politic, the perception of education was to go through a qualitative change. It would transform from being a manifestation of an unchangeable hierarchy to a vehicle of popular sovereignty providing universal and merit-based access to the state.

The Tanzimat statesmen, from the 1840s, began to envision public education as a means to securing the loyalty, fostering the unity and increasing the geopolitical usefulness of the politically equal subjects. Especially after the Crimean War, the severity of educational reform began to be felt in Ottoman elite circles. For the state's acute need to raise official cadres and loyal citizens was not only marked by the insufficiency of Quran schools, but further compounded in the wake of the Crimean War by the proliferation of autonomous non-Muslim and missionary schools, which enjoyed considerable foreign backing (Somel 2001: 42, 98; Fortna 2002: 117). Undoubtedly, one of the most significant steps in this direction was taken with the introduction of the Education Act of 1869, which set out plans for "a centralized and compulsory education system that was modeled after the French example" (Evered 2012: 1). However, fiscal difficulties did not allow for an expansion of the public school network until Abdülhamid II. The expansion of public schooling during the Hamidian period points to a sort of compromise reached between the center and the provincial elite (Somel 2001: 116). On the one hand, Abdülhamid II, having liquidated constitutional politics, attempted to introduce public education as an alternative way of integrating provincial elites into the Ottoman regime of rule and appropriation. And on the other hand, by sending their sons to public schools, local notables, relatively well-off agrarian families and Muslim merchants sought to regain access to the state as a source of income and power (Karpat 1972a: 276).[7] Although several minority communities (especially non-Muslims) continued to contest imperial visions of education, the Hamidian success in expanding the secondary school network all over the empire also points to the growing mutuality of interest between the state and provincial notables. The number of secondary school students increased from 3,000 in 1856 to roughly 40,000 in 1895 (both *rüşdiye* and *idadi* schools), while the number of those attending military, technical, medical and law schools amounted to nearly 18,000 (Shaw and Shaw 1977: 107, 112–13). On the failure side, however, reforming primary education remained a limited venture due to fiscal restrictions as well as the fear that the lower ulema, the local imams and semiindependent brotherhoods might react to the diminishing of their chances for employment and promotion (Mardin 1962: 128; Somel 2001: 61, 272).

Taken together, while the efforts to extend the state's geopolitical message to the bulk of the peasantry proved to be rather unsuccessful

---

[7] It must be noted that for all primary and secondary school students, tuition was free and room and board were provided. However, higher-level schools charged tuition, so that "only the wealthier families could afford to send their children, except the very best poor students, who could attend without charge" (Shaw and Shaw 1977: 108).

(which would be achieved forty years later by the Republic), the Hamidian state opened a new avenue of integration and appropriation for the provincial elites. The provincial elite, at least in principle, gained institutional and merit-based access to the central state as a source of income, power and status. Furthermore, the proliferation of education in a noncapitalist setting further displaced the site social reproduction from the market and became directly connected to one's level of education in, political loyalty to and geopolitical utility for the Hamidian state. That said, the irony is that that even this limited introduction of popular sovereignty, based on merit-based access to the state, bore grave consequences for the social reproduction of the sultan and his entourage. For, especially from the 1880s onward, students who were educated in provincial public schools and came from relatively modest families began to enter the ranks of the military and civil bureaucracy. Against the appropriation of higher bureaucratic posts by the sultan's associates, these lower-ranked officers, commonly known as the Young Turks, would become one of the main agents of social change as they struggled to open state careers to talent. Educated in public schools and royal academies, where they learned Western languages and sciences and became acquainted with Western political thought, the Young Turks would seek to combine Jacobinism with the social and intellectuals resources of an Ottoman-Islamic setting. The generations educated by the Hamidian schools were to remain loyal to the state, but not to Abdülhamid II. The era of rebellious officers was about to begin.

From Abdülhamid II to the Young Turks: Inventing a Jacobin Islam and a Jacobin Public

The bases of contemporary civilization are nothing but the actions and traditions of Muhammad.

                                                                Abdülhamid II

Il y a promesse de mariage entre la civilisation musulmane et la civilisation scientifique.

                                                                Ahmed Rıza

The Ottoman bureaucracy expanded remarkably in the nineteenth century. In terms of civil-military service posts, there were half a million officers in 1900 that had not existed in 1800 (Quataert 1992:

218). The fiscal cost of this bureaucratic-military expansion is note-worthy: in the 1890s, around 70 percent of government revenues was used to pay civil servant salaries and pensions, while government funds allocated for public investment remained as low as 3 percent (Tezel 1986: 85). Given this quantitative expansion, the citizen-officer, along-side the citizen-soldier, became one of the most immediate byproducts of the Ottoman engagement with Jacobinism. Public schools, in principle, injected into the Ottoman body politic of the Jacobin logic of equality and property, that is, the principle that every equal member of the nation, if they acquire certain educational credentials, was entitled to an equal share of the state, which was the main source of authority and income. Besides this, however, Abdülhamid II continued to wield personal authority through an empirewide network of spies and informers and established a cadre of loyal technocrats at the apex of the state. As the sultan centralized and personalized the appointment and promotion of the higher bureaucracy, the lower-ranked officers were bound by the law and their advancement was subjected to strict standards of merit, age and experience (Hanioğlu 2010: 125). Also, given the fiscal instability of the empire, the lower echelon of the administrative hierarchy "was often left to fend for themselves on inadequate salaries paid in arrears." The point is that from the 1880s, the lower-ranked officers would become the main agents of resistance and change in the empire. In their struggle to open the state to talent, the Young Turks would imagine progressively more radical conceptions of the "public" to oust the sultan and reinstall the Ottoman constitution (Mardin 2006: 121–2).

At this juncture, a few observations are in order that illuminate the historically specific character of Ottoman Jacobinism, in particular with regards to the politicocultural coloring of the emerging public space from the Tanzimat to the Young Turks. The most noticeable feature of the debates on the Ottoman "public" was that they all attributed a fundamental role to Islam in the constitution of the modern public space. Sultans, reformers and those in opposition (including the Young Turks), despite their conflicting interests, all imagined and attempted to create a modern public space not insulated from, but imbued by Islam. In this sense, the Tanzimat and Hamidian modernization led to the creation of a public space that was both a derivation of and a departure from the Jacobin model. In France, just as in the Ottoman Empire, elites tended to develop religion-based responses to their conditions of geopolitical backwardness. Yet, given that the theological authority in France continued to preserve some degree of autonomy even through the nineteenth century, the Church's failure to deliver geopolitical objectives could potentially generate an anticlerical and antireligious dynamic. In the Ottoman Empire, by contrast, the higher ulema were by and large dependent on worldly authority for their own reproduction, that is, for their access to vakıf lands and state offices. In the absence of an autonomous power specifically devoted to policing theology, the higher ulema especially found it harder to oppose the bureaucratic and geopolitical redefinition of Islam. The state cadres were able to reinterpret religion in conformity with their own political and geopolitical interests, as the higher ulema either had little material basis to oppose this or simply found it easier and more beneficial to accord with its bureaucratic repositioning (cf. Wood 2012: 65).

The implication is that the importation of French social, educational and legal forms into the Ottoman Empire did not inherit the Jacobin *potential* of creating an antireligious modernity, but resulted in the standardization of Islam. In other words, the combination of Jacobin and Ottoman forms of sociality from the Tanzimat to the Young Turks (then to the early Republican period) generated a historically specific modernity that repeatedly substituted the antireligious potential of Jacobinism for the bureaucratization of Islam. While transforming the agent of modernity from the individual to the nation, the Ottoman political imagination therefore did not have to operate within the framework of a politics/religion binary. Islam, bureaucratized and standardized, could be well used as a protonationalist ideology. A public space engrained in an Islamic vocabulary could mediate the tension between the rights and duties of the modern individual.

Not surprisingly, both the Tanzimat reformers and the Hamidian state tried to establish modern subjecthood by increasing the visibility of Islam both in school and in society at large (Somel 2001: 3–4; Fortna 2002: 13). Abdülhamid II went even further by explicitly linking modernization to religion by "recharg[ing] and redefin[ing] basic Islamic institutions, namely the Sharia and the caliphate, as the basis of the quest for a new national identity." He "rationalized" and standardized Islam (based on Sunni-Hanefi interpretation) both in school and court in ways that served the state's political and geopolitical objectives (Deringil 1998: 48–50). In like fashion, he consolidated the Ottoman civil code (*Mecelle*) and the new judicial system (*Nizamiye*) by fusing Islamic law and positive French law and without alienating the religious establishment (Rubin 2011: 58–9).

In the 1860s, the Young Ottomans, representing the first wave of dissident bureaucrats and intellectuals, articulated relatively inclusive, liberal and Islamic conceptions of the nation in opposition to what they considered the "Westernist dictatorship" of the Tanzimat pashas. The Young Ottomans, most of whom came from the wealthy families of İstanbul and were educated abroad, found their opportunities for advancement shrinking within the Tanzimat bureaucracy. In their quest for an alliance with the lower ulema, they formulated a form of Islamic liberalism as the precondition to the Ottoman entrance to civilization and as the basis of imperial regeneration (Mardin 1962: 105–22). They espoused the individual and constitutionalism as the basis of civilization, yet at the same time charged the Islamic establishment with the task of creating an "ethical individual" who works for the common good. As such, the Young Ottomans, while asserting their own class interests, claimed the existence of a wider "Ottoman nation" and an Islamic moral base that could guide the introduction of the abstract individual.

Competitive reframing of the nation continued throughout the Young Turk period as well. What distinguished the Young Turk theory of opposition and reform from that of the Young Ottomans was their disbelief in the presence of a public morality that could be readily provided by the existing religious establishment. In the eyes of the Young Turks, Abdülhamid II's efforts to standardize and elevate existing Islam as the new public morality had delivered nothing but inequality, tyranny and imperial decline. The inequalities of Ottoman bureaucracy, therefore, led many educated elites to disassociate themselves from the Hamidian regime and to consider the ulema as the major obstacle on the road to civilization, which is precisely why the Young Turks would increasingly invoke universalist and secular concepts such as humanity, liberty and progress in order to politicize and mobilize the lower classes against Hamidian "despotism" (Mardin 2006: 121)

Nevertheless, the Young Turks were also well aware that fighting the Hamidian regime by mobilizing the lower classes might also lead to the full activation of a Jacobin political subject whose rights and duties could undermine the position of the bureaucracy and the sultan alike.

Despite being persistently crushed by the Hamidian state, the Young Turks therefore maintained a elitist and "scientific" vision of society for a long time and remained consistently suspicious of revolutionary change. For them, it was only scientific thinking, not popular action, that could lead to personal freedom and a constitution. Referring to Robespierre as an example, they contended, "one should not show blood to the masses and should not get them used it. Otherwise no end and limit may be found for the awakened human brutality." Their ultimate objective was therefore to revolutionize "minds, schools, industry and knowledge, but not ... the streets." Moreover, they believed mass action could easily backfire in the Ottoman context, for "any appearance of chaos [in the past] had served as an excuse for [foreign] intervention, the return of despotism, or both." Accordingly, in the Young Turk journals "educating the people" and "a military takeover from the top" came to the fore as the most loudly proclaimed strategy to overthrow the Hamidian regime. Indeed, they admired and viewed another late-developer as the archetype of such "scientific" methods of transforming the state and society. Japan, in the eyes of the Young Turks, affirmed the possibility of national regeneration without invoking the "Terror" of the "bloodthirsty masses." As in the case of the Meiji restoration, they argued a "swift and bloodless" military coup and mass education could well substitute for "the violent methods of the French Revolution and the horrors of mass participation" (Sohrabi 2011: 62, 72–5, 77, 80–1).

In the Young Turk circles, then, what was deemed paramount was the problem of how to find a substitute route to "civilization," that is, "the problem of how to change the regime without a revolution" (Hanioğlu 1995: 207). They had to revive the constitutional rights and duties of the modern subject in ways conducive to the overthrow of the regime, but without lifting the lid of the revolutionary Jacobin subject. Therefore, the Young Turks considered the formation of a new ethical, scientific and Islamic public space as the prerequisite to returning to constitutional rule and halting imperial decline. They imagined a new nation led by a group of intellectual elites whose primary mission was to "educate" the masses based on "scientific" principles.

Tellingly, "science" in Young Turk discourse did not engender an anti-Islamic reaction. The common thread running through all Young Turk writings, including the writings of the most anticlerical members like Ahmed Rıza and Abdullah Cevdet, was not the rejection, but the invention of an "enlightened" Islam. In opposing Abdülhamid II, the Young Turks, especially the early members of the Committee of Union and Progress (CUP), theorized a nation, in which a "true" and "scientific" Islam, compatible with the impersonalized procedures of positivist sciences, governed and made the abstract individual politically useful . By replacing "Islamic obscurantism" with "scientific Islam," so ran the Young Turk argument, a moral and universal base for orderly progress could be established under the guidance of the intellectual elite (Hanioğlu 1995: 200–16). The Young Turks, as such, perceived modern science and education as necessary preconditions to the admission of the abstract individual into the modern public space. Distrustful of "ignorant" masses, they conditioned the equality and property of the individual to their internalization of the political morality and pedagogy of the intellectual elite. They thereby envisaged an ideal order, in which cultural-educational boundaries became and legitimized class boundaries (Mardin 2006: 123).

As time wore on, however, education, secular morality and intellectual elitism were to prove insufficient to mobilize and tame the common people. New geopolitical threats and revolutionary fervor were already in the air at the onset of the new century and would not disappear unless the Young Turks became revolutionaries themselves. And once the Young Turks unleashed the people's revolutionary energies and seized the state, they would have to water down their scientific/elitist vision of society based on a new moral and popular economy.

The Geo(politics) of Revolution: Reimagining the "People"

Up to now, no nation has been able to acquire liberty, their natural right, by means of publications. In reality, ideas are a preparatory means for evolution. However, arms speed up this evolution.

From Şura-yı Ümmet, a Young Turk journal, 1907[8]

The Young Turks, organized in the CUP, was largely composed of émigré bureaucrats.[9] Headquartered in Paris, the CUP published and

---

[8] Sohrabi (2011: 99).
[9] The Young Turks were not a monolithic movement. All Young Turk groups held grudges against Abdülhamid II's autocratic rule, yet they had no vision of a united front and no common strategy to be pursued against the sultan. The CUP

disseminated journals propagating a "scientific" transition to constitutionalism and strived to organize an empirewide underground network of constitutional resistance (Hanioğlu 2010: 144–5). From 1905, however, under the impact of domestic uprisings, new (geo)political exigencies and world historical events, the Young Turk vision of social change began to drastically alter. The constitutional revolutions in neighboring Russia (1905–6) and Iran (1906), the revolts in Anatolia (1906–7) and the imminent threat of foreign partition of Macedonia (1903–8), all combined, forced and enabled the Young Turks to develop a new repertoire of social mobilization.

The revolution in Russia was particularly decisive in shifting the Young Turks' "evolutionary positivism toward revolutionary activism" (Sohrabi 2011: 90). For one thing, the Russian upheavals made the Young Turks realize that a group of "enlightened" intellectual elites could well use and tame the revolutionary potential of the peasantry and urban poor for transformative action. The Young Turk journals extensively and affirmingly reported on the "hungry Russians coming from villages and cities [who] are like mines and torpedoes ready to ignite with a little contact." Also, the initial constitutional success of the Russian uprising, which the Russian army was reluctant to suppress, seemed to the Young Turks as confirmation of the revolutionary potential of conscripted peasants. They concluded that a people's army "can not fight against their own sons, fathers and brothers for long" and "it is only a few times that the Tzar might be able to use this force against the people" (Yaşar 2014: 119–20). Along with the discovery of the "peasant" in the Young Turk imaginary of social change, the intellectual also gained a new role. The Young Turks reasoned that if "ignorant" masses were one reason for the persistence of Hamidian despotism, the lack of "enlightened" intellectuals was the other. Intellectuals should not just wait for the people to awaken to their rights, but, as in contemporary Russia, intellectuals "were to ignite the masses against tyranny and injustice, as electricity and heat did for chemical reasons." In fact, without the intellectuals' guidance, uprisings in Russia would "express the masses' hatred of despotism

was the main organization within the Young Turks, which also played a decisive role during the 1908 revolution. Therefore, hereafter, unless otherwise stated, I will use the Young Turks and the CUP interchangeably.

and injustice but fail to achieve anything of value" (Sohrabi 2011: 80–1).

This intellectual vanguardism and peasant-based populism found further support and gained a new expression in the wake of the Iranian revolution. Tehran proved to the Young Turks the possibility of a relatively bloodless and popular revolution even in a more "backward" setting than Russia. Equally important, the fact that the ulema led the revolution in Iran not only reinforced the Young Turk belief that a "real" Islam could underpin the discourse of revolutionary leadership, but also demonstrated the existence of a local moral source that can guide and control the revolutionary subject. The Young Turks thus construed the revolution in Iran as proof that "the religion of Islam, from its inception, declared liberty, justice and equality." Indeed, precisely because Islam was originally "built upon freedom and justice, today in the government of Iran ... freedom is granted without any bloodshed," unlike in Europe and Russia where attaining freedom cost people much more dearly (Sohrabi 2011: 82–4).

While the wave of international revolutions gave the Young Turks an idea about "what must be done," the social ferment developing in Anatolia provided them with the first testing ground to adapt freshly acquired ideas and practices to new ends. Between 1906 and 1907, several provinces in the empire and especially in Central and Eastern Anatolia were shaken by popular revolts. Rising taxation demands on propertied classes, artisans and the urban poor, increasing peasant indebtedness, conscription, food scarcities and the nonpayment of salaries to military officers produced a series of reactions ranging from tax-revolts, bread riots, occupation of government buildings and mutinies (Kansu 1997: 37–41; Hanioğlu 2001: 123–4; Aytekin 2013: 324–7). Although most of these reactions were voiced through a constitutionalist discourse, they hardly produced a coherent bundle of demands. For, while wealthy merchants organized mainly to oppose tax increases, the lower classes and artisans seem to have directed their rage not only against the government, but also against the rich whom they accused of tax-evasion, hoarding and usury. For example, in Erzurum and Kastamonu, where resistance was the fiercest and lasted the longest, the rebels lynched the "profiteers" who caused food shortages and forced the wealthiest merchants to flee the town, seized government buildings and killed government representatives (Hanioğlu 2001: 114; Özbek 2010: 76; Aytekin 2013: 325).

The situation in the Eastern and Southeastern Anatolian countryside was perhaps even more unbearable and reactionary. Following the first attempts to introduce property rights in the region, the Hamidian regime had supported Kurdish tribal chiefs' claims on property and even authorized them to be a police force and tax collectors. This had, in turn, led to the reduction of most peasants (predominantly of Armenian and Kurdish origin) in the region to sharecropper status. Subjected to excessive taxation and rent and various depredations, the Armenian peasantry, from the 1880s, became a breeding ground for the spread of popular ideas and practices and the establishment of nationalist and revolutionary organizations. In particular, the Armenian Revolutionary Federation (ARF) was active in organizing armed resistance in villages and towns. During the Eastern Anatolian revolts, the ARF thus effectively put "re-possession of the peasantry" onto the list of emerging constitutional demands (Kansu 1997: 79–80; Klein 2002: 258–62, 304–5).

The CUP in particular and the Young Turk movement in general actively engaged in attempts to strengthen and spread resistance in Anatolia through underground propaganda activities (Kansu 1997: chapter 2). The Anatolian revolts "solidified the CUP resolve to move toward a more wide-ranging uprising," and in doing so, they pushed the CUP to widen the scope of their public appeal. They recognized that more peaceful means such as tax-holding by the propertied classes was not sufficient to overthrow the Hamidian regime; indeed, they congratulated the people of Erzurum and Kastamonu "for selecting the best method of ridding themselves of thirty years of Hamidian injustice and tyranny" (Sohrabi 2011: 84–5). In Anatolia, lower-class demands and methods thus began to enter the CUP's political agenda and repertoire of action. However, it would be in Macedonia where the organization would take stronger root and where the revolts turned into revolutionary uprisings.

The Ottomans had granted semiautonomous status to Macedonia after a major revolt that shook the European provinces of the empire in 1903. This left a power vacuum in the region that was filled by various rebellious groups fighting for land and independence and supported by neighboring Balkan states. Rebels organized into armed village bands and committees, initiating a competitive process of land and tax-grabbing in the region. Popularly supported and trained in guerrilla tactics, they gave a hard time to the Ottoman army and put pressure on Muslim villages (Hanioğlu 2001: 221–6). In response, the junior Ottoman officers, most of whom had been CUP members since 1907, began to penetrate Muslim villages and began to organize Muslim bands modeled after their Christian adversaries. Recruitment into village bands was assured by the backing of village notables/landowners and by providing the villagers with concrete incentives, which included the end of unjust taxes and insecurity of life and property. The process of arming peasants and creating village militias sped up, especially after June 1908 when Russia and Britain met at Reval (purportedly) to discuss the possible partition of Macedonia. The Ottoman officers took to the mountains, roamed the villages and spread the word of justice and liberty that the revolution promised to bring. Peasants and town inhabitants in Macedonia joined the CUP in increasing numbers. The Third Army, the main Ottoman military force in the region, under the leadership of CUP-related officers and with the involvement of Muslim notables and villagers, thus evolved into both a source of popular uprising and elite rebellion (Karpat 1972a: 280–1). Popular demands and elite grievances were eventually absorbed into the army that was increasingly addressed by the Young Turks as "the vanguard of the freedom movement and the public guide to the true path" (Sohrabi 2011: 96). In July 1908, an extensive military mutiny, together with a broad popular uprising, consequently forced the sultan to grant the constitution and turned the Young Turk movement into a "Jacobin revolution."

The Young Turk Revolution, War and the Jacobin "Terror" (1908–1918)

Liberty, Equality, Fraternity and Justice!

A Young Turk slogan[10]

Everyone is a soldier now.

Enver Pasha[11]

Private property is legitimate insofar as it serves social solidarity.

Ziya Gökalp[12]

Massive public celebrations, often with a strong emphasis on the fraternity of all Ottomans, took place in the first days of the revolution.

[10] Hanioğlu (2010: 150).   [11] Beşikçi (2012: 211).   [12] Barlas (1998: 46).

Hürriyet (liberty) was now declared everywhere. So was *adalet* (justice). The coupling of liberty with justice had been a usual discursive act since the beginning of the Tanzimat era. Yet, supplementing the French revolutionary trio with justice in 1908 was no longer an expression of the reforming elite's fear of social strife only, but also the result of the active incorporation of lower-class demands into the emerging constitutional agenda. The meaning of liberty and equality was thus no longer the monopoly of the Young Turk elite and their propertied allies. In this sense, the 1908 Revolution would unfold as much a revolution from "above" as a revolution from "below." That is, the dissident bureaucrats could contest the sultan and seize the state only by mobilizing and increasing their appeal to commercial and lower-class grievances caused by taxation, usury and conscription. The Muslim merchants, who were against the trading privileges enjoyed by non-Muslims, were an active force behind the CUP's revolutionary drive, so was the urban and rural poor who were exhausted by debt, taxation and war.

The sociologically amalgamated character of the revolution, combined with new geopolitical challenges, explains the specific trajectory of the development of property relations in the postrevolutionary period as well as the Young Turks' ambiguity in articulating the economic objectives of the revolution. On the one hand, "free enterprise" (*teşebbüs-i şahsi*) became one of the main code words of the revolution, which, according to many influential Young Turks and their commercial allies, could flourish only in a society wherein the rules of free contract (*serbest-i mübadelat*) and free competition (*serbest-i rekabet*) were instituted. Capital was considered as the key to bringing "civilization" to the country, which, first and foremost, required that the individual be allowed to pursue their selfish interest (Toprak 1982: 23–4). Yet, the fact that the new state elites were able to put capitalist demands into the revolutionary agenda thanks to the mobilization of lower classes put definitive limits to the regeneration of the capitalist project. For one thing, peasants and the urban poor, empowered by the revolution, consistently "misinterpreted" liberty in ways conducive to their own interests: "Liberty of property" in their hands turned into liberty from tax, liberty from debt, liberty from conscription, liberty from fares and liberty from penalties, all which brought the business of government to a standstill in the first six months following the revolution (Kayalı 1997: 59; Sohrabi 2011: 175–88).

The irony is that the lower classes themselves established many CUP branches and clubs independently of the CUP headquarters, which became the centers of opposition to taxation. Given its leadership during the revolution, the CUP was seen by the masses as the guarantor of "justice," hence organizing themselves as and through the CUP branches and clubs provided them with the legitimate means of resisting what they considered injustice (Emiroğlu 1999: 50–1; Hanioğlu 2001: 282).[13]

While the "sanctity" of property was endangered by the agitated masses and "liberty" had no stable meaning, the CUP took another initiative, which would further complicate the postrevolutionary situation. In order to overcome fiscal problems, rationalize state spending and smooth the upward mobility of educated officers loyal to the CUP, the state dismissed large numbers of officials who were "uneducated" and connected to the old regime (Sohrabi 2011: 190, 223). In addition to the soldiers and bureaucrats close to the old establishment, those especially targeted were the medrese students, the lower ulema cadres and populist religious organizations, whose inflated numbers and exemption from conscription was found hardly justifiable by the CUP. From the end of 1908, this motley crowd of disfavored officials, who enjoyed popular support from the masses disappointed by the revolution, began to organize and unite, which then culminated in a major empirewide revolt in April 1909. Three main and interrelated demands came to the fore during the revolt. First, they wanted "justice" for all those whose livelihoods were threatened by the "indiscriminate" official purges. Next, they demanded the recruitment of medrese students into the religious establishment and the continuity of their exemption from conscription. And finally, they took issue with the principle of "equality." For, in their eyes, "equality" forced them to give up their access to state-based income, while reinforcing economic advantages already enjoyed by the propertied classes, most of whom were Greeks and Armenians. They argued that by equalizing the

---

[13] From 1909, the "patriotic" clubs previously established in the provincial centers emerged as official CUP centers, while the CUP members and their propertied allies infiltrated clubs and societies established by the lower classes, most notably the ones related and contributing to the boycott movement (Shaw and Shaw 1977: 282; Çetinkaya 2014: 111–12). In early 1910, according to a prominent CUP member, the CUP had "more than 360 centers and 850,000 members, the chamber's majority and a good number of cabinet members," therefore it "constituted the Ottoman public opinion" (Sohrabi 2011: 174).

Muslim and the non-Muslim, the CUP actually countered the national interest and took sides with the "infidels," who were already supported by the European powers for the continuity of their commercial privileges. That said, it is scarcely surprising that in some provincial towns with a high interethnic composition, such as Adana, Ankara, Sivas and Aleppo, the revolt resulted in large-scale massacres, producing violent reactions against the life and property of non-Muslim imperial subjects (Astourian 2011: 77–8).

The revolt was eventually extinguished by the military, but it also signaled that most of the prerevolutionary nightmares of the CUP were coming true. The lid over the masses was lifted; and thereafter the CUP's revolutionphobia would only be further exacerbated by the outbreak of new social and geopolitical exigencies. The first external shock to the new order came in October 1908 when Austria annexed Bosnia-Herzegovina and Bulgaria declared its full independence. Perhaps much more unpleasant and unexpected than the loss of these two provinces, over which İstanbul had exercised no real control since 1878, however, was that the loss instigated a reactionary popular wave in İstanbul and the provinces. Reminiscent of the revolutionary days, massive and spontaneous popular demonstrations took place, eventually forcing the government and the CUP to find and institute a new form of legitimate protest: the boycott. As for the government, boycotting was a form of public relations practice as well as a harmless diplomatic gesture. For one thing, boycotting Austrian and Bulgarian goods fell short of declaring war, thereby not "risk[ing] the newly acquired freedom for lands that had been lost long ago." Also, it could be effective in keeping mass reactions and protests "away from a possible anticonstitutional political current" (Çetinkaya 2014: 40–1). The CUP, thus, thought of and popularized the boycott as a form of orderly and peaceful protest based on consumers' refusal to buy certain products. Just as with "liberty," however, the boycott would go much beyond what was originally advocated by the CUP and the government (Sohrabi 2011: 187; Çetinkaya 2014: 63).

The boycott often far exceeded mere consumer action, escalating to violent forms of reaction to property. Protestors picketed stores, assaulted merchants and threatened their employees and customers whenever their demands went unfulfilled. In particular, the port workers, the most active element in the boycott movement until 1912, boycotted the companies that threatened their guild privileges on the grounds that they imported goods from foreign "enemies." Especially after the government banned labor strikes (1909) and abolished guilds (1910), the boycott remained an indispensable strategy for the port workers and urban poor to maintain and advance their interests. For example, when prices of basic consumer goods imported from Austria increased, the urban poor who organized themselves in the boycott movement assaulted merchants for stockpiling goods and raising prices, hence for not being "patriotic" enough (Çetinkaya 2014: 73). Furthermore, the declaration of Cretan allegiance to Greece in 1909 and the arrival of Cretan Muslim immigrants to Anatolia further radicalized the boycott movement. In practice, Crete had been semiautonomous since 1896, therefore its union with Greece did not come as a shock. Yet, what was extraordinary was the level of mass mobilization caused by the Cretan crisis. Spontaneous mass meetings, volunteer enlistment initiatives, printed forms of agitation and the establishment of new patriotic clubs reinvigorated the popular-nationalistic setting of 1908. Boycotting, picketing and economic blockades consequently resurfaced in the lower-class agendas, this time taregeting mainly Ottoman Greek merchants (Kerimoğlu 2006: 92). The "street force" of this new wave of boycotts consisted of newly arrived Cretan immigrants who, having been forced to leave their homes, were probably the most eager to claim that "the boycott should harm the interest of the Hellenes [in general], so that they would be forced to migrate first by their own will" (Çetinkaya 2014: 119).

The CUP was directly involved in organizing some of these actions, yet was never able to exercise full control over the movement. Indeed, in several towns, "the level of mobilization instilled fear in the elites, the members of the CUP, and particularly the Ottoman government," prompting them to take (rather unsuccessful) measures to prevent the masses from beating Greek merchants, damaging their property and threatening the people not to work in or to buy from Greek stores (Çetinkaya 2014: 92, 100–1). Yet, also through the boycotts, the CUP and its propertied allies, rather hesitantly, began to embrace the opportunity to counter their own parliamentary enemies. In the parliament, while the Greek merchants and Albanian and Arab notables, as well as old-regime grandees, were suspicious of the CUP's equalizing and centralizing drive, which often led them to form anti-CUP alliances, the CUP drew its support mainly from the lesser Muslim officialdom and the Turkish propertied classes who opposed the trading privileges enjoyed by non-Muslim merchants (Ahmad 2009: 24). The boycotts, therefore, did not only mobilize the lower classes to acquire leverage in defining the "national" interest, it also provided an opportunity for the CUP to outcompete their own political and economic rivals.

Undoubtedly, the impact of these domestic struggles were amplified under worsening geopolitical circumstances. In the midst of a never-ending cycle of rebellion and war (annexation of Crete by Greece [1909–11], Albanian rebellion and independence [1910–12], Italian invasion of Tripoli [1911], British–Russian partition of Iran [1911]), the CUP was able to counter the growing parliamentary opposition only by appealing to and deepening its reach among the lower classes, that is, the masses that had already learned how to raise their own demands by playing the nationalism card (Ahmad 1988: 268). That said, however, the most radicalized moment for the boycott movement came with the Balkan Wars. No other war in Ottoman history, with the exception of the World War I, stirred up as much existential anxiety as the Balkan Wars (1912–13). The war possessed a "total" character, that is, "the home front became an integral part of warfare," and the Ottomans eventually lost virtually all their possessions in Europe as well as much of their revenues. Masses of Muslim immigrants streamed into the Ottoman Empire from the lost territories. The state was unable to pay salaries and overcome food shortages and the emergence of black markets, which not only caused a series of violent reactions and demonstrations across the empire, but also paved the way for the ultimate and most aggressive wave of boycotts (Shaw and Shaw 1977: 294; Beşikçi 2012: 3).

This time, the CUP played a much more dynamic role in the boycott movement, actively propagating the unification of rich and poor Muslims in counteracting the Greek "traitors." The boycotters accused Greek Ottomans of evading conscription and of financing and joining the Greek army during the Balkan Wars (Toprak 1995a: 109–10; Kerimoğlu 2006: 94). The CUP asserted that the movement was not even a boycott anymore, but "a duty and revival of Muslims" and "a call to reconquer the country." The national interest now demanded that consumers give up their "silly preferences" for non-Muslim goods and buy from Muslim stores only, and in turn, that Muslim merchants reinvest in the economy and hire Muslim workers. Otherwise, the CUP claimed "every penny given to non-Muslims" would become "a bullet aimed at Muslims" (Çetinkaya 2014: 168–9). Meanwhile, Muslim refugees, once again, emerged as the catalyst of the movement, extending the boycott from towns to the countryside. The earlier forms of boycott, such as picketing and physical intimidation, consequently, were replaced by banditry and gang-formation in the countryside, causing thousands of Ottoman Greek subjects to leave their land and estates.

Therefore, the postrevolutionary experimentation with capitalism was already in crisis in 1913. In the face of lower-class reactions and geopolitical challenges, the attempt to introduce liberty and equality brought nothing but chaos. The propertied classes could seize and maintain wealth only by legitimizing and presenting at least some of the lower-class demands as the interest of the nation. Private property could survive only if it was redecorated with responsibilities toward the general welfare of a new nation. Signaled here is the CUP's ever more ambitious turn to the Jacobin methods of creating equality, securing political unity and increasing geopolitical competitiveness.

Indeed, anticipating the dire social and geopolitical circumstances, the revolution had already reintroduced in 1909 the electoral law and the constitution of 1876 with the infamous Article 21. Private property was accepted, so was one's right to subsistence. Although the CUP would manipulate elections and intervene into political processes in several instances, the electoral law, in principle, allowed a greater proportion of the population to enter the new political space as either primary or secondary voters (Kayalı 1995: 268–71). Therefore, equality, subsistence and property concurrently became constitutional rights, the exercise of which was linked to military duty in 1909. The Conscription Law of 1909, once again, made military service compulsory for all Ottoman subjects, regardless of income and ethnoreligious differences. Until 1914, all fees for exemption from military service were progressively abolished. "Comradeship in arms," rather than comradeship in the marketplace, thus began to be perceived as "the most effective means for amalgamating peoples of different races, religions and sects" (Beşikçi 2012: 97). It was declared that universal conscription would enable "the most refined and the wealthiest" to enjoy the "honor" of actively "defending their motherland in the same way as the poor peasant little Mehmeds." Also, the propertyless, that is, immigrants and refugees, would "accept conscription into the Ottoman army in return for their right to be ... settled on Ottoman lands." Ultimately, everyone, "the rich and the poor, the educated and the illiterate" were brought "under the same banner" for the protection of the nation (Beşikçi 2012: 139–41, 172–3). Therefore, at a time when property and liberty were destabilized by the masses, military service, not the market, became the common denominator securing the equality, subsistence and property of all citizens. The right to subsistence and the right to property were simultaneously recognized; and both rights were conditioned to the realization of military duty. Military duty, not the capitalist contract, united and mobilized the propertied and the propertyless.

That said, however, the problem of conscription of non-Turkish elements could not be overcome until 1913 (and only partially thereafter). Many non-Muslim subjects of the Ottoman Empire continued to successfully resist conscription by either leaving the country or obtaining a foreign passport (Zurcher 1999: 89). Even during the Balkan Wars, when conscription efforts took off relatively well (except in Kurdistan and Arabia), non-Muslim resistance to conscription continued within the army. Many Greek and Bulgarian recruits were reported to have changed sides, deserted or destroyed railway tracks and telegraph lines, which then made them the scapegoat for the ultimate defeat of the Ottoman armies (Adanır 2011: 120–3). Ultimately, the Young Turks grew increasingly suspicious of and reluctant to conscript non-Muslim subjects. Non-Muslims were seen as the collaborators of foreign enemies and a source of threat of partition. The result is that while the implementation of Jacobin forms of property and equality facilitated the establishment of new bonds between the state and the Anatolian Muslim population, it also led to the further marginalization of non-Muslim groups in the newly emerging public space. With their property and existence already endangered between 1908 and 1912, non-Muslims would be subjected to another period of "Terror" for not fitting the new standards of civilization characterized by the Jacobin model.[14]

[14] Estimates for the number of Greeks who were forced to leave the Aegean region from 1913 to 1918 run between 200,000 to 1 million. Indeed, the "success" of this initial deportation encouraged the CUP to implement the same policy on the Armenian community during World War I. CUP–Armenian relations had become increasingly hostile after the Balkan Wars due to the CUP's failure to ameliorate the conditions of Armenian sharecroppers vis-à-vis the Kurdish tribal lords and the CUP's suspicion that Armenians, impressed by the Ottoman collapse in the Balkans, would cooperate with the Russians for a definitive solution to the agrarian/national question. The fear of partition further escalated

Entailed by this entanglement of subsistence, property and military service was the progressive nationalization/militarization of the rules of reproduction in Ottoman "civil" society. The creation of a "patriotic" Turkish bourgeoisie was the top priority of the Young Turks, so was the construction of forms of "private" property with new communitarian embellishments. Yet, what these exactly mean would be further clarified only during the World War I. During the war, almost half of the adult male population outside the civil service was conscripted for military service, in addition to the "hundred of thousands, both men and women, conscripted into labour battalions." Levels of production considerably diminished, which, combined with escalating war expenditures, put an enormous strain on public finances (Hanioğlu 2010: 189–90; Aksakal 2014: 468). Inflation, food shortages, price speculation, hoarding and black-marketeering developed to an unprecedented extent, rendering the provisioning of the army and the towns extremely difficult (Ahmad 1988: 274–5). Repeated attempts to stabilize the currency and prevent shortages by fiscal and punitive means did not bear fruit. Big banks and businesses, often coowned by foreigners and non-Muslim merchants, had no confidence in newly issued paper notes nor did they show any interest in funding government debt. In the countryside, while peasants were heavily indebted and barely able to maintain subsistence, Muslim landowners could not benefit from increasing demand due to commercial oligopolies dictating low prices on agricultural goods (Toprak 1995b: chapter 2). And with no funds to create and improve infrastructure and an industrial base,[15] the

in the course of World War I, resulting in massive expulsions and the almost complete annihilation of the Armenian presence in Anatolia (Akçam 2004: 141–50). In Ottoman Syria, the Young Turks were able to implement a ruthless conscription policy during World War I. In contrast to Anatolia, however, the CUP in Syria was unable to prevent food shortages, the emergence of black markets and rising inflation in basic necessities during the war. Conscription, combined with widespread famine (as a result of which one out of seven people died by the war's end), caused various riots and rebellions, culminating in the infamous Arab Revolt of 1916. The Young Turk's "Terror" eventually descended on Arab lands, causing numerous deportations and executions (Kayalı 1997: 194; Aksakal 2014: 462).

[15] In 1913, in what was to become the Turkish Republic, there were about 600 manufacturing firms employing ten or more workers. The total number of workers employed in these establishments was around 35,000, or about 0.2 percent of the population (Pamuk 2005: 113).

Ottoman state could hardly maintain, utilize and "cope with the mass army they had so diligently created" (Zurcher 1999: 91).

In the Young Turk mind, therefore, the "national bourgeoisie" would not seek its selfish interest only, but serve the nation by funding the state in its war endeavor and providing an "ethical" and "solidaristic" space of accumulation, that is, accumulation without dispossession, or better put, accumulation without infringing on the minimum subsistence reserved for patriotic, hence equal, citizens. No doubt, the redistributive impact of this "national economics" (as it came to be labeled) remained very lopsided. The Young Turks unleashed propertied interests as much as it could. They outlawed strikes, allowed Turkish merchants to massively profit from skyrocketing wartime prices without imposing extra taxes on them and permitted landowners to accumulate land to the detriment of the peasantry (Ahmad 2009: 78–80). Yet, despite all this, by leaving Article 21 intact, they also recognized minimum subsistence as a constitutional right and tried to uphold it as a public duty. Marginal lands remained expendable and divisible by the peasantry. Furthermore, by providing higher agricultural prices and credit opportunities specially designed for small producers, the state (however imperfectly) attempted to protect the peasantry from the relations of usury, thereby connecting once again the social reproduction of the poor to their (geo)political usefulness (Toprak 1995a: 73, 139–42; Ahmad 2009: 68). Also, the CUP gathered and organized former artisan and worker guilds as "national societies." This not only lent former guilds a nationa' and solidaristic base for their activities, but also enabled the CUP to obtain the support of the lower classes in establishing and enforcing commercial monopolies in basic necessities (Ahmad 1988: 271–2; Toprak 1999: 184–5). Consequently, while a system of allocation was put in place in towns to fight price speculation and food shortages, which enabled the urban poor to survive under dire wartime circumstances, the CUP elites also reaped huge profits in a system "which totally bypassed the market" (Keyder 1987: 63). Furthermore, balancing subsistence and property became an even more alarming duty in the wake of the October Revolution, which reinforced the Young Turks' fear that "untrammeled liberalism" may end with the revolutionary annihilation of property, civil war and foreign invasion (Toprak 2013: 301–3).

What to make of "national economics" then? Did it aim to establish merely a form of social liberalism or national capitalism, as often assumed? Did Young Turk solidarism simply seek to ease the Ottoman transition to capitalism by neutralizing the social costs of capitalist competition and accumulation? It is commonplace to argue that the national economics imported a solidarist ideology from Third Republic France, with Gustave LeBon and Émile Durkheim being their main source of inspiration. This view is correct insofar as it shows from where Turkish solidarism takes its cue. Yet, it is misplaced to equate the relations and objectives underlying French solidarism to those of its Turkish counterpart (e.g. Toprak 1982). The former's negation of class conflict, advocacy of social reform and emphasis on social solidarity was a response to the challenges of the transition to capitalism in France. During the Third Republic, although producers were not yet completely deprived of their customary trade and local rights, economic inequalities were "no longer as clearly and as immediately related to patent juridicopolitical inequalities as [they] used to be. Class was less and less mingled with extra-economic status relations and was increasingly mediated by property relations and market exchanges between formally equal individuals belonging to a broadening community of citizens" (LaFrance 2013: 294). While French solidarism therefore aimed to ease the social cost of destabilization generated by the advance of capitalism, the CUP asserted solidarism in a much more complex, and in my view, in an utterly noncapitalist context.

By conditioning social reproduction to serving the nation, the Young Turks not only vindicated the propertied individual in the eyes of the have-nots, but also formulated and generalized a set of nonmarket means to accessing sources of subsistence. Property was much less an economic right conditioned on successful commodity production and its productive utilization, and much more a political privilege for those who served the nation. Minimum subsistence was reserved for patriots as a constitutional right, hence a political entitlement for those who are socially and geopolitically useful to the nation. While national economics allowed for the enrichment of a 'Turkified' bourgeoisie at the expense of the non-Muslim propertied classes, it also presupposed the creation of a solidaristic space of accumulation, that is, accumulation without changing the rules of accessing land and encroaching upon the minimum subsistence requirements of "patriotic" and "equal" citizens. In this respect, the nation was the source of property, not vice versa. Patriotism, not the market, gave people land and civic status. National economics reinvented and consolidated the "Turkish nation" as a new impersonalized socioeconomic unit, a substitute abstraction between the market and the state, an alternative frame of reference according to which social reproduction would be organized. At stake, therefore, was not the creation of capitalism, but a historically specific Jacobin political economy.

National economics did not repudiate the abstract individual, but aimed to build a substitute form of individuality, an individual equipped not with market rationality, but with "national culture" (*milli kültür*) and "national morality" (*milli ahlak*). In fact, it is in relation to this challenge that the intellectual stratum of the CUP, especially after the Balkan Wars, began to give up productivist assumptions about economic development and formulate culture-based prescriptions for the Ottoman self-perception of backwardness. For example, Ziya Gökalp, who was a central committee member of the CUP and the founder of Turkish sociology, was increasingly convinced that social life could not be "oriented by rational or utilitarian standards." In this respect, continues Gökalp, "English political economy . . . did not suit the [Turkish] national spirit [and] misled [Turks]" from the onset of the Tanzimat (quoted in Barlas 1998: 45). This means that "without the cultivation (and systematization) of Turkish culture, there could be no genuine reform and modernization." What Gökalp called a "New Life" founded on a "modern national culture" was therefore needed, that it, a life whose modernness was to be defined and measured not according to some market criteria, but its level of conformity to an abstract conception of Turkishness (quoted in Berkes 1964: 364–5).

It was one's relation to the Turkish nation, instead of to the capitalist market, that became the ultimate determinant of his income and status. Therefore, it is scarcely surprising that for the Young Turks, attaining "development" was predicated not on the reform of social relations in a way conducive to the development of a market dependent society, but on the systematization of cultural, administrative and economic codes associated with Turkishness (whatever that might mean) (cf. Ülker 2005). Turkishness had to be defined in a systematic way for the smooth functioning of this new political economy, and the institutions that could not fulfill this task had to be reformed: the mosque, the school, the court and the family (not the market) had to be reorganized in order to inculcate a new socioeconomic identity and morality. Accordingly, the ulema were once again accused of not being able to "adjust" and of failing to provide a cultural-moral base for stirring the Turkish national "spirit." From 1913, "a frantic push toward secularization" was thus launched aiming at increasing state leverage over pious foundations, breaking the control of semiautonomous religious sects on primary schools, educating the ulema cadres, making access to religious posts "merit-based," modernizing the school curricula, increasing the power of lay courts and so on. Through the Family Law of 1917, likewise, the state assumed power to "modernize" matters related to all family relationships, such as marriage, polygamy, adultery, divorce and inheritance (Shaw and Shaw 1977: 306–7). That said, for reasons I explained earlier, the exhaustion of traditional sociocultural resources did not lead to the increase of antireligious sentiment in the Young Turk vision of modernization. Quite the contrary, the Young Turks thought of increasing state control over religion as an attempt to revive Islam as well as the state. Just as the prerevolutionary radicals who saw nothing incongruent between Islam and science, the later Young Turks maintained a "Turkified" Islam as the repository of ethics conducive to "civilization." Islam, cleansed from "Arabic" traditions and rescued from old-ulema interpretations, could "provide the Turks with a stable base for participation in contemporary Western civilization" (Shaw and Shaw 1977: 302). The Young Turks therefore could substitute "Turkification" of Islam for a radical secularization of the French type. "Turkification, Islamization and Contemporization," the famous trio formulated by Ziya Gökalp, could set the terms of and guide Turkish entry into modernity.

Conclusion: A Substitute Jacobin Route to Modernity

The bourgeoisie has long been the "paradigmatic" agent of modernity. The conventional view holds that without the bourgeoisie's appeal to universality, its passion for liberal democracy and its drive for capitalist development, modernization is either "incomplete" or has to take a "defensive" path. In this respect, the history of modernity "proper" is assumed to be the history of the rise of bourgeoisie. Most comparative-sociological analysis of the Young Turk Revolution subscribe to this paradigmatic view. Çağlar Keyder, for example, argues that the "peripheral" status of the Ottoman Empire in the world economy culminated in the formation of a bourgeois class whose interests rested primarily in capital accumulation in the "core" countries, rather than in the Ottoman market. Consequently, instead of "replac[ing] the bureaucracy of the old regime with state functionaries more or less given to serving capitalist interests," as was allegedly the case in revolutionary France, the Young Turks largely remained as a bureaucratic movement, failing to fully address bourgeois interests (Keyder 1987: 76). In a similar vein, Feroz Ahmad contends that given the weakness of bourgeois classes, the Young Turks had to ally with big landlords during and after the revolution, which considerably compromised the revolutionary character of the Young Turk era. This "incompleteness" of the Turkish Revolution, so continues the argument, contrasts the bourgeois revolutionaries in France, who, in cooperation with the peasantry, established the "classical path of the bourgeois revolution" (Ahmad 2008: 238–9). Şükrü Hanioğlu, in like fashion, argues for the "failure of a vital bourgeois class to emerge in the late Ottoman Empire," which he thinks also explains the CUP leaders' conservative reformation rather than "destruction" of the Ottoman old regime, "unlike the French revolutionaries of 1789" (Hanioğlu 2010: 209, 148).

Of course, the model of "classical" bourgeois revolution used by Keyder, Ahmad and Hanioğlu as the basis of comparison for analyzing the late Ottoman and Young Turk eras has lost most of its persuasiveness since the revisionist turn. Indeed, once we depart from these dated interpretations of social class and historical change in the West, which lays the foundation for the "difference" of the Young Turk Revolution, we are able to demonstrate with greater clarity the interactive character of world historical development and the multiplicity of modernities generated therein. This chapter has argued that the late Ottoman and Young Turk attempts at modernization were built on two historically distinct yet mutually restructuring projects: capitalism and Jacobinism. The Tanzimat introduced capitalism and Jacobinism into the Ottoman social fabric simultaneously. The citizen-soldier and the propertied individual were appropriated concurrently for the reconstruction of the Ottomans' military and agricultural foundations. Both capitalism and Jacobinism created acid baths in which the relations of a premodern past would be selectively dissolved. Yet, capitalism and Jacobinism were also mutually contradictory, charging the modern individual with conflicting rights and responsibilities. This internally contradictory and internationally conditioned path to modernity initiated a crisis-ridden process of modern transformation, causing massive social dislocations and reactions, selective appropriation of new ideas and their adaptation to local circumstances.

None of this was an exclusively Ottoman phenomenon; the condition of geopolitical unevenness forced the creation of similar combined projects even in Western Europe. Yet, given the character of preexistent social relations, together with the temporal and geopolitical context of modernization, the Ottoman combined project pursued a radically different path than its Western European counterparts. During the Tanzimat, the reactions from within and interventions from outside forced Ottoman elites to continuously negotiate the rights of the propertied individual and the rights of the citizen-soldier. Yet, the (geo)political risks associated with the capitalist transformation of the Ottoman sociofiscal base proved particularly formidable, which compelled the Ottoman elite, from the 1870s on, to implement more vigorously the Jacobin project. In response to the increasing exhaustion of the (geo)political and developmental promises of capitalism, Ottoman elites solidified the bridge between subsistence and nationalism, that is, they delinked the question of subsistence and equality from the market. Subsistence and equality were not necessarily derived from one's participation in the market. The market was not perceived to be the main or primary means to acquiring the means of life and civility. Instead, subsistence and equality were powerfully connected to one's (geo)political contribution to the survival of the nation. Universal conscription and universal education provided a substitute space for appropriating peasant bodies and securing the internal and external reproduction of the nation. In this sense, the abstract individual, with unhindered rights to property, was cumulatively substituted by novel political subjects whose rights and equality were constantly redefined in line with the changing requirements of an abstract political community, the nation.

Considering the persistence of noncapitalist social relations and the continuity of the centrality of the state as the main source and generator of income, even the limited introduction of different manifestations of popular sovereignty, such as political equality and merit-based access to the state, severely politicized the functioning of the Ottoman political economy. In the absence of an autonomous sphere of economic reproduction, the principle of political equality easily turned into demands for independence from all forms of "economic oppression" (rent, tax, etc.). Likewise, political equality, combined with public education, meant (at least in principle) granting all citizens equal and merit-based access to state office and the state-based income, hence an attack on the economic privileges of the ruling classes. In this light, it is little wonder that the rise of a rebellious group of bureaucrats from the 1880s (the Young Turks) led to the progressive radicalization of Ottoman political imagination, giving rise to competing and often politically explosive interpretations of the public, the nation and Islam. Afraid of the masses, the Young Turks retained for a long time an essentially elitist vision of social change, propagating a "positivist," "evolutionary," "scientific" and "reformist" path to regime change in the empire. Yet, the revolutions in Russia and Iran initiated in the Young Turk mindset a new process of intersocietal comparison and learning, forcing and enabling them to shift their vision of change from elitist reformism to revolutionary activism.

Given the uneven and combined development of Ottoman revolutionary consciousness, the 1908 Revolution began both as a revolution of capital and a revolution of the poor, a fresh attempt to reestablish a capitalist–Jacobin compound. On the one hand, the Young Turks were determined to "rationalize" the society based on the rules of free contract and free competition. Yet, the fact that the new state elites were able to conquer the state thanks to the mobilization of lower classes severely restricted the reinvigoration of the capitalist project. Furthermore, this sociologically unstable base deteriorated in the face of the existential anxieties caused by the unending wars and rebellions of the postrevolutionary period, ultimately causing the revolutionary experimentation with capitalism to collapse in 1914. In the face of lower-class reactions and geopolitical challenges brought about by the Balkan and World Wars, the attempt to "free" property from wider sociopolitical responsibilities brought the ruling elite to the verge of destruction. The new Muslim elites and merchants could seize non-Muslim wealth and maintain authority only by inventing a new form of property organized around new communitarian objectives. The locus of social reproduction, therefore, shifted from the market toward the Turkish nation. Unable to equalize "modern" subjects on the basis of the relations of the capitalist contract, the CUP eventually set the equality of service and sacrifice for the Turkish nation as the new standard of civilization, which gave the Young Turk "Terror" its sociological texture.

Overall, then, we would be amiss to understand the period from 1839 to 1918 as but a period of transition to (peripheral) capitalism in the Ottoman Empire; instead, it was the site of far-reaching efforts to develop noncapitalist (and nonsocialist) forms of modernity. Ottoman modernization opened and widened Jacobin, that is, nonmarket, channels of reproduction and accumulation. Jacobinism did not merely "shape" the relations of the market society, as was the case in Western Europe, but completely substituted them. A historically specific Jacobinism prevailed on Turkish lands, whose contradictory legacy was not only to continue to guide and trouble the early Republican elite, but also deeply impacted on the mindset of the post-Ottoman (and Iranian) reformers throughout the Middle East (e.g. Provence 2017; Viger 2019).

5 | Kemalism as the Ultimate Turkish Substitution for Capitalism (1923–1945)

"In terms of both historic impact and the laying down of an agenda," argued Fred Halliday (2005: 7), "the Turkish Revolution of 1908–23 was the most important upheaval in modern Middle Eastern history." For one thing, the revolution sent geopolitical reverberations throughout Europe and the Middle East by setting off conflict in the Balkan Wars, which, in turn, led, "through the events in Sarajevo in June 1914, to World War I, then on to redrawing of the map of the modern Middle East in 1918–26" (Halliday 2005: 7). Furthermore, the opportunities and contradictions rooted in the manner in which the Turkish Revolution was carried out (e.g. the leading role of the armed forces in state building, nationalism, the modernization of education, secularism, the construction of a modern state in a multiethnic society and the emergence of private property as a constitutional right) prompted processes of intersocietal comparison and learning throughout the Middle East, which, in turn, left an enduring impact on the way in which subsequent Middle Eastern revolutions unfolded (Halliday 2005). Halliday is certainly right in emphasizing the importance of the Young Turk seizure of the state and inauguration of the constitutional period in 1908 as the starting point for the Turkish Revolution. Yet, it is equally important to remember that the Young Turks, caught up by rebellions, wars and imperial collapse, hardly found the room of maneuver to actually carry out the revolution. Thus, for a better understanding of its social and international consequences, the revolution needs to be placed in a longer historical continuum, that is, we need to turn to the emergence of the early Republican state in Turkey, the primary heir of the 1908 Revolution.

Despite the world historical significance of the Turkish Revolution, the theoretically informed analyses of early Republican Turkey suffer from the same historical and methodological problems that trouble the analysis of the late Ottoman Empire. That is, they continue to subscribe to a highly contested and idealized conception of bourgeois

160

agency and Western European history in order to explain the specificity of the Turkish road to modernity. To reiterate, the argument is that the Turkish Revolution, due to the weakness of national bourgeois classes, remained, by and large, a bureaucratic movement. This considerably compromised the revolutionary character of the Young Turk and early Republican era, thereby leaving it either as a mere "conservative reformism" or an "incomplete bourgeois revolution" compared to the "classical path" to modernity characterized by the French Revolution' (e.g. Keyder 1987: 76; Ahmad 1988: 269–70; Boratav 2003: 46; Hanioğlu 2010: 148, 209). Consequently, a form of "state capitalism" and an authoritarian/statist modernization project prevailed under the rubric of Kemalism (e.g. Keyder 1987: 105). Of course, alternative interpretations have been advanced over time to overcome the problems associated with the antagonistic readings of Turkish Revolution and its Western counterparts. Most prominently, Aykut Kansu (1997) has uncovered the similarities between Turkish and Western European revolutions and revealed the thus-far neglected "bourgeois" and "popular" aspects of the Turkish Revolution. Accordingly, he has refused to see the Turkish Revolution as an "incomplete" revolution led only by bureaucratic classes. Instead, the Turkish Revolution, according to Kansu, should be viewed as a "full bourgeois revolution" that attempted "to establish the political and economic supremacy of a new [Muslim bourgeois] class" (Kansu 1997: 27–8). As such, Kansu, well aware of the protracted nature of bourgeois revolutions in the West, has provided an indispensable starting point to reinterpret the Young Turk revolution. Yet, in my view, Kansu's account ultimately remains unconvincing as it continues to uncritically equate the rise of the new bourgeois class with the rise of capitalism in Turkey. The transhistorical association of bourgeoise with capitalism persists, undermining the historicity of his analysis.

This chapter will depart from these interpretations of the Turkish Revolution through the theoretical and historical pointers discussed earlier. It will argue that the original Kemalist experiment with modernity (1923–45) cannot be understood as a form of (state) capitalism, but rather as a historically specific Jacobinism. Neither in the countryside nor in towns was the early Republican regime able or willing to legislate the development of a market-dependent society. The state elite were unable to impose market imperatives on the bourgeois classes and were fearful of the divorce of the peasantry from the land.

In the countryside, via a series of "people-ist" (*halkçı*) measures, such as fiscal incentives and limited land redistribution, the state elite sought to preempt peasant dispossession and labor mobility, which they perceived as the ultimate danger to the existing sociopolitical order. In the absence of a stable supply of labor power, industrialists, foreign and domestic, invested only to reap easy profits in an economy completely sheltered from competition. Organized in monopolies, they prevented competition and overproduction and even sabotaged state plans to improve industrial productivity. Combined with the crisis of the world economy and the escalating threat of war during the 1930s, the state responded to its inability to establish capitalist markets by consolidating Jacobin forms as the basis of its modernization strategy. Education, Turkification, secularization and the militarization of Republican subjects became the ultimate basis of their social reproduction. In short, after a hundred years of experimentation with "modernity," Kemalism consolidated Turkish modernity as a late Jacobin progeny.

The Prelude to the Republic: The (Geo)politics of Sharecropping

We will try to create millionaires and billionaires in our country.

Mustafa Kemal, 1923[1]

Who is the owner and master of Turkey? The peasant!

Mustafa Kemal, 1922[2]

Inconsistent as it may seem, the objective of creating a class of millionaires while declaring millions of peasants to be the masters of the country reveals two vivid expressions of the social and geopolitical challenges faced by the Kemalist elite in their ascendance to power. Geopolitically, the official end of World War I came with a considerable delay on the Ottoman Front. After the armistice treaty in 1918, it took almost two years for the Entente Powers to reach an agreement among themselves on how to partition the Ottoman Empire. The resultant treaty (the Treaty of Sevres) effectively marked the end of the empire as well as the liquidation of the Committee of Union and

---

[1] Quoted in Adanır (2001: 336).   [2] Quoted in Ataöv (1980: 31).

Progress (CUP), the ruling party in which the bureaucratic elite and the Turkish propertied classes were thus far organized. As shown in Chapter 4, before and during the war, the interests represented by the CUP had initiated and partially achieved a process of Turkification of the economy by expelling or exterminating the non-Muslim Ottoman minorities, most notably Armenians and Greeks. The treaties that ceased and ended the war contained clauses that declared the partitioning of a considerable part of Anatolia among former non-Turkish subjects of the empire, thereby implying the immediate reversal of most of the wartime wealth and property accumulated by Turkish bureaucrats, landlords and merchants. It was in this context in which the bureaucrats and Turkish propertied classes established a network of resistance organizations and a new Ankara-based assembly, contesting the sultan's acceptance of the annexation of Western Anatolia by Greece and the creation of Armenian and Kurdish states in the east (Ahmad 2002: 70).

From 1919 to 1922 the assembly, led by Mustafa Kemal, waged a series of wars against the Greek invasion of Anatolia, suppressed twenty-three domestic rebellions and tried to sideline the Istanbul government in its quest for international support and recognition. Furthermore, these dire conditions were compounded by harsh socioeconomic realities on the ground, which together complicated the Kemalist elite's socioeconomic agenda. In the wake of World War I, Turkey was overwhelmingly an agricultural society: only 0.2 percent of the population worked in manufacturing and 10 percent lived in urban centers. Moreover, the war brought about the emigration, deportation and annihilation of Ottoman minorities, which "removed those responsible for 70 per cent of the capital and 75 per cent of the labour in Turkish industrial enterprises" (Arnold 2012: 371). In the Anatolian countryside, according to one estimate, landownership was so concentrated that 87 percent of the rural population occupied only 35 percent of the cultivable land (Ahmad 2002: 43). There is every reason to assume that after almost a decade of continuous war from the beginning of World War I to the end of the War of Independence in 1922, the land question was even more alarming in the wake of the establishment of the Republic (in 1923). Most of the land and property seized from the deported and exterminated non-Muslim Ottoman subjects was appropriated by Muslim landlords, which caused several land disputes between the landlord class and the incoming immigrant population (Tezel 1986: 332–3). Tenancy was rare; the overwhelming majority of the land-hungry and landless population was heavily indebted to the landlord class, thus subject to relations of usury and involved in sharecropping to be able to meet their subsistence needs (Silier 1981: 15). "Middle peasantry," who were able to produce for their subsistence as well as for the market, were a "very thin" strata of the rural population (Silier 1981: 14). Farms employing wage labor were "extremely rare" (Keyder 1981: 13, 16). The overwhelming majority of commercial landowners were "absentee" landlords, that is, landowners who left the organization of production to sharecroppers and were not interested in investing in land (Silier 1981: 15–16; Tezel 1986: 33–9).

Perhaps more disturbing than its economic consequences, sharecropping was seen by the Turkish elite as an acute political and geopolitical problem. For one thing, "[t]he role of land-hungry peasants in the Bolshevik Revolution" was still "a fresh memory in the minds of many Turkish elites" (Karaömerlioğlu 2000: 124). Indeed, during the Turkish War of Independence (1919–22), the Bolsheviks had been involved in propaganda activities in Anatolia and exercised considerable influence over the socialist/leftist groups (most notably the "People's Group") within the first national assembly (Tunçay 1991: 90; Gökay 1997: 103–5). On the one hand, the existence of socialists and the People's Group within the parliament was the key for the Kemalist elite to obtaining the support of the Soviet Union, which stood out as the only foreign power the Ankara government could possibly rely on for military and financial support against the allied partition of Anatolia.[3] Yet, on the other hand, the assembly was a fairly "heterogeneous" and "unruly" body, exercising unprecedented control over the executive (Zurcher 2004: 159; Koçak 2005: 3, 26). In this context, the People's Group, much to the chagrin of the Kemalist elite, repeatedly radicalized the nationalist agenda, providing what

[3] The principal beneficiary of the Treaty of Sevres that ended the Ottoman Empire was Britain. In addition to granting effective control over Arab lands and Cyprus, the treaty provided Britain with free access to the Straits and the Black Sea, thereby putting the Soviets in a geopolitically insecure position. Combined with the Allied support of the anti-Bolshevik armies in Russia, the Bolsheviks grew increasingly supportive of Turkish nationalists against the Allied partition and the British-sponsored Greek invasion of Anatolia (Gökay 1997: 3; Barlas 1998: 118).

they called people-ist answers to the burning questions of what was to be done and how. For example, they advocated the principle of "occupational representation" and "women's suffrage" in order to open the parliament to interests other than the bureaucratic, commercial and religious male elite and proposed the establishment of popular assemblies/popular courts to mobilize the countryside against foreign enemies (Shaw and Shaw 1977: 351; Tunçay 1991: 90–1).

Of course, none of these demands were accepted in the assembly. And indeed, the nationalists organized around Mustafa Kemal either killed or marginalized the members of the socialist group immediately after the war of independence (1922). Yet, the point remained that the Kemalist elite, under the immense pressures of external reproduction and intense political rivalry, had to develop a competitive people-ist program in order to rapproche the Soviets themselves and to limit the socialist and sultanic influence in the assembly. In other words, although most members of the Kemalist elite originally perceived people-ism as a form of "political barbarism" or "luddite political activity" invented to prevent "progress" (Ahmad 2009: 164), the threat of domestic and external socialism and the need to appeal to and remobilize local/commercial interests as well as a war-weary and impoverished peasantry compelled them to create their own brand of people-ism (Tekeli and Şaylan 1978: 66; Kazancıgil 1981: 51). The first version of a Kemalist populist program, which became the first post-Ottoman constitution in 1921, was born in this context with strong anticapitalist and antibureaucratic undertones. Indeed, "their rhetoric was so radical that European observers initially denounced the Kemalists as Bolsheviks" (Ahmad 1995: 85).

To be sure, the radical character of Kemalist populism would be significantly watered down after the war (Tekeli and Şaylan 1978; Köker 1990: 130, 145). But one critical lesson learned during the war was to continue to guide Kemalist people-ism throughout the early Republican period. That is, although the Kemalist elite would keep claiming that Turkey was not suitable for socialism because it was a "classless" society with no bourgeois or working classes, they would remain well aware that their cunning historical "stagism" had already been proved wrong during the war by socialists both at home and abroad. Therefore, the elite perception of sharecropping and landlessness in the postwar period would be filtered through this wartime trauma of imminent socialism and geopolitical extinction. In order to remedy this, the early Republic was to formulate a historically specific people-ist ideology, which would facilitate and complicate the unfolding of the new "bourgeois" order.

Equally important, the geopolitical situation during the postwar period would make sharecropping look much more unstable and threatening than it actually was. The end of the war in 1922 had hardly brought to an end the international disputes over the new Turkish state. Most notably, the new Turkish state and the Allied Powers could not come to an agreement on two main issues: the status of the oil-rich Mosul region in Southern Kurdistan; and the status of the Turkish Straits. Britain refused to give in to Turkish demands over Mosul, while all the Allied Powers refused to recognize full Turkish sovereignty over the Straits, demanding the Straits be demilitarized and governed by an international commission. Although the official disputes over the Straits and Mosul were (temporarily) concluded during the 1920s in favor of Britain and the Allies, most of the territorial claims and disagreements over the new Turkish state were to last up to the mid-1930s, only to be magnified later by the massive insecurities caused by World War II (Barlas 1998: 123). Therefore, the fledgling Republic, unable to consolidate its borders and under threat by foreign irredentism, remained hard-pressed on the international front and unsatisfied with the international status quo (Barlas 1998: 121, 132–3). The implication is that geopolitical complications before and following the birth of the Republic (in 1923) largely shaped the elite's perception of the land question and of internal threats. The Republican cadres came to perceive landlessness and the relations of personal dependence underlying sharecropping arrangements as the ultimate hothouse for the development of alternate forms of sociality and loyalty, and hence the catalyst of domestic rebellion and foreign intervention (Tezel 1986: 344; Kuruç 1987: 158).

All that said, however, almost paradoxically, the sharecropping landlord also constituted one of the main pillars of the political alliance on which the ruling Republican People's Party (CHP) rested. While sharecropping stood out as the repository of politicocultural forms and identities potentially endangering the state, the sharecropping landlords were one of the main constitutive elements of Republican power in the countryside. Therefore, directly implicated in the establishment and consolidation of the Republican regime was the constitution of a form of production that was insulated from the (geo)politically risky consequences of sharecropping yet not based on a redistributive land reform that could have prevented the underutilization of large land-holdings and the fragmentation of smaller lands (Tezel 1986: 343). Before turning to explain what this new form of production really entailed, I first have to make clear what it did not. This is what I will discuss in the next section.

Industrialization, Monopolization, Peasantization (1923–1945): Kemalism as State Capitalism?

As indicated earlier, most scholars tend to interpret early Republican Turkey, especially its experiment with "etatism," as a form of "state capitalism" that combined elements of market society with state-led economic planning, which is then used to make sense of the manner and the outcomes of the unfolding modernity in Turket. According to Çağlar Keyder, for example, during the early Republican period, the bureaucratic class restructured the social pillars of the modernization project from above by creating a national (industrial) bourgeoisie and a middle stratum of market-oriented peasantry. The result was two-fold. First, "the bourgeoisie exchanged the right to establish ... a civil society for ... the privilege to make money" (Keyder 1987: 82). Second, while the political support extended to the middle peasantry began to generalize the relations of "petty commodity production" in agriculture, it also checked the rapid development of capitalist social relations in the countryside, thereby sanctioning a highly mediated articulation with capitalism. In short, in the absence of a strong bour-geois class and an enterprising stratum of farmers, capitalism had to be reorganized by the state from "above." The weakness of bourgeois agency and the strength of the bureaucracy is then used to explain why the process of capitalist development unfolded only limitedly and protractedly; why the Kemalist Revolution lacked "ideological coher-ence" (e.g. Zurcher 2010: 149–50); why it took an authoritarian "corporatist" form (e.g. Parla and Davison 2004: 30); and why it was largely confined to "superstructural reforms" (e.g. Timur 2001: 106).

In this respect, one may argue that Turkey was hardly an exception to the authoritarian corporatist regimes of interwar Europe: "state capitalism" was precisely what Kemalism's Western European coun-terparts carried out during the interwar period. Nazi restoration in

Germany, for example, was not a "political freeze of or simple reaction" to capitalism, but was underlined by the aim of "rationalizing" capitalism. Against what it conceived to be a "wasteful," "egoistic" and "rentier" capitalism, devoid of social harmony and subject to cycles of boom and bust, the Nazi state aimed to reorient economic life based on totalitarian "productivist" ideologies (Maier 1988: 12–15). It imposed tariffs, established monopolies, regulated the movement of labor, suppressed unions and implemented the worst forms of racism, not to annihilate market relations, but to "rationalize" them. Extraeconomic measures were used to compel and induce producers and employers to "improve" the technological and organizational setup of the production process and deepen the commodification of labor (Jessop 2013: 103). In the face of inflationary pressures, militant trade unions and geopolitical challenges, "the civic ideas of 1789" were totally discarded in favor of a new social order based on authority, discipline and economic renovation (Maier 1987: 77). The fascist commitment "to eradicate 1789 from history" manifested itself clearly "in the care taken by many fascist or semi-fascist regimes to replace the tripartite motto of the French Revolution, 'Liberté, égalité, fraternité,' with reactionary, conservative and authoritarian alternatives such the 'Credere, Obbedire, Combattere' of Italian fascism ... and the 'Travail, famille, patrie' of the Vichy regime" (Landa 2019: 47). Therefore, the important point to establish here is that notwithstanding substantial national differences, state capitalisms of the interwar period attempted to stabilize and improve capitalism, and, by doing so, they obliterated or subordinated the Jacobin interpretations of property and popular sovereignty to the capitalist project. The question to be answered, then, is whether Kemalist modernization can be subsumed under the same rubric of state capitalism.

Throughout the early Republican period, as I discussed earlier, two main (geo)political concerns marked the trajectory of Kemalist agrarian property relations. On the one hand, the fear of rebellion and geopolitical challenges forced the bureaucratic elite to stabilize the countryside and to prevent the expansion of sharecropping arrangements. On the other hand, the sharecropping landlord was one of the main pillars of the Republic, fundamental to the maintenance of the new regime in the countryside. Indeed, the Republic implemented an agrarian policy that reflected this seemingly contradictory amalgamation of interests. By enhancing the status of private property, the first

Republican constitution (in 1924) facilitated the legal consolidation of large estates. Landlords therefore obtained full legal title over their lands. Yet, neither the constitution nor the new Civil Code (in 1926) took any measures to prevent the morcellization of land. Ottoman laws prescribing partible inheritance remained in full force and effect (Tezel 1986: 340–1). More importantly, "the greatest difficulties were encountered in applying the rules relating to land"; consequently, arable land continued to be created and transferred without official registration (Versan 1984: 250; Keyder 1993: 181). This means that there was no political attempt to establish landlord/merchant monopoly over land. Marginal lands of little or no cost were readily available (Keyder 1981: 24). Viewed together, the Kemalist gambit in agriculture opened with two opposing moves. The regime attempted to maintain the minimum basis of peasant subsistence by permitting the expansion and division of small landholdings and, at the same time, officially recognized large sharecropping units, thereby forestalling a redistributive land reform.

As I elaborated in Chapter 4, depending on the transformation of the larger context of social reproduction, the existence of small producers and sharecroppers may not constitute an obstacle to the development of capitalist social relations. Peasants may become market-dependent without losing their land. Peasants may turn into "petty commodity producers" on their own land, provided that their access to land depends on their ability to compete in the marketplace, transform the conditions of production and respond to changes in commodity prices/ relative profits. Yet, it is equally true that in a sociolegal context that drains the peasantry of most of their surpluses through usury and allowing the almost unrestricted division and expansion of land, neither the peasantry nor the sharecropping landlord would be willing or compelled to increasingly depend on the market and able to reorganize/improve production according to the dictates of market competition. In the absence of a transformation of social relations and institutions that would set free alternate sources of credit and food supply, sharecropping peasants would be inherently unwilling or unable to avoid subsistence farming, respond to fluctuating market conditions, transform the conditions of production and incapable of reinvesting in land.

How conducive to capitalism was the emerging agrarian structure? From 1923 to 1929, Turkish agriculture experienced exponential growth under conditions of an open economy (Keyder 1981: 37). The state reduced agricultural taxes, distributed some state-owned lands to the landless and injected substantial loans into the agricultural sector with the hope that the small landholdings would increase production for the market and reduce their extreme dependence on the big land-lords and usurers (Hershlag 1968: 49). Under these circumstances, it seems safe to assume that the peasantry, unburdened by taxes and supported by the state, responded to favorable world market prices by increasing their level of production and surplus taken to the market. Yet, it would be a mistake to interpret the peasants' increased produc-tion for the market as necessarily leading to a "qualitative" transform-ation of their relation to land and production (cf. Keyder 1981: 33). For one thing, the state's attempts at breaking the relations of usury bore no fruit in the countryside: land distribution was too limited to generate a qualitative impact on the peasantry (Tezel 1986: 345) and the plots distributed to a limited number of cultivators were "far less than was required to maintain a family" (Hershlag 1975: 172). Likewise, most of the state-provided credit was used up by landholders with large holdings (Silier 1981: 44–5), and even when the peasantry obtained some access to these funds, most of them had to use these monies to pay off a portion of their debts, instead of investing the money in equipment, fertilizer and irrigation (Hershlag 1968: 113). In these conditions, it would be very hard to assume that majority of peasants increasingly gave up subsistence agriculture, devoted the majority of their labor-time to commodity production and reorganized their labor process according to the dictates of market competition (Duzgun 2017).

Clearly, as Keyder assumes, there must be a segment of the peasantry able to produce commodities relatively independently of the relations of debt and usury. Yet, a closer look at this so-called middle peasantry, which was engaged especially in wheat, tobacco and hazelnut produc-tion, shows that it was barely able to accumulate any surpluses (Tezel 1986: 436). This was the case because foreign and domestic merchants, organized in monopolies and trade associations, were able to collect-ively dictate prices to the peasantry that were much lower than the world average (Silier 1981: 30–1; Tezel 1986: 358–9; Toprak 1988: 22). All in all, throughout the 1920s, the continuing relations of usury and monopoly, combined with the relative availability and divisibility of land, eventually led to a pattern of agricultural development that was not conducive to the initiation of a developmental path based on "petty commodity production." Increases in commodity production were generated not by an intensive growth underlined by a qualitative transformation of the peasants' labor process and increasing dependence on the market, but by an extensive growth based on the expansion of the peasants' traditional survival strategies alongside their limited and occasional engagement with the market (Hershlag 1968: 112; Tezel 1986: 340–1, 434–5).

Throughout the 1920s, then, partly driven by increases in population and partly thanks to the improvements in security and transportation, peasants extended and divided the area under cultivation, yet remained unable or unwilling to develop a logic conducive to the rise of a market-dependent society (Hershlag 1968: 112; Tezel 1986: 340–1). Furthermore, given that there was no alternative source of labor and that the land was expandable and divisible by the peasantry, sharecropping landlords did not develop any systematic interest in supervizing and improving the labor process on large estates (which would otherwise help sharecroppers pay off their debts, thereby causing the landlord to lose their only source of labor supply). On average, 90–95 percent of the land within big estates was left uncultivated (Silier 1981: 16) and sharecropping arrangements on big estates were governed by the same subsistence-first logic that prevailed on small peasant holdings (Tekeli and İlkin 1988: 40, 89).[4]

---

[4] All this does not mean that big estates remained technologically backward. Indeed, the number of tractors in Turkey increased from 220 in 1924 to 2,000 in 1930. Yet, this increase hardly signified the rise of a capitalist landlord class. For one thing, most of these tractors were not bought according to some cost-price calculation, but obtained through state subsidies, which "amounted to close to the full price of the tractor" (Keyder 1981: 25). Also, the tractors had no practical use on large estates run by sharecroppers: in the absence of an alternate and stable labor supply, landlords "were reluctant to adopt the newly available technology, which could not be put to direct use without altering the mode of exploitation. Under conditions of sharecropping, where the grip of the landlord on the small tenant is through a perpetual indebtedness, any technology raising the productivity of the sharecropper threatens to break the cycle of usury. Thus the landlords have to control the level of technology for the perpetuation of their political and economic domination over sharecropping peasants" (Keyder 1981: 25). In any event, most landlords would find the use of tractors increasingly "noneconomical," especially after the Great Depression (Tekeli and İlkin 1988: 84–5) and the government would cease supporting the mechanization in agriculture to preempt the danger of rural unemployment (Hershlag 1968: 111). It should thus occasion no surprise that the number of tractors would drop from

If the Republic of the 1920s was not able to initiate a capitalist growth dynamic in the countryside, it was even less able to do so in the towns. For one thing, the inability/unwillingness of the state to transform agrarian property relations, together with the wartime exhaustion and exodus of non-Muslim populations, rendered the already feeble supply of industrial workers precarious. Most industrial production was carried out through temporary and seasonal peasant-workers, who came to industrial sites for a month or two at the end of the harvest season in order to supplement their household income (Makal 2007: 121; Koç 2013: 193, 213–14). Inevitably, extremely high turnover rates prevailed, undermining the prospects for the capitalist reorganization of industrial production.[5] Given the lack of a skilled and permanent workforce, industrialists had little incentive to invest in labor-saving technology, organize and manage the production process "efficiently," or to increase extremely low wages, which could otherwise have helped to stabilize the supply of labor power (Hershlag 1968: 119). From the 1920s, therefore, "efforts at reviving industrial production were largely hampered by difficulties securing workers and labor scarcity discouraged investments in new industrial enterprises" (Arnold 2012: 371).

2,000 in 1930 to 1,756 in 1948 and "the number of operating tractors barely exceeded one thousand" in 1946 (Keyder 1987: 130).

[5] Indeed, a high turnover rate was a problem in the capitalist West as well. Yet the difference is that while in the contemporary West a high turnover rate was more likely to be caused by a relatively well-established working class that was unhappy with existing wages and working conditions, in Turkey, high turnover rates were much less about low wages and more about "structural" circumstances that inhibited the formation of a permanent commodifiable workforce (Makal 2007: 53). There are several surveys and reports from the 1920s and 1930s pointing to this aspect of the problem. For example, in the coal-rich areas of the Black Sea, the average yearly number of working days for an unskilled miner was from 16 to 22. In a textile factory in Kayseri, 3,000 employees, including women and children, had to be employed in order to maintain a permanent workforce of 2,000. Across the country, annual turnover rates fluctuated between 35 and 75 percent (Hershlag 1968: 118–19, see also Koç 2013: 219). Even in the relatively well-connected commercial and manufacturing centers of Anatolia, such as İzmir, the situation seems not to have drastically differed: "as late as 1948, a textile factory in İzmir hired 2,424 workers for its 3,000-strong workforce, to replace the 2,132 labourers who left that year" (Arnold 2012: 372).

However, despite all these organizational and productive ineffi-ciencies, easy profits could still be made by the nascent bourgeoisie. During the 1920s, besides continuing to seize properties that belonged to emigrating/deported minorities, the bourgeoisie, domes-tic and foreign, received extensive support from the new state eager to create a domestic market and promote industrialization. How successful was the state at compelling and encouraging private actors to invest in and improve productive forces? Despite govern-ment support, private actors invested mainly in industries in which there was virtually no or little competition from imports despite low tariffs (Boratav 1981: 168–9; Hale 1984: 157). Furthermore, polit-ical measures aimed at strategically utilizing subsidies largely failed as local manufacturers circumvented regulations: "companies of paper acquired subsidized goods and sold them to other companies at a profit and then never began production" (Arnold 2006: 87). With easy access to political rents and no compulsion to compete, manufacturers' social reproduction hardly depended on successful commodity production and extending/deepening their hold over scarce reserves of labor power (Tezel 1986: 112). "The rent of protection ... appropriated by the local industrial bourgeoisie ... constitute(d) the basic source of accumulation" (Boratav 1981: 176). Indeed, there were attempts from the ranks of the bureaucracy to "discipline" the bourgeois class, yet to no avail. The bourgeoisie reacted in 1931 to plans that aimed to condition the protection of the internal market to the bourgeoisie's ability to sell in the inter-national market, forcing, among other things, the resignation of the then economics minister and the overhaul of economic policy in conformity with bourgeois interests (Kuruç 1987: 88–9; Şabudak 2004: 72–82; Tekeli and İlkin 2004: 217–18).

In short, during the 1920s, the state was neither able to generalize "petty commodity production," nor to initiate a sociolegal transform-ation that would release labor for permanent absorption in industrial activity. Relatedly and ironically, the state's ability to induce the reorganization of industrial activity according to market imperatives was by and large undermined by the growth of a noncapitalist indus-trial bourgeoisie whose relation to production was handicapped by chronic shortages of labor and the contraction of international markets after 1929. Because the "nascent" bourgeoisie did not invest and comply with developmental objectives, and due to the emergence of new external challenges and opportunities, the state was to directly engage in production from 1932 onward.

If anything, these socioeconomic patterns deteriorated during the Great Depression. Anatolian peasants gave up commodity production all together, reverted to subsistence farming, fell into further debt and increasingly became sharecroppers (Akçetin 2000: 93–8). Surely, in the eyes of the Republican elite, the prevailing destitution in the countryside once again resuscitated the ghost of rebellion (Emrence 2000).[6] Also, the rise of peasant movements during the 1920s in the Balkan countries, especially in Bulgaria, had further aggravated the fear of violent unrest in Turkey, forcing the ruling elite to consider new strategies to restore stability and order after the Great Depression (Karaömerlioğlu 2001: 79). Worse still, the world economic crisis revived geopolitical tensions in the Balkans. Italian and Bulgarian revisionism's return to the region with full force after 1929 heightened the perception of geopolitical threat, the fear of internal instability and the need for industrialization that had haunted the Turkish ruling elite since the 1920s (Barlas 1998: 138–43). While forcing industrialization, the escalating interimperialist rivalry also enlarged the pool of external funds available for industrialization. The Soviets, British and German states, attempting to expand their zones of influence in the Balkans and the Middle East, competitively extended low-interest credit and technical help to Turkey during the 1930s and early 1940s (Hale 1981: 74; Tezel 1986: 430).

Turkish "etatism" was born in this social and international context. What was meant by etatism was never fully clear. On the one hand, by the end of the 1930s, the state emerged as an important, if not the leading, investor and producer in iron, steel, cement, utilities and mining. It nationalized all of the previously built railroads, established state banks and investment agencies, and took back most of the state monopolies that had been run by private actors since the 1920s. On the other hand, however, all this hardly meant that "the private sector was hurt by the expansion of the state sector" (Owen and Pamuk 1999: 19). Although some distributional tensions inevitably existed between

---

[6] The perception of instability and rebellion was so imminent that Mustafa Kemal had to order the creation of an opposition party in 1930 in order to steam off the rising discontent among the rural and urban poor. Yet, even this puppet opposition party gained so much power that Kemal would have to order the party's dissolution only three months after its establishment (Emrence 2000).

the two sides, protection of and incentives for private investment was generous during the etatist period. The state stimulated the growth of private manufacturing enterprise by establishing capital-goods industries, providing the industrial bourgeoisie with subsidized inputs and granting them greater exemptions from customs (Owen and Pamuk 1999: 19). Much more importantly, the state simultaneously gave in to business demands for internal monopolies and external protection. Ever since the 1920s, "infant" industrialists attempted to "organize in cartels in order to prevent overproduction or in order to safeguard the high profit rates they enjoyed" (Keyder 1987: 103). What changed with etatism is that the state, previously unable to prevent business circumvention of productivist policies, began to deliberately encourage monopoly business practices. Etatism "responded positively to (business) demands and permitted the formation of sector-based associations which openly sought to fix prices and avoid competition" (Keyder 1987: 103). The state therefore encouraged monopolization of large industrial enterprises. Yet, at the same time, almost contradictorily, the state imposed additional taxes on mechanization as well, thereby limiting competition and preventing the dissolution of primitive manufacturing enterprises (Aydemir 1979: 454; Tekeli and İlkin 1987: 5). The overall expectation from this seemingly contradictory bundle of economic policies was that rapid industrialization could be achieved without the social costs associated with capitalist industrialization. This was also expected to promote growth and stabilization in the countryside by creating an internal market for raw materials and food, for which demand and prices had fallen since the international crisis.

As pointed out earlier, "distorting" market prices through a variety of political measures and incentives was a key element of all "state capitalisms." From this perspective, one may argue that eliminating competition and granting privileges to the industrial sector in etatist Turkey was hardly an extraordinary measure. What is striking, however, is that while the Turkish state froze competition and secured profits for industrialists, it did nothing to increase permanent labor supply. The state took virtually no measure to close the land frontier and overturn laws of partible inheritance. Peasants could still clear the land at little or no cost and, indeed, "the government aided this trend by actually distributing the land in small plots" (Birtek and Keyder 1975: 454). Furthermore, instead of systematically inducing the rise of a stratum of small commodity producers, which would have increased productivity and gradually released labor from agriculture, state support of agriculture seems to have aimed to stabilize and consolidate the "peasantry." For example, price support programs addressing especially wheat-producing peasants, which Keyder sees as the pioneer of the so-called petty commodity producers, in fact remained "limited, not exceeding 3 per cent of the wheat crop in any given year" (Owen and Pamuk 1999: 22). In other words, "the adverse terms of trade for wheat in the early 1930s were kept more or less constant until the war" (Boratav 1981: 184). In contrast to wheat, tobacco was indeed a major crop, for which the state, through its tobacco monopoly, provided relatively generous price support programs and credit (Boratav 1981: 185). Yet, the state monopoly on tobacco did not attempt to replace powerful commercial agents that were able to dictate much lower prices on the peasantry. Big private actors, buying cheap from the peasantry and selling dear to the state, therefore became the primary beneficiary of the state's encouragement of tobacco production (Silier 1981: 86–8). Unsurprisingly, there was no productivity growth even in major commercial crops produced by the peasantry, such as wheat and tobacco (Koç 1988: 86; Tekeli and İlkin 1988: 56–64). Also, beneath the surface of agricultural growth, sharecropping remained rampant. The sharecropping landlord, producing mainly cotton and beet, made huge profits thanks to state credit and price support programs (Silier 1981: 88), which were in turn spent on luxury consumption, rather than invested in production (Tezel 1986: 439). Relatedly, with peasant surpluses largely accrued to commercial agents and sharecropping landlords, "villagers did not become significant consumers of urban manufacturers" and "the national market (outside the urban areas) . . . [remained] both narrow and thin" (Keyder 1994: 152). Furthermore, these production, investment and consumption patterns inherently inimical to the transition to capitalism were further solidified during World War II under the impact of military mobilization and the forced levy on agricultural produce (Keyder 1983: 140).

Viewed in this light, it seems implausible to contend that the leitmotiv of the state support of agriculture was the creation of a rural capitalist class or the qualitative transformation of agrarian property relations. Instead, the safer argument would be that the state support of agriculture aimed to restore (however limitedly) the minimum conditions for the reproduction of peasant households by preventing seasonal price fluctuations and price speculations (Tekeli and İlkin 1988: 41), and, by doing so, it tried to promote political stability and production for industrialization without changing the essentially "peasant" character of social reproduction.[7] Furthermore, the peasantry was seen as the antidote to the potential threat of working-class and religious radicalism (Karaömerlioğlu 2000: 125). All combined, to create and sustain a peasantry that cultivates a minimum amount of land and is able to produce some surplus for industrialization was the ultimate goal of the etatist agrarian policy. The model countryside for the Kemalist elite was based on a mode of life far away from the tumultuous world of sharecropping relations and that certainly did not resemble the world of restless petty commodity producers.[8]

In short, the development of capitalism in the Turkish countryside seemed neither feasible nor desirable. The flipside of this is that the overall occupational structure and manufacturing investment remained roughly the same till the end of the 1940s,[9] which hints at the persistence of chronic labor shortages in industrial towns. Monopolization and protection of business on the one hand and the unavailability of a permanent work force on the other ultimately created an industrial structure in which "several enterprises continued to exist only thanks to government support and an artificial price structure" (Hershlag 1975: 190). Despite the enactment of highly authoritarian labor regulations and penal laws, industrialists were

[7] The unwillingness to transform agrarian relations along capitalist lines is expressed by a prominent Republican intellectual and bureaucrat as follows:

if a land reform is accomplished in our country, its end result will again be a social polarization under the impact of social differentiation and diversification, which are the tendencies and laws of the system of market economy. Lands given to the peasants will be centralized again in the hands of some farmers and city dwellers because of factors such as debt and price setbacks. For this reason, land reforms are, in fact, far from being an absolute measure to solve land issues. (İsmail Hüsrev Tökin, 1934, quoted in Karaömerlioğlu 2000: 122fn.)

[8] Tellingly, in the 1930s, despite substantial increases in agricultural output, this was achieved not by an "intensive" growth underlined by a qualitative transformation of the peasants' labor process and increasing dependence on the market, but thanks to an "extensive" growth based on demographic growth and the increase of cultivated land (Tekeli and İlkin 1988: 40–1).

[9] About 80 percent of the economically active population continued to be employed in agriculture, while the proportion of industrial employees did not exceed 8 percent of the total (Hershlag 1968: 119). The share of manufacturing in GNP increased from 12 percent in 1923 to 13 percent in 1946 (Owen and Pamuk 1999: 244).

178   Kemalism as Turkish Substitution for Capitalism

either unable or unwilling to intensify their control over the labor supply and the labor process. As a consequence, in industries approved for state support, "investments incurred created additional jobs, but no real progress was made in the level of productivity: the relative increase of output and labor was almost equal' (Hershlag 1968: 106). Productivity being stagnant, there was no ground to offer higher wages to workers. Even in state factories, where better wages could be offered, wages were not high enough to retain workers.[10] "Extremely high" turnover rates consequently prevailed in both state and private factories: workers often quit their jobs simply because they could easily return if they chose. This rendered employers' control over labor that could otherwise have been exercised through recruitment practices totally ineffective. Relatedly, in a context where workers could easily exit and reenter the labor market, the deskilling of labor and the scientific management of the labor process could backfire. Despite the preparation of several reports on how to increase productivity (Akgöz 2021), industrialists were either unable or unwilling to supervise the labor process. "Workers were not fired even after they were fined for absenteeism at various times," and in many industrial plants, there was no well-defined wage policy in place, no clear and accessible system of remuneration that would reward more productive workers and, in some factories, not even proper bookkeeping (Akgöz 2012: 93–111). This signals that industrialists were neither allowed nor compelled to transform "labor power" into "labor," systematically increase the "organic composition of capital" or reduce the "socially necessary labor time" involved in appropriating "surplus value." In such conditions, no industrialist could transform into a "capitalist," that is, a "supervisor and director of the [labor] process, as a mere function, as it were endowed with consciousness and will, of the capital engaged in the process of valorizing itself" (Marx 1996b: 1022).

It must be clear by now that early Republican etatism did not entail the development of "state capitalism." The fear of rebellion and

---

[10] The inability to retain workers becomes even more striking when one considers that industrial wages in Turkey seemed quite high compared to the industrialized countries with much higher levels of labor productivity. For example, according to a German expert who worked in the Beykoz Leather and Shoe Factory in the 1930s, "the labor time spent for tanning a kilo of leather in Germany and Turkey was . . . 12 and 37 minutes respectively, [whereas] wages per kilogram of leather were 9.9 piasters and 9 piasters" (Akgöz 2021: 21).

foreign intervention forced the ruling bloc to deliberately preempt the development of capitalist social relations. The state encouraged peasantization and monopolization as the foundation of a new industrialization strategy. The bureaucratic elite and industrial bourgeoisie allied to form a redistributive noncapitalist economy in which they themselves became the primary beneficiaries. Rural masses lived in destitution, yet the state, unable/unwilling to initiate a systematic transformation of the rules of accessing land, attempted to maintain their minimum basis of subsistence, and, by doing so, it defined social reproduction away from the market. The construction of a market society was not central to the early Republican modernization project. Instead, as I will show in the next section, the Turkish ruling elite, from the very inception of the Republic, embarked on an alternative project of modernization. By linking the population's social reproduction to their schooling and conscription, the ruling bloc created an economy underlined by and adequate for the reproduction of Jacobin forms of exploitation and mobilization.

The Army, the School and the "Terror": Redefining Property and the Citizen-Turk

If the Republic was not the political expression of an "incomplete" capitalist transformation or a "weak" bourgeoise, how to make sense of the early Republican road to modernity? What to make of Fred Halliday's remarks on the world historical significance of the agenda, contradictions and questions posed by the Turkish Revolution? In other words, how can we explain the oft-cited "paradoxical" character of the Turkish Revolution: its "ad-hoc secular-military absolutism" and "futurist democratism" (Dumont 1984: 28); its elitism and peasant-based populism (Karaömerlioğlu 2000: 116); its simultaneous emphasis on individuality and community (Kaya and Tecmen 2010: 31); its "western, democratic orientation and an inward-looking, xenophobic worldview" (Aytürk 2011: 308); and its repeated oscillation between universal and exclusionary notions of citizenship (İnce 2012)?

I suggest that what makes the Turkish modernization a revolution and lent its "contradictory" politicocultural baggage was rooted in the uneven and combined development of Jacobinism on Turkish soil. The Kemalist elite took three critical Jacobin steps at the very outset of the Republican period: they introduced conscription, public education and universal suffrage[11] (however imperfectly in a two-tier election system) as the foundation of the rights and duties of all Republican subjects. While the state's guaranteeing of private property tied the peasantry to the land and consolidated sharecropping relations, hence solidifying noncapitalist social relations in the countryside, the introduction of compulsory education, conscription and general suffrage provided the contours of an alternative model of social and ideological modernization. Put differently, the early Republic embraced political equality and universal suffrage in an utterly noncapitalist society, that is, in a society wherein the state remained the main and direct source of income and property. In such a context, wherein access to state and property was, at least in principle, universalized among politically equal subjects, the Turkish elite had to continuously reinterpret the conditions of having property and being equal. The Republic's emphasis on compulsory public education (Article 87 of the 1924 constitution) and universal conscription (enacted through the Military Service Law of 1927) was particularly important in this respect, for while the Turkish elite were unable or unwilling to initiate an organized attack on peasants' customary rights on land, they could link the enjoyment of these rights to peasants' protection of the "fatherland" and their disciplining through a centralized system of education. Given the social and geopolitical turmoil, improving the state without enclosure arose as the most urgent task, which the Republican regime tried to deliver by linking the peasants' access to land to their acquisition of skills and allegiance conducive to the social and geopolitical reproduction of the ruling elite. As such, political and geopolitical utility for the state, instead of market competition, once again, provided subjects with access to property, means of subsistence and civic status. Conscription and public education would consequently be set as the most legitimate criteria to determine one's eligibility to participate in the political community and to have access to the means of subsistence and property.

Without structural change in the rules of accessing land, using education and conscription as a way to facilitate modernity was a double-edge sword, however. On the one hand, both measures had to resort to a somewhat egalitarian and populist understanding of

---

[11] Women's suffrage was enacted in 1930 at the municipal level and in 1934 at the parliamentary level.

political community in order to broaden the mass base and increase the geopolitical competitiveness of the Kemalist regime. On the other, the potential radicalization of people-ism had to be restrained by hierarchically requalifying the rules of participation in the Republican moral economy. For, in the absence of a "self-valorizing" economic sphere, every citizen, who was educated and who proved his political allegiance by doing military service, was entitled (at least in principle) to become an equal participant in the political and economic establishment. A potential increase in the number of politically equal citizens necessarily meant a more equal sharing of the state-generated rents and income. The Republican elite thus had to hierarchically redefine equality and civility by continuously requalifying the rules of participation in the Republican political economy. This became an acute problem, especially in the face of the absorption of greater numbers of commoners into public education and the resultant glut in bureaucratic cadres.[12] The rules of accessing the state, which was by far the main source and generator of income, had to be repeatedly conditioned to credentials other than citizenship and merit. Thus, the institutionalization of military service and public education had direct and immediate implications for the economic structure and would inevitably lead to (geo)politically informed "exclusions" from the theoretically universalized political space, most notably, of Kurds and non-Muslims.

As I discussed in Chapter 4, significant steps had been taken to universalize conscription and public education before the Republic. Nevertheless, "draft evasion and army desertion remained widespread and socially acceptable" until the 1920s (Peker-Dogra 2007: 58) and public education never penetrated the primary school level; therefore, the lower ulema and semiindependent Islamic brotherhoods (*tarikats*) continued to hold considerable sway over the education of the masses (Winter 1984: 184). Traditionally, primary education, funded by land and property that belonged to charitable foundations (*vakıfs*), provided students with access to minor positions in the political and religious establishments. The heads of religious brotherhoods (*sheikhs*), together with nonreligious notables (*aghas*), exercised considerable power over the rural populace and made up the local power

---

[12] "In 1930, 34 percent of the budget went for salaries paid to civil servants, whose number was constantly increasing in the 1920s without any consideration for the financial capacity of the state" (Hershlag 1968: 68).

structure in the Ottoman provinces (Mardin 2006: 202). Since the Tanzimat, the Ottoman ruling elite had to some extent undermined the independent power of sheikhs by exercising greater control over vakıf revenues (Barnes 1974: 37) and by subjugating and coopting nonreligious notables to the central administration (Mardin 2006: 202). Deprived of independent sources of revenue and powerful non-religious allies, most dervish orders were already weakened by 1923. All that said, however, Kurds and non-Muslim Ottoman subjects stood out as exceptions all along the way. Non-Muslim Ottoman subjects, thanks to their links to foreign powers, successfully resisted universal conscription and retained their autonomous schools until 1914, which not only made them the usual victims of state violence, but also led to their marginalization in the emerging Republican order (Zurcher 1999). Likewise, Kurdistan remained relatively unscratched in the face of Ottoman centralization attempts. In Kurdistan, political and religious power holders (often the same person), with relatively independent sources of income, remained in power, and, relatedly, landlessness and sharecropping relations were more common in Kurdistan than in any other region (Keyder 1981: 13, 19). Consequently, while relations of personal dependence prevailed and persisted in the region, centralist measures like public education and conscription never took root before the Republic.

Given that religion was deeply submerged in relations of rule and property in Kurdish-dominated eastern and southeastern regions, the Republican attempt at transforming religious institutions would simultaneously mean transforming property relations, and vice versa. Indeed, it is precisely for this reason that the Republican elite increasingly framed the "agrarian question" as an ethnoreligious one. Sharecropping was increasingly associated with religious reactionism and Kurdishness, while Turkishness meant peasantization, stabilization and secularization. As one prominent Republican bureaucrat put it,

wherever small land ownership emerged, the people [in the East] wanted to rely on the government, and in such places settled administration and schooling, and therefore [the] Turkish [language], took root. Wherever the aghas and sheikhs predominated, the land and villages there passed to the control of the aghas, and administration and schooling were withdrawn from those places and in those regions Kurdish turned out to be the native language of the people. (Şevket Süreyya Aydemir, quoted in Karaömerlioğlu 2000: 129)

It was indeed this intertwining character of religion, ethnicity and the agrarian question that made many scholars perceive secularization and nationalism as the foundation stone of Turkish modernization (e.g. Berkes 1964; Gellner 1997). In this respect, nationalism and secularization should not be seen as "superstructural" attempts at transformation, but as a development and mobilization strategy peculiar to Jacobinism (cf. Webb 2007). Republican secularism and nationalism were born of an effort to turn land and property into a right for the conscripted and educated subjects of the Republic. While opening and restraining the access of the masses to the state, secularization and nationalization were also class acts that aimed to peasantize the countryside, improving the transmittability of the state's educative and geopolitical message to the agrarian masses.[13]

The first powerful centralization attempt was undertaken in 1924 with the unification and centralization of the school system. While the legislation abolished all religious schools, it also set Turkish as the only medium of instruction, thereby undermining the use of Arabic and Kurdish. In 1925, the state outlawed all religious orders, lodges and ceremonies, and criminalized religious titles apart from those endowed by the state's newly established Directorate of Religious Affairs (*Diyanet*). Likewise, from 1925 onward, a series of new laws proscribed clothing and headgear associated with hierarchies of the old religious and political establishment. The new Turkish Civil Code completed the unification of the legal system under state control, secularizing the last residues of religious regulation, especially with regards to marital and family law. In 1926, the Muslim lunar calendar was replaced by the Gregorian solar calendar. In 1928, the state introduced and enforced for all public communications the use of the new Turkish alphabet based on Latin script, replacing the previously used Persian-Arabic script. The same year, the constitutional clause that declared Islam as the state religion was removed. In 1935, the

---

[13] The fact that the so-called religious superstructure was central to those activities necessary to the reproduction of social life undermines the widely held assumption that the Kemalist vision of modernization was merely a modernization of culture or values, rather than of social structure (e.g. Anderson 2008). Trimberger tends to concur with this view by stressing that the "cultural reforms transformed the class base of the political regime, for they destroyed the institutional foundation for the power, wealth, and status of the traditional elite, and were a necessary prerequisite for recruiting a new industrial, managerial, and commercial elite" (Trimberger 1972: 200).

weekly holiday was shifted from Friday to Sunday. In 1937, secularism entered the constitution as an undisputable and unchangeable principle.

No wonder that resistance to the Republican attempts at political and religious centralization was fierce in Turkish Kurdistan. Of eighteen major revolts that broke out between 1924 and 1938, seventeen took place in the Kurdish-dominated eastern and southeastern regions. Combined with new geopolitical fears related to the British and French presence in the Middle East, Kurdistan caused a continuous perception of imminent geopolitical threat and a "civil war-like" situation during the interwar years, whose impact on the Republican psyche would, in many ways, be comparable to that of the war of independence (Tunçay 2010: 134–5). All this ultimately fed on itself through the interwar years, turning Kurdistan into the Republican powder keg, a constant target of the Kemalist "Terror." The threat of extinction forced many Kurdish notables to submit to the reforms. Indeed, if they were able to prove their allegiance to the central administration, notables could still maintain their lands and acquire an upper hand to defeat local rivals; therefore, cooptation was more likely than sheer suppression (McDowall 2004: 399). When cooptation did not work out, however, rebellions were met by the worst forms of suppression, ranging from the issuance of countrywide emergency laws to mass killings and forced deportations. The Kemalist Terror, just like its French ancestor, did not usher in an extensive land reform, however. Three laws, enacted by the Kemalist regime in 1930, 1934 and 1937, either expropriated the lands of only the most rebellious politicoreligious notables or they were limited to redistributing minimum amounts of state-owned lands to the peasantry (Barkan 1980). Either way, the ultimate point of land redistribution was not a land reform per se, but to punish rebelliousness and restore the minimum conditions of subsistence so that the link between the state's geo(political) pedagogy and peasant reproduction could be established.

Given the absence of an economic sphere, the marginalization of non-Muslims and the (geo)political threats posed by Kurds (real or perceived), it is not surprising that the Republican elite hierarchically redefined equality and civility by continuously reasserting ethnic and secular differences among "equals." While Turkishness, in principle, was defined by the Republican regime as a legal, civic and voluntarist citizenship category, in practice, it became a dual category that simultaneously encompassed "real citizens" and "potential citizens"; while the former represented the secular "Turks," the latter referred to the "untrustworthy" non-Muslims and Kurds. Needless to say, only real citizens were able to obtain bureaucratic positions, while potential citizens were tacitly yet systematically excluded from the state service. Likewise, in the private sector, most companies were required to replace non-Muslim Turkish workers with "Turks," and non-Muslim Turkish businessmen were subjected to crushingly discriminatory taxation practices (Bayır 2013: 122–3). Yet, despite all this, it is equally important to note that the Republican elite did not categorically reject the non-Turkish subjects, but saw them as "would-be-Turks." That is, while the Republican elite presented Turkishness as a unifying, secularizing and liberating force, associated with "free" peasantry, they identified other ethnoreligious groups with a sort of "false consciousness," that is, people who forgot their Turkishness as a result of centuries of "oppression" caused by the local religious authorities, sharecropping landlords and imperial powers (Karaömerlioğlu 2000: 129; İnce 2012: 45–6). Comparatively speaking, then, unlike Nazism and fascism, which attempted to annihilate the "man-the-citizen" in favor of the "man-the-improver," Kemalism, at least in principle, continued to adhere to a universalist conception of citizenship. Why?

As argued earlier, Nazism resorted to authoritarianism and racial segregation to facilitate an "organized capitalism." In the new Turkish Republic, however, property was much less a right enjoyed by those who used property "productively" and much more a privilege for those who (geo)politically served the nation. Relatedly, since a capitalist space (wherein the right to "improve" property overrides the right to equality) was socially and geopolitically unfeasible, Kemalism had to find new ways in which the right to property could be contained as well as reinforced. This is precisely why Kemalism, in contrast to fascism or Nazism, could still have a sympathy for radical conceptions of equality and claim the sharing of the "universal" values of "civilization" while continuously reinterpreting the manner of their implementation in hierarchical ways (e.g. Salmoni 2004).

The Village Institutes (VIs) were a case in point. The VIs, established in 1937, aimed to create a stratum of peasant-teachers who would act as a "peasant intelligentsia" as well as teach the peasantry in village schools. The peasant-teachers were not allowed to leave the countryside, therefore they were expected to stay within their own class and "never give up advocating the interests of the class from which [they] came" (Karaömerlioğlu 1998: 71). The VI graduates were planned to be one of the main agents of the Republican campaign for rural stabilization, Turkification and secularization. Unsurprisingly, in order to achieve these objectives, the architects of VIs emphasized the importance of learning how to struggle "against the hardships of nature" and to overcome "ignorance" rather than transforming agrarian property relations (Karaömerlioğlu 1998: 60). The "problem of low productivity" and poverty was thought to be rooted in the mere lack of "human will, voluntarism, and work with enthusiasm, devotion, diligence and passion," rather than the structure of property relations (Karaömerlioğlu 1998: 60). The flipside of this was that overcoming economic backwardness and political reactionism through education was not based on the teaching of values informed by productivist market principles, but the selective inculcation of radical citizenship practices. As one of the founders of VIs put it, the institutes and public schools should neither create "bookish intellectuals" nor merely teach techniques of production, which by themselves would be a "disaster" for the country. Rather they should teach peasants how to gain and exercise their rights so that "nobody could insult and 'exploit' them" (I. H. Tonguç, quoted in Aytemur 2007: 102). The spread of values such as "freedom of thought, freedom of expression, and equal rights which had been the well-known slogans of the French Revolution" were seen as essential to the elimination of differences that would otherwise undermine the social order (Aytemur 2007: 105–6). The Kemalist insistence on hard work, human will and voluntarism as transformative principles therefore did not hint at the rise of a "capitalist work ethic" (cf. Karaömerlioğlu 1998: 60). Instead, despite their essentially conservative agenda, the Republican elite, in the absence of a productivist space, had to engineer and contain a Jacobin citizenship ethic so that peasant labor and bodies could be expanded and tapped in ways to reproduce the Republican order.[14]

One implication is that, despite tacitly and persistently postponing their realization, Kemalism's official embracement of equality and democracy could still be used by the lower classes to radicalize these

---

[14] For a systematic analysis of the connection between the Turkish education system (1923–50) and Republican conception of equality, see Salmoni (2004).

concepts from within the official ideology.[15] This was in stark contrast to Nazi political theory, for example, which completely banished parliament and the rights of the individual in favor of a "spiritually driven" *Volk* and *Fuhrer* (Shilliam 2009: 175). Thus, while in Nazi Germany the room for popular negotiation, mobilization and sovereignty was completely obliterated in favor of hierarchy and productivity, Kemalism's bureaucratic elitism could still potentially turn into populist radicalism. Perhaps the clearest expression of this Janus-faced character of Turkish Jacobinism was people-ism, one of the main official principles of Kemalism. As mentioned earlier, the Kemalist elite, under the immense pressures of external reproduction and intense political rivalry, had to develop a competitive people-ist program during the war of independence. To be sure, the radical character of Kemalist people-ism would be significantly watered down after the war. The Kemalist elite turned people-ism by and large into a conservative phenomenon, a means to negating the existence of class differences and asserting the "indivisibility" of the nation (Köker 1990: 130, 145). Yet, in an economy driven by political redistribution of the sources of income, the lower classes could still raise their stake (as they would in the 1960s and 1970s) by reinterpreting the Kemalist negation of class differences as a blueprint for a politically more equal, if not classless, society. Kemalism, an essentially conservative and elitist venture, could potentially be led astray by the lower classes, and turn into a breeding ground for radical forms of political equality and citizenship.

Conclusion: Kemalism as a Turkish–Jacobin Synthesis

The new Republican state substituted the relations of market society within a semi-institutionalized space left over by the Young Turk

---

[15] For example, the Kemalist attempt to create a peasant intelligentsia through VIs more often than not 'created a type of student who happened to be too disobedient and self-confident despite the mainstream norms of the Single Party regime'. This also partly explains why 'many graduates of the VIs ... took part in progressive organizations and trade unions in the late 1960s and 70s' (Karaömerlioğlu 1998: 70) For a detailed survey of how the populism of the VIs became a challenge to Kemalist people-ism see also Aytemur 2007: chapter 5. Also, for the leftist interpretations of Kemalism, see Türkeş 2001.

Revolution. The act of regenerating Young Turk forms provided a shortcut to compensate for the institutions of social reproduction required for the capitalist path to modernity. Through this process of substitution, a combined political economy was produced, leading to the emergence of novel modes of appropriation and redistribution. Universal conscription and universal education provided the substitute for capitalist property and in the meanwhile, made Kemalist nationalism and secularism, alongside a Turkified Islam, the ultimate geocultural expressions of this process of substitution. In this sense, Kemalism carried the Ottoman Jacobin project to its logical conclusion. The state elite instituted education, Turkification, secularization and the militarization of Republican subjects as the ultimate basis of their social reproduction. In theory, this undertaking never relinquished its claim for the role of the individual and popular sovereignty in the making of "civilization" (whereas the totalitarian-corporatist regimes in Western Europe, to which Kemalism is often compared, aspired to eradicate the most progressive aspects of modernity in order to deepen and rationalize capitalism). Yet, given the noncapitalist character of prevailing property relations and in the face of (geo)political uncertainties, it endlessly racialized, militarized and secularized the politicocultural conditions of being civic, equal and modern. The main principles of Kemalism, etatism, people-ism, nationalism and secularism were consolidated in this context, leading to the emergence of an alternative regime of accumulation and an alternative modernity.

Overall, then, the specificities of the Turkish Revolution were rooted in the uneven and combined development of Jacobinism on Turkish soil. Kemalism was neither Turkish only, nor French, nor British. It was a combined response to the historical accumulation of the conditions of comparative backwardness. By effectively combining Jacobinism with the sociointellectual resources of a Turkish–Islamic milieu, Kemalism set a new model of authoritarian modernization, appropriation and popular mobilization that did not require the commodification of the means of life (at least for a while). As such, at a time when colonial powers sought to impose their rule in the Middle East, the Republican cadres set a relatively successful example of state-making, showing the feasibility of an alternative project of rationalization to the rest of the post-Ottoman (and Iranian) elites. For example, state elites in Arab lands were already prone to implementing reforms of Kemalist-type given "the intellectual atmosphere in which they had grown up, in schools of a western type or under the Young Turks in Constantinople." The relative success of Republican state-building in Turkey further reinforced this reformist orientation, exercising

a great influence over the political minds of the Arabs, not only because of the success of the Turks in beating back the encroachments of Europe, but because there still remained profound ties, of religion, a shared history and often a blood relationship between Arabs and Turks, and still more because of their uncompromising statement of the rights and [indivisibility] of the nation. (Hourani 1983: 296)

Thus, the Turkish Revolution and the early Turkish Republic itself became a spatiotemporal force that extended the uneven and combined development of Jacobinism into the Middle East (an analysis of which is properly a task for a separate book).[16]

---

[16] For an analysis of the transnational character of Kemalism, see Clayer et al. (2019) and Amit (2017: chapter 5).

6 | *Reinterpreting Capitalist Modernity à la Turca*

Having shown the Jacobin origins of Ottoman/Turkish path to modernity, what awaits resolution in this chapter is the historicization of the rise and consolidation of capitalist modernity in Turkey. The chapter will open by locating the origin and protracted development of capitalism in Turkey in the post-World War II period. I will show how new social and international circumstances induced the development of capitalist social relations, and how the initial Kemalist-Jacobin project and "traditional" forms of sociality were reinvented by different actors to contest and produce capitalism. In so doing, I will not presume the dominance of capitalism from the very beginning. Instead, I will take capitalist development as a process and outline its contradictory reproduction and expansion in the womb of old society. I will show how the preexistent social relations, institutions and values rooted in the early Republican experience (alongside the lateness and international context of capitalist transition) fostered and complicated the development of capitalist social relations in postwar Turkey.

Indeed, recognizing the contradictory coexistence of capitalism and Jacobinism will facilitate a new interpretation of the sociological-comparative character of Turkish modernity of the postwar period. The conventional explanations of postwar Turkish modernity tend to reproduce the methodological and historical assumptions used to analyze the earlier periods in Turkish history. For example, Şerif Mardin (2006: 62–3) describes the postwar Turkish socioeconomic system as "late neo-patrimonialism," a patrimonial system with "an increasing number of characteristics of capitalism." The political "center," according to Mardin, fostered the growth of a new class of entrepreneurs, yet the penetration of these new social elements into the center was not strong enough to change the balance of forces at the apex of the state. As a consequence, power, rather than economic production, remained the defining feature of Turkish political and economic life, hence the underdevelopment of liberal democratic conceptions of rule and governance. In like fashion, Heper (1985) and Kazancıgil (1994) emphasize the "timidity" of the bourgeois classes vis-à-vis the strength of state cadres, which made impossible the development of an "independent" civil society based on market relationships and economic rationality. Buğra (1994) and Öniş (1992) formulate a milder version of the "weak" bourgeoisie argument. Well aware of the role that the state played in the industrialization of the East Asian "tigers," they highlight the lack of a long-term industrial strategy on the part of the state cadres, which in turn led the bourgeois classes to engage in "rent-seeking activity." Eventually, they contend that what characterized Turkish society and its nonliberal ways of modernity was not the "strength" of the state per se, but a market-repressing state, instead of a "market-augmenting" one, limiting the "self-confidence" of the Turkish bourgeoisie. Keyder (1987) seems to agree with this view, as he sees bourgeois domination only in the economic sphere, with political and cultural life shaped by the rather authoritarian practices of the state cadres. This pertains to the "disinterestedness" of the bourgeois classes in enlarging the politicocultural sphere in Turkey, a consequence of their peripheral integration into the capitalist world economy.

Either way, be it the peripheral character of capitalism or the lack of indigenous sources of "proper" capitalist development, one of the main theoretical and historical issues that I diagnosed earlier equally applies to the analyses of the postwar period. That is, in searching for an explanation for the "fall" of the liberal democratic project in postwar Turkey, existing analyses reproduce idealized conceptions of bourgeois agency. The bourgeoisie can neither been seen as the transhistorical carrier of capitalist social relations nor can it be seen as the pioneer of liberal democracy. Contemporary history is replete with examples that show that even in the presence of relatively developed capitalist relations and institutions, more often than not industrialists themselves have jeopardized the further development of market relations that would have subjected them to the pressures of international economic competition (Chaudry 1993; Chibber 2005). Likewise, the consolidation of capitalist social relations hardly requires or presupposes the introduction of liberal political institutions. A diversity of regimes, state forms and ruling-class alliances are perfectly compatible with securing bourgeois predominance in political life (e.g. Blackbourn and Eley 1984; Bromley 1994). Indeed, once

I unravel the transhistorical association of the bourgeoisie with capitalism and liberal democracy and assert the distinctiveness of Jacobinism as a historically specific path, I will be able to advance a new historical narrative of the initial development and ultimate consolidation of capitalism in Turkey. This will not only provide a series of new explanations as to why Turkish modernity in the postwar period assumed the character that it did, but will also shed new light on the subsequent trajectory of Turkish modernity of the last twenty years.

Land and Democracy: World War II and the Prelude to Multiparty Politics

If we did not bring the democratic regime in 1945–46, then there could have been a bloody revolution.

İsmet İnönü, 1969[1]

I argued in Chapter 5 that the Kemalist elite viewed sharecropping relations as the harbinger of ethnoreligious separatism, proletarianization and foreign intervention. These concerns would reach their peak once the long-expected war finally broke out. During most of World War II, Turkey pursued a meticulous neutrality policy. The war had to be avoided at all costs not only because of the looming threat of German invasion, but also due to the fact the political elites were convinced that in case of war, no matter whose side Turkey was on, the Soviets would eventually occupy Turkey either as enemies or "liberators" (Aydın 1999: 105). Staying out of the war did not spare Turkey from the socioeconomic costs of preparation for war. Military expenditures increased from 30 percent of the budget in 1938 to 54 percent in 1942, while the number of conscripts increased tenfold, amounting to 1 million men in 1942 out of a total population of 17.8 million (Aydın 1999: 69). This, in turn, resulted in sharp decreases in production levels, skyrocketing inflation, and hoarding and black marketeering.[2] The state tried several measures in order to

---

[1] Quoted in Karaömerlioğlu (2006: 102).
[2] Between 1940 and 1945, industrial production decreased by 33 percent, agricultural production by 42 percent (Boratav 2003: 85). Inflation rose roughly five times between 1938 and 1945, which is an extraordinary increase "given the fact that even in countries actually in war prices increased 20 to 35 per cent only" (Karaömerlioğlu 2006: 98).

provision the army, prevent food shortages and restrain inflation, such as strict price-wage controls, forced government purchases, obligatory work practices, prolonged working hours and the introduction of a series of devastatingly high taxes.

Wartime military mobilization and economic measures led to widespread grievances in the countryside and towns. Peasants were conscripted; they were subjected to extra taxes; their draft animals were confiscated; their produce was forcefully sold at below-market prices to the state; and they were forced to work on road construction and in coal mines (Pamuk 1988: 100–7; Karaömerlioğlu 2006: 94). Large landowners, in principle, were not spared from wartime agricultural taxes, but they were able to evade government demands by bribing government officials and could still benefit from rising prices and black markets (Owen and Pamuk 1999: 25). This points to the further strengthening of large landowners' relative position vis-à-vis the peasantry, and their increasing capacity to perpetuate the sharecropping debt-cycle and relations of dependency in the countryside (Van der Lippe 2005: 86). In towns, urban dwellers deeply resented the government's freezing of wages and salaries, the rationing of basic necessities, and the rise of a new group of rich merchants who benefited from wartime inflation and black markets (Karaömerlioğlu 2006: 101, 98).

Social discontent and fiscal difficulties became particularly alarming after 1941, which forced the government to issue *Varlık Vergisi*, a onetime emergency wealth levy on leading merchants, industrialists and large landowners. The levy's declared aim was to "renew the faith of the people in the government" by "compelling those who amassed inflated (wartime) profits ... to participate in the sacrifices demanded by the extraordinary circumstances ... to an extent commensurate with their profits and capacity" (Van der Lippe 2005: 82). Despite being formulated in nondiscriminatory language, however, the levy was applied mostly to the non-Muslim minorities,[3] which was often

---

[3] Thanks to the wealth levy, state revenues increased by a third in 1943 (Keyder 1987: 113). The rate of taxation of non-Muslims amounted to ten times the rate of Muslims. Non-Muslims were charged 53 percent of the total revenue raised by the wealth tax, foreigners 10.5 percent and Muslims 36.5 percent (Van der Lippe 2005: 85). Many non-Muslims, given short notice to raise cash, were forced to sell their properties and if they failed to pay the tax, they were deported to a labor camp in Eastern Anatolia (Owen and Pamuk 1999: 26). Of the 1,400 people who were sent to the labor camp, none were Turkish Muslims (Van der Lippe 2005: 85).

justified by a typically Jacobin argument reminiscent of the Young Turk times: "for centuries Turks had fought to protect the land and the people while the minorities, who were exempt from service in the army, had time to enter business and accumulate wealth." Thus, the wealth tax, "because of their previous exemptions, should demand more from the minorities" (Van der Lippe 2005: 83). In short, faced by military threats from outside and political pressures from below, the Turkish state elite, once again, sacrificed the non-Muslim propertied classes on the altar of the citizen-soldier.

Varlık Vergisi provided (temporary) populist relief to the regime of accumulation in place, and while doing so, it reinforced the economic position of a group of favored Turkish Muslim merchants. Yet, it is important to bear in mind that Varlık Vergisi "seriously damaged business confidence" in general, raising widespread suspicion even among the Turkish propertied classes, who feared that such an arbitrary and heavy-handed taxation practice could one day also target them (Keyder 1987: 113). The fear was further magnified in 1945 when the Republican People's Party (CHP), forced by (geo)political circumstances, attempted to legislate a new land reform. At two major international conferences held by the Allied Powers in 1945, Soviet demands for territorial concessions in eastern Turkey and the need for Allied supervision of the Turkish Straits were acknowledged (Van der Lippe 2005: 127–32). Faced with Soviet hostility and let down by Britain and the United States, the CHP was forced to continue military mobilization even after the war. In this context, the CHP leaders designed a new land reform bill to preempt peasant reaction caused by continuing military mobilization and poverty (Karaömerlioğlu 2000: 131).

What differentiated the reform bill of 1945 from previous limited land reform experiments was that for the first time in Republican history, the bureaucratic elite was going beyond the mere distribution of state-owned lands and was risking alienating the landowning class by proposing nationalization of all landed property in excess of 500 dönüms (125 acres) and distributing to sharecroppers and land-hungry peasants the land that they tilled (Lewis 1975: 475; Tezel 1986: 351–7). In the face of fierce landlord reaction within the CHP, the full promises of the land reform bill never came to fruition; its implementation was halted until 1947 and the bill was significantly altered in 1950, consequently losing much of its teeth against the wealth and status of the propertied classes. Although ultimately unsuccessful, however, the reform bill was to become the last straw to break the ruling-class coalition: the ruling bloc was irreversibly shattered after the bill, with merchants and landowners beginning to loudly challenge the dominance of the "radical" bureaucrats within the CHP (Ahmad 1977: 11).

If the peasantry could not be granted land, they could, however, be endowed with democracy. Put another way, the CHP, unsuccessful at improving the conditions of peasant subsistence through land reform, could still try to regain popular support and secure the regime's (geo)political reproduction by devising a controlled transition to multiparty politics. The CHP leaders announced the opening of the era of direct elections in order to preempt "any kind of radical solutions that might (otherwise) come from below" (Karaömerlioğlu 2006: 102). Squeezed by military pressures from without and social discontent from within, the CHP eventually split in 1946 to give birth to the Democrat Party (DP), both as a shock absorber and competitor. The DP was founded by a group of nouveau riche businessmen and big landlords. This fact made the Republicans believe that the DP would not be able to obtain popular support and would be easily marginalized given the CHP's control of the state apparatus (Karpat 1964: 51). However, the DP won a decisive victory in the 1950 elections. Given its provincial roots and the fact that the Republican Party was held responsible for the poverty and authoritarianism of the last two decades, the DP proved much more successful at "mobilizing large segments of the rural and lower urban groups and set them against the Republicans" (Karpat 1964: 50).

The multiparty politics, begun in 1950, would bring about two important implications for the decades to follow. First, the rise of electoral politics would eventually lead to a process resulting in the competitive undoing of the Jacobin project, transforming the alternative political economy and subjectivity that Kemalists sought to establish during the interwar years. Second, interparty competition would operate under such intense pressures for upward social mobility that the terms of the transition to capitalism would be greatly shaped and complicated by the demands of the peasantry and urban poor. This is the argument to which I turn in the following section.

New World Order, Petty Commodity Production and the Transition to Capitalism

Greece and Turkey, without financial and other aid from either the United States or Great Britain, may become Soviet puppets in the near future.

Foreign Relations of the United States Report, 1947[4]

The leaders of the DP had fiercely opposed a radical redistribution of land in 1947, ultimately succeeding in overturning the original land reform bill. Yet they did not want agrarian relations to remain unchanged (Tezel 1986: 354). In fact, DP cadres, and above all, Adnan Menderes, the DP leader and a rich landlord from the Aegean region, came to favor an agrarian transformation that would not violate the sanctity of private property (i.e. the sanctity of large land-holdings) but would nevertheless tackle the politically dangerous and economically unsatisfactory state of agrarian relations. To revise the land law in ways mutually compatible with the interests of landlords and peasants was indeed a difficult undertaking (Ahmad 1977: 133–4). This was a burning task, especially because the DP's electoral success was achieved thanks to its appeal to the peasantry, and its recurring promise that the DP was not a "class" party but "represented all those who wanted to put an end to one-party rule" (Ahmad 1977: 16–17). In this context, it is no wonder that capitalist social relations, if created, were to be embedded within a "peasant" shell.

Yet, besides these domestic concerns, what made the state and sharecropping landlords more willing in the postwar period to initiate a capitalist growth dynamic was the radical transformation of geopolitical circumstances. As mentioned earlier, after the war, the Turkish army remained mobilized due to the perception of imminent Soviet attack. The state continued to devote 60 percent of its budget to defense expenditures. Coupled with the Greek Civil War (1946–9), the acquisition of nuclear weapons by the Soviets (1946) and the increasing importance of Middle Eastern oil fields, toward the 1950s, the United States (albeit initially reluctant to extend protection) was increasingly convinced that maintaining such a large army would cause fiscal and social destabilization in Turkey, which could eventually lead to the installation of a pro-Soviet government, thereby severely

---

[4] https://history.state.gov/historicaldocuments/frus1947v05/d33.

endangering US interests in the region (Van der Lippe 2005: 168–9). While this growing US recognition of Turkey's geopolitical importance assured Turkey against Soviet military pressure, it also allowed considerable leeway for the DP to initiate structural transformation in agriculture without being much concerned about the geopolitical troubles this transformation might have brought about. With outside pressure alleviated and foreign military assistance extended, the ruling elite could more easily control and suppress domestic reactionary movements, and without having to further invoke radical citizenship practices to defend and unite the nation. After more than a hundred years of modernization, then, Turkey finally found the (geo)political breathing space in which capitalist property relations could be established without the imminent threat of domestic rebellion and foreign intervention (cf. Karpat 1972b: 353).

If the emergence of a bipolar world order laid the (geo)political foundations for capitalist development in Turkey, American economic assistance funded by the Marshall Plan, high world market prices and favorable state policies galvanized the process of transition during the 1950s by undermining sharecropping relations and encouraging petty commodity production as the new norm in agriculture. The bulk of foreign funds were used to import agricultural machinery,[5] which led to an exponential increase of the area under cultivation especially between 1950 and 1956 (Hale 1981: 95; Hansen 1991: 360). The mechanization and expansion of the area sown was made possible by state distribution of land and credit. Throughout the 1950s, the peasantry and landowners were freed from most wartime taxes and gained access to state-provided cheap and long-term agricultural credits,[6] which gave peasants the opportunity to buy/rent agricultural machinery and draft animals without incurring too much debt. In this respect, the intensification of credit relations between the state and the peasantry not only increased peasant production and relative living

---

[5] The number of tractors increased from 1,750 in 1948 to 16,585 in 1950, 31,415 in 1952, and 41,896 in 1959 (Ahmad 1977: 135).

[6] The Agricultural Bank's credits to agriculture increased almost tenfold between 1948 and 1958 (Oktar and Varlı 2010: 12). Meanwhile, direct taxes on agricultural income were significantly reduced: "[t]he rich landowners and substantial farmers who together earned more than a fifth of the GDP, paid only 2 per cent of the total tax revenue" (Zurcher 2004: 228).

standards, but also protected them against relations of debt and usury.[7] Combined with the state provision of floor prices,[8] distribution of state-owned land[9] and infrastructural investment,[10] most landless peasants ultimately broke the cycle of debt-sharecropping: the number of owner-occupied farms increased by 30 percent between 1952 and 1963, while landlessness declined from 16 percent to 10 percent of the rural population between 1950 and 1960 (Keyder 1987: 131).

All this indicates an "extensive" expansion of agricultural production in the first half of the 1950s.[11] Mechanization, good weather conditions, price and credit support, and population increase enabled the rapid opening up of previously uncultivated lands. However, with little pressure to produce competitively, productivity levels remained more-or-less the same: producers expanded agricultural frontier land as much as possible while productivity remained almost stagnant (Owen and Pamuk 1999: 107–8). Furthermore, the extensive limits of profitable cultivation began to be tested from 1956 onward. From 1948 until 1956, the area under cultivation increased by 61 percent to 22,453,000 hectares, which is nearly the same amount of land that is

[7] A total of 88 percent of the loans, which equaled 42 percent of total credit distributed by the Agricultural Bank were received by small producers. Large loans, equal to 15 percent of total credits, were benefited by 0.48 percent of farmers (Atasoy 2005: 91).

[8] The state price policy became particularly important after the collapse of world grain prices following end of the Korean War. The overall index of grain prices paid by the state rose from 100 in 1950, to 120 in 1954, and 196 in 1959. Although these rises were more-or-less in line with increases in inflation, state purchase prices exceeded export prices by 50 percent in 1954 and 90 percent in 1959 (Hale 1981: 95).

[9] In accordance with the modified land reform act of 1946, the state distributed from 1945 to 1959 a total of about 3 million hectares (land and communal pasture land) to about 400,000 families who were the least propertied (Hershlag 1968: 158; Keyder 1983: 142).

[10] In 1950, there were only 1,600 kilometers of hard-surfaced roads. Thanks to American technical and economic aid, by 1960, "the length of hard-surfaced highways increased to over 7000 km, together with just under 35.000 km of loose-surfaced primary roads, out of a total of 61.500 km. Hundreds of previously isolated towns and villages were now integrated into the national economy" (Hale 1981: 90). Also, the improvements in road networks must have been conducive to the breaking down of territorial commercial monopolies, thereby contributing to the relative homogenization of countrywide commodity prices.

[11] The area under cultivation increased by 70 percent over the decade as a whole: from 13,900,000 hectares in 1948 to 22,453,000 hectares in 1956, and 23,264,000 hectares in 1960 (Ahmad 1977: 135).

cultivated today (Ahmad 1977: 135; Yıldırmaz 2009: 100). With the agricultural frontier more-or-less reached, producers could continue to produce only on lands of poorer quality or inferior location. This not only lowered yields and depleted investment funds, but also limited competitiveness in international markets, causing unsustainable deficits in the country's balance of payments in the latter half of the 1950s (Hansen 1991: 344).

This decade-long expansion and eventual closure of cultivable land, combined with the state's implementation of a stricter land registration system (Zurcher 2004: 227), would have four important implications on the structure of agrarian and industrial relations, which would make the 1950s a prelude to the intensive capitalist development that was to take place in the following decades. First, "with the frontier reached in the 1950s, agricultural growth became almost exclusively dependent on increased yields ... through intensification of cultivation" (Hansen 1991: 357). The shift from extensive to intensive agriculture eventually made the peasantry increasingly market-dependent for their production. During the 1960s and 1970s, agricultural productivity and yields increased, in line with increases in the use of industrial tools and products in agriculture.[12] Second, as smallholdings reached an economically feasible size and peasants were provided credit and price support, they became consumers as well as suppliers of the domestic market for the first time in Republican history. The consumption habits began to change in the countryside, going beyond the logic of minimum subsistence. Rural settlements rose as important centers of consumption for domestic industries such as agricultural machinery, textiles, processed food, consumer durables and cars (Keyder 1988: 164). This increasing market orientation was further supported by US food aid, which facilitated producers' increasing specialization in cash crop production, hence contributing to them gradually losing their ability to revert to subsistence production.[13]

---

[12] By 1976 about 88 percent of the crop land was tractor-cultivated, while 85 percent of farmers used a combination of industrial inputs (Hale 1981: 178).

[13] After the end of the Marshall Aid in 1952, the main source of US economic aid to Turkey was food aid (Atasoy 2005: 95). The volume of production increased both for cereals and industrial crops from 1950 to 1960, and yet the increases in industrial crops were more rapid: while the volume of cereal cultivation roughly doubled, industrial crop production increased by more than 350 percent (Marguiles and Yıldızoğlu 1983: 21).

Third, given the peasantry's increasing inability to meet the new standards of subsistence without recourse to the market, the 1950s witnessed the first permanent mass migrations from the countryside to the towns. Therefore, chronic labor shortages, which haunted the earlier attempts at industrialization, began to be overcome with the continuous flow of a permanent labor force.[14] Relatedly, the scientific management of the labor process began to take root in factories, which involved the introduction of piece-rate pay systems, new measures to avoid loss of time, and new methods to minimize workers' ability to negotiate the pace and sequence of the labor process (Özden 2011: chapter 4). Lastly, the emergence of a stronger labor (and consumer) market significantly contributed to the smooth transformation of sharecropping landlords into capitalist entrepreneurs. With the structural makeover of labor markets and alluring prospects for productive activity (both in agriculture and manufacturing), the sharecropping landlords finally began to find it feasible and profitable to reorganize the labor process by driving off sharecroppers and "improving" their holdings (Alexander 1960; Keyder 1987: 138; also see Zurcher 2004: 227–8).

The late 1950s thus witnessed the beginning of structural transformation in the Turkish countryside, with peasants slowly turning into petty commodity producers, that is, farmers whose access to the land and means of subsistence were increasingly determined by their ability to "improve" the conditions of production. The peasantry's political neutralization and incorporation into the capitalist project, however, brought about not too unexpected outcomes for government finances. The peasantry's growing market-dependence could be sustained only by expansionary fiscal policies and price support programs,[15] which were at least partly responsible for rapidly growing public indebtedness and inflationary pressures, especially during the second half of the 1950s. That said, however, what was more costly than the support

---

[14] As a result, while the increase in the agricultural labor force was merely 9 percent between 1950 and 1960, the number of nonagricultural laborers increased by 86 percent (Hansen 1991: 342), which means that "one out of every ten villagers migrated to an urban area during the 1950s" (Keyder 1987: 137).

[15] The overall index of grain prices paid by the state rose from 100 in 1950, to 120 in 1954 and 196 in 1959. Although these rises were more-or-less in line with increases in inflation, state purchase prices exceeded export prices by 50 percent in 1954 and 90 percent in 1959 (Hale 1981: 95).

given to the peasantry was "the credit extended from deposit banks to the private sector." In other words, the merchants, one of the leading forces behind the DP government, were the "main culprit" for the monetary expansion and the resultant macroeconomic problems (Hansen 1991: 344). While capitalism began to develop protractedly in and through the older social relations in the countryside, the urban commercial classes, enriched under the auspices of the DP, impeded the development of capitalism as much as they owed their existence to it. Let me briefly explain.

During the 1950s, "the private sector demonstrated an unprecedented flurry of activity" yet without delivering the expected developmental outcomes (Barkey 1990: 53). The DP had committed to reversing the etatism of the early Republican years under the "illusion" that the creation of a market economy was "only a matter of legislation." Once the economy was deetatized, the party assumed, "businessmen and industrialists would then do the rest and in no time a (strong) private sector would come into being" (Ahmad 1977: 128). Until 1954, the rising income and consumption levels in agriculture, combined with government encouragement and relaxation of import restrictions, indeed provided a strong stimulus for private investment. Yet, the appetite for investment continued only insofar as the Turkish lira preserved its overvalued international position (Ahmad 1993: 116). Actors involved in import business and construction sector showed no interest in earning foreign exchange or productive investment, yet received the lion's share from the distribution of bank credits.[16] Likewise, foreign companies (albeit quite few in number) were merely interested in gaining internal distribution rights, rather than engaging in productive activity (Hale 1981: 88–9). After the agricultural sector lost steam in external markets, therefore, it became increasingly difficult for the DP to continue to afford such a system of "redistribution." Electoral pressures and considerations, as well as powerful interests entrenched within the party, rendered the taxation of agriculture, the cutting back of agricultural subsidies and currency devaluation politically too risky even to try. Inflation soared, as did black markets, unemployment and indebtedness. Scarce foreign

---

[16] "Industry garnered only 2.73 per cent of these credits in 1955 while agriculture and services (basically trade and construction) scored 30.78 and 66.49 per cent respectively" (Milor 1989: 141).

currencies and fiscal resources that could have been used to foster economic growth as part of a long-term industrial strategy continued to be used merely for redistributive purposes, which would bring the state to the verge financial collapse toward the end of the 1950s.

The main beneficiaries of DP's rule were thus merchants who obtained the largest portion of bank credits, big farmers who were not taxed and agricultural petty commodity producers who were subsidized. The main losers were the members of civil and military service. For one thing, the burden of inflationary policies weighed most heavily on the salaried masses, especially in the public sector. While the salaries of functionaries and workers increased in twenty years only fourfold and twofold, respectively, wholesale commodity prices increased eleven times during the same period (Karpat 2004: 191–2). Besides suffering from high inflation, younger military officers' channels for upward mobility were blocked and became highly politicized as the DP continuously created a loyal stratum of senior officers at the apex of the military hierarchy.

In addition to the erosion of their real and relative economic standing, the Kemalist bureaucracy and intelligentsia, including most notably the junior military officers, university professors and university students, also reacted to the transformation of the ethnoreligious contours of the Republican property regime. As discussed in Chapter 5, secularism and nationalism were not mere ideologies, but the organizing principles of the Kemalist political economy characteristic of Jacobinism. The DP, under electoral pressures, made an attempt to change this regime of ethnicity and property. Throughout the 1950s, the DP carried indigenous Kurdish notables (rather than merely state-approved Kurdish elites) into parliament, even including those associated with the Kurdish rebellion of 1925. Kurds, for the first time in Republican history, thus became part of the nation and (at least vaguely) were in a position to expect the state to serve their interests and to speak, publish and educate in Kurdish (McDowall 2004: 398; Aktürk 2012: 140–2). Also, the DP reversed and relaxed some of the radical manifestations of Kemalist secularism; for example, the Village Institutes were closed for breeding radicalism; religious courses were included in formal secular education; the ban on the recitation of the call to prayer in Arabic was lifted; and the number of preacher schools (*imam-hatip*) was increased (Atasoy 2005: 73). In effect, it is hard to argue that the changes undertaken by the DP amounted to a serious challenge to Republican nationalism and secularism, but under the weight of socioeconomic problems, "the intelligentsia reacted hysterically to the (supposed) Islamic resurgence," beginning to agitate the masses for the defense of secularism and nationalism, the guarantees of their material and symbolic existence (Ahmad 1977: 373; Taşpınar 2005: 126–7).

Thus, in 1958, the DP government was not only financially insolvent, but also "totally isolated from virtually all the institutions of the state." That same year the rumors of a military coup were already circulating, yet two international developments further complicated the internal deadlock. The military coup in Iraq in July 1958 "made a deep impression on the DP leaders who now came to see military intervention backed by popular support as a potential threat to their power." This "revolution phobia" pushed the DP toward implementing increasingly authoritarian measures (Ahmad 1977: 60, 158). Restriction of the freedom of the press and assembly in 1959–60, combined with an oppressive martial law, further escalated political polarization in the country, leading to violent clashes between the opposition and government (Karpat 2004: 173) This intense political climate took another revolutionary turn in April 1960, when the press, banned from reporting on the domestic clashes, began to write about the popular uprising that forced the fall of the Syngman Rhee government in South Korea. The lesson to be drawn was clear and the Turkish intelligentsia was even further encouraged when it emerged that the United States did not try to prevent Rhee's overthrow (Ahmad 1977: 65). The writing was on the wall.

A Failed Jacobin Coup and Its Legacy: The 1961 Constitution and "Social Republic"

The Turkish Republic is a nationalistic, democratic, secular and social state.

Article 2, The Turkish constitution of 1961

Turkish society began to go through a capitalist transformation from the 1950s. Yet, given the protractedness, incompleteness and instability of this process, Jacobin social forms could easily bounce back and continue to shape the development of capitalism. Indeed, 1960 was to be the year of an attempt at restoring and radicalizing the original

Kemalist project, which, albeit unsuccessful and short-lived, would substantially mark the subsequent trajectory of capitalist modernity in Turkey.

The ten–year-long experiment with capitalism and multiparty politics collapsed with a military coup on May 27, 1960. The coup was planned and carried out predominantly by junior and mid-ranking officers. In a sense, then, the military intervention of 1960 was "in the tradition of the Young Turk revolution of 1908" (Ahmad 1993: 11). As in 1908, young officers revolted against the high military command and existing ruling-class coalition. And just as in 1908, the coup of 1960 would have hardly had any chance of success had it not incorporated other class demands into the emerging revolutionary agenda (Karpat 1970: 1672–3). However, in contrast to 1908, the 1960 coup was carried out against a democratically elected government that was still fairly popular among and generous to the peasantry. Under DP rule, the days of social discontent caused by taxation, war-making and war preparation had become something of the past (yet definitely not forgotten). Compared to the first half of the twentieth century, the 1950s were thus, in many ways, the golden age of the Turkish peasantry. In this context, junior officers, who were educated and socialized at the heart of the Kemalist establishment and marginalized during the rising capitalist order, would have to reinterpret and remobilize the social and intellectual resources of the original Kemalist project in new ways to justify the military intervention, secure their leadership of the May 27 movement and appeal to larger segments of society. And by doing so, they would set new standards for the Kemalist project, which would, in turn, initiate a new process of competitive redefinition of the social, popular and national character of the Republic.

The military committee that took power following the coup, the National Unity Committee (*Milli Birlik Komitesi* or MBK), was far from a monolithic body. For one thing, the young officers who orchestrated the coup did not represent all segments of the armed forces, they therefore still needed the presence of senior officers in the committee to be able to justify the intervention and enforce the chain of command within the military forces (Karpat 1970: 1666). The inclusion of senior officers and their entourages created a group of "moderates" within the MBK, whose sole aim was to restore power to the civilians (read the CHP) as soon as the "corrupt" elements were purged from the political system. That said, regardless of their ranks, all members were equal in the committee (Ahmad 1977: 164–5), which enabled the relatively junior officers to exercise considerable power (Weiker 1963: 127). The number of junior officers who were directly involved in the coup was fourteen. Just as the committee itself, "the Fourteen" (as they came to be called) was not a homogenous group either (Karpat 1970: 1680ff.; Hale 1994: 131). They were roughly divided into two subgroups, one populist/ultranationalist and the other populist/socialist (given the Janus-faced character of Jacobinism/Kemalism, most notably its constant oscillation between elitism and populism, and nationalism and universalism, it is perhaps not too surprising that it gave birth to two polar opposite currents of movement).

Despite obvious ideological cleavages, however, the Fourteen, en bloc, espoused "reforms which would alter the political structure of the country before party politics were once more permitted" (Ahmad 1977: 165). According to these "radical" officers, the junta's task was not simply handing back power to the civilians as the "moderates" would have, but "eliminat(ing) underdevelopment" by "completing" the Kemalist Revolution that was "interrupted" by "corrupt" politicians, "opportunistic" businessmen, and landowners and religious conservatives (Karpat 2004: 195). Fighting poverty, inflation, class conflict, "backwardness," "laziness" and "ignorance" would be the primary goal of military rule, which could be attained through a number of policies and strategies, such as by socializing the health services, undertaking fiscal modernization by taxing the landlords, implementing economic planning and, perhaps above all, by expanding and transforming the education system (Weiker 1963: 120, 133; Ahmad 1993: 128; Hale 1994: 131). The central project envisaged for this reinvigorated Kemalism was an "education mobilization programme" (Ahmad 1977: 271). The state would establish "continuing liaison in villages, cities, schools, universities, factories and the army to bring to light basic problems and to submit plans prepared for the solution of these problems," all of which were planned to "diffuse and re-instill" Kemalist secularism, nationalism and people-ism in the citizens (Weiker 1963: 133). In this regard, according to the Fourteen, the state's educational drive should go beyond mere schooling, working toward uniting the intelligentsia with the peasantry; spreading Kemalist principles throughout the country; establishing linguistic and cultural unity; reorienting and encouraging fine arts to promote the expansion of "national" culture; spreading values promoting hard work and sacrifice; and saving people from "fake sheiks" and self-interested "deviants" (Türkeş 1977: 69–71). What was at stake was the creation of a new political system and culture, and indeed until this goal was accomplished, multiparty politics must be either postponed or allowed only with the condition that educational qualifications were introduced for voters (Weiker 1963: 126ff.; Ahmad 1977: 159).

Admittedly, the overall aim of the project did not seem clear in 1960, and given that the Fourteen would lose their control over the MBK in November 1960, perhaps they did not even have the opportunity to clearly state what the political and economic implications of this educational mobilization would be. Notwithstanding this initial ambiguity, however, the Jacobin character of this educational move would be clarified later by Colonel Alparslan Türkeş, who, for many people, was the leader of the Fourteen. In 1963, Türkeş wrote that "people would be taught that they are all equal, and no one is another's slave ... Chains of slavery and tyranny, no matter what they are made of, be it platinum or gold, are chains. Revolting against such chains is the noblest thing people can do" (Türkeş 1977: 83, 73). In this regard, reviving Kemalist principles was of utmost importance in order to launch a "Turkish Renaissance" (Türkeş 1977: 87). Indeed, all this required, according to Türkeş, a radical rethinking of the ideals and principles that created "Western civilization," some of which are identified as follows: rationalism and scientific thinking; human dignity is above everything; humans must live based on their own power and labor; the use of natural resources for the interest of "humanity"; and people, if necessary, must defy injustices and counter them with force (Türkeş 1977). Vague as it may be, the clear inference from Türkeş's early writings is that in May 1960 the aim of overcoming economic backwardness and political reactionism through education was not based on the teaching of values informed by productivist market principles, but the (selective) inculcation of radical and nationalist citizenship practices. The Jacobin character of the project would be further clarified in 1965. Türkeş, while in exile, formulated a series of political principles (*Dokuz Işık* or *Ülkücülük*) that in many ways built on the model of societal and moral reorganization anticipated in the Fourteen's educational drive and claimed to be a nationalist-developmental path as an alternative to socialism and capitalism (including what he considered to be the "degenerated" variants of capitalism such as "fascism") (Türkeş 1965). This political doctrine, according to Türkeş, would recognize private property, thereby forestalling the citizens' "enslavement by bureaucracy" (i.e. socialism), but was also opposed to capitalism, which is not more than "people's enslavement by things" (Türkeş 1976: 266). Unlike capitalism, which is based on "class property" (sınıf mülkiyeti) and promotes, at best, "political democracy," Türkeş proposed an ultranationalist industrial order peculiar to "Turks," in which workers and capital-owners would jointly manage factories and share profits (Türkeş 1976: 264–6). Indeed, since this would provide every Turk a voice in economic decision-making, it would form the basis of "real," that is, economic democracy (Türkeş 1979: 60–2).

Little wonder such an ambitious "educational" drive signaled a tremendous expansion of state control over society and a major restructuring of state finances (Ahmad 1977: 271). Indeed, shortly after seizing power, the junta initiated a series of reforms aiming to reverse policies enacted by the DP, which allegedly undermined the sense of purpose and unity in the country. For the Fourteen, what needed to be done, first and foremost, was to stem inflation and eliminate taxation "injustices." This effectively meant the end of the expansionary economic policies of the previous decade. The banks were shut, bank accounts of prominent politicians and businessmen frozen, loans suspended and large construction projects stopped (Weiker 1963: 151–2; Shaw and Shaw 1977: 415). It was also rumored that the junta "intended to examine the accounts of business houses and to make the declaration of wealth obligatory," which caused "many to fear a new capital levy" or Varlık Vergisi (Ahmad 1977: 271). The measures taken to transform taxation in agriculture proved even more threatening than those targeting the urban propertied classes. The Fourteen not only increased land taxes tenfold, but also intended to lay down ceilings on landholding size, hence paving the way for an expropriative land reform (Shaw and Shaw 1977: 415). Moreover, in Turkish Kurdistan, more than 200 tribal and religious leaders associated with the DP were imprisoned and 55 were relocated to Western Turkey due to the (largely unfounded) fear that they would revolt against the military government, just as the southern Kurds engaged in military resistance in the wake of the 1958 military coup in Iraq (Taşpınar 2005: 88).

No doubt the bourgeoisie was deeply disturbed by the junior officers' "collectivist radicalism" (Ahmad 1993: 128). Business leaders, including those who were initially sympathetic to the junta, fiercely opposed the blocking of banking operations as well as investigations into their wealth and transactions, and demanded the military government "put an end to the insecurity on private property" (Karpat 2004: 196). The immediate result of this precarious economic atmosphere was an investment strike and economic stagnation: "there was scarcely any new investment, stocks of goods remained unsold, production was reduced, and without doubt the only thing that rose was unemployment" (Ahmad 1977: 271). Discontent was brewing in the streets, and even those who had initially supported the coup were now skeptical of the junta's "real" intentions. The Fourteen responded to the growing opposition by threatening to "reform" the press and purging "suspicious" university professors and military officers (Ahmad 1977: 167). The conflict within the MBK became even more intense in this context. Since the outset of the intervention, both moderates and radicals had been living "in fear of a coup by the other," but now the tide was beginning to turn against the latter (Ahmad 1977: 166). And indeed, it was this loss of societal support that finally encouraged the moderates to overthrow the radicals in November 1960. The new coup led to the purge of the Fourteen from the MBK and their appointment to missions abroad. The removal of the radicals certainly proved to be a big relief to the propertied classes, yet at the same it pushed the junior officers' radicalism underground, leading to "the re-establishment of conspiratorial groups within the armed forces" (Ahmad 1977: 168). After the November coup, therefore, "several of the 'old revolutionaries' ... drifted back to their conspiratorial habits of the late 1950s" in an effort to "revive the spirit of 27 May" (Hale 1994: 139–40).

Following the countercoup in November 1960, the army thus turned, once again, into a den of intrigue. "[T]he idea of a second takeover continued to tempt the radicals," and indeed on several occasions they challenged the high command, succeeding to shape their decisions on military appointments, economic reforms and elections (Hale 1994: 149). From November 1960 until the first elections held in October 1961, therefore, there were many rumors that the radicals were again preparing to intervene to check the growth of "reactionary" forces organized in the successor parties of the old DP

(Ahmad 1977: 170–1). The response in the high command and among the generals was one of appeasement and conciliation. Squeezed between the bourgeoisie's investment strike and the junior officers' radicalism, the high command had to both retain the program of political redemocratization and appease radical demands by making concessions. Ironically, then, the generals had to act both as democrats who would bring back civilian rule and as reformers who would implement radical changes, which the civilians would not be willing to carry out under normal circumstances. In due course, the land-owners and bourgeoisie would get their rule accepted by the military forces in general, but along the way they also had to concede to the trial and execution of their political figureheads and a constitution that they had fought hard to get rejected in the constitutional referendum (July 1961). The prime minister Menderes and two of his ministers were sent to the scaffold just before the elections (September 1961) in order to appease the Jacobin hawks in the military and to deter the neodemocrats from reversing the constitution after the elections.

In summary, the generals of November 1960 attempted to preempt both the junior officers' Jacobinism and neodemocrat revanchism, and in doing so, they paved the way for a constitution that would reset the Kemalist rules of reproduction. The new constitution, accepted in July 1961, was a "combined" beast. While it confirmed the sanctity of private property, it also incorporated populist measures invoked by the radicals. It had to appeal to new potential allies and expand the scope of freedoms in order to forestall the danger of a Jacobin or neodemocrat dictatorship. As a result, "economic and social planning" (Article 129), universal healthcare (Article 49), the right to land (Article 37), the right to work (Article 42) and a full employment policy (Article 41) entered the constitution, as did wider civil rights, greater university autonomy (Article 120), a proportional electoral system, the freedom to organize and assemble (Article 46) and the right to strike (Article 47). In addition to being "secular" and "nation-alist," the new constitution thus redefined the Kemalist Republic as a "social" and "democratic" state. Adding these two principles to the traditional Kemalist couplet would have enormous implications for the way capitalism would develop in the following two decades. The Jacobin legacy would no longer be able to stop, but complicate the development of capitalism, while at the same time providing (at least partly) the socioinstitutional framework into which capitalism would be further imposed. It was this interpenetration of the old and the new, Jacobin and capitalist, that would lend the 1960s and the 1970s their explosive and unstable character. This is the subject to which I turn in the next two sections.

Planners, Oligopolists and Workers: Contradictions of a Capitalist–Jacobin Compound

Should not private business be helped in case they incur a loss given that we live in a democracy?

An eminent Turkish industrialist, October 1960[17]

Now that the Republic was a "social" and "democratic" state, the issue of economic planning became very important. The balance of payment difficulties and foreign exchange crisis of the last decade had already shown the necessity for the strategic utilization of foreign assistance and the rational coordination of public investment. Yet it was political considerations, arising from competitive coups and competitive elections, that made it an imperative to embark on a comprehensive planning effort in the postrevolutionary period (Barkey 1990: 59–65). In this respect, planning was not only about economic development, but also about implementing policies that would facilitate the formation of a power bloc as a bulwark to the revival of Jacobins and neodemocrats. This task proved even more important after the first elections held in October 1961, which simply led to the resuscitation of old votes for new parties (Weiker 1963: chapter 5). Despite the military's clear preference for the CHP, the Republicans barely prevailed in the elections; while the CHP received obtained 173 seats in the parliament, the heirs of the DP, most notably the Justice Party (AP) and the New Turkey Party, obtained 158 and 65 seats, respectively. "In such a political climate" it would be naïve to expect that Jacobin officers "would return to barracks and watch events take their course" (Ahmad 1977: 172). Indeed, two more coup attempts were made by junior officers in 1962 and 1963, which, albeit unsuccessful, would keep the country within "the extraordinary atmosphere of an impending coup" throughout the 1960s (Ahmad 1977: 184).

---

[17] Quoted in Milor (1989: 158).

Planning, therefore, was vital to nurturing a broad social coalition that would prevent the Jacobins and neodemocrats from exploiting the country's precarious socioeconomic balances. The State Planning Organization (SPO) was established in this context. The infant industrial bourgeoisie readily embraced the SPO since planning, in principle, contained some assurance that domestic industrial production would be protected and supported in order to ease foreign exchange difficulties. Protecting and supporting domestic industries would also broaden the internal market and consumer base; hence it was an attempt to recruit salaried employees, including civil servants, military officers and the (unionized) working classes, to the emergent power bloc (Milor 1989: 152–3).

If planning itself was not a matter of dispute, "planning the plan" proved to be a highly divisive issue. Initially, the planners, who were highly educated technocrats, drafted a plan that would enable the SPO bureaucrats to exercise absolute authority over the allocation of budgetary sources for public investment and incentives for the private sector (Milor 1989: 156). By envisaging the SPO as an institution above politics, technocrats aimed to curtail the freedom of political power holders to implement economically unsound policies, and force private actors to invest in line with planning priorities, both of which they considered tantamount with the development of the country's productive and competitive power (Milor 1989: 156–7; Barkey 1990: 64–5). The planners contended that enterprises, public and private, "should . . . try to rationalize their production by minimizing their costs and increasing the productivity of labor." Protectionism, likewise, was acceptable only insofar as it fostered "the expanded reproduction of capital and the extraction of relative surplus value (respectively called 'investments' and 'innovations')." Hence technocrats designed a plan that would not only "rationalize" state intervention into the economy, but also potentially "oppose private capitalist interests in name of a collective notion of 'capital'" (Milor 1989: 158–9).

The plan was accepted by the MBK only with certain reservations and modifications. In particular, the planners' preoccupation with maximizing labor productivity was not welcomed by military bureaucrats who, given the existing political tumult, were extremely reluctant to accept policies that would cause (at least in the short-run) further sociopolitical costs such as unemployment, class conflict and ethnic tensions (Milor 1989: 159). As a result, the generals accepted the plan bill only with an administrative twist. They did not change "labor productivity" as a goal, but watered down the technocrats' authority over investment decisions by decreasing the number of experts on the main decision body of the SPO (Milor 1989: 157). After the elections, this expanded space for nonexpert control over the SPO translated into increased political leverage over the determination and implementation of developmental goals. It was particularly important that, as politicians struggled with each other to obtain the support of business groups, they transmitted (directly or otherwise) different business interests into the planning process (Hale 1981: 141–2; Milor 1989: 160).

Planning, therefore, was doomed to failure from the outset and ended with the planners' collective resignation in October 1962. Yet, the technocrats did not go down without a fight. For example, they proposed a maximum limit to land holdings and progressive taxation, which was expected to exert pressure on landowners to mechanize and prevent the underutilization of land, thereby leading to increased labor productivity, cheaper food, a larger domestic market and greater funds for agricultural and industrial investment (Ahmad 1977: 274; Milor 1989: 162–3, 165). Likewise, they took steps to institutionalize "a new conception of state economic intervention," which refused to protect, support and subsidize inefficient public enterprises and private companies whose production does not promote innovation, competitiveness and "rational" management practices (Milor 1989: 163–4). Yet, parliamentary control over the SPO eventually frustrated the attempt to expand and deepen capitalist social relations both in agriculture and manufacturing. The plan to restructure existing land, tax, credit, subsidy and investment regimes with a view to increasing innovation and international competitiveness was criticized and eventually rejected by politicians for violating freedom of property and democratic rights. Ultimately, the SPO turned into an organization whose purpose was "to achieve certain quantitative targets without altering the status quo in any drastic way" (Ahmad 1977: 275). As such, structural transformation, begun in the 1950s, would be quantitively extended but not qualitatively intensified throughout the so-called import substitution period.

As planning was reduced to mere support of the private sector, manufacturers became the staunchest supporters of import substitution policies (Barkey 1990: 60). Unsurprisingly, the country underwent a spectacular industrial expansion (roughly 9 percent a year) during the import substitution period (1962–79) and manufacturing for the first time surpassed agriculture in terms of its contribution to total growth (Barkey 1990: 80; Hansen 1991: 357). The private sector received generous support and protection from the state. Behind high tariff walls, the state provided tax rebates, scarce foreign currencies and various subsidy schemes to the manufacturing bourgeoisie so that they could import capital and intermediate goods to produce consumer products at home. However, since the SPO had no power to sanction cooperation and no control over the allocation of public funds, the state support could not be conditioned to manufacturers' ability to compete in international markets and earn foreign exchange (as was the case in successful late-late industrializers like South Korea).[18] As such, state promotion of industrialization, by and large, boiled down to mere distribution of fiscal privileges and favors with almost no gain that could have been accrued from increases in productivity and competition. "Allocations of foreign exchange ... were based solely on considerations of capacity" (Barkey 1990: 91–2). "Any firm by receiving a percentage of the total exchange allocation was automatically guaranteed a share of the domestic market" (Hale 1981: 202). Tariffs and quotas eventually led to "overprotection" and the "building of excess capacity" in many industries. "No wonder only 17.9 per cent of the total subsidies received by firms between 1968 and 1980 was invested in accordance with developmental directives" (Milor 1989: 255–6).[19]

One implication was that state economic enterprises (SEEs) in particular and public investment in general were geared to serve functions incongruent with any market or productivity criteria. That is, they

---

[18] With the exception of the textiles sector, which consistently increased its share of exports, consumer good exports decreased from 8.8 percent of production in 1967 to 6.1 percent in 1977. Investment good exports remained below 1 percent, while intermediate good exports hovered around 2 percent throughout the import substitution period. Overall, "the Turkish manufacturing sector did not achieve any significant gains in exports" (Barkey 1990: 83–6, also see Owen and Pamuk 1999: 113).

[19] The economy was characterized by a surge of investment, with very weak backward and forward linkages to the rest of the economy. The resultant lack of "vertical" investments kept the overall domestic content of the allegedly import-substituting industries as low as 23 percent (Barkey 1990: 115), hence the never-ending foreign exchange crisis and competition for import licenses throughout the import substitution period.

either supplied low price inputs to the private sector or became centers of "social" redistribution by creating public employment in cities or providing support to agricultural producers. If there had been a large pool of taxable income, perhaps the SEEs serving private and populist ends would not have hurt fiscal balances. However, although "attempts were made to introduce taxation of agricultural income ... and [indeed] taxation was established by law in 1964 ... , exemptions were considerable and evasion massive. The same was the case for the taxation of business" (Hansen 1991: 382). Tax revenues thus repeatedly lagged behind progressively increasing public expenditures. Inflationary spending and external borrowing consequently became the only means to servicing debt payments and providing the agricultural and manufacturing subsidies necessary to keep the SEEs afloat.

In many ways, what was vital to the maintenance of this property regime was the exchange rate policy that overvalued the Turkish lira (Tekin 2006: 135–6). With the exception of the immediate aftermath of devaluations, the lira was constantly maintained above its international market value. While this facilitated the import of investment goods, thereby directly benefiting import-substituting manufacturers in general, the exchange rate regime was particularly instrumental to the development of industries that assemble prefabricated goods – that is, assembly industries (Barkey 1990: 73). The assembly industries were established with very high foreign content, in the sense that, while local firms provided capital, foreign investors "bring in the patent, most of the parts to be assembled, and some managerial and engineering skill." The joint enterprise, then, "comes under state protection ... by important restrictions which make the product almost a monopoly item" (Soysal 1970 quoted in Ahmad 1977: 280). This inward-looking investment pattern was indeed reproduced by local–foreign partnerships in other sectors as well. The industries to whose development foreign capital substantially contributed such as chemicals, rubber and electrical industries, produced "goods which would cater for local customer demand" and were "in no way designed to produce goods for an export market" (Ahmad 1977: 279).

Most industrial profits were thus made behind a blanket protectionism and by "manipulating" state intervention (Tekin 2006: 133). In this context, oligopolistic manufacturers, enjoying noncompetitive prices in the domestic market thanks to state support and protection, were inherently inimical to further capitalist development: "it was perfectly rational for the industrialists to use their economic power to choke off further industrialization, rather than promoting the deepening of industrial capital" (Milor 1989: 233). If economically "unsound," however, this oligopolistic structure served to consolidate the emerging alliance between industrialists and the military bureaucracy. For, much as the bourgeoisie lived on benefits derived from a politically protected market and politically provided subsidies, the military officers also carved a special niche for themselves in this emerging economic structure. After the transition to multiparty politics in 1961, senior military officers charged themselves with an "advisory" role in the newly established "National Security Council" (MGK) whose stated function was "to assist the cabinet in the making of decisions related to national security and co-ordination." "National security," however, was understood in such a "broad and all-embracing (way) that the pashas had a say in virtually every problem before the cabinet" (Ahmad 1993: 130).

No doubt, this increasing political power translated into increased economic benefits, which, in turn, helped to neutralize the political dissent within the army, thereby forestalling another intervention from "below," and facilitated the integration of military forces (both high command and junior officers) into the oligopolistic socioeconomic structure. The benefits included but were not limited to increased pay scales, pensions and subsidized accommodation, subsidized consumer goods and also professional opportunities for retired officers both in the upper levels of the bureaucracy or private sector (Ahmad 1993: 11, 130). Another important factor contributing to the consolidation of military forces as a status quo power was the creation of the Army Mutual Assistance Association (OYAK). The association was exempted from taxes and duties and rapidly went beyond a mere mutual assistance fund "'grown into one of the largest and most profitable conglomerates in the country, providing high dividends to its investors" (Ahmad 1993: 12). In the two decades after the Revolution, it was heavily invested in several industrial and financial ventures (sometimes even in partnership with foreign investors), ranging from the production of assembled cars and tractors to cement and construction (Ahmad 1977: 281).

The Turkish military forces thus eventually lost their Jacobin potential. The citizen-officer of the past was now firmly integrated into the existing political economic structure. Furthermore, as there was no imminent geopolitical threat under NATO's protective shield, the military's long-standing need to mobilize and appeal to the lower classes by radicalizing the original Young Turk/Kemalist project became obsolete. Content with their place in the political economic establishment, there was no longer any need for military officers to invoke Jacobin forms of property, appropriation and mobilization. The citizen-soldier was dead as the citizen-officer consolidated his place as the guardian of and a partner in the new socioeconomic order. Military interventions that were to take place after 1960 would no longer seek to establish a new Jacobin order. Yet, the legacy of the failed Jacobin revolution was still there, encoded in the constitution of 1961. Clearly, one can assume that after the vanishing of the Jacobin subject, the social and democratic character of the constitution could be assimilated into a form of social democracy, and as such, the Jacobinism of the past would no longer pose any serious challenge to the emerging capitalist order. After all, a fine balance between social rights and capitalism was established in the Western countries of the time, which Turkey could emulate by "regulating" its own capitalism. Or could it?

Generous wage and social security measures and wider democratic rights were indeed consolidated in the West in the postwar period, yet, what rested at the heart of this marriage between social democracy and capitalism was that the demands for higher wages, benefits and equality were conditioned to productivity increases. Economic demands were separated from the demands for political autonomy and radical equality within the institutionalized mechanisms of wage bargaining (Maier 1977). In other words, the "limitations placed on the economy through the extension of citizenship rights and social policy were accompanied by an increasing subordination of all aspects of social life under the exigencies of the 'market'" (Lacher 2006: 144–5). In this sense, the regulated capitalism of the postwar period was much less a reaction against capitalism per se and much more a ruling-class strategy to bolster capitalist discipline of society at large within limited welfare provisions and several conditions for eligibility (Baca 2021) In short, what allowed (a diluted form of) democracy and welfare arrangements to prevail in the postwar West was the stabilization and consolidation of market society.

In Turkey, however, market society was far from being consolidated. As I argued earlier, industrialists represented an "infant" capitalist class whose very presence became an impediment to the further development of capitalism in Turkey. Their privileged access to public resources resulted in oligopolistic/monopolistic practices, which remained the ultimate basis of their social reproduction, halting the further differentiation of political processes from economic ones.[20] The paradox is that given the continuing centrality of the state in the social reproduction of the dominant power bloc, any attempt at democratizing the political space beyond its previously designated boundaries would endanger the foundations of this *partially* capitalist modernity. In this context, old Kemalist secularism and nationalism (with minor modifications) continued to be deployed to provide a sense of unity and an ethos of conduct among the business and bureaucratic elite, while being used to keep the gates of the state and economy closed to potential contenders, most notably the radical left, Kurds and political Islam (Taşpınar 2005: chapter 4; Aktürk 2012: chapter 5).

It is a historical irony that the first radical challenge to Kemalist nationalism was posed from within Kemalism itself. Two cases in point were the left turn of the CHP after the mid-1960s and the emergence of the Workers Party of Turkey (WPT or TİP). The oligopolistic economic structure had two immediate consequences for the radicalization of political life from the 1960s onward. First, given the oligopolistic character of manufacturing markets, most of the newly established industries were capital-intensive, which dramatically limited the absorption capacity of the rural masses by urban centers (Hale 1981: 215). The state tried to respond to the rising urban unemployment by siphoning off the otherwise educated-yet-unemployed mass into the bureaucracy and the SEEs.[21] The threat of unemployment and poorly paid government jobs, in the context of the relative freedom provided by the 1961 constitution, radicalized the university youth while

---

[20] It must be clear by now that what I argue here is not that the cases of successful late development were achieved without state intervention or under conditions of perfect competition. However, the state provision of oligopolistic rights and subsidies in the internal market in such countries as South Korea and Taiwan worked to ensure that capitalists became subjected to the rules of reproduction in the international market, see Chibber (2003).

[21] Manufacturing's share in GNP between 1962 and 1980 increased by more than 64 per cent, while its share in total employment rose by only 2.8 percent, see Barkey (1990: 80–1) and Şenses (1994: 53). Meanwhile, schools and institutions of higher education doubled their enrolment (Ahmad 1993: 145). The state was the employer of a third of the working population and 36 percent of the manufacturing workforce throughout the 1960s and 1970s (Güran 2011: 30).

218 Reinterpreting Capitalist Modernity à la Turca

creating a stratum of "radical" government employees (Mardin 1978: 250; 2006c: 79; Ahmad 2002: 158). Also, the state's attempts at modeling the newly established trade unions on the "American model," that is, the model that "concentrated on economic demands and discouraged political affiliations" and "linked wage increases to productivity growth," were largely unsuccessful and unable to prevent the radicalization of a growing number of workers organized mainly in and through the Confederation of Revolutionary Labor Unions (DISK) (Dereli 1968: 169; Ahmad 1993: 143).[22]

The TİP emerged in this context. Its professed aim was to transform the state into a "truly people-ist Republic" based on the rule of laborers in alliance with a people-ist intelligentsia (Sencer 1974: 313). The TİP argued for a noncapitalist path to development, which they thought would be possible by democratizing and radicalizing Kemalist statism, people-ism, nationalism and secularism. This was a planned socioeconomic order based on science and led by the laborers of Turkey regardless of their ethnic/religious origin (Sencer 1974: 326–8). Although the TİP won only 15 seats in the 1965 parliament and its seats decreased thereafter until its closure in 1971, it "played an oppositional role of historic importance totally out of proportion to its size" thanks to its organic links to the militant working class, radical university youth and intelligentsia (Ahmad 1993: 145).[23] Even more importantly, the TİP provided a platform through which one of the

[22] According to one estimate, the number of unionized workers increased from 283,000 in 1960 to 1.5 million in 1970, which equaled 38.6 percent of the wage earners. This was a degree of unionization comparable to most advanced Western European countries such as Germany and Britain (Hale 1976: 65). DISK's membership was over 300,000 workers in 1976 and 500,000 in 1980, rising from 100,000 in 1970. Given its militancy and open defiance of capitalism, however, the impact of DISK far outweighed its membership number (Bianchi 1984: 224, 229).
[23] The radicalization of university campuses during the 1960s took place under the demonstration effect of worldwide events such as the war in Vietnam and radical student movements around the world. Perhaps more important than these external factors, however, was the fact that "[t]he universities had played an important part in toppling Menderes and in formulating the constitution of the second republic. It was only logical therefore that students and teachers began to see themselves as the moving force of society" and as "an enlightened elite" (Zurcher 2004: 254–5). Unsurprisingly, student demands hardly concerned the university campus itself, varying from the reform of the "archaic" system of education and of "unjust" land ownership to the end of an alliance with the "imperialist" West (Ahmad 1977: 199).

usual suspects of the Kemalist regime, the Kurds, forcefully asserted their politicocultural rights (Aktürk 2012: 150–1).[24] The integration of Kurds into the radical left was particularly threatening for the Kemalist political and economic elite, not only because Kurdish politicocultural demands, tinged with socialism, would amount to an overhaul of the Kemalist regime of property and ethnicity, but also because the prospect of a radicalized Kurdish population heightened Ankara's never-ending geopolitical anxieties about Kurdish-dominated eastern and southeastern regions, especially in the wake of 1970 Baath–Barzani Accord in Iraq (McDowall 2004: 411; Taşpınar 2005: 93).[25]

That said, what was perhaps much more disturbing for the ruling elite was that as societal actors attempted to reinterpret and revive the Jacobin legacy of Kemalism, CHP itself was becoming a hotbed for leftist radicalism. In the 1960s, oligopolistic economic structure caused a chronic need for and an ever-intensifying political competition among different business groups over the scarce foreign currencies. Business interests were organized in and through different associations and political parties, yet the majority of big businesses were members of and represented by the AP, the main descendant of the DP (Ahmad 1977: 244). The AP won the elections in 1965 and 1969, and was able to form majority governments thanks to its appeal to the bulk of businessmen, big landlords and middle farmers. The JP's main rival was the CHP. Unsuccessful at recruiting larger segments of the

---

[24] Kurdish youth and intellectuals were another example of the potentially universalist and explosive character of Kemalist people-ism and education. Until the end of the 1950s, the rate of extension of public school system in Kurdish-dominated regions remained relatively low compared to other regions. The MBK, in an attempt to Turkify the region, began to establish area boarding schools in the region after 1960, which provided young Kurdish peasants not only an opportunity to obtain state-based income, but also (indirectly) a greater room of engagement in national (radical) politics. And indeed, given the strong legacy and relative prevalence of sharecropping relations and the state–landowner alliance in the region, Kurdish students and intellectuals substantially contributed to the formulation of TİP demands on land reform, end of "internal colonialism," and so on (McDowall 2004: 409–10). After the closure of TİP in 1971, Kurds were largely pushed to underground organizations, a process further accelerated by the subsequent incorporation of the Turkish left into the CHP.

[25] The significance of the geopolitical factor becomes clearer when one considers that despite the proliferation of various leftist journals in the Turkish language, severe restrictions on Kurdish political and cultural expression remained in place throughout the 1960s and 1970s (Taşpınar 2005: 91).

business world as well as farmers (most likely due to its association to the May 27 movement and the earlier Kemalist project in the popular psyche), the CHP had no choice but to turn left by reinventing Kemalist people-ism. The CHP became the conduit through which the under-privileged, who were forcing the gates of the state in the 1970s, radicalized and turned Kemalism's solidaristic and nonclass vision of nation into an outcry for greater political and economic equality (Sencer 1974: 281). Obviously, the CHP's turn to the left had its limits, as it remained attentive of dominant bureaucratic and bourgeois interests. Yet, to some degree, it succeeded in including the previously marginalized segments of society, such as the radical working class, poor peasants and leftist university youth as well as Kurds and Alevis into the CHP constituency. By doing so, the CHP transformed existing conceptions of secularism and nationalism as understood thus far by the political and economic elite.

The implication is that coming into the 1970s, business and political elites were not only concerned about rising real wages,[26] but alarmed by the rise of a militant left even in such establishment parties like the CHP. Given the constitutional rights and freedoms, however, the only thing that they could do (at least for a while) was to exert pressure on governments and tolerate, if not unwillingly support, the formation of a Kemalist ultranationalism. Informed by a virulent anticommunism and ultranationalism, the Nationalist Action Party (established by Alparslan Türkeş, one of the Fourteen) and its militant youth organization ("commandos" as they came to be known) stirred up political violence to an unprecedented level. When the commandos proved unsatisfactory and perhaps too unruly, the military intervened once again through a "coup by memorandum," asking for the resignation of the AP government and the formation of a "strong" government "inspired by Ataturk's principles" that would end "anarchy" and "social and economic unrest" (Ahmad 1993: 147–8).

A technocratic government ruled the country from 1971 to 1973, but achieved almost no success in economically "disciplining" the bourgeoisie (Tekin 2006), nor was it able to alter the course of political

---

[26] For example, despite significantly lower higher levels of productivity, manufacturing wages in Turkey were three times the level of South Korean wages in 1974, double in 1977 and still higher by half than Korean wages in 1979 (Keyder 1987: 159–61). Also, the number of workdays lost due to industrial dispute increased threefold from 1973 to 1980 (Keyder 1987: 191–2).

developments despite utilizing considerable brutality (Zurcher 2004: 5). In particular, the junta dissolved the TİP, which contributed only to the further radicalization of former TİP supporters. In addition to mass demonstrations, university occupations and general strikes, the militant left began to engage in guerilla activities after 1973, killing US officers, kidnapping prominent businessmen and robbing banks. Ultimately, militant trade unionism and escalating violence between the left and "commandos" on the one hand, and the OPEC (Organization of the Petroleum Exporting Countries) crisis and unemployment on the other reinforced one another, causing a strong stagflationary spiral and political polarization verging on civil war.[27] This further deteriorated the political atmosphere, only to pave the way for another military intervention in 1980. It would fall onto the new junta to change the constitution and initiate a radical economic restructuring by decisively reformulating the dominant conception of political economy and sovereignty.

In summary, the widening of political space alongside the tightening of the economic sphere through the 1960s and 1970s forced and allowed social forces from below to radicalize prevailing discourses on popular sovereignty and the nation. Partly due to the legacy of Jacobinism encoded in the 1961 constitution and partly due to the incompleteness of capitalist transformation, struggles over otherwise strictly economic issues were easily and almost immediately translated into struggles over political rule and political rights (and vice versa). And this was further complicated by the fact that both the support for and critiques of the existing order were raised through the ruling ideology – Kemalism. As in the 1971 coup, Kemalism was often invoked to maintain the stability of an oligopolistic capitalism. Yet, given Kemalism's Jacobin past, the lower classes also used Kemalism, the most easily justifiable ideology, to counter Kemalism's own elitism. In this Jacobin–capitalist compound, therefore, Kemalism was used either to defend an oligopolistic order or to smash capitalism

---

[27] Inflation rise from 10.1 percent in 1975 to 85 percent in 1979. The debt–service ratio increased from 7 percent in 1975 to 26.7 percent in 1978, with short-term borrowing, nonexistent in 1970, amounting to 60 percent of the total borrowing in 1977 (Atasoy 2005: 113). From 1970 to 1980, twelve governments were formed, and no single party was able to form a majority government (Arat 1991: 143). The escalation of political violence costed the lives of more than 5,000 people between 1976 and 1980.

altogether. Kemalism was either oligopolist or socialist (the CHP, trying to be both, perhaps ended up being neither), hence unable to provide a reliable political-cultural base for the deepening of capitalist social relations. What is equally interesting, however, is that the blueprint for a capitalism "proper" was being cooked elsewhere in an entirely non-Kemalist sociointellectual milieu. Completely breaking away from Kemalism, a new bourgeois class was in the making in Anatolian towns, which would use local Islamic values to create a "just," "productive," "competitive" and "national" order against the existing "Masonic" and "imitator" capitalism, and against "socialist" and "atheist" populism. A discussion of the rise of Islamic capitalism is in order.

Capitalism of the Oppressed: Reinterpreting the National View Movement

There is no real planning in Turkey. For 25 years we have not established institutions conducive to real industrialization. The state has supported only those who seek to reap easy profits from the market..[in this sense] the motor of Turkish industrialization is not the state, but a small happy minority. None of the factories they built are real factories, because none of them can compete with world market prices. We have to resolve this issue at the root ... All of the existing laws related to industrialization are obsolete.

Necmettin Erbakan, 1973[28]

Coming to the end of the 1970s, a new bourgeois class, mainly based in Anatolian towns, comprised of small and medium-sized enterprises (SMEs), and in close connection with certain Islamic Sufi sects, began to formulate a new conception of Islam and the state as the foundation of a new industrialization strategy. After more than 100 years of modernization, the political and intellectual outlines of a capitalist development strategy would be finally laid out without combining it with Jacobinism. Capitalism would no longer be substituted for, nor would it be instituted in addition to, Kemalism. Indeed, a purely capitalist future, unfettered by the legacies of the Jacobin past, was being imagined. Herein lay the origins of the present times.

[28] Quoted in Erbakan (2013d [1973]: 60).

Let me begin by contesting an all-too-common conception about this new class of merchants and its political demands organized in the "National View" movement (NVM). The conventional interpretation holds that the Anatolian bourgeoisie of the 1970s was essentially a protectionist, inward-looking and noncompetitive group of entrepreneurs in favor of a pseudoetatist industrialization strategy. According to Keyder, for example, the National View's (NV's) conception of development "combined a shopkeeper ideology with demands for state interventionism in large industry, thus guaranteeing that the transition to monopoly capitalism should occur without the destruction of small business" (Keyder 1979: 35). Ahmad tends to concur with this view by arguing that the NVM was disturbed by the expansion of modern capitalist industries and threatened by the looming threat of international competition due to the state's plans to form a customs union with the European Economic Community (EEC) (Ahmad 1977: 382). In this respect, so the argument goes, the new bourgeois class was the opposite image of TUSIAD, the business association formed by big, mainly İstanbul-based secular capitalists that supported an outward-looking industrial strategy, including Turkey's integration with the EEC (Atasoy 2005: 119; 2009: 53). To be able to preserve their small-sized and technologically backward enterprises in the face of domestic and international competition, the NV translated "the discontent of the small town traditional petty bourgeoisie into a platform of Islamic revivalism ... (in lieu of) the nostalgic image of community lost through uncontrolled capitalism" (Keyder 1979: 35; also see Gülalp 2001: 435). The NVM demanded greater state protection and larger shares of bank credits, hence their constant emphasis on Islamic "justice," conservative values, rejection of the West, the dislike of Kemalism and so on.

There is a kernel of truth in the conventional interpretation: the Anatolian bourgeoisie reacted against the İstanbul-based industrial monopolies and the state's "unjust" credit policies favoring big business. They also fiercely rejected "Western" values and showed great dismay toward Kemalism, while remaining fearful of the possibility of abolition of quotas and tariffs between Turkey and the EEC. What is misleading, however, is the assumption that the Anatolian bourgeoisie was merely an inward-looking class of entrepreneurs trying to defend "petty bourgeois" interests against competition from big domestic and foreign industrialists.

The size of an industrial firm is far from being a clear indicator of its investment and productive patterns, nor does its owners' demand for economic openness necessarily equate with support for structural economic reform. By way of example, the TUSIAD, the presumably mostly free-trade–oriented interest association of large industrialists, actually had a completely ambivalent stance toward economic reform throughout the 1970s and early 1980s. As noted, from the 1960s, import restrictions on consumer goods produced a class of oligopolists (most of which were TUSIAD members).[29] These big industrialists were completely protected from foreign competition while generating almost no foreign exchange. Also, they were the main beneficiaries of import quotas and subsidies (Barkey 1990: 118; Tekin 2006: 139), while enjoying highly privileged access to bank credits, first as a result of state policies encouraging banks to offer low-interest funds for industrial investment,[30] and then due to the establishment of "holding corporations" that included one or more banks. That industrial enterprises could now borrow unlimited sums from banks that belong to their own holding corporations further added to the oligopolistic controls over the economy (Barkey 1990: 123–5).[31] In these circumstances, TUSIAD members had little incentive to go truly "international." For example, they supported Turkey's integration with the EEC, mainly because of the prospect of cheaper imports and additional foreign funds, while remaining adamant that the integration should not bring about the lira's devaluation (Tekin 2006: 140, 145–6). It is little wonder that at least until the late 1970s, industrialists "across-the-board" fiercely opposed and systematically undermined government initiatives to devalue the lira, selectively expose the private sector to international competition and so on (Barkey 1990: 119; Tekin 2006).

Still, it is true that things began to change, especially after 1978, when the foreign exchange and debt crisis reached its tipping point. At

[29] In 1969, according to one estimate, more than half of the total production belonged to three enterprises in 236 of the 251 mass consumption goods (Öztürk 2015: 123).

[30] The government credits allocated to large industrialists in 1973 was equal to 44 percent of their total capital, although only 3 percent of their production stemmed from exports (Atasoy 2005: 117).

[31] Of the existing 24 private banks in 1980, 19 were part of holding corporations. In 1982, the top 10 banks accounted for 90 percent of saving deposits (Barkey 1990: 124).

this point, the loss of profit caused by the lack of foreign exchange and underutilized capacity was even greater than the increased cost of imported inputs (Tekin 1997: 219). Cleavages in the existing power bloc eventually deepened, and TUSIAD became increasingly and vocally critical of import substitution policies, charging the government and trade unions with sacrificing the country's future for their short-term gains (Barkey 1990: 117; Arat 1991: 140; Tekin 1997: 239). For all this change in discourse, however, TUSIAD's "long-term commitment to the outward oriented measures was doubtful" (Tekin 1997: 220–1; Barkey 1990: 178, 184). TUSIAD conceded some limited reform measures as long as "they resulted in infusion of foreign exchange (thus imports of their inputs) into the economy," yet once foreign exchange became easily accessible after the military coup, they reverted to their old stance of criticizing the government for continuing with reform measures at their expense. During the 1980s, TUSIAD would by and large (though not entirely) remain as the association of noncompetitive, protectionist and inward-looking industrialists, opposing (yet no longer able to completely derail) the economic restructuring begun in 1980 (Tekin 1997: 249–50).

The NV, and the two political parties established as its offspring, the National Order Party (MNP, 1969–71) and the National Salvation Party (MSP, 1973–80), developed as a reaction to the dominance of big industrialists (Landau 1976: 21). Small firms were almost completely excluded from state-generated credit and subsidy circles, although they produced 25 percent of total industrial production and 88.3 percent of the total manufacture of footwear, apparel and textiles (which were three of the few industrial sectors showing strong export potential) (Atasoy 2005: 119; Tekin 2006: 153). Furthermore, although Anatolian industrialists were much less dependent on foreign imports for their production and consumption, their share of public (manufacturing) investment remained much lower than their counterparts based in İstanbul and İzmir (Barkey 1990: 132–3). Despite being subjected to various politicoeconomic exclusions, however, the Anatolian bourgeoisie largely operated outside centrally supervised industrial relations, thereby having access to a nonunionized (hence cheaper) workforce. Also, their willingness to export to the relatively less competitive markets in the Middle East was improving, especially after the rise in oil prices in the 1970s. Given these constraints and opportunities, it was perhaps a fairly foreseeable phenomenon that the

Anatolian industrialists were calling for a fairer distribution of state support and an end to interregional discrepancies in terms of their access to credit and markets. What needs to be emphasized, however, is that this disgruntled "petty bourgeoisie" believed that the answer to these ills lied not in less, but more, capitalism.

Necmettin Erbakan, a mechanical engineer trained in West Germany, was the intellectual father of the NV, and the leader of the MNP and MSP. Erbakan argued that industrialization was much less a matter of "planning" and "engineering" than of transforming the obstructive "structure" and "climate" of the general order (Erbakan 2013b [1971]: 404).[32] The key to this transformation was neither "statism" per se nor "liberalism" (Erbakan 2013d [1973]: 63). Statism and liberalism have both been tried in Turkey, yet they bene-fited either only bureaucrats or a small minority of businessmen. These two groups, together with their foreign partners, squandered the scarce resources of a poor country by establishing low productivity and noncompetitive industries (Erbakan 2013d [1973]: 50). Moreover, both statism and liberalism came to promote a "materialistic" lifestyle and education by slavishly mimicking the West (*taklitçilik*), which resulted in "interest-based exploitation" of the masses (*sömürücü faiz-cilik*) and their drift toward anarchism and communism (Erbakan 2013b [1971]: 403; 2013d [1973]: 68). In this view, the economic system is thus led by a "Masonic," "Zionist," "Jewish-like" "Comprador" minority that heavily taxed and borrowed from the people, but did not offer any payback by creating jobs and "real" investment. As such, Turkish industrialization was marked by a "vege-tative growth" (*nebati inkişaf*), which structurally inhibited an over-whelming majority of the people from participating as manufacturers, and even when people became workers, their wages were not based on "strong money," thereby rapidly eroding under inflation (Erbakan 2013d [1973]: 51, 62; 2013a [1975]: 105).

Thus, without a wholesale transformation of existing sociopolitical organization, rules and mentality (*teşkilat, mevzuat, zihniyet*), no plan could deliver expected economic outcomes in Turkey (Erbakan 2013d [1973]: 53–5). "Real industrialization" was then not only about eco-nomic planning, but required the transition to a "horizontal statism" (*ufki devletçilik*) and moralism (*maveviyatçilik*) that together would

[32] All translations of Erbakan are mine unless otherwise stated.

promote the development of an "intensive" (*yoğun*) private sector. To accomplish this goal, Erbakan proposed a number of politicocultural measures, some of which are as follows: The credit system will be overhauled in such ways that the allocation of credit will be commensurate with the level of productivity of industrial undertakings (Erbakan 2013b [1971]: 403). The state will lead and induce the deepening and spread of private industrial investment with the condition that production will be made contingent on "satisfactory profit" and "world market prices" (Erbakan 2013d [1973]: 63). The profitability of state institutions will be increased by shifting redundant state employees to more productive enterprises (Erbakan 2013d [1973]). Public investments are vital to encouraging productive investment in the private sector, therefore public funds should not be directed to unproductive and uncompetitive venues (quoted in Landau 1976: 16–17). The SEEs, unless they have a "leading" function in the economy, will operate in the same way private enterprises do, and those with leading functions will be privatized once they complete their tasks (Erbakan 2013c [1976]: 127). Taxes will be imposed on wealth, not on profits. The interest rate system will be abolished. Banks will be directly involved in production and share profits with industrialists by establishing joint productive ventures. With interest rates replaced by profit-sharing, bank operations will not only facilitate production, but also decrease the cost of borrowing and inflation, thereby increasing export competitiveness (Erbakan 2013a [1975]: 105–6). The presidency and prime ministry will be combined in a presidential system and the president will be directly elected by the people (instead of by parliament) (Erbakan 2013a [1975]: 59). The number of members of parliament will be decreased, and the electoral system that prevents parliament from working in harmony and decreases its productivity will be remedied (Erbakan 2013a [1975]). Ministries dealing with economic issues will be combined and reorganized in line with the requirements of rapid industrialization and export growth (Erbakan 2013a [1975]: 60; 2013b [1971]: 402). "Communists" and "freemasons" will be removed from state service (Erbakan 2013b [1971]: 402).

Erbakan's conception of "horizontal statism" signals a political economy in which state support and protection is conditioned to a firm's competitiveness in international markets. In this sense, he did not espouse protectionism per se; instead, he was in favor of a "selective" and strategic protectionism: For example, he says "as opposed to struggling with the EEC to be able to sell some parsley ... we should sell our agricultural and manufactured goods to Muslim states [and] build their industries [and] their roads" (Erbakan 1975 quoted in Atasoy 2005: 128). Instead of being Europe's "servant," we should lower tariffs with our neighbors in the Middle East and Africa. "We should be men and ... sell our products to the markets that we can control" (Erbakan 2013d [1973]: 70–1). And indeed, "if Turkey insists on integrating with Europe, I am afraid – Allah forbid – instead of joining the EEC, anarchy will prevail in the country and we will become just another province of communist Russia" (Erbakan 2013d [1973]: 57).

Revealingly, Erbakan's conception of social justice (*içtimai adalet*) has nothing to do with some universal values pertaining to human dignity per se, but is more-or-less a natural outcome of the order prescribed. That is, Erbakan sees social justice by and large as a derivation of the political transformation that would spread the fruits of increased competition, productivity, currency stability and an improved investment climate. Social justice, according to Erbakan, cannot be maintained through minor social fixes to existing "masonic" "corrupted" "liberal" capitalism (Erbakan 2013d [1973]: 52), and in fact, any attempt to do so is doomed to failure, for they would lead in the long run to nothing but higher inflation, higher unemployment, higher taxes on the poor and, thereby, communism (Erbakan 2013a [1975]: 102). Social justice, therefore, requires a radical departure from the existing economic and political order toward the establishment of a productivity-based system that, by increasing international competitiveness, would create jobs for the unemployed, cut waste and increase opportunities of enrichment for hardworking people while enabling workers to earn better pay and even get a share of profits (*kardan hisse*) (Erbakan 2013a [1975]: 105). Needless to say, all this depends on disciplining not only the rich through productivity-based credit and state-support policies, but also the workers and small farmers. Small farmers "should be able to sell their produce at its real value" (Landau 1976: 17), unions will operate independently of "political" influences, and workers and employers will treat each other like brothers who cooperate and work for the common goal (Erbakan 2013a [1975]: 104–6). Indeed, in such an order, there should not be an immediate need for a welfare state. The brotherly love and mutual help, ingrained in the nation's consciousness by God, will be the primary guarantor of social justice, while the state's role in redistribution will be "secondary" and "complementary" (National Salvation Party 1975: article 5).

Therefore, in Erbakan's mindset, social justice was not a goal by itself, but was part and parcel of a process of subordinating the poor to the imperatives of market competition. It is in this context that the meaning of Erbakan's call for "moral" transformation also begins to become clear. Against the "moral invasion" of Western values that brought nothing but "exploitation" and "anarchy" to the country (Erbakan 2013b [1971]: 400), Erbakan proposes a "radical re-interpretation" of secularism. He argues that secularism turned into a means of "oppressing the believers" and protecting the "usurer" (Erbakan 2013a [1975]: 62). Secularism promotes corruption, oppression and anarchy, as it removed from people's minds and hearts the love for their traditions, customs and national character. As a consequence, the education system was totally corrupted. Especially disturbing are sociology courses and curricula, most of which are based on the ideas of "a man called Durkheim (a man who had the very same ideas as a French rabbi)" (Erbakan 2013b [1971]: 405). Sociology in particular, and the education system in general, foster "materialism" hence legitimizing corruption and anarchy among the youth in the name of "reason" and "intelligence." As such, generations have been brought up with no respect for existing moral and cultural values. Corrupted here is not only religion itself but also "science." For, "real science" must be done not for science's sake, but "people's use." In this context, Erbakan makes an interesting reference to Henry IV of England (*sic*), who purportedly said in 1569 to the Royal Society of Science not to do science "over the clouds," but produce science that has practical utility for national development (Erbakan 2013d [1973]: 71). The solution to all these problems, according to Erbakan, lies in reinterpreting secularism to signify the state's tolerance for religious differences, rather than religion's exclusion from the state. This is indeed what democracy and human rights, two principles encoded in the 1961 constitution, would also presuppose as a logical conclusion (Erbakan 2013d [1975]: 61–2).

Erbakan, in short, sees secularism as the gatekeeper of a usurious or corrupted capitalism and consequently his own conception of secularism hints at the undoing of property relations and subjectivities

that Kemalism came to support. Erbakan's secularism implies the
beginning of state restructuring according to the requirements of a
"nonusurious" and "productive" order and the combining of science
and education with religion in ways to create politically loyal, scientif-
ically "useful" and economically "productive" subjects. In this respect,
Erbakan's semantic move from Durkheim to Henry IV is very mean-
ingful. Durkheim was perhaps the most important intellectual source
that inspired the "solidarism" or "populism" of the original Kemalist
project, whereas the Royal Society of Science, which the English king
was allegedly addressing, was the champion and orator of the culture
of "improvement." Therefore, while Erbakan points to the centrality
of secularism in maintaining and changing existing property relations,
his preference of Henry over Durkheim serves as a reminder of the type
of socioeconomic order that the NVM propagated.

All in all, Erbakan offered a totally fresh foundation for capitalist
development in Turkey. While short of a comprehensive economic
plan, his conception of social justice, his strategic reordering of state
support and credit in ways to subordinate production to the dictates
of international market competition, his proposal to shift power
from parliament toward the executive and his reinterpretation of
secularism provided the outlines of a novel project of capitalist
development. Erbakan sought to unburden "modernization" or
"Westernization" from its Jacobin yoke, which he saw as responsible for causing "anarchy" and creating a corrupted capitalism.
Erbakan's contempt for the "West" and his blatant anti-Semitism
were thus rooted in his effort to destroy the remnants of Jacobinism
and enthrone *fully* capitalist property relations. Part and parcel of
the destruction of Jacobinism was a new legal and moral order that,
by linking social and economic rights to productivity increases,
aimed to subordinate the poor ever more powerfully to the dictates
of capitalist competition. The moral improvement and material welfare of the poor was imagined as a direct derivation of their subordination to the discipline of capitalist accumulation. In this sense, by
linking the welfare of the poor to the "improvement" of property,
Erbakan wanted a definitive solution to the necessarily ambiguous
character of Jacobin property. Erbakan's attack on "interest-based
exploitation," and his drawing of new boundaries between the
moral and the immoral was just the flip side of his attempt to deepen
capitalist property relations.

Regardless of its intentions, however, the NV would not muster enough power to materialize its societal vision until the 2000s. Although the NV's call for a productive and just order found a strong resonance among the urban poor (especially the nonunionized workers and religious Kurds), from the 1970s to the end of the 1990s, the political parties associated with the NVM either acted only as minor partners in coalition governments or were prevented by the status quo powers from taking control of the state. The NV's societal vision would have to wait till the 2000s to be realized.

Turkey's (Not-So) Great Transformation, 1980–2002: Secularism against Capitalism

We have protected industry for too long (and) ... excessively ... It is not acceptable to produce garbage behind the customs walls and sell your garbage at the price you want. No, we will not let that happen anymore. You should compete, bro!

Turgut Özal, prime minister, 1987[33]

In many ways, the 1980 military takeover represented a watershed in Turkish political economy. Unlike the fragmented character of the 1960 intervention, the 1980 coup was led by a unified chain of command and organized well ahead of time, with a clear action plan to be implemented during and after the intervention (Karpat 1988: 149). The coup decisively suspended the constitution, shut down political parties and unions and brutally repressed the left. A transitionary government, consisting of retired military officers and technocrats, was put in place, while overall power was conducted by the MGK, which was composed of the military high command. The new constitution reversed the liberties contained in the constitution of 1961, reasserting Kemalism in ways that criminalized all leftist currents, including radical interpretations of Kemalism itself. It perceived almost everything as a threat to the security of the state and the territorial/ cultural integrity of the nation. The left, in general, suffered serious injuries after the coup. However, the Kurds, who were closely allied with the socialist movements of the 1970s, proved to be better organized and resilient than the rest of the militant left, reacting to political

[33] Quoted in Özel (2014: 65).

and military repression through armed insurgency organized by the Kurdistan Workers' Party (PKK). Also, the emergence of Turkish Kurdistan as a "common front of communist and nationalist activities" coincided with the increased perception of a geopolitical threat over the region; first as a result of the outbreak of a rebellion in Iranian Kurdistan following the Islamic Revolution, and then Syria's hosting and tacit support of the PKK leadership throughout the 1980s and the 1990s (Taşpınar 2005: 97, 137–8, 171).

If the left in general and the Kurds in particular were the main victims of the coup, the Islamic movement received only a slight blow. As in the 1970s, the military tried to remove "radical" elements from the former MSP constituency, while tolerating, if not reviving, the Islamic movement as a bulwark against the Left (Aktürk 2012: 164–5). This trend was further encouraged by the United States, which, threatened by the fall of Iran and Afghanistan, had plans to create a moderate Sunni Islamic bloc in the Middle East led by Saudi Arabia and with ties to NATO through Turkey (Atasoy 2005: 150). It is no wonder that typical Kemalist methods of containing and utilizing Islam followed the military intervention. The number of preacher schools and Koranic courses sharply rose between 1980 and 1983, as did the *Diyanet*'s (Director of Religious Affairs') budget and personnel. Also, compulsory religious lessons were introduced in all primary and middle schools (Taşpınar 2005: 138). Likewise, "secular-track school curricula recorded a marked about-face in the national educational system." While the curricula of the earlier period "distanced the republic from the Ottoman ancien regime (which students were taught had been overthrown by a 'revolution')," after 1980 it began "a gradual reversal on the question of the Ottoman-Islamic heritage which culminated in advocacy for the integration of Islamic values into the nation's political culture" (Kandiyoti 2012: 520). Given that Kemalism, as previously understood, had turned into a breeding ground for leftist radicalism, the junta and successive governments thus increasingly resorted to Islam to create a new type of subjectivity incorruptible by leftist currents.

In a sense, this quest for a new "Turkish-Islamic synthesis," although pursued in a more authoritarian manner, was not different from previous state attempts at reinterpreting Islam as an element in the making of obedient subjects. Nevertheless, the transformation of Turkish secularism in the early 1980s was underlined by an additional factor that would change the momentum of Turkish political economy. For the transformation of secularism from the 1980s signaled the breaking down of the power bloc that ruled Turkey since 1960. Given the fiscal and debt crisis, the military regime had to create a new state–society complex that would create, strengthen and rely on groups and classes with stakes in structural reform, international competition and an outward orientation.

The first step in this direction was taken with the appointment to the transitional cabinet of Turgut Özal, a proreform technocrat and engineer, as minister of state in charge of economics. Özal had acted as the head of the SPO between 1969 and 1971 and worked as an economist for the World Bank during the 1970s. He had initially been involved in Erbakan's MSP, where his brother was a leading figure, and later in 1980, the AP government put him in charge of preparation for an economic reform package, which failed to materialize due to the political stalemate preceding the coup. Already in the 1970s, Özal had thus witnessed the politics of economic reform first hand. One lesson Özal drew from the failure of stabilization packages in the 1970s and 1980s was that "steadfastness [was needed] against demands from all groups, and especially from the private sector, as the cardinal ingredient for his measures' success" (Barkey 1990: 184). Relatedly, Özal was also aware that previous reforms had failed to take off because there was no significant private-sector group pressing for their full implementation, that is, he knew that once the balance of payments crisis was over, the protectionist pressures from both the private and public sector would resuscitate, resulting in the reversal of reforms (Tekin 1997: 236).

In short, what was at stake was a radical reorganization of public and private powers in the postcoup period, which aimed at selective seclusion of the state from popular pressures and the creation of a coalition whose interests rested on the expansion and deepening of export-oriented production and expanded reproduction of capital. The first task, that is, the building of the state's relative autonomy, was partly achieved through institutional and legal changes designed to overcome potential political clashes within the state and restrict the influence of societal groups over economic policy-making. These measures included, albeit were not limited to: empowerment of the presidency; the constitution of a unicameral legislature; strengthening of the executive through the issuance of decree laws (*kanun hükmünde kararname*); the centralization of economic decision-making in a number of state ministries to bypass the control of parliament; restrictions of constitutional freedoms; curbing of trade unions' power; centralization of decision-making in higher education; and the establishment of a 10 percent electoral threshold (Barkey 1990: 187–9; Oğuz 2008: 163–4). The sustainability of these legal and institutional changes was also dependent on the realization of the second task, which indeed proved to be much more formidable than the first. For, already in 1982, there was resistance to Özal's market reforms from the largest holding corporations with strong import substitution concerns, which in fact, by exerting pressure on the military, led to Özal's resignation from the transitional government (Barkey 1990: 184; Tekin 1997: 247–8, 250). Big business was interested in increasing Turkey's "credit-worthiness" yet not structural reform, that is, a reform that would lead to the reproduction of the import-substituting industrial structure by ensuring the continuous availability of external funds for import-dependent industries (Aydın 2005: 112).

Özal came back with an election victory in 1983, however. While all precoup politicians were banned from electoral politics for ten years, Özal, as a technocrat highly respected by Western creditors, was allowed by the junta to enter the elections with his brand-new Motherland Party (ANAP). The commercial elite supported the ANAP in the elections as they believed the military-backed parties could hinder the arrival of foreign funds. As a result, the ANAP managed to win, especially the constituency of the old AP and MSP, gaining over 35 percent of the votes, and (given the new electoral system) 60 percent of the seats in parliament. Özal's electoral success assured him the power to reinitiate the economic reform process and the building of a proreform coalition of bourgeois interests (Barkey 1990: 190).

Özal took several measures to "discipline" the bourgeois class and to create a broad social base that could support the expansion and deepening of capitalist social relations. Through funds provided by international financial institutions and foreign governments, he designed new incentives (subsidies, credits, foreign exchange allocations and tax exemptions) to reinforce and deepen the proreform groups within the business community. No wonder most TUSIAD members remained suspicious of Özal during the 1980s, criticizing him for frequent devaluations (hence rising prices for their imports), import liberalization (hence increasing foreign competition) and the government's support for "exporters" over the "investing industrialists" (Tekin 1997: 249).[34] This is not to deny that the policies encouraging export-led growth initiated a protracted transformation within the group of big industrialists: some import substitution holding companies, encouraged by generous export subsidies, lowere wages and the devalued lira,[35] began to take an outward orientation from the mid-1980s. Yet, it is equally true that given their immense resources and political links, the bulk of export subsidies were still received by large holding companies with almost no export potential (Milor and Biddle 1995: 6; 1997: 291). Likewise, the domestic markets for manufactured goods continued to be governed by an oligopolistic pricing structure, "abated by arms-length connections with the company owned/managed banking conglomerates" (Boratav et al. 2000: 18–19; Yeldan 2001: 1). In other words, in spite of the emergence of a number of strongly export-oriented sectors in competitive industries with smaller producers (especially textiles and ready-to-wear clothing), most export support policies and the domestic market benefited noncompetitive and monopolistic actors, who did not have to compete to survive. As a result, various forms of incentives, such as tax rebates, preferential credits and grants, ended up becoming "giveaways," "pure and simple" (Milor and Biddle 1995: 57). "Rent-oriented networks" that appeared to have no economic rationale continued to be "the norm with respect to the Turkish incentive regime" (Milor and Biddle 1995: 6).

At any event, the private sector's unwillingness to export further increased in the context of the late 1980s. As the Iran–Iraq War came to an end and oil prices dropped after 1986, Turkey's initial "export

---

[34] The number of TUSIAD members increased from 12 in 1971 to 243 in 1987. In the 1980s, "the Association accounted for about half the production and employment of private manufacturing industry" (Arat 1991: 137). In the first half of the 1980s, according to Tekin, there were only two TUSIAD members (ENKA Holding and IZDAS) who were heavily involved in export activities, while others either took an ambiguous stance or did not change their antiexport position (Tekin 1997: 249–50).

[35] From 1980 to the end of 1988, the real effective rate of depreciation of the lira was about 55 percent. Given the highly prohibitive environment for unionized labor and suspension of free collective agreements, real labor costs declined from 100 in 1980 to 65.8 in 1988 (Şenses 1994: 56–7).

miracle" subsided (İlkin 1991: 95).[36] This, in turn, increased the cost
of export subsidies and foreign debt due to continued real depreciation
of the lira (Boratav et al. 2000: 8). Combined with meager private
manufacturing investment, public expenditure and inflation came
under serious pressure from 1986 onward.[37] Furthermore, mass protests erupted against the suppression of real wages and agricultural
subsidies, which in turn reinforced the hands of precoup political
leaders who were allowed to return to electoral politics in 1987 (Özel
2003: 106). In this context, Özal had no choice but to reinitiate the
cycle of electoral populism, which would lead to important wage and
subsidy increases until 1994. Thus, toward the end of the 1980s, the
strategy of "restraining incomes of popular classes to encourage capital
accumulation and gaining international competitiveness, was increasingly becoming inoperative" (Türel 1996: 167). The most typical
response by the business elite to declining export earnings, increasing
wages and inflation was to mark up their prices, begin an investment
strike and shed labor, which exacerbated the ongoing political and
economic crisis. At this juncture, the state liberalized the capital
account in 1989 to finance its deficits, which would in fact provide
big business with a golden opportunity for turning potential losses into
profits (Boratav et al. 2000: 6–7).

After the opening of the capital account in 1989, the holding banks
became the central benefactors of state-borrowing practices. Lured by

[36] In the period 1980–88, the real value of exports grew 19 percent annually,
which then declined 5 percent between 1989 and 1993 (Boratav et al. 2000: 30).
This seemingly impressive export growth has to be qualified in two respects,
which also shows the shaky foundations of Turkish export performance. First,
"the extent of state intervention through export incentive schemes was so large
that it probably led to much time and effort devoted to obtaining export
incentives" (Şenses 1994: 58). According to one estimate, for example, "the
subsidy effect of government incentives equaled roughly 55 per cent of the value
of exports" (Atasoy 2005: 149, also see Yeldan 1994: 82). Second, given the
generosity of government support, overstating export earnings to take
advantage of the export rebate schemes was a commonplace practice. The
"fictitious exports" are estimated to have reached to almost 13 percent of total
exports to OECD (Organization for Economic Cooperation and Development)
countries during 1981–5 (Şenses 1994: 58).

[37] Inflation decreased from 108 percent in 1980 to 28 percent in 1983, and then
increased back to 75 percent in 1988 (Waldner 1999: 220–1). The national debt
between 1980 and 1990 increased from US$13.5 billion to US$40 billion, while
yearly repayment reached to US$7 billion, which was approximately 60 percent
of export earnings (Taşpınar 2005: 142).

high interest rates, these banks, almost all of which were parts of holding companies with industrial bases, made profits by purchasing government securities and exploiting the difference between the exchange rate and the interest rate (Oğuz 2008: 110–12).[38] That is, they first obtained funds on international markets as credit denominated in dollars, converted this into Turkish lira and then lent to the government at high interest rates. It does not require great foresight to predict that an increasingly high proportion of profits were obtained in the financial activities associated with the holding of government securities. With holding companies enjoying oligopolistic markets and financial rents, there was eventually only little need for reinvestment, which is an indicator of the degree of stagnation of investment levels throughout the 1990s.[39] Furthermore, the privatization of SEEs took place only very slowly until the 2000s, in part due to the unwillingness of large businesses to buy into the privatization process, and their opposition to the sale of SEEs to foreign competitors (Öniş 1991: 171, 173). The point is that throughout the 1980s and 1990s, the social reproduction of the big bourgeoisie, in spite of their rhetorical support for structural reforms, remained by and large dependent on the state's systematic transfer of monopoly and financial rents. This created a vicious rent-debt cycle, which ultimately prevented the completion of the capitalist restructuring process begun in 1980. As the state's attempt at strategically leading capitalist development degenerated into the mere distribution of tax revenues, the restructuring of

---

[38] "Private commercial banks" annual interest income from securities steadily increased from under US$0.5 billion in 1987 to over US$9 billion by 1999. On average, this income was about twice as big as the net profits of these banks throughout the 1990s, putting into perspective their structural dependence on and vested interest in Turkey's perpetual fiscal crisis (Güven 2009: 238–9).

[39] While real gross domestic product grew only by 3.4 percent per annum between 1990 and 2000, the annual real rate of growth of banking-sector assets exceeded 13 percent. This enormous divergence between the performance of the real economy and the financial sector was clearly a result of the short-term foreign capital inflows that were made possible by very high rates of interest offered by the state: 100 percent in January 1996; 80 percent in March 2000 (see Cizre and Yeldan 2005: 391–5). This brought in its train catastrophic consequences for public finance. The ratio of interest payments to tax revenues rose from 28 percent in 1992 to 77 percent in 2000, while the public sector's real disposable income declined by 39 percent through the 1990s (Boratav and Yeldan 2006: 424)

productive capacity of the economy via the deepening of capitalist social relations was undermined.

In spite of their rhetorical support for structural reforms throughout the 1990s, big business thus prevented the transfer of public resources from finance to internationally competitive manufacturing sectors. Mirroring the economic problems of the 1990s was the extreme polarization of political life. Having failed to remedy inflation and sufficiently support SMEs, the ANAP's former electoral base rapidly eroded in the 1990s. The cleavages between the large industrialists and the Islamic bourgeoisie, who had temporarily united under ANAP rule during the 1980s, began to deepen (Taşpınar 2005: 144). Especially after Turgut Özal became the president of Turkey in 1989 (thereby having to keep out of party politics), the party lost most of its appeal among its conservative constituency (Ahmad 1993: 198). The precoup political leaders had also returned to active politics by the 1991 elections, which led to the reemergence of the old political fault lines. The center-right and center-left were both fragmented among two major parties, which rendered the formation of a broad-based coalition to fix the ailing economy very difficult. From 1991 to 1999, nine coalition governments were formed; and besides the political instability, the intensity of electoral competition forced the centrist parties of both right and left to engage in a form of "double redistribution" (Güven 2009). While trying to appease the big bourgeoisie through financial rents, they also strived to win rural votes (still one of the most important segments of electoral politics) by resorting to agricultural populism, especially from 1994 onward. "Rather than neutralize losers by bringing together potential winners under a pro-reform coalition," double redistribution "rallied traditional and new style rent seekers behind an odd political alliance dedicated to forestalling reform and the reinforcement of the emergent institutional status quo" (Güven 2009: 258). Financial and rural transfers enabled volatile coalition governments to survive, yet at the same time "exacerbated the fiscal dependence on commercial banks" and "insulated agriculture from world markets via an expensive currency" (Güven 2009: 248, 254). Given that economic reproduction was immediately related to intense political competition, corruption also took devastating forms, further adding to the never-ending economic and political crisis of the 1990s (Gülalp 2001: 438; Güven 2009: 193–4).

The urban poor and SMEs were excluded from the channels of double redistribution. Worker activism, which tended to resuscitate at the end of the 1980s, petered out through the second half of the 1990s. The growing inability of both private and public sectors to tolerate wage increases, as well as the repression of the radical left and the informalization of labor markets, rendered labor-based populism politically futile. The urban poor, who used to be the support base of leftist currents in the 1970s, were increasingly impoverished and marginalized, and left with no hope of social mobility and the political representation of their interests. In addition, the expansion of the informal sector paralleled the rise of SMEs "both in the metropolitan and Anatolian heartlands, in which wage levels were (and still are) much lower" (Güven 2009: 192).The SMEs, most of which were ventures associated with so-called Islamic capital, gained access to a larger pool of cheap labor, which helped them improve their ability to "establish themselves as significant exporters of manufactures" despite the fact that they had "received little or no subsidy from the state" (Öniş 1997: 759).

Indeed, the most consistent support for the postcoup export drive came from these SMEs, which, "frequently in conflict with TUSIAD, lobbied for the maintenance and increase of incentives presented to exporters" (Ünay 2006: 74). Among these, the most prominent were Turkish construction companies and industrialists (predominantly textile and to a lesser extent iron and steel manufacturers) operating in or producing for the expanding Middle Eastern markets, where "a company's religious affiliation mattered a great deal to potential customers" (Barkey 1990: 178). Indeed, the Middle Eastern markets and financial institutions provided ample opportunities for the expansion of Anatolian SMEs (or Anatolian Tigers as they came to be called) closely linked to Islamic brotherhoods and networks (Hoşgör 2011: 345). The Islamic bourgeoisie, previously deprived of credit and state support, strongly responded to these opportunities and the export incentives provided by Özal's ANAP. The business association representing the interests of Islamic capital, MUSIAD, opposed the "uncompetitive environment created by state support of TUSIAD and big business in general" (Yavuz 1997: 72), while advocating for the free accumulation of profit "as long as profit comes from productive activities" (Hoşgör 2011: 349). In their opposition to TUSIAD, they appealed to and sought to discipline the urban poor with a new understanding of "justice" congruent with the competitive and productive relations of a "moral" capitalism. In this conception, the key to peace and prosperity was considered to be the Islamic regulation of the marketplace, which prevents injustices stemming from industrial monopolies, financial speculation and radical unionism, while promoting productive industrial relations, innovation and hence economic growth for everyone. Workers should avoid conflict and confrontation at the workplace, and instead, should "share the risk and responsibility with the employers in quantity and quality of the products produced." Justice, in this sense, was strongly tied to the attainment of "harmony and productivity," hence the abolishing of all institutions and practices that cause "hoarding," corruption and "laziness." Indeed, MUSIAD argued that if profit was used productively and not solely for individual consumption, wealth did not cause "oppression" nor did the wealthy constitute a "class." There was "capital" in this new order, but there were no capitalists (Hoşgör 2011: 349–50).

Clearly, MUSIAD echoed the NVM of the 1970s; and it is not by accident that MUSIAD's call for justice strongly resonated with the NV of the 1990s, which was revamped in Necmettin Erbakan's Welfare Party (RP). The RP was both a product and a foe of the new Kemalist order established in 1980. As mentioned earlier, since the 1980 coup, the bureaucratic and business elite had begun to see Islam as a bulwark against the left. While Erbakan's Islam grew in the space espoused by the Kemalist political and economic elite against communism, it also charged the Kemalist establishment with moral degeneration, which was considered to be the root cause of rentier interests and anarchist currents. According to Erbakan, what needed to be done was to establish a "Just Order" (*Adil Düzen*), an order underlined by distinct social and moral patterns conducive to productivity and "justice" in the economy. Interest, money printing, the present financial system and monopolies all cause poverty and social injustice (Erbakan 1991: 22–7). In the Just Order, by contrast, the state would prevent monopolization by ensuring that every entrepreneur would benefit from state services, while private enterprise would be a right available to everyone. The Just Order thus implied a transition from a monopolist to a "truly pro-private enterprise" order in which the state would play a significant role in assuring productivity and competitiveness (Erbakan 1991). Relatedly, according to Erbakan, given the strong role of the state in maintaining a truly competitive order, the prospect of Turkey joining the Customs Union without being a full member of the European Union must be avoided at all costs. "Turkey's entry into the Customs Union without being a member of the European Union, the decision-making body of the trading bloc" would inevitably lead to the dissolution of productive sectors and the strengthening of a corrupted capitalism in Turkey. Entering the Customs Union would "amount to accepting to live in the servants' quarters next to the doghouse in the garden of a manor" (Erbakan quoted in Cook 2007: 106–7). Instead, stronger economic relations must be forged with the relatively more penetrable markets such as the Middle East, post-Soviet Central Asia and the dynamic economies of Southeast Asia with predominantly Muslim populations, such as Malaysia and Indonesia (Öniş 1997: 754).

The Just Order was founded upon a new political structure and new morality. The former pertained to a state that would promote production, investment and competitiveness, maintain a balanced budget, establish a progressive taxation system, pursue an anti-inflationary monetary policy and implement privatization more "justly" (Erbakan 1991: 22–7). All this, in turn, was conditioned on the cultivation of a national moral consciousness distinct from Western politicocultural influences. The Just Order rejected Westernization as a prerequisite for economic development, seeing that imitating Western models for almost two centuries brought Turkey nothing but "exploitation" and "anarchy." In this respect, transforming secularism was vital to the restructuring of both the state and economy. "Production mobilization" was possible only if a spiritual transformation could be achieved and the old transnational Muslim community (*umma*), uncorrupted by Western influences, could be recovered. The *umma* would replace Western-imposed rights and duties in society with religiously sanctioned yet voluntarily implemented networks of trust and solidarity. This new sociality and morality would not only ensure free competition, productivity and loyalty, but also provide a space wherein Western-imposed social differences such as nation and race are transcended (Duran 1998). Transforming secularism therefore was not about asserting a new interpretation of religion only, but reconstructing the regime of property and ethnicity based on sociointellectual resources untroubled by the legacy of Kemalism.

The RP mobilized the urban poor (most of whom were Kurds)[40] and the Islamic bourgeoisie around its Just Order program, ultimately succeeding from a mere 7.2 percent of the national vote in 1987 to become the first party with 21.3 percent in 1995. In a context where winning votes through union-based working-class populism was no longer feasible, and redistributive policies were associated with inflation and unemployment, the left was increasingly crippled in delivering anything substantial to the urban poor whose numbers grew tremendously since the 1980s. By contrast, the RP offered a way out of the existing system by invoking a world wherein the secular privileges that sustain the Kemalist political economy are destroyed. The popular appeal of replacing the "unjust" and "materialist" system with Islamic equity and transnational brotherhood augmented the RP's organizational capabilities linked to its close relations with Islamic brotherhoods (Yavuz 1997: 67). As such, the RP was not simply reproducing social democracy with an Islamic face, as often argued (e.g. Öniş 1997), but in its quest for power against the Kemalist political and economic elite, the RP derived from Islam the structure of a fully capitalist society, that is, one that recognizes no secular privilege for property. Overcoming injustice and poverty was intrinsically linked to the deepening of capitalist social relations.

Naturally, the RP's rise to power in 1995 as the major partner in a coalition government deeply disturbed the Kemalist political and economic elite. The perception of the threat was framed either as the danger of Islamic fundamentalism undermining secularism or as the looming possibility of a serious "social explosion" caused by adverse socioeconomic circumstances (Cizre-Sakallıoğlu and Yeldan 2000: 482). The military intervened once again on February 28, 1997 with a "soft coup." They did not suspend the constitution or dissolve the parliament; instead, they issued a number of policy "recommendations" to the RP-led government aimed at preventing the rise of Islamic "reactionaries" within the state and economy. This left Erbakan with no room, leading to his resignation. February 28 brought about the closure of middle-level imam-hatip schools through

---

[40] The population of big cities had rapidly increased in the two decades following the military coup. The rural population decreased from 55 percent of total population in 1980 to 40 percent in 1990 and to 35 percent in 2000. Likewise, İstanbul's population increased from about 5 million in 1988 to 10–12 million in 1997.

the extension of obligatory public schooling from five to eight years, closer inspection of religious orders, strict observation of secular dress codes in "public spaces" and supervision of government recruitment practices. The Constitutional Court shut down the RP in January 1998, while Erbakan was banned from politics for five years. Although the remaining RP members of parliament formed the Virtue Party, the military made sure that the RP would be excluded from future governments. On the economic front, the assets of some Islamic holding companies were frozen, while many Islamic firms were excluded from state contracts and their financial operations put under greater scrutiny. Islamic reactionism (*irtica*) was now considered by the MGK as the most important "internal" threat to the Republic, alongside the "external" threat of Kurdish separatism (Taşpınar 2005: 156–7). TUSIAD was either indifferent to or supportive of the February 28 process, an indicator of their perception of the threat from Islamic capital and their prioritization of "secularism" over "democracy" (Özel 2012: 22–3).

In short, the legacies of a Jacobin past were invoked once again to reinforce an oligarchic capitalism against the vision of a more market-dependent society. The soft coup of 1997 turned secularism into a bulwark against the deepening of capitalist social relations. However, economic and political privileges safeguarded by secularism could not be protected through political and juridical means only. Indeed, following the soft coup, "a new sense of alarm and urgency" prevailed among the Turkish political and economic elite "about the need for discipline in the government's fiscal management." For, the existence and sustainability of the regime in the face of Islamic resurgence depended, above all, on the state's capability to restrain inflation and alleviate economic problems (Cizre-Sakallıoğlu and Yeldan 2000: 481–2). Inflation and corruption scandals were posing severe systemic challenges to the Republican regime as a whole; therefore, fixing these problems began to be considered by the secularist establishment as a matter of "virtually life and death" (Cizre-Sakallıoğlu and Yeldan 2000: 504). Unlike the earlier economic crisis, the state's (potential) financial default was no longer a matter of a temporary illiquidity of funds, but a matter of survival in the face of a powerful contender with mass support. Therefore, even before the wave of the global crisis, which had begun in Asia (1997) and Russia (1998), reached Turkey in 2000–1, the technocratic space for structural reform was widened perhaps as never before due to these pressures from "below."

Consequently, in December 1999, for the first time in its postwar history, Turkey accepted a reform program in the absence of an explicit crisis (Aydın 2005: 119; Oğuz 2008: 117). Under close supervision by the International Monetary Fund (IMF), the Turkish government pledged to target hemorrhaging public expenditures in order to reduce inflation to single digits by the end of 2002, which would ultimately require a radical restructuring of the banking sector and thus the reorganization of holding companies (Aydın 2005: 120). Based on this picture, there is no question that when the economic crisis finally hit Turkey in February 2001, the ability of big business to stop or slow down the pace of structural reforms was already diminished. Nevertheless, it would be mere speculation to argue that the majority of big businesses would continue to give sustained support to the reform process. Indeed, there were signs of reform fatigue already in the summer of 2002, marked by the resignation of the technocratic head of the reform programme. "Even ministers from the governing party were fleeing by July 2002 and early elections were called for November 2002" (Özdemir 2013: 57). Therefore, we cannot tell whether the big bourgeoisie would have retained its reformist stance had a government in their favor been elected in November. In any event, the elections completely crushed the political parties of the 1990s, pushing big business to the margins of future power arrangements. Islamists with a brand-new party (AKP, or Justice and Development Party), established only nineteen months before the elections and with a brand-new leader (Recep Tayyip Erdoğan), secured 34 percent of the votes and 66 percent of the seats in parliament. Islamists, forced out of the government in 1997, thus reseized it in 2002. In the decades to follow, Islamists would breathe new life into capitalism, as they eliminated the last remnants of Kemalist secularism.

Consolidation of Capitalist Modernity: From Neo-Ottoman Commonwealth to Capitalist Authoritarianism

Turkey should be administered like an incorporated company. If not, there are shackles tied to your ankles and you cannot walk further.

Recep Tayyip Erdoğan, president, 2015[41]

---

[41] https://tr.sputniknews.com/20150315/1014435942.html.

Once the 2001 crisis subsided, therefore, what replaced reformist technocrats was not a fragmented political structure susceptible to reproducing the oligarchic redistribution of the 1990s, but a single-party government with organic links to a new capitalist class (Güven 2009). A new capitalist class, previously excluded from the official credit channels and privileges enjoyed by the old elite, has emerged with a distinct project of capitalist transformation. Its previous exclusion from state-generated rents forced it to envision a society in which economic competitiveness, underlined by a specific politicoreligious subjectivity, would be the ultimate basis for societal reproduction. In short, the AKP signaled the rise of a new capitalist class whose social reproduction was conditioned on the deepening of capitalist social relations.

The new bourgeois class became the supporter of structural reforms initiated in December 1999, helping to consolidate the reform process and ensure its irreversibility. In turn, the AKP provided various incentives to the Islamic bourgeoisie, reversing their unfavorable treatment in public contracts and privatization bids, leading to their further enrichment and internationalization. With the AKP and Islamic bourgeoisie converging on an antimonopolist agenda, the big bourgeoisie was to make strategic compromises to the Islamic bourgeoisie concerning the political and institutional structure of the economy (Hoşgör 2011: 355). Forced by the new configuration of political power, and encouraged by prospects for economic expansion under a single-party government and European Union membership, the large conglomerates ceded their resistance to structural reform, which indeed has enabled them to become the main beneficiaries of state investment incentives and privatization processes since 2002 (Karatepe 2015: 57–8).

On the whole, such a sociopolitical restructuring signaled the reorganization of holding companies in such a way as to promote "productive capital-based accumulation" through increasing competitiveness in the international market (Oğuz 2008: 118; Aydın 2013: 100). The introduction of banking reform[42] and the deregulation of the energy and telecommunication sectors reinforced the tendency toward subjecting the private sector to the rules of competition in an

---

[42] Akın et al. (2009) note that in the postcrisis period, declining inflation rates, fiscal prudence and the European Union's insistence on compliance with BASEL II requirements forced Turkish banks to assume their intermediation role, transferring the weight in their portfolios from government securities to loans.

increasingly internationalizing market. What was underway, in other words, was a departure from the previous pattern of accumulation based on the redistribution of profits through the state toward a mode of accumulation based on production through increasing international competitiveness.[43] Emerging is a historically specific political economy, which, despite the continuity of corruption and extensive use of political power for personal economic advantage,[44] is ultimately premised on the ability of public and private powers to achieve material reproduction through the world market and on the capacity to reproduce the fiction of self-regulating markets.[45]

Relatedly, the period under AKP rule witnessed massive privatizations[46] and the implementation of measures designed to shield economic decision-making from popular measures and party politics, for example, the centralization of decision-making power in the executive branch of the state, the creation of "independent" economic institutions such as the Central Bank, the Competition Board and the Privatization Administration, and above all, the recent shift from the long-standing parliamentary system to a centralized Russian-style presidential one. In particular, until the mid 2010s, the "independence" of economic decision-making was propped up by the favorable credit conditions worldwide: the global liquidity has eased the socioeconomic costs of restructuring at home and helped finance the chronic capital account deficit, and the credit requirements of the private sector

[43] Between 2002 and 2021, exports and imports of Turkey increased from US$35 and 51 billion to US$225 and 271 billion, respectively.

[44] The fact that the public procurement law has been changed 192 times between 2003 and 2021 is perhaps the bleakest reminder of the continued nontransparency of state interventions and the use of personal power for economic gain, see www.birgun.net/haber/kamu-ihale-kanunu-192-kez-degistiriliyor-343171.

[45] My intention here is not to exaggerate the performance of the Turkish economy in the post-2001 period. And certainly the continuing crisis of the world economy, increasing depletion of global liquidity and domestic corruption would not permit optimistic assessments of the Turkish economy at all. All that said, however, all of these factors must not obscure the qualitative changes the Turkish economy and society has undergone in the last two decades, which is the main focus in this chapter.

[46] While annual privatization income amounted to US$380 million between 1980 and 2003, after 2003 it would reach US$6 billion annually. Also, privatization entered the constitution in 1999, countering for the first time the explicit constitutional references to "nationalization" and "use for public good" (Güran 2011: 23, 38; Zaifer 2020).

and the households without having to tweak the independence of "independent" institutions (Bedirhanoğlu 2021). While this eventually caused the national debt to skyrocket from around US$100 billion in 2005 (15 percent of GDP) to US$450 billion in 2020 (62 percent of GDP), it also ensured the acceptability and "neutrality" of market outcomes. The global liquidity helped, at least for a while, to reproduce the impersonal, depoliticized and rule-based appearance of the markets, hence signaling the qualitative transformation of state–business relations under AKP rule.

The transformation of state–business relations has been accompanied by corresponding changes in the countryside. Since the 2000s, Turkey has witnessed an immensely rapid period of dissolution of petty commodity production driven by neoliberal market reforms. The state ceased to provide support for buying at floor prices, input subsidies and subsidized credits to agricultural producers. It largely withdrew its support from the production of widely cultivated crops such as sugar and tobacco. Instead of buying agricultural products at politically constituted prices, the state provides only temporary income support to peasants, expecting them to produce goods highly demanded in the world market at competitive rates (Aydın 2005: 158–9). In addition to the erosion in the amount of state support,[47] income support now took on a temporary character that increasingly exposed small farmers to the imperatives of market competition, thereby precipitating the divorce of peasants from land. Furthermore, the Agrarian and Seed Laws passed in 2006 have further contributed to the commodification of land and labor in the Turkish countryside. Upholding intellectual property rights in agricultural crops and seeds, these two complementary laws have deprived small farmers of the traditional seed varieties used for centuries. Small producers turned into "contract farmers," increasingly producing crops demanded by agroindustrial corporations in exchange for information, credits, seeds and other inputs. Contract farming has put agribusiness firms in a position to determine the conditions of production and impose the type, quality and quantity of production over the remaining segments of the rural population. All combined, the political support given to small farmers since the 1950s has rapidly faded away, with the

---

[47] State support for agriculture decreased from 3.2 percent of GDP in 1999 to 0.45 percent in 2009 (Günaydın 2009: 183).

consequence that even the remaining farmers have completely lost their autonomy, becoming totally subjected to the imperatives of capital accumulation (Aydın 2010; Keyder and Yenal 2011). With large portions of small farmers dispossessed, the remainder subordinated to full market discipline on their own land, capitalism has permeated the Turkish countryside more than ever before.

The social aspect of the Republic has also been significantly altered under the AKP rule. New forms of flexible and insecure work such as part-time and temporary work and subcontracting were legalized from 2003 in order to formalize the massive informal sector.[48] This was accompanied by legal changes that deteriorated the organizational power of labor in the formal sector. Collective rights, bargaining processes and institutions have been undermined so much so that "trade union density decreased from 20% in 1998 … to 6.3% in 2013," while "the number of workers covered by collective agreements decreased by half to 4% in 2015" (Özdemir 2020: 10–11). Besides the growing insecurity and flexibility of labor, the AKP considerably increased welfare spending, which further weakened opposition to neoliberal policies, hence facilitating the deepening of capitalist social relations. That is, while "the first generation neoliberal reforms in the 1980s and 1990s decreased formal employment opportunities and increased social exclusion and insecurity in Turkey," the second round of neoliberal restructuring begun in the 2000s "contained social policies which have benefited the poor and socially excluded groups, helping AKP and Erdoğan gain popularity among the poor masses" (Özdemir 2020: 2). Although state-funded and "universal" in appearance, some of the healthcare and welfare services have been subcontracted to private actors and Islamic-oriented charity groups, and replaced by "means-tested social assistance measures that are commonly regarded as incompatible with social citizenship rights, which ought to entail universal benefits to all citizens regardless of their financial condition" (Bozkurt 2013: 391). Indeed, these government–charity partnerships have been particularly successful in reaching those who were previously excluded from formalized channels of public welfare, which is another key variable used to explain the AKP's series of electoral successes from 2002 to the present. Furthermore, the state

---

[48] The number of subcontracted workers increased from 358,000 in 2002 to 1.5 million in 2011 (Özdemir 2020: 10).

has mobilized the financial sector to extend credit to poorer segments of the society. The ratio of household debt to disposable income increased from 4.7 percent in 2002 to 52 percent in 2015, with the result that citizens whose incomes are at or below the poverty line have accessed sources of consumption that they otherwise could not have (Güngen 2017: 9). All that said, although these welfare and financial measures seem to have lifted the poor out of the worst forms of poverty,[49] this success is just the other side of the qualitative redefinition of citizenship rights under AKP rule, that is, the material welfare of the poor has been directly linked to their acceptance of the logic of workfare, charity, credit-dependence and the discipline of capitalist accumulation (Coşar and Yeğenoğlu 2009).

The overall result is the consolidation of capitalist social relations for the first time in Turkish history. In this context, given that economic competition and compulsion has become the main determinant for the social reproduction of all echelons of society (bourgeoise included), one may expect that cultural, religious and political hierarchies of the previous period would lose their centrality in the production and distribution of socioeconomic power, and concomitantly, a political arena in which subjects enjoy wider (yet strictly) political and cultural rights would emerge and expand. Clearly, the point here is not that the more capitalism, the more democracy or that capitalism is necessarily less authoritarian than other modes of socioeconomic organization. Capitalism can and has been compatible with different forms of political rule and labor control, such as fascism and coerced wage labor (Post 2013; Bruff 2014; Kiely 2017). Yet, the opposite is also true: as capitalism effectively denies any rights of participation in decisions related to the organization of production, thereby shielding itself from any kind of democratic accountability at the workplace, it may also create a wider space of citizen involvement in which political and cultural rights can be exercised without overstepping the productive use of property. While other class societies are structurally antithetical to political equality due to the fusion of political and economic powers, capitalism is not. Hence capitalism's possible, yet not necessary,

---

[49] According to the World Bank, the number of citizens living at or under the poverty threshold (US$5.50 a day) has decreased from 31.8 percent of the population in 2002 to 9.9 percent in 2016 (Özdemir 2020: 16).

congruity with the requirements of liberal democracy (Wood 1991: 174–6; 1995: 237).

Indeed, the very trajectory of the AKP rule since 2002 has confirmed how quickly the prospect of capitalist democracy can vanish, to be replaced by capitalist authoritarianism. The 2000s have witnessed perhaps the most revolutionary political and cultural changes ever made in the history of the Turkish Republic. The dominance of the Kemalist bureaucracy in key state institutions has been eliminated, as have the economic privileges enjoyed by OYAK. Most military spending has been made subject to review by civil auditors. Constitutional amendments have been passed to increase parliamentary control over the system of appointments to the high courts. The decisions taken by the Supreme Military Council, the body with authority over promotions and dismissals in the army, have been opened to judicial and parliamentary review, which had not been possible previously. Likewise, the MGK's "monitoring" function has been significantly curtailed through the appointment of a civilian secretary-general and an increased number of nonmilitary members on the council. The retirement age has been lowered in some key positions within the security, higher-education and scientific establishments in order to replace old cadres with bureaucrats close to the AKP (Cizre 2011; Polat 2013).

It is important to note that none of this would be possible without the assistance of an Islamic brotherhood known as the Gülenists. Although active since the 1970s, this Islamic cult, led by a US-based preacher, Fettullah Gülen, have had a formidable presence in the police, judiciary, education, military and media since the 2000s. In particular, between 2007 and 2011, the Gülenists entrenched in the police and judiciary system initiated a series of anticoup investigations against (mostly) Kemalist-minded high-ranking military staff, politicians, civil society actors and journalists, which not only led to their detention for years on fake charges, but also enabled the AKP government to fully consolidate its power within the state and civil society.

Considering the "success" of the AKP–Gülen alliance in transforming the state and civil society, no wonder the main parameters of Kemalist modernity have been opened to public debate. Secularism has been largely overhauled, as the AKP cadres and Islamic intellectuals have reinterpreted secularism away from the French-inspired Kemalist laïcité toward the Anglo-Saxon model (Türkmen 2009:

394), where secularism is understood not as "freedom from religion," but "freedom of religion" (Kaya 2015: 55). Headscarf bans in universities and the civil service have been lifted. The discrimination against religious school students in the university entrance exam, effective since 1997, has been brought to an end. Additional religion-based courses have been added to secular public school curriculums (Kaya 2015: 57). Also, plans have been floated to convert most secular high schools into preacher schools and introduce compulsory religious education in primary schools. In a similar fashion, the dominant conception of nation seems to have gone through a drastic change, as the AKP initiated a "peace process" with the aim of resolving the long-lasting Kurdish question. Indeed, in April 2013, the negotiation with the PKK came to the brink of a historic peace deal, securing the disarmament of the PKK in exchange of the wider recognition of Kurds' political and collective rights. In this sense, the AKP set in train a radical process of redefining the main parameters of the earlier period, nurturing a new subjectivity and collectivity as the foundation of a new political economy.

The *initial* outcome of such a restructuring of state–society relations was a form of Islamic multiculturalism, inspired by a romanticized Ottoman imperial pluralism and encouraged by the accession process to the European Union. Islamic values and old imperial forms of rule were reformulated to prepare the ground for a form of liberalism, which sought to promote new forms of political community, subjectivity and space. This involved the creation of a new citizenship ethic largely derived from narratives based on the prophet Muhammad's life (the Sunna), especially with regard to his "tolerance" for non-Muslims (Türkmen 2009) and the fact that he was a merchant. Meanwhile, Koranic verses were transformed into slogans that provide the moral basis for "economic competition" and fairness of market outcomes (Yavuz 2003: 95). "Tolerance," "fairness" and "economic competition" related to a community where the subjects internalize a capitalist competition ethic and *some* liberal democratic values based on a narrative of peaceful social coexistence derived from an imagined Ottoman-Islamic past. Entailed in this reorganization of sociality was the emergence of a religiously represented and politically empowered individuality unencumbered by the Kemalist organization of social reproduction (Atasoy 2009). It is this ground on which a shift occurred, at least for a while, from the monolithically understood political space toward a new collective subjectivity based on the peaceful coexistence of different ethnoreligious and cultural groups; indeed as some commentators like to call it, a new "Ottoman Commonwealth." As a result, the AKP government, at least initially, adopted a relatively more tolerant approach to political and cultural freedoms, taking steps toward resolving the most recurrent problems in Turkish political life regarding the rights of ethnic and religious minorities (Aktürk 2012: 193–4; Keyman and Gümüşçü 2014; Boyraz 2019).

Furthermore, the Ottoman commonwealth was not only a domestic project, but part of an attempt at regional respatialization, with serious implications on Turkey's foreign policy orientation.[50] That involved the emergence of a "trading state," which sought to unburden itself from the costs of the most chronic issues in Turkey's international affairs by promoting economic and cultural integration in the old Ottoman geography while respecting the existing political boundaries, a policy fashionably labeled as "Neo-Ottomanism" (Çolak 2006; Kirişçi 2009). Until the early 2010s, Turkey pursued a "zero problems with neighbors" policy, and in doing so, it amplified its soft power in the Balkans, the Middle East, Central Asia and Africa by increasing its economic engagement, providing developmental assistance, and acting as an impartial broker for such thorny regional disputes as the Iranian nuclear proliferation and the Israel–Palestine conflict. The AKP's foreign policy activism by and large conformed to the expectations of the Western alliance, playing the role of "a benign regional power" and "a good citizen of the liberal order" (Kutlay and Öniş 2021).

The AKP's initial approach to governance, both at home and abroad, was predicated on the reproduction of a historically specific political economy and subjectivity. Domestically, rights were tolerated

---

[50] The term was most explicitly used by Hüseyin Çelik, the minister of education, who called for the establishment of an Ottoman commonwealth under Turkish leadership:

Britain has its commonwealth. So Russia, France, and Spain. So where is our commonwealth? ... We are a nation that has created great states. We are not just another state on the earth's surface. But unfortunately, most of us are not even aware of Turkey's mission. If the Middle East, Africa, and the Balkans are not our hinterland, then our claim to be a great state will remain just words. (Bakan Çelik, "'Commonwealth' istiyor," *Radikal*, November 15, 2007)

only insofar as they did not disrupt the reproduction of this new mode of life, which was itself conditioned on the availability of global liquidity and successful competition in the global marketplace. Modes of life, inspired by past or alternative experiences, can be tolerated only if they are assimilated into capitalist values and subordinated to the requirements of capitalist competition. Needless to say, behaviors, thoughts and habits rooted elsewhere, say in the early Kemalist project, in the institutions and constitution of 1961 or in the dream of an ecosocialist Kurdistan, sit uneasily with the idea of Islamic multiculturalism. And, considering that capitalist social relations are being consolidated in such a globally competitive and (geo)politically fragile context, perhaps there has been only little room for even a temporary toleration of these radically different forms of sociality.

From this angle, it is hardly surprising that since the last decade, the AKP has resorted to increasingly authoritarian and arbitrary measures to undermine existing constitutional rights as well as the "rule-based" and "impersonal" appearance of economic institutions. In particular, since the Gezi Park Revolt in 2013 and the collapse of the Kurdish peace process in 2015, the AKP has responded to societal demands for economic and political rights by attacking civil liberties and freedoms. In addition, the alliance between the AKP and Gülenists ended in 2013. Having disagreed over issues related to the control of the state, education and foreign policy, both parties increasingly drifted apart, culminating in the Gülenist coup attempt in July 2016. The AKP suppressed the putsch attempt and declared a two-year–long country-wide state of emergency, which it has used not only to clean the state from the Gülenists, but also as an excuse to stifle all opposition to Erdoğan's increasingly authoritarian rule.

Testimony to this are not only the thousands of political activists, dissident students, investigative journalists and radical academics who have faced police violence, imprisonment and job loss since 2013. Erdoğan has on a daily basis been intimidating the supporters of even the most "ordinary" center and center-left political parties by accusing them of treason, terrorism, cooperation with imperialism and the like. Furthermore, the electoral rights of a significant portion of the Kurdish population have been tacitly yet effectively cancelled, as the government removed from power almost all of the democratically elected mayors of the Peoples' Democratic Party (whose electoral base is largely Kurdish) on terrorism charges. Through systematic prosecutions and harassment campaigns against dissenting voices,[51] the AKP has considerably limited civil liberties and freedom of expression while invoking monolithic conceptions of the nation.

On the economic front, especially after 2010, the AKP has increasingly perceived the "independence" of "independent" economic and juridical institutions such as the Central Bank and the Constitutional Court more as a problem than a solution to its domestic and international woes, regularly intervening to the election of their board members (Özel 2015: 5). With the downturn in global economy and the concomitant draining of available credit channels, the AKP is no longer able to solve the heightening social contradictions through the financialized, impersonal and rule-based forms of economic management. The shift from the long-standing parliamentary system to a centralized Russian-style presidential one in 2018 has helped to consolidate this new trend, further centralizing and personalizing the processes of economic decision-making (Bedirhanoğlu 2021: 2). With the removal of checks and balances on the president's power, economic management has become more and more short-termist, arbitrary and unaccountable, all to meet the government's debt recycling requirements, the needs of an expansionary monetary policy and electoral concerns. The lack of a clear and consistent economic strategy has made the economic management look increasingly random, leading to currency crisis, inflation and widespread poverty.[52] Furthermore, economic issues have been increasingly securitized, framed as matters of national survival, which no social actor should try to "politicize." Moreover, beyond the econonomic sphere, there is a clear tendency toward the unification of the party and the state, which raises the

---

[51] Emblematic of these systematic prosecutions is the investigations against those who commit the crime of "insulting the president." Between 2014 and 2019, roughly 36,000 people were investigated for "insulting" President Erdoğan, of whom 12,000 were tried, and 4,000 were sentenced to imprisonment from one to four years ("36 bin kişiye 'cumhurbaşkanına hakaret' soruşturması," *Bianet*, September 13, 2020).

[52] Annual Inflation increased from 8.6 percent in 2004 to 48 percent in January 2022. The Turkish lira has been almost in a freefall since 2018. The US dollar–TRY exchange rate was roughly 3.5 in 2017, increasing to over 14 in December 2021. GDP per capita decreased from US$12,600 in 2013 to US$8,500 in 2020.

suspicion of whether or not the AKP would peacefully leave the government even when it is not successful at the ballotbox.

In fact, the randomization of AKP's economic policy has been fueled by the randomization of its foreign policy and vice versa. That is, the AKP has been utilizing foreign policy as an economic crisis management tool in the domestic sphere and as a way of capitalizing on nationalist sentiments, which further undermined and randomized the Turkish economy. Since the last decade, neo-Ottomanism, as "soft-power" has lost most of its relevance, turning into an increasingly assertive foreign policy strategy. Empowered by a rapidly growing indigenous arms industry, the AKP cadres saw the Arab Spring as an opportunity to improve Turkey's geopolitical standing and prop up the ailing popular support to the government at home. Also, the emergence of rival spatialization strategies in the Middle East and Eastern Mediterranean has forced the further militarization of Turkish foreign policy. As a result, Turkish foreign policy has become increasingly assertive, adventurist and unilateral. Turkey has not hesitated to seek alliances outside the West, and to force regime change and get militarily involved in various conflict zones in Turkey's (extended) neighborhood such as Iraq, Syria, Libya, Nagorno-Karabagh, Somalia and Qatar (Hoffmann and Cemgil 2016). While scoring easy geopolitical points seemed to have paid off for some time in terms of mustering domestic popular support, they led to Turkey's increased diplomatic isolation within the Western alliance and the region. Overconfident, arbitrary and short-termist foreign policy decisions have, in turn, further undermined the already ailing economy, aggravating the authoritarianism and randomization of Erdoğan's regime at home (Kutlay and Öniş 2021).

In short, the space temporarily opened for the realization of the Islamic-liberal dream in the early years of AKP rule has shuttered. The initial liberal project, which envisioned a transcultural and transnationally defined space of accumulation unbounded by the hitherto prevailing conceptions of nationhood and public space, is rapidly assimilating into a form of capitalist authoritarianism. Partly driven by the world economic crisis and partly due to the rapidly changing geopolitical context, the AKP has had no problem with resorting to extremely authoritarian and arbitrary measures. There has been a clear shift from a "rule-based" neoliberalism toward an arbitrary, militarized and fascist-like neoliberal regime of governance. Indeed, in this context, given that Kemalism no longer poses any existential challenge to the propertied classes embedded within the AKP, it is not surprising that under new social and geopolitical dictates, the AKP has selectively and pragmatically reloaded early Kemalist nationalism and anticolonialism with ideological support and value. The AKP has reinforced its already existing authoritarian tendencies by selectively recalling some of the most readily available forms of unity and inequality rooted in the Kemalist conceptions of fatherland (*vatan*) and nation (*millet*). The AKP has revived the specter of Kemalism to undermine the demands for a more democratic future as well as the last remnants of a Jacobin past.

Coming full circle, is the transition from Kemalism to Erdoğanism merely a transition from one form of authoritarianism to another? Is all this only another phase of "modernity" marked by a shift from one form of "crony capitalism" to another? Is this just a shift from Kemalist modernity to Islamist modernity based on new markets, new technologies, new ideologies and so on? Is the neo-Ottoman commonwealth just a natural culmination of the eruption of the Kemalist conceptions of political space and collectivity? Or are we talking about two fundamentally distinct societal projects, Jacobin modernity and capitalist modernity, with transition from one to the other requiring nothing less than an epochal transformation (cf. Atasoy 2009; Esen and Gümüşçü 2016; Oğuz 2016; Tuğal 2016; Bedirhanoğlu et al. 2020)?

The origin of Kemalism was rooted in Jacobinism, which had much less to do with capitalism and much more to do with substituting capitalist forms of appropriation with novel conceptions of space and subjectivity. By contrast, the new Ottoman commonwealth and authoritarianism has less to do with modernity per se and much more to do with the universalization of capitalism, its social relations and its contradictions, and the subjection of all human existence and values to its commodifying logic. After almost a seven-decade–long complicated and complementary coexistence, Kemalism completely lost its ability to restructure capitalism. A historically distinct space of accumulation looms on the horizon, which not only marks a rupture in the socio-spatial organization of Turkish society, but also makes imaginable a political economy and subjectivity deeply embedded in capitalist social relations. As such, liberal democracy and fascism become real possibilities for the first time in Turkish history (given the recent unfolding of events the latter seems much more likely than the former). What is approaching is not an "alternative modernity" per se, but what is facing Turkey today is a fully capitalist modernity underlined by the authoritarian consolidation of capitalist social relations.

7 | Conclusion

The global breakthrough to modernity was a highly variegated process. The starting point for this book was the argument that the debates surrounding the making of the modern world had so far failed to fully capture the radically multilinear character of world historical development. The reason for this failure is a methodological tendency to take for granted the categories and divisions created by modernity itself. The "domestic," "international," "economic" and "political" are sociospatial categories peculiar to (capitalist) modernity; therefore, using them to historicize modernity tends to impose the structure of the modern present onto a premodern past. In this sense, the real challenge of social and international theory, today, is to reconsider modernity by engaging in a radical historicization of the categories that the social sciences have tended to take at face value. Overcoming modern binaries and categories through transdisciplinary methodologies is the key to historicizing the process of becoming modern. In this book, I have sought to make a contribution to this task by developing a systematic critique of methodological presentism and methodological internalism. I have shown that both critiques are essential in order to collapse the artificial divisions between the economic and the political, and the internal and the international.

This twofold methodological critique, if systematically applied, enables a fuller understanding of the internationally conditioned and multilinear character of world historical development. For one thing, the critique of internalism helps us theorize the coconstitution of social and international relations and, by doing so, it takes us beyond the logic of static comparisons, registering the interactive, processual and sequential constitution of global modernity. Yet, I have argued that for a sociologically "plural" and historically "dynamic" conception of modernity, we also need to avoid the epistemological trap of presentism. Presentist readings of modernity tend to extrapolate capitalism back in time, forcing the contemporary differentiation of

258

economics and politics onto history. As such, presentism overburdens the agents of modern transformation with capitalism, that is, it freezes the ambiguity, resistance and sociopolitical alternatives involved in the process of modern transformation though a pregiven conception of capitalism. Presentism impairs international historical sociological imagination, obscuring the liminality and generative potential of the international through an all-absorbing conception of capitalism. Indeed, International Historical Sociology (IHS), once freed from retrospective and deterministic readings of history, is able to demonstrate with more accuracy the spatially and temporally interactive character of world historical development.

In this book, the principal outcome of this process of reinterpreting the international relations of modernity was Jacobinism. I have argued that although the prior development of capitalism in Britain generated tremendous fiscal/geopolitical pressures on the European continent for emulation, it also led to the outbreak of revolutionary ruptures that fostered qualitatively different conditions of being "modern," that is, it generated "substitutional" forms that advanced qualitatively different forms of rationalization, mobilization and appropriation as alternatives to market society. In particular, the substitutions associated with Revolutionary/Napoleonic France were characterized by the innovation of one of the most radical ways of competing with capitalism, that is, the subjection of the peasantry to universal conscription and public education, and the attendant rise of the citizen-soldier and citizen-officer as agents of an alternative (geo)political economy, which I called Jacobinism. More precisely, the French elite, unable or unwilling to initiate an organized attack on peasants' customary rights on land, linked the enjoyment of these rights to peasants' service and socialization in the army and public school. Through the citizen-army and public education, the Jacobin project instituted a set of new rules of social reproduction embedded in institutions, laws and cultural practices that reinforced the decommodified character of land and labor. In this context, access to income and property was, at least in principle, universalized among politically equal citizens; therefore, the French elite had to continuously reinterpret the conditions of access to the state (which, unlike in Britain, remained and expanded as the main, if not the direct, source of income and property). New popular and disciplinary discourses of nation and religion were mobilized in order to increase the citizens' contribution to the geo(political) survival of the state, as well as restrain their access to it. As a result, nationalism and secularism in France, in a way unheard of in Britain, were used as principles governing property relations.

Therefore, it was not 1917, but 1789 that marked the first long-lasting anticapitalist moment in modern European history. Jacobinism produced an alternative modernity, intrinsically related to capitalism because of the international dimension of social transformation, but at the same time qualitatively different due to the generative and liminal nature of this international dimension. From the French Revolution onward, European modernity never expanded in a singular fashion. Modernity was always "combined"; its constitution and movement were deeply impacted by the contradictory rights and duties of the individual entailed by capitalism and Jacobinism (Shilliam 2009: 9). Overall, then, much of the history of "modernity" would be fundamentally obscured if we presume a universality of capitalist dynamics in many European societies as well as in non-Western societies. Furthermore, capitalism and Jacobinism posed distinctive alternatives; yet they were also interactive and entailed forms of substitution as much as mechanisms of emulation. The outcomes they generated, in turn, became critical reference points for subsequent "modernizing" projects (often as counterpoints as much as models).

In Western Europe, Jacobinism blazed brightly yet rapidly (Shilliam 2009: 201). After the first half of the nineteenth century, Jacobinism lost most of its transformative force, with Jacobin conceptions of nation, citizen, army and school turned into merely political and cultural aspects of the rising capitalist modernities. Yet, elsewhere, as I have shown in the case of the Ottoman Empire and Turkey, Jacobinism could emerge as a force much more obstinate than its French predecessor. Over the course of the nineteenth century, as more states began to develop military and fiscal capabilities fostered by Jacobinism and/or capitalism, it became imperative for the Ottoman elite to "reform" the state in ways that could not simply be tapped from the sphere of possibilities present in the existing Ottoman socioeconomic order. The Ottomans had to go beyond the mere importation of military techniques and equipment, and "modernize" the state and society based on principles structurally antithetical to the politico-cultural privileges and obligations that came to constitute the Ottoman socioeconomic order.

In this context, the Ottomans introduced capitalism and Jacobinism concurrently. The initial phase of Westernization, the Tanzimat, was carried out through these two distinct and potentially contradictory projects. The Ottoman ruling classes continuously attempted to negotiate and reconcile the rights of the propertied individual and the rights of the citizen-soldier during the Tanzimat. Yet, the outcome of this combined project was not the consolidation of "petty commodity production," as conventionally argued. The threat of revolt and foreign intervention rendered the capitalist project too risky for the Ottoman elite. The right to property could not triumph over the right to subsistence (and vice versa). Neither capitalism nor Jacobinism took root during the Tanzimat. From the end of the 1860s, however, the state became increasingly reluctant to commodify land and transform the agrarian structure, while increasingly turning to mass conscription and mass education to boost its geopolitical power.

In the absence of the relations of market society, wherein market competition could be expected to deliver socially acceptable and geopolitically beneficial results, the equality and property of the "abstract individual" were inevitably coupled with duties toward the state and a repeatedly reimagined "abstract collectivity," the nation. The enjoyment of property was not conditioned on successful commodity production and its productive utilization, but to the fulfillment of duties toward the state and the nation. As the state and the nation were instituted as the ultimate loci of social reproduction, struggles over sources of income predictably launched a competitive and increasingly radicalizing process of reframing the "Ottoman nation" and "national interest." Thus, the cumulative radicalization of the Ottoman modernization project and the growing Jacobin influence on the formation of Ottoman intellectuals and bureaucrats cannot be reduced to an ideological preference or mentalité only, but was, at least partly, rooted in the noncapitalist character of property relations and the mounting geopolitical challenges of the late nineteenth and early twentieth centuries.

The first round of radicalization of the nation was carried out by a large group of low-ranking officers and bureaucrats. Having graduated from public schools, trained in the positive sciences and organized in the so-called Young Turk Movement, these rebellious officers strived to open the state to talent. However, challenging the sultan and the higher bureaucracy depended on the Young Turks' ability to mobilize the lower classes and incorporate lower-class demands into their essentially elitist-conservative vision of national rule and regeneration. The demonstration effect of the Russian and Iranian revolutions, combined with new geopolitical exigencies and internal opportunities, led the Young Turks eventually to set in motion a revolutionary process in which contradictory popular interests would be amalgamated as the interest of the nation. When Abdülhamid II was taken down in 1908, the rights of the modern subject therefore entered the new Ottoman constitution not on the shoulders of bureaucrats and commercial classes only, but through the active involvement of the lower classes.

That said, initially, it was the rights of the propertied individual that the Young Turks most vigorously tried to institute. Like the Tanzimat, however, the period between 1908 and 1913 witnessed a series of mass uprisings caused by the radicalized interpretations of equality and liberty. This resulted in violent reaction against property and propertied classes (most of whom were non-Muslims), which the Young Turks were barely able to control. Combined with severe geopolitical dangers, the Young Turks, once again, had to find new ways in which the "dangerous" masses and foreign enemies could be prevented from completely derailing the reproduction of the new political community. Consequently, they partially conceded to the lower-class reframing of the nation and national interest, and while doing so, they also learned how to make use of lower-class clubs/organizations to outcompete and exterminate their own political and economic rivals. The "national economics" of the Young Turk era could not annihilate the political basis of subsistence, but attempted to solve the tension between subsistence and property, that is, between equality and liberty, by reorganizing social classes in a "solidaristic" space of accumulation that allowed for the minimum subsistence requirements of "patriotic" and "equal" citizens.

In 1923, when the Turkish Republic was established, property was less a right enjoyed by those who used property "productively" and much more a privilege for those who geo(politically) served the nation. Fulfillment of military and political duties, rather than productive activity, was the basis of social reproduction. Chapter 5 turned to the question of how successful the early Republican regime was in changing the structure of property relations. I have discussed "state capitalism" with particular reference to Germany and Italy during the interwar years, while questioning whether early Republican Turkey can be subsumed under the same rubric of state capitalism. I have argued that state elites in Turkey were unable to impose market discipline on the bourgeois classes, and given the continuous threat (actual or perceived) of foreign intervention and domestic rebellion, they were unwilling to initiate a capitalist transformation of agriculture. Unable and/or unwilling to establish "institutionalized markets" in the 1930s, state elites, in alliance with a noncapitalist industrial bourgeoisie, once again, turned to consolidate education, Turkification and the militarization of Republican subjects as the ultimate basis of their social reproduction. As such, I have suggested that after 100 years of experimentation with "modernity," Kemalism consolidated Jacobinism on Turkish lands. In principle, Kemalism never gave up its claim for the role of private property and popular sovereignty in the making of modern "civilization," yet given the noncapitalist character of prevailing property relations and in the face of geopolitical challenges, it continually racialized, militarized and secularized the conditions of possessing property and being civic, equal and modern.

In this book, the analysis of the "international" dimension of social change has been critical in recovering and making sense of the emergence, importation and transformation of Jacobinism across borders. And another world historical development, the rise of a bipolar world order, further marked the international codetermination of Turkey's internal development, heralding the end of Jacobinism. For, after a century of "substitute" modernization, the Turkish elite could establish capitalist property relations thanks to the geopolitical protection and monetary support provided by the United States. In this sense, the 1950s signified the beginning of the end of Jacobinism and the rise of capitalism in Turkey. Yet, the preexistent social relations, institutions and values rooted in the early Republican experience, combined with the lateness and international context of capitalist transition, greatly complicated the development of capitalist social relations. The original Kemalist project gave birth to radically different interpretations formulated to contest as well as produce capitalism. In the 1970s, there was also another form of capitalism developing in provincial Anatolian towns, however. Disgruntled by their systematic exclusion from state-generated economic rents, commercial groups in Anatolian towns organized themselves in and through the Islamic National View

Movement (NVM). The movement, in its various incarnations from the 1970s to the 1990s, envisioned a fully capitalist future unencumbered by Kemalism's Jacobin yoke. Against a "corrupted" and "anarchic" capitalist order, the movement formulated a novel capitalist development strategy, which was a harbinger of the end of capitalism's complicated coexistence with Jacobinism in Turkey. With the neoliberal turn in the 1980s, the classes associated with and mobilized by the NVM became increasingly important in the political and economic spheres. In the meantime, secularism turned into the main ideological safeguard used to protect the political-economic privileges of the Kemalist elite. In 2002, a less-militant heir of the NVM, the Justice and Development Party (AKP), came to power. The AKP has either dispensed with the main contours of Kemalist modernity or transformed them in such ways to serve its own strategic and societal goals. A disciplinary, authoritarian and productivist Islam is rapidly replacing and transforming the politicocultural legacies of the earlier period. What we are witnessing is the authoritarian consolidation of capitalist modernity à la Turca.

What are the implications of this book's argument for historical sociology and International Relations (IR)? First and foremost, Jacobinism has to be factored into both disciplines for a deeper understanding of the historical roots and legacies of the modern world. Jacobinism, sometimes in competition and sometimes in collaboration with capitalism, put its stamp on the formation of the modern social and international order in and beyond Europe. A nonpresentist and noninternalist reading of Jacobinism releases "modernity" from the cage of capitalism, shedding new light on the content, tempo and multilinearity of world historical development. As such, it not only enables us to depart from one-dimensional narratives of the transition to modernity, but also provides a valuable starting point for us to rethink the combined and processual constitution of the modern social and international order.

Second, the case of the Ottoman Empire lends support to an argument I invoked in the introduction: For a long time, it was not capitalism but Jacobinism that introduced the majority of the world to the relations and institutions of modernity. As shown, the first 100 years of Turkish modernization generated property relations and subjectivities that were consciously designed to achieve a Jacobin form of late development. Furthermore, Turkish Jacobinism's demonstration effect had important implications for the quality and manner of the arrival of modernity in the Middle East. The Turkish Revolution became a vector itself, constituted by and constitutive of the uneven and combined development (UCD) of Jacobinism in a wider regional context. Therefore, Jacobinism may have the potential to recover a big chunk of the history of modernity in the non-Western world. Further research may show that Jacobinism opens up the possibility of critically reconsidering and reconstructing the debate on non-Western modernities.

Third, the book has shown that a critical dialogue between IR and historical sociology could generate crucial implications for the broader field of IR. Since the postpositivist turn in IR, several attempts have been made to challenge the mainstream approaches' reification of structures and processes of IR. Yet, critiques of mainstream theories have failed to provide an alternative international theory that systematically overcomes the inside/outside ontology pervasive in the field of IR. In general, IHS and UCD, in particular, were born/revived as precisely such attempts to formulate a unitary theory of domestic and international relations. However, as I have shown above, UCD's potential to contribute to the formation of an international social theory is precluded by the persistence of methodological presentism among its proponents. Presentism not only reads capitalism back into history, but also impoverishes our conception of international interactivity and heterogeneity. The international, without overcoming presentism, imprisons our imagination of international hybridity and multiplicity in an all-absorbing conception of capitalism. A deeper understanding of the generative and contested nature of the international is occluded by an ever-present capitalism. The book has sought to remedy this weakness, equipping IR with a sociology of the international that is both noninternalist and nonpresentist. Such a critique and reconstruction of (critical) IR theories, in turn, has paved the way for a more accurate theorization of the origin and development of the modern international order, hence contributing to a deeper understanding of the "international relations of modernity" (Teschke 2003; Lacher 2006; Matin 2013a).

Finally, the argument presented here has sought to concretize the meaning of modernity by problematizing its relation to capitalism. A central, albeit implicit, argument of this book has been that the transition to modernity cannot be equated with the transition to capitalism. There have, indeed, been many explanations for the capitalism–modernity relationship, yet the general tendency in historical sociology and IR scholarship is to subsume capitalism under modernity, or vice versa. While some approaches assume that capitalism, in the course of economic development, laid the groundwork for the political and cultural modernization that generated modernity, others see the political and cultural "rationalization," driven by geopolitical competition, as responsible for the economic rationalization associated with capitalism. In short, capitalism is either conflated with or understood simply as the economic aspect of modernity. Indeed, it is the precisely the conceptual assimilation of capitalism into modernity that has led several social theorists to charge modernity with the worst atrocities in modern history such as imperialism, fascism and genocide (e.g. Bauman 2000). In a similar fashion, the postcolonial literature has often associated these atrocities with the Enlightenment tradition rooted in the ideas of instrumental rationality and the modern state (cf. Chibber 2013).

There is obviously a grain of truth in these interpretations. Many modern principles and technologies indeed deserve criticism and their (selective) implementation, in many ways, has put modernity at the service of existing power structures and colonialism. Nevertheless, equating modernity and the Enlightenment as a whole to these atrocities leaves us to wonder how to make sense of, for example, a whole gamut of eighteenth- and early nineteenth-century developments in Europe such as the emergence of an extended "public sphere" beyond the participation of the propertied elite, new conceptions of political community, universal citizenship, universal equality and such Enlightenment principles as "resistance to all arbitrary power, a commitment to universal human emancipation, and a critical stance towards all kinds of authority" (Wood 1991: 24; 1997b; 2012: 222).

The analysis offered in this book lends support to the argument that a more fruitful solution to the capitalism–modernity relation in history can be found by distinguishing between capitalist modernities and non-capitalist modernities (Wood 2002: 182–9; Lacher 2006: 110; cf. de Sousa Santos 1995: 1). For example, as this book has shown, capitalism and Jacobinism did not represent merely quantitative variants of the same process of "instrumental rationalization." Rather, they were geopolitically related yet historically distinct projects, activating mutually incompatible interpretations of property and equality.

Recognizing the distinct genealogies of capitalism and Jacobinism allows us to evaluate the historical trajectory and balance sheet of modernity in a more precise manner. For one thing, once we register the incommensurability of capitalism and Jacobinism, we realize that most of the worst outcomes of modernity were indeed the byproducts of capitalist modernity entrenched in the ethic of productivity or the culture of "improvement." As I have briefly discussed in Chapter 5, fascism and Nazism were definitely modern in the sense that they were a product of the modern era and were driven (at least partly) by the imperatives of capitalist accumulation. Yet, it is also important to note that fascism and Nazism sought to obliterate the most progressive aspects of modernity rooted in 1789. "Proud of its role as the executioner of modernity, seen as a process of destructive egalitarianism, abstract rights, and international brotherhood," fascism mobilized a political and intellectual counter movement against the Jacobin (and socialist) aspects of modernity (Landa 2019: 47). Surely, Jacobin modernity could be violent and oppressive too. After all, Jacobinism established unprecedented apparatuses of administration, rule and war, technically for the people or the nation, but always on the backs of impoverished masses. Yet, for reasons I discussed earlier, Jacobins did not or could not completely dispense with the potentially radical elements of the Enlightenment and modernity. Indeed, it is precisely because of this potentially progressive legacy that fascism, while deeply indebted to capitalism, was zealously opposed to the Jacobin dimension of modernity (Landa 2019: 63).

From this angle, it is perhaps unsurprising that although capitalism has taken off its fascist hat and achieved a certain degree of stabilization since the postwar period in the West, it has continued to eviscerate the radical interpretations of equality and citizenship. Demands for property and income have been effectively separated from the demands for radical equality and political autonomy. A hypercompetitive, consumerist and politically docile subjectivity, fortified and controlled by new technologies of surveillance and debt, has ultimately prevailed, rendering increasingly difficult to imagine a modernity beyond capitalism in the West. In the Global South, such as in Turkey, due to social, temporal and international circumstances, the destruction of Jacobinism (and socialism) could be achieved only by reviving the specter of fascism. In an attempt to preempt and suppress societal reactions (spontaneous or organized) to global capitalism's problems, most states have resorted to increasingly authoritarian measures, leading to the rise of fascist-like regimes across the Global South. These states are very likely to respond to societal reactions against global warming, pandemics, economic woes and lack of democracy by sending the last crumbs of equality and democracy to the dustbin of history. New security concerns, legitimized through nationalist and medicalized discourses, are gaining prominence within and among polities. These new forms of governance will seek to vindicate capitalism by ever more aggressively individualizing, externalizing and medicalizing the responsibility for capitalism's failures. It is quite likely that civic universal ideas will be totally discarded to maintain the health of capitalism.

The bottomline is that most of the vagaries of modernity, ranging from the racist violence of the interwar period to the chronic democratic deficit, resurgent authoritarianism, persistent risk of unemployment, ecological degradation and pandemics of the more contemporary times have been rooted not in modernity per se, but in the ascension of capitalism to the driving seat of modernity. And if this is correct, which I believe it is, imagining and realizing a new non-capitalist modernity, albeit a Herculean task, remains the only feasible solution to the economic, political and ecological deadlock in which we have found ourselves today.

Bibliography

Abbott, Andrew. 1995. "Defining the Boundaries of Social Inquiry," *Social Research*, 62 (4): 857–82.

2001. *Chaos of Disciplines.* Chicago: University of Chicago Press.

Abrams, Philip. 1982. *Historical Sociology.* Ithaca, NY: Cornell University Press.

Acemoglu, Daron, and James Robinson. 2012. *Why Nations Fail: The Origins of Power, Prosperity, and Poverty.* New York: Crown Business.

Acomb, Frances. 1980. *Anglophobia in France, 1763–1789: An Essay in the History of Constitutionalism and Nationalism.* New York: Octagon Books.

Adanır, Fikret. 1998. "The Ottoman Peasantries 1360–1860." In *The Peasantries of Europe: From the Fourteenth to the Eighteenth Centuries,* edited by Tom Scott, 269–310. London: Longman.

2001. "Kemalist Authoritarianism and Fascist Trends in Turkey during the Inter-war Period." In *Fascism outside Europe,* edited by Stein Ugelvik Larsen, 313–61. New York: Columbia University Press.

2011. "Non-Muslims in the Ottoman Army and the Ottoman Defeat in the Balkan War of 1912–1913." In *A Question of Genocide,* edited by Ronald Grigor Suny, Fatma Müge Göçek and Norman M. Naimark, 113–25. Oxford: Oxford University Press.

Agnew, John. 1994. "The Territorial Trap: The Geographical Assumptions of International Relations Theory," *Review of International Political Economy,* 1 (1): 53–80.

Ahmad, Feroz. 1977. *The Turkish Experiment in Democracy, 1950–75.* London: C. Hurst & Co. Publishers Ltd.

1988. "War and Society under the Young Turks," *Review (Fernand Braudel Center),* 11 (2): 265–86.

1993. *The Making of Modern Turkey.* New York: Routledge.

1995. "The Development of Class Consciousness in Republican Turkey, 1923–45." In *Workers and Working Class in the Ottoman Empire and the Turkish Republic 1839–19,* edited by Donald Quataert and Erik J. Zurcher, 75–94. New York: I. B. Tauris.

2002. *Modern Türkiye'nin Oluşumu.* İstanbul: Kaynak.

2008. *From Empire to Republic: Essays on the Late Ottoman Empire and Modern Turkey*, vol. 1. İstanbul: Bilgi University Press.

2009. *İttihatçılıktan Kemalizme*. İstanbul: Kaynak.

Akçam, Taner. 2004. *From Empire to Republic: Turkish Nationalism and the Armenian Genocide*. New York: Zed Books.

Akçetin, Elif. 2000. "Anatolian Peasants in the Great Depression, 1929–1933," *New Perspectives on Turkey*, (23): 79–102.

Akgöz, Görkem. 2012. Many Voices of a Turkish State Factory: Working at Bakirköy Cloth Factory, 1932–50. PhD thesis. Amsterdam: Amsterdam Institute for Social Science Research.

2021. "Experts, Exiles, and Textiles: German 'Rationalisierung' on the 1930s Turkish Shop Floor," *International Social History Review*, 66 (2): 179–216.

Akın, Güzin Gülsün, Ahmet Faruk Aysan and Levent Yıldıran. 2009. "Transformation of the Turkish Financial Sector in the Aftermath of the 2001 Crisis." In *Turkey and the Global Economy: Neo-liberal Restructuring and Integration in the Post-crisis Era*, edited by Ziya Öniş and Fikret Şenses, 73–100. London: Routledge.

Aksakal, Mustafa. 2014. "The Ottoman Empire." In *The Cambridge History of the First World War*, vol. 1, edited by Jay Winter, 459–78. Cambridge: Cambridge University Press.

Aksan, Virginia. 2007. *Ottoman Wars 1700–1870: An Empire Besieged*. London: Longman/Pearson.

2013. "Mobilization of Warrior Populations in the Ottoman Context, 1750–1850." In *Fighting for a Living: A Comparative Study of Military Labour 1500–2000*, edited by Erik-Jan Zürcher, 331–52. Amsterdam: Amsterdam University Press.

Aktürk, Şener. 2012. *Regimes of Ethnicity and Nationhood in Germany, Russia, and Turkey*. Cambridge: Cambridge University Press.

Alexander, Alec P. 1960. "Industrial Entrepreneurship in Turkey: Origins and Growth," *Economic Development and Cultural Change*, 8 (4): 349–65.

Allinson, Jamie, and Alexander Anievas. 2010. "The Uneven and Combined Development of the Meiji Restoration," *Capital & Class*, 34 (3): 469–90.

Amit, Bein. 2017. *Kemalist Turkey and the Middle East: International Relations in the Interwar Period*. Cambridge: Cambridge University Press.

Anderson, Kevin. 2010. *Marx at the Margins: On Nationalism, Ethnicity, and Non-Western Societies*. Chicago: University of Chicago Press.

Anderson, Perry. 1974. *Lineages of the Absolutist State*. London: New Left Books.

1978. *Passages from Antiquity to Feudalism*. London: Verso.

1992. *English Questions*. London: Verso.

2008. "Kemalism," *London Review of Books*, September 11.

Anievas, Alexander. 2015. "Revolutions and International Relations: Rediscovering the Classical Bourgeois Revolutions," *European Journal of International Relations*, 21 (4): 841–66.

Anievas, Alexander, and Kamran Matin. 2016. "Historical Sociology, World History and the 'Problematic of the International.'" In *Historical Sociology and World History: Uneven and Combined Development over the Longue Durée*, edited by Alexander Anievas and Kamran Matin, 1–16. London: Rowman & Littlefield.

Anievas, Alexander, and Kerem Nişancıoğlu. 2015. *How the West Came to Rule*. London: Pluto Press.

Arat, Yesim. 1991. "Politics and Big Business: Janus-Faced Link to the State." In *Strong State and Economic Interest Groups: The Post-1980 Turkish Experience*, edited by Metin Heper, 135–47. Berlin: Walter de Gruyter.

Arnold, Caroline E. 2006. Claims on the Common: Social Services and Late Industrialization in India and Turkey. PhD thesis. Berkeley: University of California–Berkeley.

2012. "In the Service of Industrialization: Etatism, Social Services and the Construction of Industrial Labour Forces in Turkey (1930–50)," *Middle Eastern Studies*, 48 (3): 363–85.

Ashley, Richard. 1984. "The Poverty of Neorealism," *International Organization*, 38: 225–86.

1989. "Living on Border Lines: Man, Poststructuralism, and War." In *International/Intertextual Relations: Postmodern Readings of World Politics*, edited by James Der Derian and Michael Shapiro, 259–321. Lexington, MA/Toronto: Lexington Books.

Astourian, Stephan. 2011. "The Silence of the Land: Agrarian Relations, Ethnicity and Power." In *A Question of Genocide*, edited by Ronald Grigor Suny, Fatma Müge Göçek and Norman M. Naimark, 55–81. Oxford: Oxford University Press.

Ataöv, Türkkaya. 1980. "The Principles of Kemalism," *The Turkish Yearbook of International Relations*, (20): 19–44.

Atasoy, Yıldız. 2005. *Turkey, Islamists and Democracy: Transition and Globalisation in a Muslim State*. London: I. B. Tauris.

2009. *Islam's Marriage with Neo-liberalism: State Transformation in Turkey*. London: Palgrave Macmillan.

Aydemir, Şevket Süreyya. 1979. *Ikinci Adam*, vol. 1. İstanbul: Remzi Kitabevi.

Aydın, Mustafa. 1999. "Determinants of Turkish Foreign Policy: Historical Framework and Traditional Inputs," *Middle Eastern Studies*, 35 (4): 152–86.

Aydın, Zülküf. 2005. *The Political Economy of Turkey*. London: Pluto Press.

———. 2010. "Neo-liberal Transformation of Turkish Agriculture," *Journal of Agrarian Change*, 10 (2): 149–87.

———. 2013. "Global Crisis, Turkey and the Regulation of Economic Crisis," *Capital & Class*, 37 (1): 95–109.

Aytekin, E. Attila. 2008. "Cultivators, Creditors and the State: Rural Indebtedness in the Nineteenth Century Ottoman Empire," *The Journal of Peasant Studies*, 35 (2): 292–313.

———. 2012. "Peasant Protest in the Late Ottoman Empire: Moral Economy, Revolt, and the Tanzimat Reforms," *International Review of Social History*, 57 (2): 191–228.

———. 2013. "Tax Revolts during the Tanzimat Period (1839–1876) and before the Young Turk Revolution (1904–1908): Popular Protest and State Formation in the Late Ottoman Empire," *Journal of Policy History*, 25 (3): 308–33.

Aytemur, Nuran. 2007. The Populism of the Village Institutes: A Contradictory of Kemalist Populism. PhD thesis. Ankara: Middle East Technical University.

Aytürk, İlker. 2011. "The Racist Critics of Atatürk and Kemalism, from the 1930s to the 1960s," *Journal of Contemporary History*, 46 (2): 308–35.

Baca, George. 2021. "Neoliberalism's Prologue: Keynesianism, Myths of Class Compromises and the Restoration of Class Power," *Anthropological Theory*, 21 (4): 520–40.

Baker, Keith Michael. 1990. *Inventing the French Revolution: Essays on French Political Culture in the Eighteenth Century*. Cambridge: Cambridge University Press.

Barkan, Ömer Lütfi. 1980. "Çiftçiyi Topraklandırma Kanunu ve Türkiye'de Zırai Bir Reformun Ana Meseleleri." In *Türkiye'de Toprak Meselesi*, edited by Ömer Lütfi Barkan, 449–521. İstanbul: Gözlem Yayınları.

Barkey, Henri J. 1990. *The State and the Industrialization Crisis in Turkey*. Boulder, CO: Westview Press.

Barlas, Dilek. 1998. *Etatism and Diplomacy in Turkey: Economic and Foreign Policy Strategies in an Uncertain World, 1929–1939*. Leiden: Brill.

Barnes, John Robert. 1986. *An Introduction to Religious Foundations in the Ottoman Empire*. Leiden: Brill.

Bauerly, Bradley. 2016. *The Agrarian Seeds of Empire: The Political Economy of Agriculture in US State Building*. Leiden: Brill.

Bauman, Zygmunt. 2000. *Modernity and the Holocaust*. Ithaca, NY: Cornell University Press.

Bayır, Derya. 2013. *Minorities and Nationalism in Turkish Law*. London: Ashgate.

Bedirhanoğlu, Pınar. 2021. "Economic Management under the Presidential System of Government in Turkey: Beyond the Depoliticization versus Repoliticisation Dichotomy," *Journal of Balkan and Near Eastern Studies*, 10.1080/19448953.2021.1992183.

Bedirhanoğlu, Pınar, Çağlar Dölek, Funda Hülagü and Özlem Kaygusuz (eds.). 2020. *Turkey's New State in the Making: Transformations in Legality, Economy and Coercion*. London: Zed Books.

Beik, William. 1985. *Absolutism and Society in Seventeenth-Century France: State Power and Provincial Aristocracy in Languedoc*. Cambridge: Cambridge University Press.

2009. *A Social and Cultural History of Early Modern France*. Cambridge: Cambridge University Press.

Berberoğlu, Berch. 1982. *Turkey in Crisis: from State Capitalism to Neocolonialism*. London: Zed Books.

Berkes, Niyazi. 1964. *The Development of Secularism in Turkey*. Montreal: McGill University Press.

Berman, Harold J. 1983. *Law and Revolution: The Formation of the Western Legal Tradition*. Cambridge, MA: Harvard University Press.

Bertaud, Jean Paul. 1988. *The Army of the French Revolution: From Citizen Soldiers to Instruments of Power*. Princeton, NJ: Princeton University Press.

Beşikçi, Mehmet. 2012. *The Ottoman Mobilization of Manpower in the First World War: Between Voluntarism and Resistance*. Leiden: Brill.

Bhaduri, Amit. 1973. "Agricultural Backwardness under Semi-feudalism," *The Economic Journal*, 83 (329): 120–37.

Bhambra, Gurminder. 2010. "Historical Sociology, International Relations and Connected Histories," *Cambridge Review of International Affairs*, 23 (1): 127–43.

2016. "Undoing the Epistemic Disavowal of the Haitian Revolution: A Contribution to Global Social Thought," *Journal of Intercultural Studies*, 37 (1): 1–16.

Bianchi, Robert. 1984. *Interest Groups and Political Development in Turkey*. Princeton, NJ: Princeton University Press.

Birtek, Faruk, and Çağlar Keyder. 1975. "Agriculture and the State: An Inquiry into Agricultural Differentiation and Political Alliances: The Case of Turkey," *The Journal of Peasant Studies*, 2 (4): 446–67.

Blackbourn, David, and Geoff Eley. 1984. *The Peculiarities of German History: Bourgeois Society and Politics in Nineteenth-Century Germany*. Oxford: Oxford University Press.

Blaney, David, and Arlene Tickner. 2017. "International Relations in the Prison of Colonial Modernity," *International Relations*, 31 (1): 71–5.

Blaufarb, Rafe. 2016. *The Great Demarcation: The French Revolution and the Invention of Modern Property*. New York: Oxford University Press.

Bloch, Marc. 1961. *Feudal Society*. Chicago: University of Chicago Press.

1966. *French Rural History: An Essay on Its Basic Characteristics*. Berkeley: University of California Press.

Block, Fred, and Margaret Somers. 1984. "Beyond the Economistic Fallacy: The Holistic Social Science of Karl Polanyi." In *Vision and Method in Historical Sociology*, edited by Theda Skocpol, 47–84. Cambridge: Cambridge University Press.

Bonney, Richard. 2012. "The Rise of the Fiscal State in France, 1500–1914." In *The Rise of Fiscal States: A Global History, 1500–1914*, edited by Bartolomé Yun-Casalilla, Patrick K. O'Brien and Francisco Comín Comín, 93–100. Cambridge: Cambridge University Press.

Boratav, Korkut. 1981. "Kemalist Economic Policies and Etatism." In *Ataturk: Founder of a Modern State*, edited by Ali Kazancigil and Ergun Ozbudun, 165–90. London: C. Hurst & Co. Publishers Ltd.

2003. *Turkiye Iktisat Tarihi*. Ankara: İmge Kitabevi.

Boratav, Korkut, and Erinç Yeldan. 2006. "Turkey, 1980–2000: Financial Liberalization, Macroeconomic (In)-stability, and Patterns of Distribution." In *External Liberalization in Asia, Post-socialist Europe and Brazil*, edited by Taylor Lance, 417–55. Oxford: Oxford University Press.

Boratav, Korkut, Erinç Yeldan, and Ahmet Kose. 2000. "Turkey: Globalization, Distribution and Social Policy, 1980–1998." CEPA Working Paper Series, New School University. www.researchgate.net/publication/5014165_Globalization_Distribution_and_Social_Policy_Turkey_1980-1998.

Bourde, André J. 2013. *The Influence of England on the French Agronomes, 1750–1789*. Cambridge: Cambridge University Press.

Boyraz, Cemil. 2019. "The Alevi Question and the Limits of Citizenship in Turkey," *British Journal of Middle Eastern Studies*, 46 (5): 767–80.

Bozkurt, Umut. 2013. "Neoliberalism with a Human Face: Making Sense of the Justice and Development Party's Neoliberal Populism in Turkey," *Science & Society*, 77 (3): 372–96.

Brenner, Robert. 1977. "The Origins of Capitalist Development: A Critique of Neo-Smithian Marxism," *New Left Review*, 104: 25–92.

1985a. "Agrarian Class Structures and Economic Development in Pre-industrial Europe." In *The Brenner Debate: Agrarian Class Structure and Economic Development in Pre-industrial Europe*, edited by Trevor

Henry Aston and Charles H. E. Philpin, 10–63. Cambridge: Cambridge University Press.

1985b. "The Agrarian Roots of European Capitalism." In *The Brenner Debate: Agrarian Class Structure and Economic Development in Pre-industrial Europe*, edited by Trevor Henry Aston and Charles H. E. Philpin, 213–327. Cambridge: Cambridge University Press.

1986. "The Social Basis of Economic Development." In *Analytical Marxism*, edited by John Roemer, 23–53. Cambridge: Cambridge University Press.

1989. "Bourgeois Revolution and Transition to Capitalism." In *The First Modern Society: Essays in English History in Honor of Lawrence Stone*, edited by A. L. Beier, David Cannadine and James M. Rosenheim, 271–304. Cambridge: Cambridge University Press.

2003. *Merchants and Revolution: Commercial Change, Political Conflict, and London's Overseas Traders, 1550–1653*. London: Verso.

2006. "From Theory to History: 'The European Dynamic' or Feudalism to Capitalism." In *An Anatomy of Power: The Social Theory of Michael Mann*, edited by John A. Hall and Ralph Schroeder, 189–232. Cambridge: Cambridge University Press.

Brewer, John. 1989. *The Sinews of Power: War, Money and the English State 1688–1783*. London: Routledge.

Briggs, Robin. 1998. *Early Modern France, 1560–1715*. Oxford: Oxford University Press.

Bromley, Simon. 1994. *Rethinking Middle East Politics*. Austin: University of Texas Press.

Bruff, Ian. 2014. "The Rise of Authoritarian Neoliberalism," *Rethinking Marxism*, 26 (1): 113–29.

Bryant, Joseph. 2005. "Grand, Yet Grounded: Ontology, Theory, and Method in Michael Mann's Historical Sociology." In *An Anatomy of Power: The Social Theory of Michael Mann*, edited by John A. Hall and Ralph Schroeder, 71–99. Cambridge: Cambridge University Press.

2006. "The West and the Rest Revisited: Debating Capitalist Origins, European Colonialism, and the Advent of Modernity," *The Canadian Journal of Sociology*, 31 (4): 403–44.

Buğra, Ayşe. 1994. *State and Business in Modern Turkey: A Comparative Study*. Albany: State University of New York Press.

Buzan, Barry, and George Lawson. 2015. *The Global Transformation*. Cambridge: Cambridge University Press.

Buzan, Barry, and Richard Little. 2010. "World History and the Development of Non-Western International Relations Theory." In *Non-Western International Relations Theory: Perspectives on and beyond Asia*, edited by Amitav Acharya and Barry Buzan, 197–220. London: Routledge.

Calhoun, Craig. 2003. "Comments," *Current Anthropology*, 44 (4), 461–62.

Carr, Edward H. 1981. *The Twenty Years' Crisis 1919–1939*. London: Macmillan.

Chakrabarty, Dipesh. 2000. *Provincializing Europe: Postcolonial Thought and Historical Difference*. Princeton, NJ: Princeton University Press.

Chaudry, Kiren. 1993. "The Myths of the Market and the Common History of Late Developers," *Politics and Society*, 21 (3): 245–77.

Chibber, Vivek. 2003. *Locked in Place: State-Building and Late Industrialization in India*. Princeton, NJ: Princeton University Press.

2005. "Reviving the Developmental State: The Myth of the National Bourgeoisie," *Socialist Register*, 41: 144–65.

2013. *Postcolonial Theory and the Specter of Capital*. London: Verso.

Clayer, Nathalie, Fabio Giomi and Emmanuel Szurek (eds.). 2019. *Kemalism Transnational Politics in the Post Ottoman World*. London: I. B. Tauris.

Cobban, Alfred. 1964. *The Social Interpretation of the French Revolution*. Cambridge: Cambridge University Press.

Cox, Robert. 1986. "Social Forces, States and World Order." In *Neorealism and Its Critics*, edited by Robert Keohane, 204–54. New York: Columbia University Press.

Cizre-Sakallioglu, Umit, and Erinç Yeldan. 2000. "Politics, Society and Financial Liberalization: Turkey in the 1990s," *Development and Change*, 31 (2): 481–508.

Cizre, Ümit, and Erinç Yeldan. 2005. "The Turkish Encounter with Neo-liberalism: Economics and Politics in the 2000/2001 Crises," *Review of International Political Economy*, 12 (3): 387–408.

Clark, Edward. 2012. "Osmanlı'da Sanayi Devrimi." In *Tanzimat: Değişim sürecinde Osmanlı İmparatorluğu*, edited by Halil İnalcık and Mehmet Seyitdanlıoğlu, 755–72. İstanbul: İş Bankası Yayınları.

Collins, James B. 1995. *The State in Early Modern France*. Cambridge: Cambridge University Press.

Comninel, George C. 1987. *Rethinking the French Revolution: Marxism and the Revisionist Challenge*. London: Verso.

2000. "English Feudalism and the Origins of Capitalism," *Journal of Peasant Studies*, 27 (4): 1–53.

2019. *Alienation and Emancipation in the Work of Karl Marx*. New York: Palgrave Macmillan.

Cook, Steven. 2007. *Ruling but not Governing: The Military and Political Development in Egypt, Algeria, and Turkey*. Baltimore: Johns Hopkins University Press.

Corrigan, Philip, and Derek Sayer. 1985. *The Great Arch*. Oxford: Basil Blackwell.

Coşar, Simten, and Metin Yeğenoğlu. 2009. "The Neoliberal Restructuring of Turkey's Social Security System," *Monthly Review*, 60 (11): 36–49.

Crouzet, Francois. 1990. *Britain Ascendant: Studies in British and Franco-British Economic History*. Cambridge: Cambridge University Press.

2003. "The Historiography of French Economic Growth in the Nineteenth Century," *Economic History Review*, 56: 215–42.

Çadırcı, Musa. 2008. *Tanzimat sürecinde Türkiye'de askerlik*. Ankara: İmge Kitabevi.

Çakır-Kantarcıoğlu, Meryem. 2018. "Ortak Toprakların Özel Mülkiyete Dönüşmesi mi? İngiliz Çitleme Hareketleri ile 1858 Arazi Kanunnamesi'ne dair bir Karşılaştırma," *Memleket, Siyaset, Yönetim*, 13 (30): 103–40.

Çetinkaya, Doğan. 2014. *The Young Turks and the Boycott Movement*. London: I. B. Tauris.

Cizre, Umit. 2011. "Disentangling the Threads of Civil–Military Relations in Turkey: Promises and Perils," *Mediterranean Quarterly*, 22 (2): 57–75.

Çolak, Yılmaz. 2006. "Ottomanism vs. Kemalism: Collective Memory and Cultural Pluralism in 1990s Turkey," *Middle Eastern Studies*, 42 (4): 583–98.

Dahrendorf, Ralf. 1958. "Out of Utopia: Toward a Reorientation of Sociological Analysis," *American Journal of Sociology*, 64 (2):115–27.

Darling, Linda T. 2006. "Public Finances: The Role of the Ottoman Centre," in *The Cambridge History of Turkey*, vol. 3, edited by Suraiya Faroqhi, 118–31. Cambridge: Cambridge University Press.

2013. *A History of Social Justice and Political Power in the Middle East*. London: Routledge.

Daunton, Martin. 2012. "The Politics of British Taxation, from the Glorious Revolution to the Great War." In *The Rise of Fiscal States: A Global History, 1500–1914*, edited by Bartolomé Yun-Casalilla, Patrick K. O'Brien and Francisco Comín Comín, 111–44. Cambridge: Cambridge University Press.

Davidson, Neil. 2012. *How Revolutionary Were the Bourgeois Revolutions?* Chicago: Haymarket.

Dereli, Toker. 1968. *The Development of Turkish Trade Unionism*. İstanbul: Sermet Matbaasi.

Deringil, Selim. 1998. *The Well-Protected Domains: Ideology and the Legitimation of Power in the Ottoman Empire 1876–1909*. London: I. B. Tauris.

De Vries, Jan. 1976. *The Economy of Europe in an Age of Crisis: 1600–1750*. Cambridge: Cambridge University Press.

Dimmock, Spencer. 2014. *The Origin of Capitalism in England, 1400–1600.* Leiden: Brill.

2019. "Expropriation and the Political Origins of Agrarian Capitalism in England." In *Case Studies in the Origins of Capitalism,* edited by Xavier Lafrance and Charles Post, 39–62. London: Palgrave Macmillan.

Dinler, Demet. 2003. "Turkiye'de Güçlü Devlet Geleneği Tezinin Eleştirisi," *Praksis,* 9: 17–54.

Duby, Georges. 1968. *Rural Economy and Country Life in the Medieval West.* Columbia: University of South Carolina Press.

Dufour, Frédérick Guillaume. 2007. "Social-Property Regimes and the Uneven and Combined Development of Nationalist Practices," *European Journal of International Relations,* 13 (4): 583–604.

Dumont, Paul. 1984. "The Origins of Kemalist Ideology." In *Ataturk and the Modernization of Turkey,* edited by Jacob Landau, 25–44. Leiden: Brill.

Dunn, John. 2009. "Conscription in Mehmed Ali's Egypt: A Napoleonic Legacy." In *Conscription in the Napoleonic Era,* edited by Donald Stoker and Frederick C. Schneid, 175–88. London: Routledge.

Duran, Burhanettin. 1998. "Approaching the Kurdish question via adil düzen: An Islamist Formula of the Welfare Party for Ethnic Coexistence," *Journal of Muslim Minority Affairs,* 18 (1): 111–28.

Duzgun, Eren. 2012. "Class, State and Property: Modernity and Capitalism in Turkey," *European Journal of Sociology,* 53 (2): 119–48.

2013. "Capitalist Modernity a la Turca: Turkey's Great Transformation Reconsidered," *Critical Sociology,* 39 (6): 889–910.

2017. "Agrarian Change, Industrialization and Geopolitics: Beyond the Turkish *Sonderweg,*" *European Journal of Sociology,* 58 (3), 405–39.

2018a. "Property, Geopolitics, and Eurocentrism: The 'Great Divergence' and the Ottoman Empire," *Review of Radical Political Economics,* 50 (1): 24–43.

2018b. "The International Relations of 'Bourgeois Revolutions': Disputing the Turkish Revolution," *European Journal of International Relations,* 24 (2): 414–43.

2018c. "Capitalism, Jacobinism and International Relations: Re-interpreting the Ottoman Path to Modernity," *Review of International Studies,* 44 (2): 252–78.

2020. "Against Eurocentric Anti-Eurocentrism: International Relations, Historical Sociology and Political Marxism," *Journal of International Relations and Development,* 23: 285–307.

2021. "Debating 'Uneven and Combined Development': Beyond Ottoman Patrimonialism," *Journal of International Relations and Development,* DOI: https://doi.org/10.1057/s41268-021-00232-0.

Eisenstadt, Samuel. 1999. *Fundamentalism, Sectarianism, and Revolution: The Jacobin Dimension of Modernity.* Cambridge: Cambridge University Press.

2000. "Multiple Modernities," *Daedalus*, 129: 1–29.

Eley, Geoff. 2002. *Forging Democracy: The History of the Left in Europe, 1850–2000.* Oxford: Oxford University Press.

Emrence, Cem. 2000. "Politics of Discontent in the Midst of the Great Depression," *New Perspectives on Turkey*, 23: 31–52.

Erbakan, Necmettin. 1991. *Adil Ekonomik Düzen.* Ankara: Semih Ofset.

2013a. *Erbakan Külliyatı*, vol. 1. İstanbul: MGV Yayınları.

2013b. *Erbakan Külliyatı*, vol. 2. İstanbul: MGV Yayınları.

2013c. *Erbakan Külliyatı*, vol. 3. İstanbul: MGV Yayınları.

2013d. *Erbakan Külliyatı*, vol. 5. İstanbul: MGV Yayınları.

Emirbayer, Mustafa. 1997. "Manifesto for a Relational Sociology," *American Journal of Sociology*, 103 (2): 281–317.

Emiroğlu, Kudret. 1999. *Anadolu'da Devrim Günleri, vol. 2, Meşrutiyet'in İlanı.* Ankara: İmge Kitabevi Yayınları.

Esen, Berk, and Şebnem Gümüşçü. 2016. "Rising Competitive Authoritarianism in Turkey," *Third World Quarterly*, 37 (9): 1581–606.

Esping-Andersen, Gosta. 1990. *The Three Worlds of Welfare Capitalism.* London: Polity.

Evans, Jessica. 2016. "The Uneven and Combined Development of Class Forces: Migration as Combined Development," *Cambridge Review of International Affairs*, 28 (3): 1061–73.

Evered, Emine Ö. 2012. *Empire and Education under the Ottomans: Politics, Reform and Resistance from the Tanzimat to the Young Turks.* London: I. B. Tauris.

Fahmy, Khaled. 1998. "The Era of Muhammad Ali Pasha." In *The Cambridge History of Egypt*, vol. 2, edited by M. W. Daly and Carl F. Petry, 139–79. Cambridge: Cambridge University Press.

Feher, Ferenc. 1987. *The Frozen Revolution: An Essay on Jacobinism.* Cambridge: Cambridge University Press.

Findley, Carter V. 2006. "Political Culture and the Great Households." In *The Cambridge History of Turkey*, vol. 3, edited by Suraiya N. Faroqhi, 65–80. New York: Cambridge University Press.

Fitzsimmons, Michael P. 1987. "Privilege and the Polity in France, 1786–1791," *The American Historical Review*, 92 (2): 269.

1993. "The National Assembly and the Invention of Citizenship." In *The French Revolution and the Meaning of Citizenship*, edited by Renée Waldinger, Philip Dawson and Isser Woloch, 29–42. Westport, CT: Greenwood Press.

Forrest, Alan. 1989. *Conscripts and Deserters the Army and French Society during the Revolution and Empire.* New York: Oxford University Press.

——— 2002. "Conscription as Ideology: Revolutionary France and the Nation in Arms." In *The Comparative Study of Conscription in the Armed Forces,* edited by Lars Mjøset and Stephen Van Holde, 95–116. Amsterdam; New York: JAI Press.

Fortna, Benjamin C. 2002. *Imperial Classroom: Islam, the State, and Education in the Late Ottoman Empire.* Oxford: Oxford University Press.

Friedmann, Harriet. 1980. "Household Production and the National Economy: Concepts for the Analysis of Agrarian Formations," *Journal of Peasant Studies,* 7 (2): 158–84.

Furet, François. 1981. *Interpreting the French Revolution.* Cambridge: Cambridge University Press.

Gaonkar, Dilip Parameshwar (ed.). 2001. *Alternative Modernities.* Durham, NC: Duke University Press.

Gellner, Ernest. 1997. "The Turkish Option in Comparative Perspective." In *Rethinking Modernity and National Identity in Turkey,* edited by Sibel Bozdoğan and Reşat Kasaba. Seattle: University of Washington Press.

Gerstenberger, Heide. 2007. *Impersonal Power: History and Theory of the Bourgeois State.* Leiden: Brill.

Giddens, Anthony. 1973. *The Class Structure of the Advanced Societies.* London: Hutchinson.

——— 1985. *A Contemporary Critique of Historical Materialism.* Berkeley: University of California Press.

——— 1987. *The Nation-State and Violence.* Berkeley: University of California Press.

——— 1990. *The Consequences of Modernity.* Stanford, CA: Stanford University Press.

Gilroy, Paul. 1993. *The Black Atlantic: Modernity and Double Consciousness.* Cambridge, MA: Harvard University Press.

Go, Julian. 2016. *Postcolonial Thought and Social Theory.* Oxford: Oxford University Press.

Go, Julian, and George Lawson. 2017. *Global Historical Sociology.* Cambridge: Cambridge University Press.

Göçek, Fatma Müge. 1995. *Rise of the Bourgeoisie, Demise of Empire: Ottoman Westernization and Social Change.* New York: Oxford University Press.

Godelier, Maurice. 1986. *The Mental and the Material.* London: Verso.

Goody, Jack. 2004. *Capitalism and Modernity: The Great Debate.* London: Polity Press.

Gökay, Bülent. 1997. *A Clash of Empires: Turkey between Russian Bolshevism and British Imperialism, 1918–1923.* London: I. B. Tauris.

Gözler, Kemal. 1999. *Türk Anayasaları.* Bursa: Ekin Kitabevi Yayınları.

Green, Jeremy. 2012. "Uneven and Combined Development and the Anglo-German Prelude to World War I," *European Journal of International Relations,* 18 (2): 345–68.

Gross, Jean-Pierre. 1997. *Fair Shares for All: Jacobin Egalitarianism in Practice.* Cambridge: Cambridge University Press.

Gülalp, Haldun. 2001. "Globalization and Political Islam: The Social Bases of Turkey's Welfare Party," *International Journal of Middle East Studies,* 33 (3): 433–48.

Günaydın, Gokhan. 2009. "Türkiye Tarım Politikalarında Yapısal Uyum," *Mülkiye,* 262: 175–222.

Güngen, Ali Rıza. 2017. "Financial Inclusion and Policy-Making: Strategy, Campaigns and Microcredit a la Turca," *New Political Economy,* 23 (3): 331–47.

Güran, Mehmet Cahit. 2011. "The Political Economy of Privatization in Turkey." In *The Political Economy of Regulation in Turkey,* edited by Cetin Tamer and Fuat Oğuz, 23–50. New York: Springer.

Güran, Tevfik. 1992. "Zirai Politika ve Ziraatte Gelismeler 1839–1876." In *150: Yılında Tanzimat,* edited by Hakkı Dursun Yıldız, 219–33. Ankara: Turk Tarih Kurumu Yayınları.

1998. *Osmanlı Tarımı.* İstanbul: Eren Yayıncılık.

Güven, Ali Burak. 2009. Peasants, Bankers and the State: Forging Institutions in Neo-liberal Turkey. PhD thesis. Toronto: University of Toronto.

Hale, William M. 1976. "Labour Unions in Turkey: Progress and Problems." In *Aspects of Modern Turkey,* edited by William M. Hale, 59–74. London: Bowker.

1981. *The Political and Economic Development of Modern Turkey.* New York: St. Martin's Press.

1984. "The Traditional and the Modern in the Economy of Kemalist Turkey." In *Ataturk and the Modernization of Turkey,* edited by Jacob Landau, 153–70. Leiden: Brill.

1994. *Turkish Politics and the Military.* London: Routledge.

Halliday, Fred. 1999. *Revolution and World Politics.* London: Macmillan.

2002. "For an International Sociology." In *Historical Sociology of International Relations,* edited by Stephen Hobden and John M. Hobson, 244–64. Cambridge: Cambridge University Press.

2005. *The Middle East in International Relations.* Cambridge: Cambridge University Press.

Halperin, Sandra. 1997. *In the Mirror of the Third World: Capitalist Development in Modern Europe.* Ithaca, NY: Cornell University Press.

2004. *War and Social Change in Modern Europe.* Cambridge: Cambridge University Press.

2006. "International Relations Theory and the Hegemony of Western Conceptions of Hegemony." In *Decolonizing International Relations*, edited by Branwen G. Jones. Plymouth: Rowman & Littlefield.

Hampson, Norman. 1991. "The Idea of the Nation in Revolutionary France." In *Reshaping France: Town, Country, and Region during the French Revolution*, edited by Alan Forrest and Peter Jones, 13–25. Manchester: Manchester University Press.

Hanioğlu, Şükrü. 1995. *The Young Turks in Opposition*. Oxford: Oxford University Press.

2001. *Preparation for a Revolution: The Young Turks, 1902–1908*. Oxford: Oxford University Press.

2010. *A Brief History of the Late Ottoman Empire*. Princeton, NJ: Princeton University Press.

Hansen, Bent. 1991. *Egypt and Turkey: The Political Economy of Poverty, Equity and Growth*. New York: Oxford University Press.

Heinzelmann, Tobias. 2009. *Cihaddan Vatan Savunmasına: Osmanlı İmparatorluğu'nda Genel Askerlik Yükümlülüğü 1826–1856*. İstanbul: Kitap Yayınevi.

Heper, Metin. 1985. *The State Tradition in Turkey*. Huntingdon: Eothen Press.

Hershlag, Zvi Yehuda. 1968. *Turkey: The Challenge of Growth*. Leiden: Brill.

1975. *Introduction to the Modern Economic History of the Middle East*. Leiden: Brill.

Higonnet, Patrice. 1998. *Goodness Beyond Virtue: Jacobins during the French Revolution*. Cambridge, MA: Harvard University Press.

Hill, Christopher. 1961. *The Century of Revolution, 1603–1714*. Edinburgh: Thomas Nelson.

1992. *Reformation to Industrial Revolution*. London: Penguin Books.

Hirsch, Jean-Pierre. 1994. "Terror and Property." In *The French Revolution and the Creation of Modern Political Culture*, vol. 4, edited by Keith Michael Baker, 211–22. Oxford: Pergamon Press.

Hobden, Stephen, and John M. Hobson (eds.). 2002. *Historical Sociology of International Relations*. Cambridge: Cambridge University Press.

Hobson, John M. 1997. *The Wealth of States: A Comparative Sociology of International Economic and Political Change*. Cambridge: Cambridge University Press.

1998. "For a 'Second-Wave' Weberian Historical Sociology in International Relations," *Review of International Political Economy*, 5 (2): 354–61.

2002. "What's at Stake in 'Bringing Historical Sociology Back into International Relations?'" In *Historical Sociology of International*

Relations, edited by Stephen Hobden and John M. Hobson, 3–41. Cambridge: Cambridge University Press.

2004. *Eastern Origins of Western Civilization*. Cambridge: Cambridge University Press.

Hobson, John, George Lawson and Justin Rosenberg. 2010. "Historical Sociology." In *The International Studies Encyclopedia*: vol. 8, edited by Robert Denemark. Oxford: Wiley-Blackwell.

Hoffman, Philip T. 1996. *Growth in a Traditional Society: The French Countryside, 1450–1815*. Princeton, NJ: Princeton University Press.

Hoffmann, Clemens. 2008. "The Balkanization of Ottoman rule: Premodern Origins of the Modern International System in Southeastern Europe," *Cooperation and Conflict*, 43 (4): 373–96.

Hoffmann, Clemens, and Can Cemgil. 2016. "The (Un)making of the Pax Turca in the Middle East: Understanding the Social-historical Roots of Foreign Policy," *Cambridge Review of International Affairs*, 4: 1279–302.

Holstun, James. 2000. *Ehud's Dagger: Class Struggle in the English Revolution*. London: Verso.

Hoşgör, Evren. 2011. "Islamic Capital/Anatolian Tigers: Past and Present," *Middle Eastern Studies*, 47 (2): 343–60.

Hourani, Albert. 1983. *Arabic Thought in the Liberal Age, 1789–1939*. Cambridge: Cambridge University Press.

İlkin, Selim. 1991. "Exporters: Favored Dependency." In *Strong State and Economic Interest Groups: The Post-1980 Turkish Experience*, edited by Metin Heper, 89–98. Berlin: Walter de Gruyter.

İnalcık, Halil. 1954. "Ottoman Methods of Conquest," *Studia Islamica*, 2: 103–30.

1978. *The Ottoman Empire: Conquest, Organization and Economy*. London: Variorum Reprints.

İnce, Başak. 2012. *Citizenship and Identity in Turkey: From Atatürk's Republic to the Present Day*. London: I. B. Tauris.

İrem, Nazım. 2008. "Klasik Osmanlı Adalet Rejimi ve 1839 Gülhane Kırılması," *Muhafazakâr Düşünce, Sayı*, 15: 149–74.

Isett, Christopher, and Stephen Miller. 2016. *The Social History of Agriculture: From the Origins to the Current Crisis*. Lanham, MD: Rowman & Littlefield.

İslamoğlu, Huri. 2000. "Property as a Contested Domain: A Revaluation of the Ottoman Land Code of 1858." In *New Perspectives on Property and Land in the Middle East*, edited by Roger Owen, 3–62. Cambridge, MA: Harvard University Press.

İslamoğlu, Huri, and Çağlar Keyder. 1977. "Agenda for Ottoman History," *Review*, 1 (1): 31–55.

Issawi, Charles. 1980. *The Economic History of Turkey, 1800–1914*. Chicago: University of Chicago Press.

Itzkowitz, Norman. 1980. *Ottoman Empire and Islamic Tradition*. Chicago: University of Chicago Press.

Jessop, Bob. 2013. "The Complexities of Competition and Competitiveness." In *Asian Capitalism and the Regulation of Competition*, edited by Michael W. Dowdle, John Gillespie and Imelda Maher, 96–120. New York: Cambridge University Press.

Jones, Peter M. 1988. *The Peasantry in the French Revolution*. Cambridge: Cambridge University Press.

1991. "The Agrarian Law: Schemes for Land Redistribution during the French Revolution," *Past and Present*, 133 (1): 96–133.

1995. *Reform and Revolution in France: The Politics of Transition, 1774–1791*. Cambridge: Cambridge University Press.

2012. "The Challenge of Land Reform in Eighteenth- and Nineteenth-Century France," *Past & Present*, 216 (1): 107–42.

Kafadar, Cemal. 1981. Yeniçeri-Esnaf Relations: Solidarity and Conflict. MA thesis. Montreal: McGill University.

1995. *Between Two Worlds: The Construction of the Ottoman State*. Berkeley: University of California Press.

1997. "The Question of Ottoman Decline," *Harvard Middle East and Islamic Review*, 4 (1–2): 30–75.

Kandiyoti, Deniz. 2012. "The Travails of the Secular: Puzzle and Paradox in Turkey," *Economy and Society*, 41 (4): 513–31.

Kansu, Aykut. 1997. *The Revolution of 1908 in Turkey*. Leiden: Brill.

Karaman, K. Kıvanç, and Şevket Pamuk. 2010. "Ottoman State Finances in European Perspective, 1500–1914," *The Journal of Economic History*, 70 (3): 593–629.

Karaömerlioğlu, Asım. 1998. "The Village Institutes Experience in Turkey," *British Journal of Middle Eastern Studies*, 25 (1): 47–73.

2000. "Elite Perceptions of Land Reform in Early Republican Turkey," *Journal of Agrarian Change*, 27 (3): 115–41.

2001. "Agrarian Populism as an Ideological Discourse of Interwar Europe," *New Perspectives on Turkey*, 26: 59–93.

2006. "Turkey's 'Return' to Multi-party Politics: A Social Interpretation," *East European Quarterly*, 40 (1): 89–107.

Karatepe, İsmail Doğan. 2015, "Türkiye'de Devlet, Burjuvazi ve Yatırım Teşvikleri." In *Finansallaşma, Devlet ve Politik İktisat*, edited by Hakan Mıhçı, 243–70. İstanbul: Nota Bene.

Karpat, Kemal H. 1964. "Society, Economics, and Politics in Contemporary Turkey," *World Politics*, 17 (1): 50–74.

1970. "The Military and Politics in Turkey, 1960–64: A Socio-cultural Analysis of a Revolution," *The American Historical Review*, 75 (6): 1654–83.

1972a. "The Transformation of the Ottoman State, 1789–1908," *International Journal of Middle East Studies*, 3 (3): 243–81.

1972b. "Political Developments in Turkey, 1950–70," *Middle Eastern Studies*, 8 (3): 349–75.

1988. "Military Interventions: Army–Civilian Relation in Turkey before and after 1980." In *State, Democracy, and the Military: Turkey in the 1980s*, edited by Metin Heper *and* Ahmet Evin, 137–58. Berlin: Walter de Gruyter.

2004. "Reflections on the Social Background of the Turkish Revolution of 1960." In *Studies on Turkish Politics and Society: Selected Articles and Essays*, edited by Kemal H. Karpat, 172–200. Leiden: Brill.

Kasaba, Reşat. 1988. *The Ottoman Empire and the World-Economy: The Nineteenth Century*. Albany: State University of New York Press.

Kaya, Yücel Alp. 2015. "On the Çiftlik Regulation in Tırhala in the Mid-nineteenth Century: Economists, Pashas, Governors, Çiftlik-holders, Subaşıs, and Sharecroppers." In *Ottoman Rural Societies and Economies*, edited by Kolovos Elias, 333–80. Rethymno: Crete University Press.

2021. "Balkanlar ve Batı Anadolu'da ilk Birikimin Gelişimi," *Devrimci Marksizm*, 45–6: 11–66.

Kaya, Ayhan. 2015. "Islamisation of Turkey under the AKP Rule: Empowering Family, Faith and Charity," *South European Society and Politics*, 20 (1): 47–69.

Kaya, Ayhan, and Ayşe Tecmen. 2010. "Turkish Modernity: A Continuous Journey of Europeanisation." In *Europe, Nations and Modernity*, edited by Atsuko Ichijo, 13–36. New York: Palgrave Macmillan.

Kaya, Ibrahim. 2004. *Social Theory and Later Modernities: The Turkish Experience*. Liverpool: Liverpool University Press.

Kayalı, Hasan. 1995. "Elections and the Electoral Process in the Ottoman Empire, 1876–1919," *International Journal of Middle East Studies*, 27 (3): 265–86.

1997. *Arabs and Young Turks: Ottomanism, Arabism, and Islamism in the Ottoman Empire, 1908–1918*. Berkeley: University of California Press.

Kazancıgil, Ali. 1981. "The Ottoman-Turkish State and Kemalism." In *Ataturk: Founder of a Modern State*, edited by Ali Kazancıgil and Ergun Özbudun, 37–57. London: C. Hurst & Co. Publishers Ltd.

1994. "High Stateness in a Muslim Society: The Case of Turkey." In *Comparing Nations*, edited by Dogan Matter and Ali Kazancıgil, 213–38. Oxford: Blackwell.

Keddie, Nikki. 1994. "The French Revolution and the Middle East." In *Global Ramifications of the French Revolution*, edited by Joseph Klaits and Michael H. Haltzel, 140–57. Cambridge: Cambridge University Press.

Kennedy, Geoff. 2008. *Diggers, Levelers, and Agrarian Capitalism: Radical Political Thought in Seventeenth Century England*. Lanham, MD: Lexington Books.

Keohane, Robert. 1986. "Realism, Neorealism and the Study of World Politics." In *Neorealism and Its Critics*, edited by Robert Keohane, 1–27. New York: Columbia University Press.

Kerimoğlu, Hasan. 2006. "1913–1914 Rumlara Karşı Boykot," *Çağdaş Türkiye Tarihi Araştırmaları Dergisi*, 13 (Fall): 91–107.

Kestnbaum, Meyer. 2002. "Service and the Mass Army." In *The Comparative Study of Conscription in the Armed Forces*, edited by Lars Mjøset and Stephen van Holde, 117–44. Amsterdam; New York: JAI Press.

Keyder, Çağlar. 1979. "The Political Economy of Turkish Democracy," *New Left Review*, 115: 3–44.

1981. *The Definition of a Peripheral Economy: Turkey 1923–1929*. Cambridge: Cambridge University Press.

1983. *Toplumsal tarih çalışmaları*. Ankara: Dost Kitabevi.

1987. *State and Class in Turkey: A Study in Capitalist Development*. London: Verso.

1988. "Türk Tarımında Küçük Meta Üretiminin Yerleşmesi, 1946–1960." In *Türkiye' de Tarımsal Yapılar 1923–2000*, edited by Şevket Pamuk and Zafer Toprak, 163–73. Ankara: Yurt Yayınları.

1991. "Introduction: Large Scale Commercial Agriculture in the Ottoman Empire?" In *Landholding and Commercial Agriculture in the Middle East*, edited by Çağlar Keyder and Faruk Tabak, 1–16. Albany: State University of New York Press.

1993. "Genesis of Petty Commodity Production in Agriculture: The Case of Turkey." In *Culture and Economy: Changes in Turkish Villages, edited by* Paul Stirling, 171–86. Huntingdon: Eothen Press.

1994. "Manufacturing in the Ottoman Empire and in Republican Turkey, ca. 1900–1950." In *Manufacturing in the Ottoman Empire and Turkey, 1500–1950, edited by* Donald Quataert, 123–64. Albany: State University of New York Press.

Keyder, Çağlar, and Zafer Yenal. 2011. "Agrarian Change under Globalization: Markets and Insecurity in Turkish Agriculture," *Journal of Agrarian Change*, 11 (1): 60–86.

Keyman, Fuat, and Gümüşçü, Şebnem. 2014. *Democracy, Identity, and Foreign Policy in Turkey: Hegemony through Transformation*. Basingstoke: Palgrave Macmillan.

Kiely, Ray. 2017. "From Authoritarian Liberalism to Economic Technocracy: Neoliberalism, Politics and 'De-democratization,'" *Critical Sociology*, 43 (4–5): 725–45.

Kirişçi, Kemal. 2009. "The Transformation of Turkish Foreign Policy: The Rise of the Trading State," *New Perspectives on Turkey*, 40: 29–57.

Klein, Janet. 2002. Power in the Periphery: The Hamidiye Light Cavalry and the Struggle over Ottoman Kurdistan, 1890–1914. PhD thesis. Princeton, NJ: Princeton University.

Knafo, Sam. 2013. *The Making of Modern Finance: Liberal Governance and the Gold Standard.* Abingdon: Routledge.

Knöbl, Wolfgang. 2003. "Theories That Won't Pass Away: The Never-ending Story of Modernization Theory." In *Handbook of Historical Sociology*, edited by Delanty Gerard and Engin Isin, 96–109. London: Sage.

Kocabicak, Ece. 2022. *The Political Economy of Patriarchy in the Global South*, London: Routledge, forthcoming.

Koçak, Cemil. 2005. "Parliament Membership during the Single-Party System in Turkey (1925–1945)," *European Journal of Turkish Studies: Social Sciences on Contemporary Turkey*, (3). http://ejts.revues.org/497.

Koç, Mustafa. 1988. Persistence of Small Commodity Production in Agriculture: The Case of Tobacco Producers in Aegean Turkey. PhD thesis. Toronto: University of Toronto.

Koç, Yıldırım. 2013. *Kemalist Devrim CHP ve İşçi Sınıfı (1919–1946).* İstanbul: Kaynak.

Kosik, Karel. 1976. *Dialectics of the Concrete: A Study on Problems of Man and World.* Boston: Reidel.

Köker, Levent. 1990. *Modernleşme, Kemalizm ve Demokrasi.* İstanbul: İletişim Yayınları.

Kuran, Timur. 2001. "The Provision of Public Goods under Islamic Law: Origins, Impact, and Limitations of the Waqf System," *Law & Society Review*, 35 (4): 841–98.

2004. "Why the Middle East Is Economically Underdeveloped: Historical Mechanisms of Institutional Stagnation," *The Journal of Economic Perspectives*, 18 (3): 71–90.

Kuruç, Bilsay. 1987. *Mustafa Kemal Döneminde Ekonomi.* Ankara: Bilgi Yayınevi.

Kutlay, Mustafa, and Ziya Öniş. 2021. "Understanding Oscillations in Turkish foreign Policy: Pathways to Unusual Middle Power Activism," *Third World Quarterly*, 42 (12): 3051–69.

Lacher, Hannes. 2006. *Beyond Globalization: Capitalism, Territoriality and the International Relations of Modernity.* London: Routledge.

Lacher, Hannes, and Julian Germann. 2012. "Before Hegemony: Britain, Free Trade, and Nineteenth-Century World Order Revisited," *International Studies Review*, 14 (1): 99–124.

Lafrance, Xavier. 2013. Citizens and Wage-Laborers: Capitalism and the Formation of a Working Class in France. PhD thesis. Toronto: York University.

2019a. *The Making of Capitalism in France: Class Structures, Economic Development, the State and the Formation of the French Working Class, 1750–1914*. Leiden: Brill.

2019b. "The Transition to Industrial Capitalism in 19th Century France." In *Case Studies in the Origins of Capitalism*, edited by Xavier Lafrance and Charles Post, 111–38. New York: Palgrave Macmillan.

Landa, Ishay. 2019. "The Magic of the Extreme: On Fascism, Modernity, and Capitalism," *The Journal of Holocaust Research*, 33 (1): 43–63.

Landau, Jacob M. 1976. *Politics and Islam: The National Salvation Party in Turkey*. Salt Lake City: Middle East Center, University of Utah.

Lapointe Thierry, and Frédérick G. Dufour. 2012. "Assessing the Historical Turn in IR: An Anatomy of Second Wave Historical Sociology," *Cambridge Review of International Affairs*, 25 (1): 97–121.

Lawson, George. 2004. *Negotiated Revolutions: The Czech Republic, South Africa and Chile*. London: Routledge.

2007. "Historical Sociology in International Relations: Open Society, Research Programme and Vocation," *International Politics*, 44 (4): 343–68.

2012. "The Eternal Divide? History and International Relations," *European Journal of International Relations*, 18: 203–36.

Lefebvre, Henri. 1961. *The Coming of the French Revolution*. New York: Vintage.

Lerner, Daniel. 1958. *The Passing of Traditional Society: Modernizing the Middle East*. New York: Free Press.

Lewis, Bernard. 1975. *The Emergence of Modern Turkey*. Oxford: Oxford University Press.

Lewy, Claude. 1956. "The Code and Property." In *The Code Napoleon and the Common Law World*, edited by Bernard Schwartz, 162–76. New York: New York University Press.

Lucas, Colin. 1973. "Nobles, Bourgeois and the Origins of the French Revolution," *Past and Present*, 60 (1): 84–126.

Maier, Charles S. 1977. "The Politics of Productivity: Foundations of American International Economic Policy after World War II," *International Organization*, 31 (4): 607–33.

1987. *In Search of Stability: Explorations in Historical Political Economy*. Cambridge: Cambridge University Press.

1988. *Recasting Bourgeois Europe*. Princeton, NJ: Princeton University Press.

Makal, Ahmet. 2007. *Ameleden İşçiye: Erken Cumhuriyet Dönemi Emek Tarihi Çalışmaları.* İstanbul: İletişim Yayınları.

Mann, Michael. 1986. *The Sources of Social Power: Volume 1, A History of Power from the Beginning to AD 1760.* Cambridge: Cambridge University Press.

1993. *The Sources of Social Power: Volume 2, The Rise of Classes and Nation-States, 1760–1914.* Cambridge: Cambridge University Press.

2012. *The Sources of Social Power: Volume 3, Global Empires and Revolution, 1890–1945.* Cambridge: Cambridge University Press.

Mardin, Şerif. 1962. *The Genesis of Young Ottoman Thought: A Study in the Modernization of Turkish Political Ideas.* Princeton, NJ: Princeton University Press.

2006. *Religion, Society and Modernity in Turkey.* Syracuse, NY: Syracuse University Press.

Marguiles, Roni, and Ergin Yıldızoğlu. 1983. "Agrarian Change in Republican Turkey: Evidence and Interpretation." Working paper, University of East Anglia.

Martin, James Kirby, and Mark Edward Lender. 2015. *"A Respectable Army": The Military Origins of the Republic, 1763–1789.* Chichester: Wiley Blackwell.

Marx, Karl. 1975. *German Ideology.* London: Penguin Books.

1976. *Communist Manifesto.* London: Penguin Books.

1993. *Grundrisse.* London: Penguin Books.

1996a. "'Preface' to *A Contribution to the Critique of Political Economy.*" In *Marx: Later Political Writings*, edited by Terrell Carver, 158–62. Cambridge: Cambridge University Press.

1996b. *Capital*, vol. 1. London: Penguin Books.

1997. *Capital*, vol. 3. London: Penguin Books.

Matin, Kamran. 2013a. *Recasting Iranian Modernity.* London: Routledge.

2013b. "Redeeming the Universal: Postcolonialism and the Inner Life of Eurocentrism," *European Journal of International Relations*, 19 (2): 353–77.

2020. "Deciphering the Modern Janus: Societal Multiplicity and Nation-Formation," *Globalizations*, 17 (3): 436–51.

Mayer, Arno. 1981. *The Persistence of the Old Regime: Europe to the Great War.* New York: Pantheon Books.

McDowall, David. 2004. *A Modern History of the Kurds.* New York: I. B. Tauris.

McMichael, Philip. 1990. "Incorporating Comparison within a World-Historical Perspective: An Alternative Comparative Method," *American Sociological Review*, 55 (3): 385–97.

2000. "World System Analysis, Globalization, and Incorporated Comparison," *Journal of World System Research*, 6 (3): 68–99.

McNally, David. 1988. *Political Economy and the Rise of Capitalism*. Berkeley: University of California Press.

2011. *Monsters of the Market: Zombies, Vampires and Global Capitalism*. Chicago: Haymarket Books.

McPhee, Peter. 2006. *Living the French Revolution*. New York: Palgrave Macmillan.

Mills, C. Wright. 1959. *The Sociological Imagination*. Oxford: Oxford University Press.

Milonakis, Dimitris, and Giorgos Meramveliotakis. 2012. "Homo Economicus and the Economics of Property Rights: History in Reverse Order," *Review of Radical Political Economics*, 45 (1): 5–23.

Milor, Vedat. 1989. A Comparative Study of Planning and Economic Development in Turkey and France: Bringing the State Back In. PhD thesis. Berkeley: University of California, Berkeley.

Milor, Vedat, and Jesse Biddle. 1995. "Institutional Influences on Economic Policy in Turkey: A Three-Industry Comparison." World Bank PSD Occasional Paper No. 3.

1997. "Economic Governance in Turkey: Bureaucratic Capacity, Policy Networks and Business Associations." In *Business and the State in Developing Countries*, edited by Sylvia Maxfield and Ben Ross Schneider, 277–310. New York: Cornell University Press.

Miller, Stephen. 2008. *State and Society in Eighteenth-Century France: A Study of Political Power and Social Revolution in Languedoc*. Washington, DC: Catholic University of America Press.

2012. "French Absolutism and Agricultural Capitalism," *Historical Materialism*, 20 (4): 141–62.

2019. "Peasant Farming in Eighteenth- and Nineteenth-Century France and the Transition to Capitalism under Charles de Gaulle." In *Case Studies in the Origins of Capitalism*, edited by Xavier Lafrance and Charles Post, 87–110. New York: Palgrave Macmillan.

Mjøset, Lars, and Stephen van Holde. 2002. "Killing for the State, Dying for the Nation." In *The Comparative Study of Conscription in the Armed Forces*, edited by Lars Mjøset and Stephen Van Holde, 3–94. Amsterdam; New York: JAI Press.

Mooers, Colin. 1991. *The Making of Bourgeois Europe: Absolutism, Revolution, and the Rise of Capitalism in England, France, and Germany*. London: Verso.

Moore, Barrington. 1966. *Social Origins of Dictatorship and Democracy: Lord and Peasant in the Making of the Modern World*. Boston: Beacon Press.

Moreau, Odile. 2010. *Reformlar Çağında Osmanlı İmparatorluğu: Askeri "Yeni Düzen"in İnsanları ve Fikirleri.* İstanbul: Bilgi Üniversitesi Yayınları.

Morton, Adam David. 2007. "Waiting for Gramsci: State Formation, Passive Revolution and the International," *Millennium: Journal of International Studies*, 35 (3): 597–621.

2011. *Revolution and State in Modern Mexico: The Political Economy of Uneven Development.* Lanham, MD: Rowman & Littlefield.

Morton, Adam David, and Andreas Bieler. 2018. *Global Capitalism, Global War, Global Crisis.* Cambridge: Cambridge University Press.

Mundy, Martha, and Richard Saumarez Smith. 2007. *Governing Property, Making the Modern State: Law, Administration and Production in Ottoman Syria.* London: I. B. Tauris.

Murphey, Rhoads. 2012. "The Ottoman Economy in the Early Imperial Age." In *The Ottoman World*, edited by Christine Woodhead, 25–40. Abingdon: Routledge.

National Salvation Party. 1975. *Party Program.* İstanbul: Dergah Yayınları.

Nicolaus, M. 1973. "Foreword" In *Karl Marx, Grundrisse: Foundations of Political Economy.* London: Penguin Books.

North, Douglass. 1981. *Structure and Change in Economic History.* New York: W. W. Norton.

Oğuz, Şebnem. 2008. Globalization and the Contradictions of State Restructuring in Turkey. PhD thesis. Toronto: York University.

2016. "Yeni Türkiye'nin Siyasal Rejimi." In *"Yeni" Türkiye: Kapitalizm, Devlet, Sınıflar*, edited by Tolga Tören and Melahat Kutun, 81–127. İstanbul: SAV.

Oktar, Suat, and Arzu A. Varlı. 2010. "Demokrat Parti'nin tarim politikasi, 1950–1954," *Marmara Üniversitesi I.I.B.F Dergisi*, 28 (1): 1–22.

Öniş, Ziya. 1991. "The Evolution of Privatization in Turkey: The Institutional Context of Public-Enterprise Reform," *International Journal of Middle East Studies*, 23 (2): 163–76.

1992. "The East Asian Model Development and the Turkish Case: A Comparative Analysis," *METU Studies in Development*, 19 (4): 495–528.

1997. "The Political Economy of Islamic Resurgence in Turkey: The Rise of the Welfare Party in Perspective," *Third World Quarterly*, 18 (4): 743–66.

Ortaylı, İlber. 1978. "Osmanlı İmparatorluğu'nda sanayileşme anlayışına bir örnek: Islah-ı Sanayi Komisyonu olayı," *METU Studies in Development, Special Issue on Turkish Economic History:* 123–30.

1998. *İmparatorluğun En Uzun Yüzyılı.* İstanbul: İletişim.

Overton, Mark. 1989. "Agricultural Revolution? England, 1540–1850." In *New Directions in Economic and Social History*, edited by Anne Digby and Charles Feinstein, 9–21. London: Macmillan.

Owen, Roger. 1981. *The Middle East in the World Economy, 1800–1914*. New York: Methuen.

Owen, Roger, and Şevket Pamuk. 1999. *A History of Middle East Economies in the Twentieth Century*. Cambridge: I. B. Tauris.

Owens, Patricia. 2015. *Economy of Force: Counterinsurgency and the Historical Rise of the Social*. Cambridge: Cambridge University Press.

Özbek, Nadir. 2010. "Osmanlı İmparatorluğu'nda Gelir Vergisi: 1903–1907 Tarihli Vergi-i Şahsi Uygulaması," *Tarih ve Toplum Yeni Yaklaşımlar*, 10: 43–80.

Özdemir, Yonca. 2013. "Is 'Consensus' Necessary for Inflation Stabilization? A Comparison of Israel and Turkey," *Middle Eastern Studies*, 49 (1): 47–62.

2020. "AKP's Neoliberal Populism and Contradictions of New Social Policies in Turkey," *Contemporary Politics*, 26 (3): 245–67.

Özden, Barış Alp. 2011. Working Class Formation in Turkey, 1946–1962. PhD thesis. İstanbul: Boğaziçi University.

Özel, Işık. 2003. "The Breakup of State–Business Coalitions in Turkey in the 1980s," *Journal of International Affairs*, 57 (1): 97–112.

2012. "Is It None of Their Business? Business and Democratization, the Case of Turkey," *Democratization*, 20 (6): 1081–116.

2014. *State-Business Alliances and Economic Development: Turkey, Mexico and North Africa*. New York: Routledge.

2015. "Reverting Structural Reforms in Turkey: Towards an Illiberal Economic Governance?," *Global Turkey in Europe Policy Brief*, May: 1–7.

Öztürk, Özgür. 2015. "The Islamist Big Bourgeosie." In *The Neoliberal Landscape and the Rise of Islamist Capital in Turkey*, edited by Neşecan Balkan, Erol Balkan and Ahmet Öncü, 117–41. New York: Berghahn Books.

Pal, Maia. 2020. *Jurisdictional Accumulation: An Early Modern History of Law, Empires, and Capital*. Cambridge: Cambridge University Press.

Palmer, R. Robert. 1985. *The Improvement of Humanity: Education and the French Revolution*. Princeton, NJ: Princeton University Press.

1988. "Translator's Preface." In *The Army of the French Revolution: From Citizen Soldiers to Instruments of Power*, edited by Jean Paul Bertaud, xi–xvi. Princeton, NJ: Princeton University Press.

2005. *Twelve Who Ruled : The Year of the Terror in the French Revolution*. Princeton, NJ: Princeton University Press.

Pamuk, Şevket. 1987a. *The Ottoman Empire and European Capitalism, 1820–1913: Trade, Investment and Production.* Cambridge: Cambridge University Press.

1987b. "Commodity Production for World-Markets and Relations of Production in Ottoman Agriculture, 1840–1913." In *The Ottoman Empire and the World-Economy*, edited by Huricihan İslamoğlu-İnan, 178–202. Cambridge: Cambridge University Press.

1988. "İkinci Dünya Savaşı Yıllarında Devlet, Tarımsal Yapılar ve Bölüşüm." In *Turkiye' de Tarimsal Yapilar 1923–2000*, edited by Şevket Pamuk and Zafer Toprak, 91–108. Ankara: Yurt Yayınları.

2005. "The Ottoman Economy in World War I." In *The Economics of World War I*, edited by Stephen Broadberry and Mark Harrison, 112–36. Cambridge: Cambridge University Press.

2008. "Agriculture and Economic Development in Turkey, 1870–2000." In *Agriculture and Economic Development in Europe since 1870*, edited by Pedro Lains and Vicente Pinilla, 375–95. London: Routledge.

Parker, David. 1983. *The Making of French Absolutism.* New York: St. Martin's Press.

1996. *Class and State in Ancien Regime France: The Road to Modernity?* London: Routledge.

Parla, Taha, and Andrew Davison. 2004. *Corporatist Ideology in Kemalist Turkey.* Syracuse, NY: Syracuse University Press.

Patriquin, Larry. 2007. *Agrarian Capitalism and Poor Relief in England, 1500–1860.* Basingstoke: Palgrave Macmillan.

Peker-Dogra, Asli. 2007. The Soldier and the Civilian: Conscription and Military Power in Turkey. PhD thesis. New York: New York University.

Polanyi, Karl. 1957a. "The Economy as Instituted Process." In *Trade and Market in the Early Empires: Economies in History and Theory*, edited by Karl Polanyi, Conrad M. Arensberg and Harry W. Pearson, 243–70. New York: The Free Press.

1957b. *The Great Transformation.* Boston: Beacon Press.

1957c. "Aristotle Discovers the Economy." In *Trade and Market in the Early Empires: Economies in History and Theory*, edited by Karl Polanyi, Conrad M. Arensberg and Harry W. Pearson, 64–94. New York: The Free Press.

1977. *The Livelihood of Man*, edited by Harry W Pearson. New York: Academic Press.

Polat, Necati. 2013. "Regime Change in Turkey," *International Politics*, 50 (3): 435–54.

Post, Charles. 2011. *The American Road to Capitalism: Studies in Class-Structure, Economic Development, and Political Conflict, 1620–1877.* Leiden: Brill.

2013. "Capitalism, Laws of Motion and Social Relations of Production," *Historical Materialism*, 21 (4): 71–91.

Post, Charles and Xavier Lafrance (eds.). 2019. *Case Studies in the Origins of Capitalism*. Basingstoke: Palgrave Macmillan.

Prendergast, Christopher. 2003. "Codeword Modernity," *New Left Review*, 24: 95–111.

Provence, Michael. 2017. *The Last Ottoman Generation and the Making of the Modern Middle East*. Cambridge: Cambridge University Press.

Quataert, Donald. 1992. "Main Problems of the Economy during the Tanzimat Period." In *150. Yılında Tanzimat*, edited by Hakkı Dursun Yıldız, 211–18. Ankara: Türk Tarih Kurumu Yayınları.

1994. "The Age of Reforms." In *An Economic and Social History of the Ottoman Empire*, vol. 2: 1600–1914, edited by Suraiya Faroqhi, Bruce McGowan, Donald Quataert, Şevket Pamuk and Halil İnalcik, 759–934. Cambridge: Cambridge University Press.

2005. *The Ottoman Empire, 1700–1922*. Cambridge: Cambridge University Press.

Rioux, Sébastien. 2009. "International Historical Sociology," *Rethinking Marxism*, 21 (4): 585–604.

2015. "The Collapse of 'The International Imagination,'" *Research in Political Economy*, 30: 85–112.

Rosenberg, Justin. 1994. *The Empire of Civil Society: A Critique of the Realist Theory of International Relations*. London: Verso.

1996. "Isaac Deutscher and the Lost History of International Relations," *New Left Review*, 215: 3–15.

2006. "Why Is There No International Historical Sociology?," *European Journal of International Relations*, 12 (3): 307–40.

2007. "International Relations – The 'Higher Bullshit,'" *International Politics*, 44: 450–82.

2008. "Uneven and Combined Development: An Exchange of Letters" (with Alex Callinicos), *Cambridge Review of International Affairs*, 21 (1): 77–112.

2013. "The 'Philosophical Premises' of Uneven and Combined Development," *Review of International Studies*, 39 (3): 569–97.

2016a. "Uneven and Combined Development: "The International" in Theory and History." In *Historical Sociology and World History: Uneven and Combined Development over the Longue Durée*, edited by Alexander Anievas and Kamran Matin, 17–30. London: Rowman & Littlefield.

2016b. "Confessions of a Sociolator," *Millennium: Journal of International Studies*, 44 (2): 292–9.

2020. "Uneven and Combined Development: A Defense of the General Abstraction," *Cambridge Review of International Affairs*. DOI: 10.1080/09557571.2020.1835824.

Rostow, Walt W. 1960. *The Stages of Economic Growth: A Non-Communist Manifesto*. Cambridge: Cambridge University Press.

Rubin, Avi. 2011. *Ottoman Nizamiye Courts: Law and Modernity*. London: Palgrave Macmillan.

Runciman, Walter G. 1989. *A Treatise on Social Theory*, vol. 2. Cambridge: Cambridge University Press.

Ruggie, John. 1993. "Territoriality and Beyond," *International Organization*, 47 (1):139–74.

Salgado, Pedro. 2020a. "The Transition Debate in Brazilian History: The Bourgeois Paradigm and Its Critique," *Journal of Agrarian Change*. DOI: 10.1111/joac.12394.

2020b. "Agency and Geopolitics: Brazilian Formal Independence and the Problem of Eurocentrism in International Historical Sociology," *Cambridge Review of International Affairs*, 33 (3): 432–51.

Salmoni, Barak. 2004. "Ordered Liberty and Disciplined Freedom: Turkish Education and Republican Democracy, 1923–50," *Middle Eastern Studies*, 40 (2): 80–110.

Salzmann, Ariel. 2004. *Tocqueville in the Ottoman Empire: Rival Paths to the Modern State*. Leiden: Brill.

de Sousa Santos, Boaventura. 1995. *Toward a New Common Sense: Law, Science and Politics in the Paradigmatic Transition*. London; New York: Routledge.

Sayer, Derek. 1987. *The Violence of Abstraction*. London: Basil Blackwell.

1990. *Capitalism and Modernity*. London: Routledge.

Schwartz, Bernard. 1956. "The Code and Public Law." In *The Code Napoleon and the Common-Law World*, edited by Bernard Schwartz, 247–66. New York: New York University Press.

Seipp, David J. 1994. "The Concept of Property in the Early Common Law," *Law and History Review*, 12 (1): 29–91.

Sencer, Muzaffer. 1974. *Türkiye'de Siyasal Partilerin Sosyal Temelleri*. İstanbul: Geçiş Yayınları.

Sewell, William H. 1980. *Work and Revolution in France: The Language of Labor from the Old Regime to 1848*. Cambridge: Cambridge University Press.

1988. "Le Citoyen/la citoyenne: Activity, Passivity and the Revolutionary Concept of Citizenship." In *The French Revolution and the Creation of Modern Political Culture*, vol. 2, edited by Colin Lucas, 105–24. Oxford: Pergamon Press.

1994. "The Sans-Culotte Rhetoric of Subsistence." In *The French Revolution and the Creation of Modern Political Culture*, vol. 4, edited by Keith Michael Baker, 249–71. Oxford: Pergamon Press.

Shaw, Stanford J., and Ezel Kural Shaw. 1977. *History of the Ottoman Empire and Modern Turkey: Volume 2, Reform, Revolution, and Republic: The Rise of Modern Turkey 1808–1975*. Cambridge: Cambridge University Press.

Shilliam, Robbie. 2009. *German Thought and International Relations: The Rise and Fall of a Liberal Project*. London: Palgrave Macmillan.

Silier, Oya. 1981. *Türkiye'de Tarımsal Yapının Gelişimi (1923–1938)*. İstanbul: Boğaziçi Üniversitesi Yayınları.

Slack, Paul. 2015. *The Invention of Improvement: Information and Material Progress in Seventeenth Century England*. Oxford: Oxford University Press.

Smith, Anthony D. 1979. *Nationalism in the Twentieth Century*. Oxford: Martin Robertson.

Skocpol, Theda. 1977. "Wallerstein's World Capitalist System: A Theoretical and Historical Critique," *American Journal of Sociology*, 82 (5): 1075–90.

  1979. *States and Social Revolutions: A Comparative Analysis of France, Russia, and China*. Cambridge: Cambridge University Press.

  1984. "Sociology's Historical Imagination." In *Vision and Method in Historical Sociology*, edited by Theda Skocpol, 1–21. New York: Cambridge University Press.

  1994. *Social Revolutions in the Modern World*. Cambridge: Cambridge University Press.

Skocpol, Theda, and Meyer Kestnbaum. 1990. "Mars Unshackled: The French Revolution in World-Historical Perspective." In *The French Revolution and the Birth of Modernity*, edited by Ferenc Feher, 13–29. Berkeley: University of California Press.

Sohrabi, Nader. 2011. *Revolution and Constitutionalism in the Ottoman Empire and Iran*. Cambridge: Cambridge University Press.

Somel, Selçuk Akşin. 2001. *The Modernization of Public Education in the Ottoman Empire, 1839–1908: Islamization, Autocracy, and Discipline*. Leiden: Brill.

Sommerville, John. 1992. *The Secularization of Early Modern England*. Oxford: Oxford University Press.

Stone, Bailey. 2002. *Reinterpreting the French Revolution: A Global-Historical Perspective*. Cambridge: Cambridge University Press.

Stone, Lawrence. 1965. *Social Change and Revolution in England, 1540–1640*. London: Barnes and Noble.

Sugar, Peter. 1977. *Southeastern Europe under Ottoman Rule, 1354–1804.* Seattle: University of Washington Press.

Şabudak, Özcan. 2004. Bir Ekonomi Bürokratının Portresi: Mustafa Şeref Özkan. MA thesis. İstanbul: Marmara University.

Şenses, Fikret. 1994. "The Stabilization and Structural Adjustment Program and the Process of Turkish Industrialization: Main Policies and Their Impact." In *Recent Industrialization Experience of Turkey in a Global Context,* edited by Fikret Şenses, 51–74. Westport, CT: Greenwood Press.

Taşpınar, Ömer. 2005. *Kurdish Nationalism and Political Islam in Turkey: Kemalist Identity in Transition.* London: Routledge.

Taylor, George V. 1967. "Noncapitalist Wealth and the Origins of the French Revolution," *America Historical Review,* 72: 469–96.

Tekeli, İlhan, and Selim İlkin. 1987. "Savaşmayan Ülkenin Savaş Ekonomisi," *METU Studies in Development,* 14 (1): 1–48.

1988. "Devletçilik Dönemi Tarım Politikaları: Modernleşme çabaları." In *Türkiye'de Tarımsal Yapılar 1923–2000,* edited by Şevket Pamuk and Zafer Toprak, 37–89. Ankara: Yurt Yayınları.

2004. *Cumhuriyetin Harcı: Köktenci Modernitenin Doğuşu.* İstanbul: İstanbul Bilgi Üniversitesi Yayınları.

Tekeli, İlhan, and Gencay Şaylan. 1978. "Türkiye'de Halkçılık İdeolojisinin Evrimi," *Toplum ve Bilim,* 6–7: 44–110.

Tekin, Ali. 1997. The Political Economy of Foreign Trade Policy Reforms. PhD thesis. Pittsburgh, PA: University of Pittsburgh.

2006. "Turkey's Aborted Attempt at Export-Led Growth Strategy: Anatomy of the 1970 Economic Reform," *Middle Eastern Studies,* 42 (1): 133–63.

Tenbruck, Friedrich. 1994. "Internal History of Society or Universal History?," *Theory, Culture and Society,* 11 (1): 75–93.

Teschke, Benno. 2003. *The Myth of 1648: Class, Geopolitics, and the Making of Modern International Relations.* London: Verso.

2005. "Bourgeois Revolution, State Formation and the Absence of the International," *Historical Materialism,* 13 (2): 3–26.

2014. "IR Theory, Historical Materialism, and the False Promise of International Historical Sociology," *Spectrum: Journal of Global Studies,* 6: 1–66.

2015. "After the Tilly Thesis." In *Does War Make States? Investigations of Charles Tilly's Historical Sociology,* edited by Lars Bo Kaspersen and Jeppe Strandsbjerg, 25–51. Cambridge: Cambridge University Press.

2019. "The Social Origins of 18th Century British Grand Strategy: A Historical Sociology of the Peace of Utrecht." In *The 1713 Peace of*

Utrecht and Its Enduring Effects, edited by Alfred H. A. Soons, 120–55. Leiden: Brill.

Teschke, Benno, and Hannes Lacher. 2007. "The Changing 'Logics' of Capitalist Competition," *Cambridge Review of International Affairs*, 20 (4): 565–80.

Tezcan, Baki. 2010. *The Second Ottoman Empire*. Cambridge: Cambridge University Press.

Tezel, Yahya. 1986. *Cumhuriyet Döneminin İktisadi Tarihi (1923–1950)*. İstanbul: Tarih Vakfı Yurt Yayınları.

Thirsk, Joan. 1978. *Economic Policy and Projects: The Development of a Consumer Society in Early Modern England*. London: Clarendon Press.

Thompson, Edward P. 1965. "The Peculiarities of the English," *Socialist Register*, 2 (2): 311–62.

  1990. *Whigs and Hunters: The Origin of the Black Act*. London: Penguin Books.

  1991a. *Customs in Common*. London: Merlin Press.

  1991b. *The Making of the English Working Class*. London: Penguin Books.

  1995. *The Poverty of Theory*. London: Merlin Press.

Tickner, Arlene, and Ole Waever (eds.). 2009. *International Relations Scholarship around the World*. London: Routledge.

Tilly, Charles. 1984. *Big Structures, Large Processes, Huge Comparisons*. New York: Russell Sage Foundation.

  1990a. *Coercion, Capital and European States: AD 990–1992*. Oxford: Wiley-Blackwell.

  1990b. "State and Counterrevolution in France." In *The French Revolution and the Birth of Modernity*, edited by Ferenc Feher, 49–68. Berkeley: University of California Press.

  1991. "How and What Are Historians Doing." In *Divided Knowledge across Disciplines, across Cultures*, edited by David Easton and Corinne Schelling, 86–117. Newbury Park, CA: Sage.

Timur, Taner. 2001. *Türk Devrimi Ve Sonrası*. Ankara: İmge Kitabevi.

Tokay, Gül. 2019. "The Ottoman Army during the Hamidian Period: An Assessment." In *Abdülhamid II and His Legacy*, edited by Ş. Tufan Buzpınar and Gökhan Çetinsaya, 65–82. İstanbul: ISIS Press.

Toksöz, Meltem. 2010. *Nomads, Migrants and Cotton in the Eastern Mediterranean*. Leiden: Brill.

Toprak, Zafer. 1982. *Türkiye'de "millî^ iktisat", 1908–1918*. İstanbul: Yurt Yayınları.

  1988. "Türkiye Tarımı ve Yapısal Gelişmeler (1900–1950)." In *Türkiye'de Tarımsal Yapılar*, edited by Şevket Pamuk and Zafer Toprak, 19–36. Ankara: Yurt Yayınları.

1995a. *Milli iktisat, milli burjuvazi*. İstanbul: Tarih Vakfı Yurt Yayınları.
1995b. *İttihat Terakki ve Devletçilik*. İstanbul: Tarih Vakfı Yurt Yayınları.
1999. "From Liberalism to Solidarism: The Ottoman Economic Mind in the Age of the Nation State." In *Studies in Ottoman Social and Economic Life,* edited by Raoul Motika, Christoph Herzog and Michael Ursinus, 171–90. Heidelberg: Heidelberger Orientverlag.
2013. *Türkiye'de Popülizm*. İstanbul: Doğan Kitap.
Trimberger, Ellen K. 1972. "A Theory of Elite Revolutions," *Studies in Comparative International Development,* 7: 191–207.
Tuğal, Cihan. 2016. "In Turkey, the Regime Slides from Soft to Hard Totalitarianism," *Open Democracy,* February 17.
Tunçay, Mete. 1991. *Türkiye'de Sol Akımlar-I (1908–1925)*. İstanbul: B. D. S. Yayıncılık.
2010. *Türkiye Cumhuriyeti'nde Tek Parti Yönetiminin Kurulması 1923–1931*. İstanbul: Tarih Vakfı Yurt Yayınları.
Türel, Oktar. 1996. "Has Anybody Seen Robin Hood in Post-1980 Turkey? Comments on Leander's Paper," *Review of International Political Economy,* 3 (1): 164–78.
Türkeş, Alparslan. 1965. *Dokuz Işık*. İstanbul: Dokuz Işık Yayınları.
1976. *Dokuz Isik ve Turkiye*. İstanbul: Kervan Yayınları.
1977. *27 Mayıs, 13 Kasım, 21 Mayıs ve gerçekler*. İstanbul: Dokuz Işık Yayınevi.
1979. *Gonul Seferberligine*. Ankara: Hasret Yayınları.
Türkeş, Mustafa. 2001. "A Patriotic Leftist Development Strategy Proposal in Turkey in the 1930s: The Case of the Kadro (Cadre) Movement," *International Journal of Middle East Studies,* 33: 91–114.
Türkmen, Buket. 2009. "A Transformed Kemalist Islam or a New Islamic Civic Morality? A Study of 'Religious Culture and Morality' Textbooks in the Turkish High School Curricula," *Comparative Studies of South Asia, Africa and the Middle East,* 29 (3): 381–97.
Ülker, Erol. 2005. "Contextualising 'Turkification': Nation-Building in the Late Ottoman Empire, 1908–18," *Nations and Nationalism,* 11 (4): 613–36.
Ünay, Sadik. 2006. *Neoliberal Globalization and Institutional Reform: The Political Economy of Development and Planning in Turkey*. Hauppauge, NY: Nova Publishers.
Üstel, Füsun. 2004. *"Makbul Vatandaş"ın peşinde: II. Meşrutiyet'ten bugüne Türkiye'de Vatandaş Eğitimi*. İstanbul: İletişim.
Van der Lippe, John M. 2005. *The Politics of Turkish Democracy: Ismet Inonu and the Formation of the Multi-Party System, 1938–1950*. Albany: State University of New York Press.

Vaughan, Michalina, and Margaret Archer. 1971. *Social Conflict and Educational Change in England and France 1789–1848*. Cambridge: Cambridge University Press.

Versan, Vakur. 1984. "The Kemalist Reform of Turkish Law and Its Impact." In *Ataturk and the Modernization of Turkey*, edited by Jacob Landau, 247–50. Leiden: Brill.

Viger, Jonathan. 2019. "The Eighteenth Brumaire in Historical Context: Reconsidering Class and State in France and Syria," *Theory and Society*, 48: 611–38.

Vitalis, Robert. 2015. *White World Order, Black Power Politics: The Birth of American International Relations*. Ithaca, NY: Cornell University Press.

Vries, Peer. 2012. "Does Wealth Entirely Depend on Inclusive Institutions and Pluralist Politics?," *Tijdschrift voor Sociale en Economische Geschiedenis*, 9 (3): 74–93.

Waldner, David. 1999. *State Building and Late Development*. Ithaca, NY: Cornell University Press.

Walker, Robert B. J. 1993. *Inside/Outside: International Relations as Political Theory*. Cambridge: Cambridge University Press.

Wallerstein, Immanuel. 1974. *The Modern World-System, volume I: Capitalist Agriculture and the Origins of the European World-Economy in the Sixteenth Century*. Berkeley: University of California Press.

   1980. *The Modern World-System, volume II: Mercantilism and the Consolidation of the European World-Economy, 1600–1750*. New York: Academic Press.

   1989. *The Modern World-System, volume III: The Second Great Expansion of the Capitalist World-Economy, 1730–1840*. San Diego, CA: Academic Press

   2001. *Unthinking Social Science: The Limits of Nineteenth-Century Paradigms*. Philadelphia: Temple University Press.

   2003. "Anthropology, Sociology, and Other Dubious Disciplines," *Current Anthropology*, 44 (4), 453–60.

   2011. *The Modern World-System, volume IV: Centrist Liberalism Triumphant, 1789–1914*. Berkeley: University of California Press.

Waltz, Kenneth N. (1979). *Theory of International Politics*. Reading, MA: Addison-Wesley.

Webb, Ed. 2007. Civilizing Religion: Jacobin Projects of Secularization in Turkey, France, Tunisia, and Syria. PhD thesis. Philadelphia: University of Pennsylvania.

Weber, Eugen. 1976. *Peasants into Frenchmen: The Modernization of Rural France, 1870–1914*. Stanford, CA: University of Stanford Press.

Weiker, Walter. 1963. *The Turkish Revolution, 1960–1961: Aspects of Military Politics*. Washington, DC: The Brookings Institution.

Wendt, Alexander. 1999. *Social Theory of International Politics*. Cambridge: Cambridge University Press.

Winter, Michael. 1984. "The Modernisation of Education in Kemalist Turkey." In *Ataturk and the Modernization of Turkey*, edited by Jacob Landau, 183–94. Leiden: Brill.

Wolf, Eric R. 1997. *Europe and the People without History*. Berkeley: University of California Press.

Woloch, Isser. 1993. "The Right to Primary Education in the French Revolution: From Theory to Practice." In *The French Revolution and the Meaning of Citizenship*, edited by Renée Waldinger, Philip Dawson and Isser Woloch, 137–52. Westport, CT: Greenwood Press.

1994a. *The New Regime: Transformations of the French Civic Order, 1789–1820s*. New York: W. W. Norton.

1994b. "The Contraction and Expansion of Democratic Space during the Period of the Terror." In *The French Revolution and the Creation of Modern Political Culture*, vol. 4, edited by Keith Michael Baker, 309–26. Oxford: Pergamon Press.

Wood, Ellen Meiksins. 1981. "The Separation of the Economic and the Political in Capitalism," *New Left Review*, 127: 66–95.

1986. *Retreat from Class*. London: Verso.

1991. *The Pristine Culture of Capitalism: A Historical Essay on Old Regimes and Modern States*. London: Verso.

1995. *Democracy against Capitalism: Renewing Historical Materialism*. Cambridge: Cambridge University Press.

1997a. "The Non-history of Capitalism," *Historical Materialism*, 1 (1): 5–21.

1997b. "Modernity, Postmodernity or Capitalism?," *Review of International Political Economy*, 4 (3): 539–60.

1998. "The Agrarian Origins of Capitalism," *Monthly Review*, July/ August, 14–31.

1999. *The Origin of Capitalism*. New York: Monthly Review Press.

2001a. *The Origin of Capitalism: Longer View*. London: Verso.

2001b. "Eurocentric Anti-Eurocentrism," *Against the Current*, May–June.

2002. "The Question of Market Dependence," *Journal of Agrarian Change*, 2 (1): 50–87.

2005. *Empire of Capital*. London: Verso.

2012. *Liberty and Property: A Social History of Western Political Thought from Renaissance to Enlightenment*. London: Verso.

Woodiwiss, Anthony. 1997. "Against 'Modernity': A Dissident Rant," *Economy and Society*, 26 (1): 1–21.

Wrigley, Edward A. 1985. "Urban Growth and Agricultural Change: England and the Continent in Early Modern Europe," *Journal of Interdisciplinary History*, 15: 683–728.

Yalvaç, Faruk. 1991. "The Sociology of the State and the Sociology of International Relations". In *State and Society in International Relations*, edited by Michael Banks and Martin Shaw, 93–113. New York: Harvester Wheatsheaf.

Yaşar, Murat. 2014. "Learning the Ropes: The Young Turk Perception of the 1905 Russian Revolution," *Middle Eastern Studies*, 50 (1): 114–28.

Yavuz, Hakan. 1997. "Political Islam and the Welfare (Refah) Party in Turkey," *Comparative Politics*, 30 (1): 63–82.

2003. *Islamic Political Identity in Turkey*. Oxford: Oxford University Press.

Yeldan, Erinc. 1994. "The Economic Structure of Power under Turkish Structural Adjustment: Prices, Growth and Accumulation." In *Recent Industrialization Experience of Turkey in a Global Context*, edited by Fikret Senses, 75–90. Westport, CT: Greenwood Press.

2001. "On the IMF-Directed Disinflation Program in Turkey." Social Science Research Network Working Paper, http://papers.ssrn.com/sol3/papers.cfm?abstract_id=290539.

Yeşil, Fatih. 2007. "Looking at the French Revolution through Ottoman Eyes: Ebubekir Ratib Efendi's Observations," *Bulletin of the School of Oriental and African Studies*, 70 (2): 283–304.

Yıldırmaz, Sinan. 2009. From "Imaginary" To "Real": A Social History of the Peasantry in Turkey (1945–1960). PhD thesis, İstanbul: Boğaziçi University.

Yıldız, Gültekin. 2009. *Neferin adı yok: zorunlu askerliğe geçiş sürecinde Osmanlı Devleti'nde siyaset, ordu ve toplum, 1826–1839*. İstanbul: Kitabevi.

Zacares, Javier Moreno. 2018. "Beyond Market Dependence: The Origins of Capitalism in Catalonia," *Journal of Agrarian Change*, 18 (4): 749–67.

Zaifer, Ahmet. 2020. "Variegated Privatisation: Class, Capital Accumulation and State in Turkey's Privatisation Process in the 1980s and 1990s," *Critical Sociology*, 46 (1): 141–56.

Zarakol, Ayşe. 2011. *After Defeat: How the East Learned to Live with the West*. Cambridge: Cambridge University Press.

Zmolek, Michael A. 2019. "'Compelled to Sell All': Proletarianization, Agrarian Capitalism and the Industrial Revolution." In *Case Studies in the Origins of Capitalism*, edited by Xavier Lafrance and Charles Post, 63–86. London: Palgrave Macmillan.

Zurcher, Erik J. 1999. "The Ottoman Conscription System in Theory and Practice." In *Arming the State: Military Conscription in the Middle East and Central Asia, 1775–1925*, edited by Erik J. Zurcher, 79–94. London: I. B. Tauris.

2004. *Turkey: A Modern History*. London: I. B. Tauris.

2010. *The Young Turk Legacy and Nation Building*. London: I. B. Tauris.

Index

Abdülhamid II, 129–30, 133–4, 136, 262
Abrams, Philip, 36
absolutism, 14, 54–5, 64, 68, 70–1, 73–4, 76, 93, 95, 179
absolutist France, 5, 47, 50, 54–5, 61, 64, 68, 70, 72, 75–6
absolutist France (economy), 61
absolutist France (state), 61, 64
comparative backwardness vis-à-vis Britain, 72
labor productivity, 62
tax/office structure, 61
venal office, 61, 64
abstract collectivity, 55, 75, 78, 95, 261
abstract individual, 54–5, 74, 78, 94–5, 137, 139, 154, 157, 261
Agrarian and Seed Laws, 247
Ahmad, Feroz, 156
Alevis, 220
Anderson, Perry, 37
Anievas, Alexander and Kerem Nişancıoğlu, 44
Arab Revolt of 1916 151
Armenian Revolutionary Federation (ARF), 142
assembly industries, 214
Atatürk, Mustafa Kemal, 162, 174
Austria, 103–4, 146

Baath–Barzani Accord of 1970 219
Balkan Wars, 148, 150, 154, 158, 160
Bentham, Jeremy, 85
Black Act, 65
Black Death, 33
Bolsheviks, 164
Bolshevism, 5, 260
bourgeois revolution, 10, 15, 44–5, 56, 156

incomplete bourgeois revolution, 10, 14, 155, 161, 179
revisionist historiography of, 45, 56, 101
boycott movement, 145–6, 148
Brenner, Robert, 3, 30
Britain, 4, 6, 14, 34, 54, 63–4, 67–9, 71–2, 74, 78, 80, 87, 91–2, 95, 99, 108, 110, 143, 164, 174, 194, 218, 252, 259
British capitalism, 54
English Poor Law, 84
idiosyncrasy of the early modern state, 68
Reformation, 65
Speenhamland Law, 63
Buğra, Ayşe, 191
Burke, Edmund, 85

capitalism, 1, 3, 5, 8, 10–11, 14–16, 19–20, 22, 25, 28, 30–1, 34, 44, 46–8, 50, 54–5, 57, 60, 63, 69, 71, 82, 85, 93, 95, 98–9, 101, 110, 112, 117, 120, 126, 156–8, 161, 167, 169, 176–7, 185, 188, 190–1, 195, 201, 204, 206, 209, 216, 218, 221, 223, 226, 228, 230, 240–1, 243–4, 248–9, 253, 256, 258, 260, 262–3, 265–6
as a break in human history, 25
capitalism–democracy relation, 31, 249
capitalist accumulation, 46, 63, 85, 230, 249, 267
capitalist authoritarianism, 250, 255
capitalist modernity, 4, 43, 56, 69, 102, 190, 256, 264, 266
capitalist social relations, 5, 11, 15, 27–8, 43, 45, 49–50, 56–7, 64, 70, 93–4, 99, 102, 122, 157, 167, 169,

304